A History of Chess in the English Civil Service

Kevin Thurlow

A History of Chess in the English Civil Service

Published by The Conrad Press in the United Kingdom 2021

Tel: +44(0)1227 472 874
www.theconradpress.com
info@theconradpress.com

ISBN 978-1-913567-69-9

Copyright © Kevin Thurlow, 2021

The moral right of Kevin Thurlow to be identified as author of this work has been asserted in accordance with the Copyright, Designs and Patents Act 1988.

All rights reserved.

Typesetting and Cover Design by: Charlotte Mouncey, www.bookstyle.co.uk
The Conrad Press logo was designed by Maria Priestley.

Printed and bound in Great Britain by Clays Ltd, Elcograf S.p.A.

Dedicated to everyone ever involved in Civil Service chess

Contents

Preface and Acknowledgements	7
Abbreviations and Acronyms	10
Chapter 1 1845 - 1927 Beginnings	13
Chapter 2 1927 – 1939 CSCA Merger to World War II	60
Chapter 3 1939 – 1946 Espionage, World War II and the Advent of Computers	94
Chapter 4 1946 – 1967 Hitting the Heights	111
Chapter 5 1967 – 1983 Modernization	162
Chapter 6 1983 – 1998 Drama follows Drama	216
Chapter 7 1999 – 2016 Decline and Fall	283
Annex Articles by E C Baker, M.B.E.	333
Club Histories	
Correspondence Chess	390
Biographies	397
Trophy Winners & Officials	487
Literature Sources etc.	527

Preface and Acknowledgements

This book has been a long time coming. The author was in regular correspondence with EC Baker and received a letter containing this (dated 7/8/1987),

'I have not collected chess memorabilia & long ago sought to complete CSCA records from 1922 plus a stray CS & Metropolitan League item and had them bound as far as practical & passed them to the safekeeping of succeeding Secretaries. In such circumstances I could not attempt an official history but in all histories, we miss the small personal details, the odd incidents that often give us a clearer picture of how things were than all the match reports and minutes of meetings. The ordinary club members are the raison d'être of our organization so it seems appropriate to record a few of their chess experiences.'

When the centenary of the league approached, there were a number of proposals on how to celebrate the milestone, including a book on the history of the league. The Annual General Meeting dismissed this idea, but a few days later the Chairman (Ian Pheby) received a telephone call from someone saying that there should be a book. Ian explained that the AGM had rejected the idea so the league could not spend money on it. The caller said that he wanted a book and he was willing to make a sizeable donation to ensure it happened. In view of this amazing generosity, the Committee decided to proceed with a book and asked the author to write it. All the clubs including some defunct ones were invited to contribute and a large number of individuals provided information, or searched archives. The author visited the BCF Chess Library in Hastings, and spent several days at the *British Chess Magazine* premises, reading every copy of their magazine from the late 19th Century onwards. The staff provided many cups of tea to help. Ian Pheby and Roland Smith visited Civil Service Sports Council and trawled through their archives at great length.

Juggling the production of a book with full-time work is not easy, which has caused some delays, but here it is at last. Retirement and the Covid-19 outbreak have produced some spare time.

Many people and organizations have helped, and they are listed alphabetically below. Any omissions are accidental and much regretted.

Kevin Thurlow

Aircrew Remembered, Tony Ashby, EC Baker, Geoffrey S Barker, *British Chess Magazine*, British Newspaper Archive, BTHQ (British Telecom Headquarters CC), Susie Cairns, '*Chess*', Chess Scotland website, Civil Service Sports Council, *DHSS Chess,* Paul Efstathiou, Essex CCA (Ivor Smith, Steve Wedlock, Howard Grist, John Philpott), *Falkirk Herald*, Ron Fleming, The Fowler Family, Richard Fries, Raymond Gedling, David Gilbert, Bernard Glaze, Edward Godly, Greater London Chess Club, Angela Hales, Hastings University, Eric Hazell, Home Office Chess Club, Inland Revenue, John James, Ian Jewesbury, Kingston Cemetery, Kingston History

Centre, Marian Holmes, Paula Keay, Gary Kenworthy, Gerard Killoran, John McAllister, Meteorological Office Chess Club, David Mills, Steve Murray, National Rifle Association, Danny O'Byrne, Malcolm Pein, Tim Pelling, Ian Pheby, Tim Paulden (Chess Devon), Ray Pomeroy, Carl Portman, Chris Reeve, John Sargent, John Saunders, *The Scotsman*, Martin Smith, Roland Smith, St Paul's Church, Kingston, *Surrey Comet*, *Surrey Mirror*, *Sussex Agricultural Express*, Wilf Taylor, David Thomson, *The Times*, James Toon, Chris Torrero, UNATS Chess Club, Gareth Ward, Paul Watson, *Westmorland Gazette*, Edward Winter (creator of Chesshistory.com)

Abbreviations and Acronyms

BCF	British Chess Federation
BCM	*British Chess Magazine*
BFCC	British Federation for Correspondence Chess
BT	British Telecom
BTHQ	British Telecom Headquarters
Centels	Central Telecommunications
COMPOST	Cabinet Office, Management & Personnel Office, Central Statistical Office, Treasury, formerly Civil Service Department/Treasury.
Credex	Export Control Guarantee Department
CS	Civil Service
CSCA	Civil Service Chess Association
CSD	Civil Service Department
CSRC	Civil Service Recreation Centre
CSSC	Civil Service Sports Council
DETR	Department of the Environment, Transport and Regions
DHSS	Department of Health and Social Security
DOE	Department of the Environment
DSIR	Department of Scientific and Industrial

	Research
DSS	Department of Social Security
DTI	Department of Trade and Industry
EC	Executive Committee
ECF	English Chess Federation
EFCC	English Federation for Correspondence Chess
Fortels	A telephone department
GCHQ	Government Communications Headquarters
GLC	Greater London Council
GLCC	Greater London Chess Club
GPO	General Post Office
ICCF	International Correspondence Chess Federation
IR	Inland Revenue
LCC	London County Council
LCCL	London Commercial Chess League
MCCA	Middlesex County Chess Association
NALGO	National Association of Local Government Officers
PO	Post Office
SBD	Savings Bank Department
SCCA	Surrey County Chess Association
SCCU	Southern Counties Chess Union

CHAPTER 1

1845 - 1927 Beginnings

There have been links between the Civil Service and chess for many years. The famous Russian player Mikhail Chigorin was a civil servant, as was Petroff, but we will confine ourselves to these shores in this work.

Although the Civil Service League started in 1904, there was chess activity before that, both for individuals and teams. There were other associations as well. An article in *British Chess Magazine* in 1975 reported that on 9th April 1845, chess was played over an electric telegraph line between London and Gosport, play ending after seven hours, 'perhaps because the Post Office clerk wanted to get home'. This drew a mild rebuke from EC Baker, who commented that the Post Office did not become responsible for telegraphs until 1870, and that the Admiralty had paid for the line and managed it up until then.

The *Wells Journal* of 19th October 1867 reported,

'It is in contemplation to start a chess club for the Civil Service. A preliminary meeting has been held in the Post Office library, which was well-attended, and sundry forms were agreed to be submitted at a subsequent meeting.'

An identical report appeared in a Kent newspaper, and the *London Daily News* added that the meeting was held on 17th October at 5 pm. This clearly led to something, as *The Era* reported on 27th December 1868 that there was,

'Talk of the Civil Service Chess Club using the venue of St. George's Chess Club.'

Chess was played in a cabinet meeting in 1872, when Gladstone's Cabinet was awaiting a tribunal's decision on the 'Alabama' case. America was demanding compensation from Britain for selling warships to the Confederacy in the American Civil War, and Gladstone suggested international arbitration. The 'Alabama' had captured or destroyed 55 Union ships, so it had been quite successful. After a few hours waiting for the decision, Lord Granville summoned a chess set, to stop the members of the Cabinet arguing amongst themselves. Granville and William 'Buckshot' Forster settled down to play whilst the remainder watched. (He was nicknamed 'Buckshot' by the press, due to his alleged approach to a troublesome crowd in Ireland.) No news came through, but nobody argued! Britain lost and paid 15.5 million dollars, which was a lot of money in those days, and actually more than USA was claiming.

The *Morning Post* of 2nd October 1873 said that the Postmaster General's report had drawn attention to the Crystal Palace chess tournament, where wires transmitting the moves had communicated with Glasgow, Hull, Nottingham, Birmingham and Bristol. Nowadays, we are used to live coverage of games on the internet, but clearly the basic idea is not new. The *North Wales Chronicle* reported on 18th October 1873, in a section called 'London News', that,

'Another new club, called the Belgrave, for the use of the Civil Service, is about to be established in the Buckingham Palace Road, within two minutes' walk of Victoria Station. It provides two spacious dining rooms, billiards and smoking rooms, library, reading and writing rooms, rooms for chess, cards etc., lavatories, and sleeping accommodation for about twenty members.'

In the late 1870s, the 'Civil Service Publishing Co.' was publishing chess books. A former civil servant in India was a prime mover in the 1883 London Congress. The *Pall Mall Gazette* reported on 30th July 1884 that SJ Stevens and GA Hooke ('both of the third class') had shared the chief prize in a tournament of one hundred members of the City of London Chess Club. The first-rate players said that many of the prize winners should become first class players in due course, and, 'will be required to give odds'. It was not unusual in those days for championships to be played at odds, i.e. a player might start with fewer pieces or pawns than his opponent, which is unthinkable nowadays. We will hear of Mr Hooke again. Players of the 'third class' were probably quite good. Within a couple of years Hooke was probably of master strength.

The *Manchester Evening News* reported on 8th September 1887,

'The Speaker has so far accommodated the sporting instincts of members as to give his consent to chess being played in the Smoke-room of the House of Commons; and last night the first chess party was made up consisting of Lord Carmarthen, Mr Evelyn, Mr Boord and Mr CS Parker. The noble marquis is a young gentleman of decidedly sporting tendency, though he keeps it well under control. Since he has been in the House he has shown that he is quite capable of developing into a useful matter of fact, business-like member, and having the advantage of being son & heir to a duke, will no doubt have a fairly brilliant ministerial career.'

The newspaper did not seem to like him much. In fact when the marquis (originally George Osborne) inherited his father's title, becoming 10th Duke of Leeds in 1895, he left Parliament. He was briefly treasurer of the household, which gave him membership of the Privy Council.

The London Chess League started in 1887, and Somerset House fielded a team in 1890. The Civil Service Rifles (based at Somerset House) were also active in the 1890s. They played London School Board and the Post Office amongst others. In December 1893, they lost 5½-3½ to London Schools Board (presumably with an unfinished game), Matthews, Herbert and Smith providing the wins.

Civil Service Rifles October 1894		Sydenham and Forest Hill
1. Waters	½-½	Latter
2. Redman	½-½	Larfent
3. Brooks	0-1	Topham
4. Holmes	0-1	Manners
5. Clarke	½-½	Del Mar
6. Addison	0-1	Anderson
7. Watkins	½-½	Feldon
8. Thurgood	½-½	Atkinson
9. Oppler	½-½	Troughton
10. Stoker	0-1	Spagnoletti
11. Etheridge	0-1	Blake
12. Smith	½-½	Smith
	3½-8½	

The Morning Post (30th September 1895) reported,

'The Civil Service Rifles Chess Club, of which Lord Albemarle is the President, has issued a programme of fixtures and entertainments for the ensuing season, which includes a number of matches with various organizations. The club being engaged in the league competition will take an active part in the winter contests.'

They did not seem to be particularly successful, but played in the London League for some years. On 21st October 1895, it was reported that they had lost 7½-4½ to Insurance in the 'B' division. *London Daily News* reported on 28th November 1895 that Somerset House had drawn 4-4 with London County Council. This particular battle was to continue for well over a century, although the teams changed names. Individuals who would later play in the CS League were making their mark in league chess. RP Michell played (Board 12) for Metropolitan and GA Hooke (Board 10) for City of London in 1895. The *Standard* reported in February 1896 that the Lord Chief Justice (Baron Russell of Killowen) was interested in chess.

The (London) Ladies Chess Club played a huge number of matches towards the end of the 19th Century, (usually one a week!), and in December 1898 they beat the Local Government Board 5-3, but lost 2.5-7.5 to London County Council. The Local Government Board and London County Council were well-placed in 'D' division in 1900. We are informed by the *Manchester Courier and Lancashire General Advertiser* of 12th February 1902 that,

'It was decided yesterday that for the Inter-Parliamentary chess tournament between Great Britain and Australia, the English team should consist of two Peers and three Commoners.'

That year, chess was being played in the tea-room of the Houses of Parliament. Mr A Bonar Law presented a trophy to be held by the winner of the Parliamentary chess tournament. According to BCM,

'The trophy is a beautifully designed silver vase, the summit of which is an exact reproduction of the Clock. The side of the bowl is a view in relief of the Houses of Parliament as seen from the river, and on the other the following inscription:- 'House of Commons Chess Championship. Presented by A. Bonar Law, MP., 1902. Won 1901-1902. Reginald McKenna, MP.'; space being reserved for the name of the winners in succeeding years.'

In 1948, a question in the House from Sir John Maitland (Horncastle) 'asked the Minister of Works of what metal the bronze-coloured cup in the Chess Room is made; and when it was last cleaned.'

Mr Charles Key (Poplar, Bow and Bromley) responded, 'This silver cup is understood to have been presented to the Chess Club by Mr. Bonar Law and has never been placed in my Department's care. I will, however, have it cleaned.'

Sadly, the trophy seems now to be 'lost'.

In 1903, the London League 'Early' division featured such teams as Local Government Board, London County Council, London School Board and Post Office (Stores Department). Western Postal District and Customs were also playing in the London League at the time.

So it was quite natural for a Civil Service League to start. The 'Civil Service and Municipal League (London)' was formed in 1904. The first secretary of the league was WHM Kirk (Local Government Board) and he had a long and distinguished career. His address was Studland, Gartmoor Gardens, Wimbledon (near Wimbledon Park). Unfortunately, the match scores for the first season are not available, but we do have a league table.

1904-1905 London Civil Service League - Inaugural Season

		1	2	3	4	5	6	7	8	9	Tot
1	Admiralty	X	1	1	1	1	1	1	1	1	8
2	India Office	0	X	½	1	1	1	1	1	1	6½
3	Local Government Board	0	½	X	0	1	1	1	1	1	5½
4	Savings Bank	0	0	1	X	0	1	1	1	1	5
5	Government Laboratory	0	0	0	1	X	1	1	½	1	4½
6	GPO Stores Department	0	0	0	0	0	X	1	1	1	3
7	Returned Letter Office	0	0	0	0	0	0	X	½	1	1½
8	Customs	0	0	0	0	½	0	½	X	0	1
9	GPO Engineering	0	0	0	0	0	0	0	1	X	1

GPO = General Post Office

Much has changed over the intervening hundred years. Of the nine original clubs, only Customs remain in the league, and then only as part of Revenue and Customs. The Admiralty now comes under the Ministry of Defence, which does not play in the league. The India Office ceased to exist many years ago and the Local Government Board was the forerunner of NALGO, (National Association of Local Government Officers), who played for many years in the London Commercial League. The Savings Bank started in 1861 as part of the Post Office, but became its own department in 1969. The Laboratory of the Government Chemist (then Government Laboratory) was privatized in 1995, but had left the league in 1989. Even the Post Office, which provided four teams in the first season, no longer has any teams in the league in stark contrast to 1904. The Returned Letter Office had only recently changed its name from the slightly alarming 'Dead Letter Office'.

The lack of continuity is not surprising. Government departments do change, either through alterations in policy or just through circumstance. This has become particularly true in the last 50 years. New Governments or Ministers have been known to make changes because they look good or in an attempt to prove that something is being done. There are reorganizations that are entirely justified of course. There was no need for an India Office once India achieved independence. The War Office ceased to exist some years ago, although Ministry of Defence continues its duties. The Ministry of Defence oversees all the armed services, rather than each having its own department. The author's previous employer, the Government Chemist, started as part of Revenue, then Customs, (at one stage it was effectively part of both, as each had its own analysts), then as its own department, before becoming part of DSIR (Department of Scientific and Industrial Research), then part of Ministry of

Technology, Board of Trade, Department of Trade and Industry, Department of Industry, Board of Trade (again), Department of Trade and Industry (again), then an agency of Department of Trade and Industry, before being privatized. Ironically, the Government continued to be the biggest customer. The Departments of Health and Social Security merged and separated so often that the chess club just kept going as DHSS whatever the status of the parent department(s).

The second season of the league was down to seven teams as Customs and India Office dropped out temporarily. However, the league had a couple of representative matches. On 12th October 1905, they took on Bohemians, winning 17-8. The scores on the top ten boards were as follows.

Civil Service		Bohemians
1. RP Michell	1-0	HW Shoosmith
2. GE Wainwright	1-0	W Schartan
3. HS Barlow	1-0	HW Smith
4. GA Felce	1-0	FS Michell
5. T Crassweller	½-½	WM Bussell
6. GR Snowden	0-1	EW Brennand
7. WHM Kirk	1-0	WC Squire
8. FW Osborne	1-0	HE Wood
9. TL Adamson	1-0	GH Bentley
10. EK Skerrett	½-½	Mr Ogg
	8-2	

Both the top board players were good enough to play in the British Championship, which was a 12-player invitation event then. Shoosmith drew with Blackburne and Atkins, so these were quality players. Michell was top board for Middlesex and Wainwright top board for Surrey. Michell worked for Admiralty and had won the British Amateur Chess Championship in 1902. On 26th October, CS lost 9½-5½ to Metropolitan. To put this in perspective, Metropolitan were London League champions, (which was contested over 20 boards) and had had over 300 members in the 1890s!

The Civil Service League was now a going concern and it was announced that subscriptions would be increased so that a permanent trophy could be purchased.

1891 had seen the formation of the 'Junior Civil Service Prayer Union', which turned into the 'Junior Civil Service Christian Union' in 1897. This organization published a monthly magazine called the *Union Observer*. In 1905, it was reported at the Annual Conference of the Union that the *Observer* had a shortfall of £23. The editor (Vernon Peacock) was not worried, 'If it were necessary to make the paper pay it could be done; but the object was to turn out the best possible paper for a penny.' He argued that the paper encouraged membership of the Union, and defended the chess column as 'popular'.

The magazine changed its name the following year to *The Civil Service Observer*, describing itself as the 'Organ of the Junior Civil Service Christian Union and Post Office Total Abstinence Society', not qualities one immediately associates with chess. In 1908, H Polman of Local Government Board took over as editor.

1905-1906 London Civil Service League

		1	2	3	4	5	6	7	Tot
1	Admiralty	X	1	1	1	1	1	1	5
2	Savings Bank	0	X	1	0	1	1	1	4
3	Local Government Board	0	0	X	1	1	1	1	4
4	GPO Stores Department	0	1	0	X	0	1	1	3
5	GPO Engineering	0	0	0	1	X	1	1	3
6	Government Laboratory	0	0	0	0	0	X	½	½
7	Returned Letter Office	0	0	0	0	0	½	X	½

The sharp-eyed reader will perhaps be puzzled that Admiralty had won all six matches, but only scored five points. The reigning champions of the league were fined a match point for the following season, to give the others a chance. Admiralty were enormously strong so they took this in their stride. However, they had lost to Patent Office in a friendly match and the latter now entered the league for the first time. Michell and Wainwright both beat Blackburne in the 1906 British Championship.

The entry for the 1906-07 league was slightly different, with Admiralty, Customs, GPO Stores, GPO Accountant General's Department, GPO Engineering Department, Local Government Board, Patent Office and Savings Bank. Early results included, Patent Office 8-4 Savings Bank, Local Government Board 8½-1½ Customs, Local Government Board 7½-4½ GPO Engineering, Admiralty 7½-4½ Savings Bank, and GPO Accountant General's Department 6½-5½ GPO Stores.

At this stage the chess clubs of London County Council (which had been playing in the London League) and London School Board merged, under the name of LCC. LCC would later become GLC, and then GLCC when the GLC was abolished. It had started life as the Metropolitan Board of Works

Chess Club in 1887. The new club had 116 members and a further 28 joined shortly afterwards. These are figures which most clubs can now only dream about. The Local Government Board was also playing in the London League. Patent Office club met at Southampton Buildings on Tuesday and Fridays from 5 pm to 9 pm. One club that did not play in the league was the 'Civil Service Rifle Volunteers Chess Club', based in Somerset House. It is not clear when they became 'Volunteers'. The history of CS chess is riddled with clubs with remarkable names. Andrew Bonar Law MP won on top board for House of Commons vs Oxford University. RP Michell became the first President of Middlesex CCA.

1907-1908 London Civil Service League

		1	2	3	4	5	6	7	8	9	10	Tot
1	GPO North	X	1	1	1	1	1	1	0	1	1	8
2	Savings Bank	0	X	1	1	1	1	1	1	1	1	8
3	LCC	0	0	X	1	½	1	1	1	1	1	6½
4	Patent Office	0	0	0	X	1	1	1	½	1	1	4½
5	India Office	0	0	½	0	X	1	0	1	1	1	4½
6	Paymaster General	0	0	0	0	0	X	1	1	1	1	4
7	GPO Stores	0	0	0	0	1	0	X	1	1	1	4
8	Local Government Board	1	0	0	½	0	0	0	X	0	1	2½
9	Customs	0	0	0	0	0	0	0	1	X	1	2
10	GPO Engineering	0	0	0	0	0	0	0	0	0	X	0

Patent Office were fined one point for winning the previous year. The LCC team was admitted by special resolution, possibly because of their recent merger. There was a play-off match to decide the champions, in which GPO North beat Savings Bank by 6½-3½. On 19th May 1908, a House of Commons

Team defeated a Combined Oxford and Cambridge University team 5½-4½. Board 2 for the House was Andrew Bonar Law, then the Shadow Spokesman for Tariff Reform, and later the Prime Minister. Bonar Law was a keen supporter of Joseph Chamberlain, who believed that Customs Tariffs should be set so that they were the same throughout Europe. This was a remarkable idea for its time.

In 1908-09 the league had developed into the London Civil Service and Municipal Chess League, and had two divisions for the first time, and a record total of 17 teams. For many years, the divisions were called sections, but the term divisions will be used throughout this work.

1908-1909 London Civil Service and Municipal Chess League, Division 1.

		1	2	3	4	5	6	7	Tot
1	Savings Bank	X	0	1	1	1	1	1	5
2	GPO North	1	X	1	½	1	1	1	4½
3	Patent Office	0	0	X	1	1	1	½	3½
4	LCC	0	½	0	X	1	1	1	3½
5	Local Government Board	0	0	0	0	X	1	½	1½
6	Board of Education	0	0	0	0	0	X	1	1
7	GPO Stores	0	0	½	0	½	0	X	1

GPO North's one point fine for winning the previous year proved decisive.

1908-1909 London Civil Service and Municipal Chess League, Division 2.

		1	2	3	4	5	6	7	8	9	10	Tot
1	Patent Office II	X	0	1	1	1	1	1	1	1	1	8
2	GPO Engineering	1	X	1	½	1	1	0	1	1	1	7½
3	LCC II	0	0	X	1	1	1	1	1	1	1	7
4	GPO North II	0	½	0	X	1	1	1	1	1	1	6½
5	Paymaster General	0	0	0	0	X	1	1	1	0	1	4
6	India Store Depot	0	0	0	0	0	X	1	1	1	1	4
7	Metropolitan Water Board	0	1	0	0	0	0	X	1	½	1	3½
8	Local Government Bd II	0	0	0	0	0	0	0	X	1	1	2
9	National Telephone	0	0	0	0	1	0	½	0	X	½	2
10	GPO Stores II	0	0	0	0	0	0	0	0	½	X	½

Twenty teams played the following year, including Exchequer and Audit, the Board of Agriculture and Fisheries, and the Central Telegraph Office. On the 6th October 1909, the Civil Service League lost 22-28 to Hampstead. It was reported that CS were weakened as although there were many leading players in public service, a large number worked for departments which did not play in the league. The CS team was only selected from people who played in the league. You could be the best player in the country, but if your department had no team, you would not be selected.

1909-1910 London Civil Service and Municipal Chess League, Division 1.

		1	2	3	4	5	6	7	8	9	Tot
1	GPO North	X	1	1	1	1	1	1	1	1	8
2	Patent Office	0	X	1	1	1	1	1	1	1	7
3	Local Government Board	0	0	X	1	0	1	½	1	1	4½
4	LCC	0	0	0	X	1	0	1	1	1	4
5	GPO Engineering	0	0	1	0	X	0	1	1	1	4
6	Savings Bank	0	0	0	1	1	X	1	0	1	3*
7	Board of Education	0	0	½	0	0	0	X	1	½	2
8	Exchequer & Audit Dept	0	0	0	0	0	1	0	X	½	1½
9	GPO Stores	0	0	0	0	0	0	½	½	X	1

* Savings Bank fined a point for winning the previous year.

1909-1910 London Civil Service and Municipal Chess League, Division 2.

		1	2	3	4	5	6	7	8	9	10	11	Tot
1	GPO North II	X	1	1	1	0	1	1	1	1	1	1	9
2	Patent Office II	0	X	1	1	1	1	1	1	1	1	1	9
3	LCC II	0	0	X	0	1	1	1	0	1	1	1	6
4	Paymaster General	0	0	1	X	0	0	1	1	1	1	1	6
5	Central Telegraph Off.	1	0	0	1	X	0	0	1	1	1	1	6
6	Local Government Bd II	0	0	0	1	1	X	0	1	0	1	1	5
7	Metropolitan Water Board	0	0	0	0	1	1	X	0	1	1	1	5
8	India Stores Depot	0	0	1	0	0	0	1	X	0	1	1	4
9	Board of Agriculture & F	0	0	0	0	0	1	0	1	X	1	0	3
10	GPO Stores II	0	0	0	0	0	0	0	0	0	X	1	1
11	National Telephone	0	0	0	0	0	0	0	0	1	0	X	1

The top two teams shared the title. The prize-winning teams in both divisions decided not to accept the prizes they were due, instead suggesting the money be used to buy a permanent trophy for division 2.

The league had grown to 23 teams in 1910, including Westminster City Council Offices. There was sufficient confidence in the league's future to permit the purchase of a trophy for division 2.

BCM's report of the 1911 British Championship said, 'Mr Michell played, as he always does with thoughtfulness and accuracy. He had a wider theoretical knowledge of the game than the majority of the players and is therefore always dangerous. His only losses were against Yates and McKee, and with the latter he might have drawn by perpetual check had he not played to win.' Yates shared first place with Atkins, but lost the play-off. He went on to win the British Championship six times. The 1911-12 season again saw 23 teams play in the league, including a new team from the Office of Works. There were discussions about the inclusion of a third division the following year. By the end of 1911, Bonar Law had become the leader of the Conservative Party, despite never having held a Cabinet post. The long-serving secretary of the league, WHM Kirk, won the 'First Class Amateurs Section B' at the British Championship in 1912, and also won the Surrey Individual Challenge cup, which is the county championship.

The 1912-13 League now had 25 teams. Division I was won by Somerset House with an impressive 8½/9, well ahead of LCC on 7, and Local Government Board 6½. Somerset House had an impressive team, with HG Cole, EG Sergeant, E Macdonald and D Miller. However, league records show 'Inland Revenue' winning the league, certainly they had a large presence at Somerset House. Patent Office II won division 2 with 7½/9, ahead of Customs and Somerset House II on 6½. Local Government Board II scored 4/4, ahead of Patent Office III 3, in division 3.

Records are sketchy for the 1913-1914 season. Somerset House had a close battle with Board of Education, but the former emerged victorious. Customs (or Custom House) won division 2 and Customs II won division 3 ahead of Somerset House II and III. *BCM* commented, 'The enthusiasm of the players in this league may be judged from the fact that it is not at all uncommon for a man to win (or lose) his game in a CS League match and then rush off to take part in a London League contest!' As matches might start at 5 pm, this was just about feasible.

Trophies were awarded the following season to GPO (division 1), Board of Agriculture and Fisheries (division 2) and a Somerset House team (division 3). By now World War I was well underway and Civil Service League chess fell into abeyance.

In 1916 a Liberal/Conservative Government was in power, (although there were a couple of Labour posts as well), with Lloyd George as Prime Minister. Andrew Bonar Law became Leader of the House, as well as Chancellor of the Exchequer (the latter post until 1919). He spoke at Bootle on 3rd December 1918, three weeks after the end of the war, 'One of the results of the war must be to make it plain that men who deliberately, as in a game of chess, plunged the world into a conflict for the sake of gain to themselves should always be held guilty of bloodshed.' It became known in the House that Capablanca had been invited there to do a simultaneous display on 2nd December 1919. James Hogge MP asked Bonar Law about this and enquired if a prize fight would also be allowed. Bonar Law was considered somewhat dour, so his unusually witty reply was that, 'If my Hon. Friend wishes to take part in a prize-fight, and will make application in the usual way, I am sure it will have consideration.' Bonar Law clearly loved his chess, but had difficulty fitting in games. He used to send a message when he was free and players would travel to Westminster to give him a game. When he had worked in Kidstons' Queen Street Office in Glasgow, he had lunch at Lang's Coffee House nearby and sometimes had time for a game of chess before afternoon work. He was devoted to indoor games, like chess, billiards and whist, later bridge. He was a good chess player and would solve problems on trains when there was nobody to play. The very strong player Jacques Mieses said Bonar Law was a good amateur, which was intended as a compliment.

In 1921, he played at the Café de la Regencé, a renowned chess venue, which had been visited by such luminaries as Philidor, Morphy and Anderssen. It was said Bonar Law played with :-

'Great recklessness, flashes of brilliance, but in a manner dangerously unsound by ordinary standards.'

This was in great contrast to his golf, bridge and most of his life...

WHM Kirk played in the third section of the Hastings 'Victory' Congress, winning with 9.5/11. Back on 7 was 18 year-old Max Euwe, later to be world champion. The top section was won by Capablanca, with RP Michell scoring a respectable 50 %. The *CSCA Annual Report* for 1919-1920 begins, 'the resumption of the league's activities after the War found 15 clubs ready to play.' RP Michell played a 16-board simultaneous display against Admiralty on 20th February 1920, winning 13 games, and conceding only two draws and a loss. The league was now underway again.

1919-1920 London Civil Service and Municipal Chess League, Division 1.

		1	2	3	4	5	6	7	8	Tot
1	GPO North	X	0	1	1	1	1	1	1	6
2	Ministry of Health	1	X	0	1	½	1	1	1	5½
3	LCC	0	1	X	1	1	½	1	1	5½
4	Patent Office	0	0	0	X	1	1	1	1	4
5	Board of Education	0	½	0	0	X	1	0	1	2½
6	Somerset House	0	0	½	0	0	X	½	1	2
7	Paymaster General	0	0	0	0	1	½	X	0	1½
8	Customs	0	0	0	0	0	0	1	X	1

GPO North retained their title, as they had won the previous competition in 1914-15. The second division had 11 teams, and was won by Post Office Stores 8½/10, ahead of Ministry of Agriculture and Fisheries 8, Metropolitan Water Board 7½, Post Office Engineering 6½, Office of Works 5, Somerset House II 5, Patent Office II 4½, Ministry of Health II 3½, Overseas Trade Department 3, Ministry of Labour, Kew 2½, Customs II 1.

The league grew significantly the following year, to 29 teams. Division 1 was closely contested. Board of Education and Patent Office shared first with 7½/9, Post Office Stores 6, GPO North 5½, Customs 4½, Ministry of Health, LCC, Admiralty 3½, Somerset House 2, Ministry of Agriculture and Fisheries 1½. Board of Education drew three matches, against PO Stores, GPO North and LCC. Patent Office lost to Board of Education and drew with Ministry of Health. The play-off match resulted in another victory for Board of Education. Division 2 was won by PO Engineering with 8½/11, only just ahead of GPO North II and Savings Bank (who beat the winners) on 8. Division 3 was won by Home Office on 6 (probably out of 7 matches), closely followed by PO Stores II

5½ and LCC II 5. The league's success was widely attributed to the continuing hard work of WHM Kirk.

The London Chess League AGM was held on 6th July 1921 and considered altering its constitution to include the affiliation of other leagues, including the London Civil Service and Municipal League, the Postal Services League, the Banks League etc. It was agreed that this should happen, subject to any alterations that may be necessary. For example, a chess centre was desirable which could be open all day, and where league matches could be played. Refreshments had to be provided as well. Initially, a suitable venue could not be found.

Few details remain of individual clubs, but it is interesting to note that at this time GPO North was open to employees of the Accountant General's Department and Secretaries Office. They met at the GPO North Refreshment Rooms and paid a subscription of 5/- (25 p). The club secretary was GT Womack. GPO Engineering met at the same venue on the same night, but their employees paid only 3/- (15 p). Their club secretary was LG Farries. This may seem inequitable, but one assumes the office staff were paid considerably more than the engineers. In their 9th year in the league (1920/21) the Ministry of Agriculture and Fisheries Chess Club was thriving with 37 members and most of these entered the club tournaments. They entered a team in division 1 of the CS Chess League and also had a team in division 3. By September 1921 their membership ('including ladies') had increased to 50.

CS chess was booming in London. The Post Office deserves a special mention in these early years because of the number of chess clubs which had been formed in different sections of the same department. Prior to 1914 the Post Office had only one good club but this led to lack of interest. The creation of many smaller chess clubs in the Post Office had widened interest and led to a rapid expansion of separate clubs in many workplaces such as sorting and parcel offices scattered around London, engineering works and so on. They had eight teams from six independent clubs competing in the Civil Service and Municipal Chess League. Such was the degree of interest that in June 1921 in addition to playing in the Civil Service League, they formed their own league, 'The London Postal Chess League'. It should be clarified that this was a league for Post Office employees to play 'over the board' chess, not a league for 'correspondence chess'. Their first President was the Controller of the Post Office, CC Sanderson, who in 1922 was elected a vice–president of the newly formed Civil Service Chess Association (CSCA) and who was later knighted. Initially the London Postal Chess League comprised 6 clubs - ECDO (East Central District Office), Phoenix (GPO Parcels), SEPO (South-Eastern Post Office), WCDO (West Central District Office), NWDO (North-West District Office) and Paddington District Office, but interest spread rapidly and soon two divisions were formed. Two of their clubs, City of London Postal Clubs and Paddington DO also entered teams in division C of the London Chess League.

In October 1921 the following teams entered the 'London Postal Chess Challenge Cup' : Northern DO, Phoenix (Parcels), Excelsior (GPO) – who were the defending champions, West Central, Western DO, Foreign Section (GPO), St. Georges (SEDO), Waverly (Peckham), Buckingham (SWDO), Chelsea DO, Crescent (Eastern DO), and North West DO. Twelve teams participated in a knock-out competition for the 'London Postal Challenge Cup' later that year, and this was in addition to the teams competing in the Civil Service and Municipal Chess League.

The Civilian reported on 26th November 1921,

'Proposed formation of a CIVIL SERVICE CHESS CLUB – A meeting will be held in the Conference Room 'A' at the Mines Department, Hotel Windsor, Victoria Street, S.W., at 6pm on the 28th instant, with a view to the above. It is hoped there will be a large attendance of Civil Service chess players.'

This seems rather short notice, but it obviously worked, as at the meeting two days later, it was proposed that a Civil Service Chess Club be formed. This recognized that the league, which was now in its 17th year, had 38 teams, 11 in division 1, 14 in division 2 and 13 in division 3. The various sections of the Post Office, including Post Office Savings Bank, had 9 teams with three teams in each division. It is interesting to compare the departmental teams with those of today. The rules governing in which divisions teams could play were very different in those days and it was often left to the clubs to indicate in which division their teams should play. There was no automatic promotion or relegation and Ministry of Health apparently had a 2nd team in both division 2 and 3, although that may have been a printing error.

Division I
1. Board of Education, 2. Patent Office, 3. GPO North, 4. Somerset House, 5. Customs, 6. PO Stores, 7. Ministry of Health, 8. London County Council I, 9. Ministry of Agriculture & Fisheries, 10. PO Engineering, 11. Admiralty I.

Division 2
1. PO Savings Bank, 2. Paymaster General's Office, 3. GPO North II, 4.Office of Works, 5. Metropolitan Water Board, 6. Home Office, 7. Patent Office II, 8. Ministry of Health II, 9. Customs II, 10. PO Stores II, 11. Admiralty II, 12.

LCC II, 13. Department of Overseas Trade, 14. Ministry of Labour (L.S & E).

Division 3
1. Somerset House II, 2. Ministry of Health II, 3. Ministry of Labour (Kew), 4. Home Office II, 5. Mines, 6. Ministry of Agriculture & Fisheries II, 7. Royal Mint, 8. Denman (GPO Engineering), 9. Metropolitan Water Board II, 10. Patent Office III, 11. PO Engineering II, 12. GPO North III, 13. Board of Trade.

An unusual (and rather splendid) event occurred on the 6th January 1922. RP Michell and EG Sergeant (Inland Revenue) met in 'Bath's Hall, Wood Street, Kingston' at 8pm for a demonstration of living chess. A map of that time shows that the Public Baths were in Wood Street, hence 'Bath's Hall'. Wood Street is now dominated by a very large shopping centre. Details were available from Mrs Michell (the former Edith Tapsell, a strong player in her own right) at 26 Alexandra Road, Kingston Hill. An alarming report said that the performance would be postponed, due to 'sickness in the neighbourhood', which appears to have been a flu outbreak. The concerns are understandable as there had been a flu pandemic a couple of years earlier, which had killed at least 50 million people worldwide (more than died in World War I). However, the event went ahead in the presence of the Mayor and Mayoress and a moderate attendance of the general public, which included several strong local players. The event was in support of the 'Church Completion Fund', presumably the Church next door to where the Michells lived in Kingston. A school now occupies the site of their house. Miss Dorothy Cushon designed the costumes in crusader style, the white pieces wearing white costumes with gold decoration, and the black pieces wearing red with silver decoration. The kings and queens marched on to the board attended by their pawns. The four bishops followed and formed a square with their croziers under which marched the knights and rooks to salute their sovereigns. Michell had white and won on the 57th move. A strong local player, Mr EH Cumberland acted as 'shouter' (conveying the moves from the players) and Mrs Michell and Mr E Cox-Hartnell acted as 'shovers' (pointing the pieces to the correct squares). In the interval, the Kingston Hill Orchestra, led by Mr Jack Hatch played a variety of music, and a game of Capablanca's was demonstrated. The 3rd Kingston Hill Troop of Girl Guides acted as attendants.

It was about now that changes were approaching in CS sport. Warren Fisher (1879-1948) was permanent secretary to Treasury and Head of the Civil Service 1919 – 1939. He was asked to improve morale in the CS as it was recognised that staff were unhappy. He had a rather startling solution to this problem. Fisher thought that Civil Service staff were run down and fed up and he suggested that the Government should pay for staff to have a short holiday in Paris to see life! Unfortunately, everyone whom he consulted said it was unthinkable. Fisher commented that he was supposed to raise staff morale... According to O'Halpin's biography,

'He believed that sport could break down barriers of rank and department, and also that it increased a sense of common identity in the service as a whole. The founders of the Civil Service Sports Association were allowed to use offices in the Treasury for their meetings, and in 1921 he launched an appeal among his fellow heads of departments to raise £150 towards the cost of establishing the new body. In 1925 he persuaded the Government, despite Churchill's objections, to give a grant of £200000 over four years to finance the purchase of suitable grounds. This was announced by Austen Chamberlain at the annual Civil Service dinner on 12th February 1926. Leo Amery, who attended the dinner, 'doubted very much this is the right moment for such a concession and I think the doubt is widely shared.' '

The Cabinet withdrew the grant. Fisher was furious, 'If the Government do not intend to give the £50000 per year as promised, there seems to be nothing to be said for vague references to the future.' The Civil Service Sports Association was formed in 1921 and later renamed the Civil Service Sports Council (CSSC) and it bought the Chiswick grounds anyway.

In 1938, the Government started a grant of £20000 a year. At least Fisher was still in post then, but the 16-year wait must have rankled. He did not think much of Bonar Law. When Bonar Law stepped down as Prime Minister, Fisher shouted, 'Thank God!'

The Civil Service Chess Association was formed in 1922. GA Felce (President of Surrey) took the chair at a general meeting of Civil Service chess players held on 27th February 1922 with the object of approving rules and a constitution for an Association comprising the whole of the chess players within the Civil Service and to elect a provisional committee. The principal objects of the Association were to arrange matches for teams representing the Service as a whole and to obtain a central club room. It was announced in *The Civilian* on 11th March 1922 that 'ASSOCIATIONS had been formed for the following forms of Sport :- Cricket, Swimming, Rugby Football, Rowing, Chess, Shooting, Golf, and Athletics.' CSSC's own records said that CSCA was formed in 1921, but post-war this was amended to 1922, which looks correct.

The first meeting of the CSCA Council was held 24th April 1922. Sir Horace P Hamilton KCB (Customs & Excise) was elected president. Sir TK Rose, DSc, (Royal Mint) and CC Sanderson (GPO) were elected as vice-presidents. In those days, such honours were more associated with seniority in Civil Service than activities in chess, although Rose was an enthusiastic and useful player. AJ Spencer (Science Museum) was elected secretary and T Hipkins (London Postal Chess League) treasurer. It was decided to arrange a Civil Service chess championship for the autumn, and also representative matches with the Universities, House of Commons and a 50-board match GPO v Rest of the Civil Service at the Postal Festival at Crystal Palace on 26 August 1922. It also planned to arrange exhibition games against Capablanca. The Association now embraced 22 clubs and about 500 players but activities were initially confined to the London area. In July 1922 WHM Kirk (Ministry of Health) was elected chairman and it was suggested that unattached players contact the secretary with a view to forming a group for individual members. The CSCA had a Council of 22 members, the three main officers, and representatives of 19 clubs. Matches were arranged against Surrey, Kent, Middlesex, and Oxford and Cambridge Universities. RC Griffith (President of Middlesex) gave an interesting lecture and the chair was taken by Sir George L Barstow KCB (Treasury) who was himself a player of considerable ability. Such was the high level of interest in chess that the Prime Minister, The Rt. Hon. Andrew Bonar Law presented a trophy for a Civil Service departmental knock-out competition. The first AGM of the Civil Service Chess Association (CSCA) was held on 23rd October 1922 at the Treasury. An interesting programme was arranged for the coming season including club, individual and representative matches. The rules for the Bonar Law competition were agreed and these differed from the present-day rules. The competition was open to clubs outside London and the entry fee was 2/6 (12½ p). The clubs arranged a date by mutual agreement and results had to be reported within 24 hours. According to reports, 'A large number of CS clubs have already affiliated (to CSCA) and it is hoped that the remainder will follow, when the objects and proposals of the Association become better known. Individual membership of the Association is open to civil servants who do not belong to affiliated or other clubs. The Hon. Secretary is Mr AJ Spencer (Science Museum), who is anxious to get in touch with all such unattached chess players and will gladly answer any enquiries.' This last action was a splendid idea as it will be recalled that previous CS teams had been weakened as they only fielded members who were able to play in the league. A club called UNATS (for unattached players) duly appeared a quarter of a century later! The first individual championship was scheduled for 1923. In addition to holding a cup, the winner would receive a gold medal, the runner-up a silver medal and the two losing semi-finalists a bronze medal. The Prime Minister (Bonar Law) had accepted office as a vice-president of the CS Sports Council. He promised to arrange a match between the Houses of Parliament and the Civil Service. Another new club was formed, Royal Arsenal, which met on Mondays from 5 pm – 8.30 pm, and welcomed all workers from the Arsenal and allied departments. Individual tournaments and club matches were arranged.

With the increase in the number of clubs and 41 teams, it was necessary to have a fourth division for 1922/23. The representative matches included 50 board matches against both Middlesex and Surrey and a 20-board match against a combined team from Oxford and Cambridge Universities. CS beat Middlesex 28 – 22 on 27th January 1923 and the team included RP Michell (City of London Chess Club), HS Barlow (Surrey Champion), GA Felce (Surrey President), Sir George Barstow (Treasury) and Sir Thomas Rose (Royal Mint).

The 1922/23 season started on 26 August with a Post Office family fete and fun fair held at Crystal Palace and the many activities included a 33-board match v Rest of Civil Service. The match was held in a Committee Room overlooking the South Terrace but the players had to contend with considerable noise from the fun of the fair! The result was a win for the Civil Service 19½-13½. The top four boards were

Civil Service		Post Office
1. ET Jesty	½-½	EW Osler
2. EG Twitchett	1-0	AC Challenger
3. BHN Stronach	½-½	CS Shaw
4. CM Cordingley	½-½	G Henson

Civil Service chess was also thriving elsewhere in the UK and in 1922/23 the Edinburgh CS club (founded 1909) had three teams in the Edinburgh Chess League, finishing runners-up in A division and as champions of C division. The following season did not get off to a good start in A division when the team lost 4-2 to Edinburgh Ladies but in a friendly 12 board match the Service won 7½-4½.

The Post Office played a 40-board match v Hampstead Chess Club with boards 1-20 played at Stansfield House and 21-40 at Diviani's Restaurant, Hampstead winning 23½ -16½. Western DO won both the magnificent HL Forster Trophy and also the division 2 championship. By 1923, the Postal league had 18 teams in it.

The Post Office individual champion was AC Challenger

(SWDO) and he also had the best score in division 1. The league was indebted to the Editor of the *British Chess Magazine (BCM)* for fully annotating the games. Many members played in County and CSCA representative matches and frequently competed with considerable success in the CSCA individual championship.

On 13th February, Kostich defeated Somerset House 18-1, conceding just two draws. Bonar Law delivered a speech to the International Congress players on 29th July 1922, on the qualities necessary for chess players,

'The power of looking ahead and seeing further than one's opponent; concentration as great, if not greater, than in any other human occupation; it required also and no great player was without it, a great deal of imagination. It demanded in addition, patience and vigilance, more perhaps than any other quality.'

As the International Tournament was taking place, the British Championship did not, but other sections did, and RP Michell won the Major Open and his wife won the British Women's Championship.

HC Griffiths delivered a lecture to the Royal Mint Chess Club on Ruy Lopez. The club had arranged a large programme of matches and they also entered the CS League. On 12 March 1923, the Middlesex President RC Griffith (a former British champion) gave a lecture to CSCA, entitled 'King's Side Attacks', and the Council hoped, 'to increase the number of events of this character during the coming Season'.

The London-based league had done a lot for CS chess, but obviously was only really interested in the London area. The CSCA was the national body for CS chess. Of course, London activities still tended to predominate, owing to the geographical concentration of players. The first season of the CSCA

(1922/23) was an undoubted success as 19 clubs affiliated with a membership of 532, plus ten individual members. The *First Annual Report* of the Civil Service Chess Association lists the officers as, President Sir George Barstow KCB, Vice-Presidents Sir TK Rose DSc and Chas C Sanderson Esq., Hon. Treasurer WH Hipkiss and Hon. Secretary AJ Spencer. The AGM was scheduled for Monday 24th September at 6 pm, at Treasury Chambers, Whitehall. The affiliated clubs were: Admiralty, Board of Customs and Excise, Board of Education, Home Office, Ministry of Health, Royal Mint, Dept. of Overseas Trade, Patent Office, Paymaster General's Office, GPO North, GPO Engineering (Denman), PO Savings Bank, Western Postal Office of GPO, GPO Parcels (Phoenix CC), Inland Section of GPO, Western Parcel Office of GPO, Somerset House, GPO Stores, Office of Works.

According to the annual report,

'The question of correspondence chess matches has been considered by the Council, and an invitation to play such a match has been received from Bedfordshire, but the Council felt that the Association had hardly settled down sufficiently to embark on matches of this character. Reference should be made, however, to the fact that the Phoenix Chess Club, affiliated to the Association, defeated the Birmingham PO in a correspondence match of six boards.

The Council feel that the thanks of the Association are due to Sir Aubrey Symonds KCB, the Chairman of the Sports Council, for his kindness in placing at the disposal of the Association a room at the Ministry of Health for chess purposes.

In accordance with the revised rules of the Civil Service Sports Council, the Association is entitled to three representatives on that Council, and your Council elected Messrs. Dark,

Poor and the Hon. Secretary to represent the Association.

The financial position of the Association is sound inasmuch as there is a small balance in hand, but increased revenue is necessary if the Association is to enlarge its scope by offering additional attractions to its members.

With regard to the coming Season, the Council wish to urge all affiliated clubs to send in to the Secretary as soon as possible any revision of membership lists they may wish to make. The Council also express the hope that clubs not affiliated may see their way to do so in order to give that further support to the Association which it needs.

By order of the Council,
AJ Spencer
Hon. Secretary
10th September 1923'

Patent Office were first winners of the knockout competition and the Council gratefully acknowledged the gift of a trophy from Bonar Law. Fourteen teams entered the competition, which was played over ten boards.

Round 1
GPO Stores beat Royal Mint
Inland Section beat Denman
Patent Office beat Home Office
GPO North beat Phoenix
Ministry of Health beat Somerset House
Board of Education beat HM Office of Works
Admiralty bye
Department of Overseas Trade bye

Round 2
Ministry of Health beat Inland Section
Patent Office beat GPO Stores
GPO North beat Overseas Trade
Board of Education beat Admiralty

Semi final
Patent Office beat GPO North
Board of Education beat Ministry of Health

Patent Office played four matches against GPO North before triumphing and reaching the final. In those days there was no method of determining winners by the elimination rules for splitting ties and there were many replays. Tie-breaks, like board count and bottom board elimination, only became a permanent fixture in the late 70s.

Final

Patent Office

Board of Education

1.	HF Lowe (w)	½-½	CEC Tattersall
2.	FW Dunn	½-½	ET Jesty
3.	WO Woodfield	½-½	BHN Stronach
4.	P Clarkson	½-½	F Dark
5.	RF Whitehead	1-0	JA Graham
6.	A Burns	1-0	WS Elphick
7.	GH Green	1-0	JM McCullough
8.	W Langstaff	1-0	SG Duffell
9.	H Harding	1-0	FL Snow
10.	LM Rampal	½-½	E Lancaster Jones
		7½-2½	

It was hoped at that stage that Bonar Law would present the trophy himself, indeed he was eager to do so, but his untimely death occurred before the event's completion. According to the 'Times', 'It takes the form of a silver rook, mounted on a rectangular stepped plinth, the piece itself being copied from a rook in a carved ivory set now in the Victoria and Albert Museum. This set is from Berhampore, Bengal, and is believed to have been made about 1800.' After a commemorative tablet had been added to the trophy it was presented informally, with CSSC being invited to organize a more formal presentation if it desired.

A later description read,

'Mausoleum, 4½ inch in height, 2 inch square base. First step around bottom decorated with rose pattern, then two plain steps leading to a square door on every side, surmounted with mosque like dome decorated with leaves on which there is a spire. This is an intricate piece of work requiring well thought out method of manufacturing. London Hallmarked 1923. Weight 140 g. It is mounted on wooden base, square with steps leading to the mausoleum. Each flat part of the step having a silver plate suitable for engraving. Whole subject is set up in its own wooden case with glass door and brass handle.'

Leading league positions were:-

Division 1, Somerset House 9, Patent Office 7½, GPO North and Board of Education 7, Ministry of Health 5 (after being penalized a point for winning the previous year).

Division 2, GPO North II 11, LCC II 8, GPO Stores II and Ministry of Health II 7½.

Division 3, Mines and Customs 6½ (Mines won the play-off), GPO North III 5.

Division 4, Crown Agencies for Colonies 6½, LCC III 6, Patent Office III 5½.

The amalgamation of the Civil Service Chess Association and the Civil Service and Municipal Chess League had now been effected. Mr W Kirk and Mr F J Colman, both of the Ministry of Health, were secretary and assistant secretary, respectively.

The CS league now had four divisions. Mines Department were part of the Board of Trade. Many of the club names reflect their time.

There were 37 entries in the individual championship and ET Jesty (Education Board 2) defeated CEC Tattersall (Education Board 1) in the final. The strength of the competition can be judged by the semi-finalists which included the Surrey champion HS Barlow (Ministry of Pensions) and EW Osler (Inland Section, GPO). An unusual feature of the individual championship was the Council's right to exempt from the preliminary rounds players of established ability. Tattersall joined Victoria and Albert Museum in 1915 and became 'Keeper of the Department of Textiles' in 1934, three years before he retired. He did write the highly-regarded *A History of British Carpets* in 1934. It is not clear if museums came under 'Education' or if his qualification came from earlier employment.

After the win v Middlesex, CS lost narrowly 9 -11 on 24th March 1923 to the Combined Oxford and Cambridge teams (the full match score appearing in the 'Times' two days later) and on April 7th 1923 lost 23½ – 26½ to Surrey. The chess match against the Houses of Parliament was cancelled because after the election, the new House did not have enough chess players!

Combined Universities		Civil Service
1. EE Colman (C)	½-½	G A Felce
2. TA Staynes (O)	½-½	EW Osler
3. A Oppenheim (O)	0-1	BHN Stronach
4. EA Coad-Pryor (C)	0-1	EJ Price
5. JM Bee (C)	1-0	EG Twitchett
6. PI Wyndham (C)	1-0	F Dark
7. GW Knight (O)	0-1	WO Woodfield
8. AM Ewbank (C)	1-0	CM Cordingley
9. JE West (C)	½-½	GA Shoobridge
10. J Edwards (O)	0-1	E Daly
11. AH Crothers (O)	½-½	EC Taylor
12. RM Dowdeswell (C)	½-½	WH Taylor
13. EH Gateman (C)	0-1	TL Adamson
14. AH Wykeham-George (O)	1-0	SJ Holloway
15. E Lob (O)	0-1	FH Jerram
16. S Goldstein (C)	1-0	LA Paish
17. JW Harmer (C)	1-0	EE Parsons
18. LM Fraser (O)	½-½	A Gunsberg
19. E Lancaster-Jones (C)	1-0	WH Sealy
20. DE Littlewood (C)	1-0	H Polman
	11-9	

The University players on boards 1, 4, 5, 14, 15, 19 were past members of the universities.

PS Milner-Barry won the inaugural British Boys (Under 18) Championship at Hastings and BCM commented, 'He is a player of the attacking type and may go far.' He certainly did, and his exploits and fame were not limited to chess. The 26th March saw a 'Centipede Simultaneous Display' at the Royal

Mint. The 'centipede' consisted of FFL Alexander, Harold Brown, EW Davies and ME Goldstein, and they would make moves in turn against the opposition. Despite the presence of strong players, this can cause confusion. The author took part in a tandem simultaneous where one of the masters aggressively posted a piece, only for his colleague to rapidly retreat it the next move, rather than sacrificing it as the first master intended. Nevertheless, the centipede triumphed by 14½-1½. The sole winner was the Royal Mint captain, Sir Thomas Kirk Rose, who had formerly been in an assayer for the Mint and had given evidence as an expert witness in forgery cases some 30 years earlier. One expert forger had made some convincing coins, but after Rose's evidence and a partial plea of 'Guilty', a sentence of 8 years Penal Servitude resulted. Rose also wrote *The Metallurgy of Gold*, published in 1915.

The 1923 British Championship was played at Southsea and GE Wainwright finished a respectable 5th. The Major Open saw ET Jesty finish 6th with 5/11, the runaway winner being Alexander Alekhine on 10½! Jesty put up a good fight against the future world champion.

CS played Surrey over 50 boards at the Ministry of Health in November 1923, winning 25½-24½, and it was hoped it would become an annual event. Top results were:-

	Civil Service		Surrey
1.	RP Michell	½-½	RCJ Walker
2.	GA Felce	½-½	HB Uber
3.	EW Osler	1-0	GE Wernick
4.	BHN Stronach	½-½	HC Griffiths
5.	EJ Price	½-½	FF Alexander
6.	EG Twitchett	0-1	EW Davies
7.	F Dark	½-½	PJ Allingham

8. HF Lowe	0-1	WL Brierley
9. WC Woodfield	½-½	P Howell
10. TG Edmund-Smith	1-0	AW Fisher
11. CM Cordingley	½-½	EA Limming
12. J Cooke	0-1	GC Evans

When 'time' was called, Civil Service led 20½-19½ and the remaining games were either settled by agreement, or adjudicated by Amos Burn, who had been one of the world's leading players. Michell lived in Surrey so the result of the match would probably have been different if he changed sides. Losses followed against Middlesex by 18-32 and Kent by 25½-34½.

RP Michell had a fantastic tournament result at Margate in 1923. Gruenfeld won with 5.5/7, ahead of Alekhine (World Champion just four years later), Bogolyubov, Muffang and Michell 4.5, Reti 3, Colman 1, Mueller 0.5. Michell's only loss came against Gruenfeld, and he drew against Alekhine, Muffang and Mueller. Curiously, Michell faced the Gruenfeld Defence when he played Alekhine, and Alekhine's Defence when he played Reti. It has to be remembered that Michell was now 50 years old. He also played at the Hastings (1923/24) tournament, which was won by future World Champion Max Euwe with 7½/9, but Michell scored 5.

The London Commercial Chess League was founded in 1924. The initial teams were Cornhill, Lloyds Ports (Royal Exchange), Anglo-Mex, Morton's, Motor Union, Nestanglo, St Helen's Court, Sedgwick Collins, CT Bowrings, Shell-Mex. Shell agreed to a condition that six of Shell's best players were barred from the league to make the competition more interesting, which was to be played over at least 9 boards. The weakening of Shell certainly worked as they did not finish in the top two. At this stage, there were no CS teams in the Commercial League, but there was considerable overlap in later years. The CS individual competition continued and in 1924, both the finalists were from Post Office clubs with G Wernick (GPO North) defeating EW Osler (Mount Pleasant), after several draws. W Woodfield and J Mahood were the losing semi-finalists. Post Office also encouraged chess outside London and a correspondence chess match was won by London Phoenix against Birmingham Post Office, and Bath Post Office lost a conventional match against Bristol Civil Service 4½ – 9½.

1923/4 was a very successful year for Ministry of Health who not only won the league championship with 9/10 but defeated the holders Patent Office 6½-3½ in the final of the Bonar Law. The 'Times' reported the result the following day! Not to be outshone the Health 2nd team won division 2 with 11/12.

Bonar Law Final 15th April 1924

Min. of Health		Patent Office
1. EJ Price	0-1	WO Woodfield
2. WHM Kirk	1-0	W Dunn
3. C Cordingley	1-0	P Clarkson
4. R Daly	1-0	W Langstaff
5. CA Thorogood	1-0	RF Whitehead
6. HG Dowden	1-0	SE Chisholm
7. HJ Pearman	½-½	LM Rampal
8. Dr JE Chapman	0-1	A Burns
9. LE Fitzgerald	1-0	GH Green
10. RJ Harrison	0-1	H Harding
	6½-3½	

Patent Office II succeeded in the inaugural year of the Minor club championship (in 1936, this was later called the 'Post Annual Cup') defeating GPO Parcels (Phoenix CC).

A few days earlier, Surrey defeated Essex 11-6 in the semi-final of the Southern Counties Chess Union championship, both sides making use of strong Civil Service players, e.g. Woodfield, Michell, Felce, Shoobridge, Stronach etc.

In June 1924 CS played a match against Kent in somewhat unusual surroundings - the roof of Australia House in the Strand. Most of the boards were placed next to the parapet overlooking the Strand and the players enjoyed a marvellous view of London. Fortunately, the rain held off until the match was concluded! When the 100-board match was arranged, it was overlooked that the date coincided with a Saturday holiday for the Civil Service and many players refused to travel to London. Saturday working for the Civil Service was still usual then, and continued for many years. The match was reduced to 60 boards and Kent won 34½-25½. Lord Dunsany made one of his rare appearances for Kent and drew his game on board 15. CSCA was eager to acquire its own premises, as it was not possible to furnish a playing room properly, when it was used for meetings on a daily basis.

The 1924/5 season for the London CS & Municipal Chess League got off to a good start with a record entry of 21 affiliated clubs, 60 teams and 640 members, and a 5th division was created. Three new clubs entered – Ministry of Pensions, Air Ministry and Central Telegraph Office and there were five teams from Health and four from both GPO North and London County Council. Michell took on the War Office on 14th October 1924 in a simultaneous display, winning 15, drawing three, and losing to EG Trowbridge and QMS Bell. Surrey gained revenge that month for the previous year's defeat, the top board clash between

RP Michell and FFL Alexander being drawn.

The Ministry of Health retained the Bonar Law winning 7-3 against Education in what was a high class final:-

Health		Education
1. WHM Kirk	1-0	CEC Tatterstall
2. EJ Price	½-½	ET Jesty
3. CM Cordingley	0-1	BHN Stronach
4. R Daly	1-0	AJ Spencer
5. HJ Pearman	½-½	WW Hunt
6. HG Dowden	0-1	JA Graham
7. FA Jerram	1-0	JM McCullough
8. LE Fitzgerald	1-0	SG Duffell
9. RJ Harrison	1-0	FE Douglas
10. TE Davies	1-0	J Tucker
	7-3	

Health won the bottom two boards early in the evening and never looked back.

The minor club championship was won by GPO North II who defeated Patent Office II in the final. Middlesex won the 50-board match with CS held in March 1925.

The semi-final stage of the individual championship of Civil Service was reached, with EJ Price due to play W Gooding and ET Jesty playing WO Woodfield. ET Jesty went on to win the title, having won the inaugural event in 1923.

The Customs & Excise Chess Club commenced their season in October 1925 with a simultaneous display by T.G. Edmund – Smith. Two teams were entered in the league and the club intended to hold both a senior and junior championship.

In these early days the CSCA benefited from the interest

shown by the former Prime Minister (Bonar Law) and having such worthy government officials as Sir George L Barstow (President) who took the chair at the Annual General Meeting held on 13 October 1925. The Council reported a successful season. Chess players unattached to clubs were invited to enter the individual championship and the Area Associations were invited to cooperate in spreading the word for entries in both team and individual competitions. A match versus Surrey was played on 24 October 1925 and the Service lost 22-29. The results in other large matches were 23½ – 24½ v Kent and a win v Essex 33½ –18½ . A match was also arranged against London University. The secretary offered to hold a Lantern Lecture at the Science Museum on *The evolution of chess*.

Michell was back at Hastings in 1925/26, where Alekhine and Vidmar dominated, finishing equal first on 8½/9, but Michell was third on 5. WHM Kirk took time off from organizing to win the Surrey championship.

There was a clash of two CS teams on 3rd February 1926.

Bristol Civil Service		Bath Post Office
1. WG Stevens	0-1	W Palmer Jones
2. FJ Brown	0-1	GJ Beaven
3. H Wear	1-0	G Milne
4. HJ Bragg	½-½	C Hutchings
5. WH Field	0-1	R Davis
6. EE Cary	1-0	LR Coles
7. OJ Smith	1-0	H Honey
8. EH Head	1-0	J Midgley
9. A Gillespey	1-0	E Quinton
10. CC Roberts	1-0	O Parfitt
11. HR Parsons	1-0	GJ Blacker
12. WAJ Thomas	0-1	H Allen
	7½-4½	

The former organization was rather bigger, so that was not a bad performance by Bath. They did even better in November of that year.

Bath Post Office		Bristol Civil Service
1. W Palmer Jones	½-½	H Weir
2. GJ Beaven	½-½	FJ Brown
3. G Milne	½-½	JJ Wood
4. R Davis	1-0	HJ Bragg
5. H Honey	1-0	WH Field
6. O Parfitt	0-1	OJ Smith
7. E Quinton	0-1	WG Stevens
8. L Horne	0-1	E Filer
9. GJ Blacker	1-0	A Gillespy
10. A Adams	1-0	CC Roberts
11. V Rosenburg	½-½	WA Lee
12. A Cressey	0-1	JS Vowles
13. W Robins	0-1	SC May
14. SE Hacke	0-1	G Pearson
15. RWJ Mayles	1-0	G Coles
	7-8	

Some of the names differ slightly, (Wear/Weir and (Gillespey/Gillespy) but the responsibility lies with either the *Bath Chronicle* and *Weekly Gazette* or one of the captains, unless there were players with extremely similar names. The *Western Daily Press* reported that the Bristol Civil Service team led the league at the start of January, but then slipped to last after a couple of losses.

In June 1926 Patent Office were the victors 5½–4½ against Somerset House in the Bonar Law Final after the famous international Znosko-Borovsky adjudicated a win for Patent Office on board 7 and a draw on Board 9.

Patent Office		Somerset House
1. WO Woodfield	0-1	EG Sergeant
2. FW Dunn	½-½	D. Miller
3. P Clarkson	0-1	MA Prentice
4. RF Whitehead	1-0	WH Taylor
5. HW Hilliar	0-1	WS Wallis
6. SF Chisholm	½-½	EW Harris
7. A Burns	1-0	WW Brougham
8. W Langstaff	1-0	GE Marler
9. EA Lynn	½-½	WS Jackson
10. GH Green	1-0	E Robert
	5½-4½	

In April 1957, more than thirty years later, Inland Revenue won the Bonar Law final against GPO by 5½-4½ and as in 1926, Sergeant was on board 1 and Miller on board 2!

Patent Office II defeated GPO North II in the final of the minor club competition.

The clubs in 1925/26 were so different from those nowadays; e.g. Admiralty, Royal Arsenal, Customs & Excise, Trade, Clearing Office Sports Association, Home Office, India Stores, Health, Office of Works, Patent Office, Paymaster General's Office, Royal Mint, GPO Engineering (Denman CC), GPO North, GPO Parcels (Phoenix CC), GPO Stores, GPO SW District Office, PO Savings Bank, Somerset House, War Office. Ministry of Labour (Headquarters) affiliated for the 1926/27 season. There were 65 teams and 640 individual players.

Division 1 featured Somerset House (Inland Revenue), Board of Trade, Post Office Savings Bank (POSB), Ministry of Health, Ministry of Agriculture, Patent Office, GPO North, Ministry of Pensions, Admiralty, London County Council.

Division 2 comprised Crown Agents, Woolwich Arsenal, Metropolitan Water Board, Ministry of Labour, Paymaster General, GPO North 2, Office of Works, PO Stores, Ministry of Health 2, War Office.

The Council very much appreciated the kindness and generosity of G Middleton JP (on behalf of the Post Annual League) in presenting a trophy to the CS Sports Council. This was allocated to the minor club knock-out competition which thereafter was known as the 'Post Annual' Cup. It was a purchase from proceeds of the Union of Post Office Workers' *The Post* magazine. The Bonar Law and Post Annual trophies were very welcome, but did cause some difficulties. Ron Fleming (Treasurer for a great many years) wrote, 'Coming now to the CSCA itself, I recall that this started life as the London Civil Service and Municipal Chess League, and incorporated various London Civil Service chess clubs plus the London County Council and the Metropolitan Water Board. It bought or acquired various shields and competed for them. After the Great War the then Prime Minister, Bonar Law, presented a trophy to the Civil Service Sports Council, and the Post Annual League presented a cup to the Sports Council. These were passed on to the CSCA for competition between Civil Service chess clubs. However, they remained the property of the CS Sports Council. This point arose when the question of insuring them arose, and a meeting took place between representatives of the Sports Council and CSCA at which a declaration to this effect was drawn up and signed. I signed for the CSCA (together with, I believe, Ted Baker), and Middleton and another signed on behalf of the Sports Council. All later cups, trophies etc. were bought by the CSCA or by benefactors and are the property of the CSCA.'

This became an issue when a CS League committee later proposed to 'return' the trophies to CSSC, causing loud complaints from those with more knowledge of history.

There were 23 entries for the individual championship which was won by BHN Stronach (Education) who defeated WH Taylor (Somerset House) in the final. Invitations to play in representative matches were sent to members of all affiliated clubs, not just directed to the strongest players. The British Boys Championship was won by CHO'D Alexander.

Civil Service defeated Kent 32½-22½ on 4th December 1926 in 'Mr (Neville) Chamberlain's own room at the Ministry of Health, Whitehall.' Civil servants are well-used to their political masters enjoying considerably better conditions than them, but having a room which can accommodate 110 chess players seems extraordinary. Possibly the Minister had a large meeting room, or 'room' meant the whole building. A few weeks later, the players were presumably occupying a small corner of the room as they defeated London University by 17½-13½ on 27th January 1927.

London University		Civil Service
1. EG Sergeant	1-0	G Wernick
2. ME Goldstein	1-0	J Mahood
3. RF Goldstein	1-0	WO Woodfield

Again, high quality players were on show. The Post Office player, EW Osler, won the Essex Championship in 1927. On 12th February, CS lost heavily to Surrey 16½-33½.

Patent Office Chess Club held a dinner on 1st March 1927 and the programme was based on the idea that chess would provide the entertainment. An informal reception preceded the dinner and trophies held by the club, as well as unusual books, were on display. JW Barker demonstrated 'four magic square chess tours'. After dinner, a series of toasts was proposed, and illustrated by playing through games on a demonstration board. S Reed talked of the 'Old Masters', demonstrating a game between MacDonnell and de la Bourdonnais, and M Rampal covered the 'Masters of the Middle Period', showing Steinitz vs L Paulsen (Baden-Baden 1870). OC Muller replied, being well qualified to do so as he had known Steinitz and Zukertort. HF Lowe showed Alekhine vs Yates in tribute to 'Modern Masters'. RP Michell expressed the highest admiration for Capablanca and Lasker. The fourth toast, 'The Men and the Board' was proposed by the club President FW Dunn and was a surprise presentation to WO Woodfield, who had worked hard for the club over many years. The toast of the evening, 'The Civil Service and Municipal League' was proposed by the Comptroller General of HM Patent Office and replied to by WHM Kirk, secretary of the league since its inception.

64 teams played in the league (one fewer than 1925-26) and GPO North won the championship after a play-off.

Division 1, GPO North 10/12, Patent Office 10, Somerset House (Inland Revenue) 8, Board of Education 7, Ministry of Health 6, Office of High Commissioner for India 6, PO Savings Bank 6, Admiralty 5½, Customs 5½, Ministry of Pensions 5, Ministry of Agriculture and Fisheries 3½, Board of Trade 3, London County Council 2½.

Division 2, Paymaster General's Office 10½/13, Crown Agents for the Colonies 8½, GPO North II 8½, PO Savings Bank II 8½, London County Council II 8, Somerset House II 7½, Woolwich Arsenal 7½, Office of Works 6½, Patent Office II 6½, Metropolitan Water Board 5, War Office 4½,

Ministry of Labour 3½, PO Stores 3½, Ministry of Health II 2½.

Division 3, Denman 11/13, Ministry of Pensions (Acton) 11 (Denman won the play-off), Centels 10½, Admiralty II 10, London County Council III 9, Board of Trade II 8, PO Savings Bank III 7½, Home Office 7, Ministry of Agriculture and Fisheries II 5, Stationery Office 4½, Ministry of Health III 3, GPO North III 2½, PO Stores II 1½, Foreign Office ½.

Division 4, Somerset House III 8/9, Ministry of Labour (Kew) 7½, Ministry of Pensions (Westminster) 7½, Ministry of Labour II 4½, Customs II 4, Ministry of Health IV 3½, Air Ministry 3, London County Council IV 3, PO Savings Bank IV 3, Royal Mint 1.

Division 5, Board of Trade III 11/12, Ministry of Pensions (Acton) II, 10½, Office of Works II 10½, Metropolitan Water Board 8½, Woolwich Arsenal II 7, PO Savings Bank V 6, Centels II 5½, Denman II 5½, Crown Agents for the Colonies II 5, Home Office II 5, Ministry of Health V 2, Paymaster General's Office II 1, Ministry of Agriculture and Fisheries III ½.

In the semi-finals of the Bonar Law, Somerset House beat Patent Office 6-4 and Board of Education beat GPO North 7½-2½. This was the third time Board of Education had reached the final, but Somerset House took the trophy by the narrowest possible margin.

Bonar Law Trophy Final
8th April 1927

Somerset House		Board of Education
1. EG Sergeant	1-0	CEC Tattersall
2. D Miller	0-1	ET Jesty
3. MA Prentice	1-0	F Dark
4. WS Wallis	1-0	BHN Stronach
5. KW Harris	½-½	AJ Spencer
6. GE Marier	0-1	WW Hunt
7. WW Brougham	0-1	JA Graham
8. JD Todd	1-0	FL Snow
9. LR Bush	1-0	W Elphick
10. TS Gillon	0-1	SG Duffell
	5½-4½	

CHAPTER 2

1927 – 1939 CSCA Merger to World War II

From 1922 to 1927, the CSCA and London CS League were running separately, but now it was thought a good idea to merge the bodies. A Special General Meeting of the CSCA was held at Treasury Chambers on 29 April 1927, with Sir George Barstow presiding, at which, 'On the recommendation of the Council the following resolutions were passed unanimously:-

(1) That the C.S. Chess Association accepts with regret the resignation of Mr Spencer as Secretary as from August 31st next, in view of his duties as Secretary to the C.S. Sports Society Ltd., and desires to thank him most cordially for his services.

(2) That (subject to satisfactory arrangements with regard to the two municipal clubs) the CSCA would welcome the amalgamation of the CS and Municipal League with the Association and would gladly offer the post of Secretary to the present Secretary of the league.

(3) That the C.S. Chess Association authorizes the Council to make recommendations to the next general meeting for any desirable modification of the Capitation fee.'

This was reported in the *Civil Service Sports Journal*, June 1927, and the same publication in November stated, 'The amalgamation of the Civil Service Chess Association and the Civil Service and Municipal Chess League has now been effected. Mr W Kirk and Mr F J Colman, both of the Ministry of Health, are secretary and assistant secretary, respectively.'

W O Woodfield took over as chairman.

Although satisfactory arrangements were made relating to the two municipal clubs, the whole issue would lead to huge problems some 60 years later.

On 26 May 1927 LCC proposed a motion (a) to reorganise the league from 5 divisions into 3 and (b) increase the number of boards in division 1 to 20; in division 2 to 15 boards and division 3 to 10 boards. This was resoundingly defeated because clubs were worried about the dual issues of accommodating 20 boards and the strength of their teams. There was a rule which gave a 1 point penalty to teams which had won their division but remained in the same division. POSB (Post Office Savings Bank) proposed that this rule should not apply where teams were in their correct division but this proposal was carried forward to the next meeting. At the time, clubs could not field more than one team in the same division. If you had a team in division 1, and a second team won Division 2, they could not be promoted. At a meeting on 16 September 1927 to agree the fixture list and make the draw for the cup competitions the name of the league was changed from the Civil Service Chess League to the London Civil Service and Municipal Chess League. The team entry fee was reduced from 10/- (50p) to 7/6d (37½p) and the affiliation fee per player was fixed at 1/- (5p) for the first 10 players and 6d (2½p) for each other player. A motion to make both adjudication fees payable by the team whose claim failed was defeated. In other words, your opponent could insist on sending a game for adjudication, when you had mate in 1, and you had to pay half the cost!

1927 also saw the CS prepare for the biggest match ever seen in this country. H Meek and RHS Stevenson organised the 'Rest of England', although it was mainly London and the

Home Counties, against the CSCA over 500 boards. This took place on the 22nd October 1927 and the Rest won comfortably by 297½-210½ at the Ministry of Health. The *Surrey Mirror* reported that 26 rooms were used. Obviously, the organisers arranged for a few reserves and allowed them to play as well. The match was intended to lessen the deficit of £400 incurred with the recent International Team Tournament, and doubtless succeeded. The match was reported as far away as in the *Hull Daily Mail*. At the time, CSCA had more than 1100 members. There were proposals to ask the Postmaster General for special rates to be applied to telephone matches. It was all very well for 50 and 100 (or more!) board matches to take place in London, but once wider travel was involved, telephone matches became more desirable.

CS went on to beat Essex 31½-18½, but the latter were somewhat miffed as several Essex players who had dual qualification played for CS. CS also beat Surrey 26½–23½, Kent 32-17, Oxford University 9-6 and London University 22-18. In fact, CS won all the matches that (27/28) season, except the massive one.

At the AGM of the Civil Service Chess Association held on 31 October 1927 Sir George Barstow expressed his willingness to present a cup to the Association and it was agreed that the Barstow cup would be for the individual championship and be competed for annually.

1927/8 saw a slight decrease to 61 teams in the 5 divisions.

Division 1, Patent Office 10/12, GPO North 9½, Admiralty 9, PO Savings Bank 8½, Ministry of Health 8, Office of High Commissioner for India 6½, Somerset House (Inland Revenue) 6, London County Council 5, Board of Education 5, Customs 4½, Board of Trade 4, Ministry of Pensions 1, Ministry of Agriculture 1.

Division 2, GPO North II 11/13, Paymaster General's Office 10½, Metropolitan Water Board 10½, PO Savings Bank II 8, Patent Office II 8, Denman 7, London County Council II 6½, Woolwich Arsenal 6, Crown Agents 5, Ministry of Pensions II 5, PO Stores 4½, Admiralty II 4½, Somerset House II 3½, Office of Works 1.

Division 3, War Office 10/12, Board of Trade II 7½, Ministry of Health II 7½, Ministry of Labour 7, London County Council III 6½, Centels 6, Home Office 6, Stationery Office 6, Somerset House III 6, Ministry of Pensions III 4½, PO Savings Bank III 4½, Ministry of Labour (Kew) 3½, Ministry of Agriculture II 3.

Division 4, Air Ministry 7/8, Ministry of Pensions IV 6½, Customs II 5½, Ministry of Labour II 4½, GPO North III 3½, London County Council IV 3½, Board of Trade III 2½, Denman II 1½, Ministry of Health III 1½.

Division 5, Office of Works II 11/11, Woolwich Arsenal II 8½, Crown Agents II 7, PO Savings Bank IV 6½, Metropolitan Water Board II 6, Ministry of Labour III 6, Ministry of Agriculture III 5, Ministry of Pensions V 5, Centels II 4, Somerset House IV 3, Ministry of Health IV 2½, Paymaster General's Office II 1½.

11 teams entered the Bonar Law, which Somerset House won. 16 teams entered the Post Annual, which was won by GPO North II. The individual champion was ES Jesty (Education).

The 1928/9 season was not so successful in representative matches, but seven matches were played, with four wins and a draw - National Association of Local Government Officers (NALGO) 6-6, Essex 24-20, Surrey 21-29, London University 24-16, and losses to Kent 24½ -20½ and Oxford University 4-8.

Top ten boards of CSCA vs Surrey.

Civil Service		Surrey
1. J Mahood	1-0	JH Blake
2. WHM Kirk	0-1	G Wernick
3. TE Smith	1-0	HC Griffiths
4. R Cook	0-1	E Macdonald
5. G Dunn	0-1	HB Uber
6. B Mooney	½-½	G Tregaskis
7. C Cordingley	½-½	P Howell
8. RC Taylor	1-0	J Hunter
9. W Henderson	½-½	AD Barlow
10. E Bailey	0-1	C Colliver
	4½-5½	

CS also beat London Commercial Chess League (LCCL), by 101½ – 48½ at Finsbury Circus, on 6th November 1928. *BCM* reported that each of the games was 'played in comfort amid the marble pillars and oak beams of the finely appointed headquarters of the Oil Kings'. T Noakes captained LCCL and H Polman captained CSCA. Top 20 boards were as follows:-

Civil Service Chess Association		London Commercial Chess League
1. J Mahood (w)	½-½	FJ Whitmarsh
2. EW Osler	½-½	GF Hawkins
3. WHM Kirk	1-0	FP Dangerfield
4. WO Woodfield	1-0	VJ Scholes
5. BJ Mooney	0-1	HD Callender
6. CM Cordingley	½-½	AJ Miles
7. GE Marler	0-1	W Veitch
8. RCS Taylor	1-0	AA Craswell
9. Clarkson	1-0	RT Chamberlain

10. WH Hipkiss	½-½	FD Downton
11. HG Rogers	1-0	WJ Benge
12. CEP Brooks	1-0	RG Tollett
13. EG Gillett	1-0	CA Cazaly
14. P Riley	1-0	E Gare
15. AE Colvil	0-1	AE Challis
16. AH Duffy	1-0	J Bennett
17. RJ Mumford	1-0	FT Tillott
18. H Harding	½-½	J Cantor
19. FH Fish	0-1	RJ Prince
20. FE Douglas	1-0	FS Groom
	13½-6½	

League positions for 1928/29 were :-

Division 1 – GPO North 9½/12, Admiralty, Ministry of Health, and PO Savings Bank 8½ each, Board of Education and Patent Office 7½ each, Customs, Ministry of Pensions, and Office of High Commissioner for India 5½ each, Somerset House 4½, Board of Trade and London County Council 3½ each, Ministry of Agriculture and Fisheries 0.

Division 2 – Woolwich Arsenal 10½/12, Metropolitan Water Board 10, Crown Agents for Colonies 8½, GPO North II and Office of Works 6½ each, Paymaster General's Office, Denman, and Savings Bank II 6 each, War Office 5, Patent Office II 4½, London County Council II 3½, Admiralty II 2½, PO Stores 1½. GPO North II were penalized a point for winning the division the previous year.

Division 3 – Ministry of Health 9/11, Centels 8½, Air Ministry 7½, London County Council III and Ministry of Pensions II 6½ each, Stationery Office 6, Ministry of Labour and Somerset House II 5 each, Board of Trade II and

Ministry of Agriculture and Fisheries II 4 each, Ministry of Labour (Kew) 3, Home Office 1.

Division 4 – Customs II 9½/11, Ministry of Pensions III 9, GPO North III and Savings Bank III 7½ each, Office of Works II 7, London County Council IV 6½, Crown Agents II and Ministry of Labour III 5 each, Foreign Office and Ministry of Health III 3½ each, Woolwich Arsenal II 2, Board of Trade III 0.

Division 5 – Denman II 12/13, Ministry of Pensions IV 10½, Metropolitan Water Board II and Ministry of Labour III 9½ each, Centels II and Somerset House III 8 each, Office of Works III 6½, Stationery Office (D) 6, Savings Bank IV 5½, Woolwich Arsenal III 5, War Office II 4, Stationery Office II 3½, Ministry of Health IV 3, Paymaster General's Office II 0.

Patent Office beat Education in the final of the Bonar Law and the Post Annual was won by PO Stores. J Mahood (Paymaster General's Office) was the individual champion for the second time in succession and held the Barstow trophy. The junior (i.e. second) individual competition was won by J Webb, who also won the prize for the highest individual score in league matches (Division I). ET Jesty won the West London Chess Club championship.

In 1929, CS was refused permission to play in the Amboyna, a Southern Counties Chess Union (SCCU) competition over 50 boards. The rules state now that the competitions are open only to counties (although other organizations may affiliate) and one imagines that was the reason the decision was made. The 3rd Class Section A at the British Championship was won by a schoolboy, HJ Poupard, with 9½/11, who was playing for Government Chemists half a century later.

CS lost to Essex 28½-15½, on 25th January 1930, as this time Essex fielded many civil servants. The 1930 Bonar Law cup final was won by Patent Office, who had already won the league.

Patent Office		Somerset House
1. FW Dunn	0-1	EG Sergeant
2. WO Woodfield	1-0	D Miller
3. RF Whitehead	½-½	WS Wallis
4. P Clarkson	1-0	EW Harris
5. HW Hilliar	½-½	WS Jackson
6. JR Harman	1-0	JP Todd
7. W Langstaff	½-½	LS Bush
8. RJ Mumford	1-0	E Roberts
9. EA Lynn	1-0	J Johnstone
10. H Harding	½-½	G Jones
	7-3	

The representative matches got off to a bad start when illness prevented CS turning out a strong team against Surrey and CS lost 33½ –19½. Although CS scored three draws and a win on the top four boards, the results then went in favour of Surrey who had Golombek on board 6. CS lost 23-25 to Kent on 8th November 1930, but fared rather better on the 30th December, when they overcame Commercial League 52½-47½. 100-board matches were more common in those days, although the match was originally intended to be over 150 boards. CS won the match against Essex 31½-18½ on 31st January 1931, but were helped considerably, as 13 Essex players defaulted. CS also beat Kent 25-23.

Meanwhile, RP Michell was in Hastings, where he finished 4th, behind Euwe, Capablanca and Sultan Khan, drawing with

Capablanca. Alexander and Broadbent were in the Premier Reserves.

There was a slight drop in entries with only 57 teams in the league, 11 for the Bonar Law and 12 for the Post Annual. There were two newcomers – Middlesex County Council in division 4 and Scotland Yard in division 5. CS lost the match versus Surrey and again the match captain Mr Polman (Health) appealed for more support from players in division 1.

The league winners for 1930/31 were division 1- Admiralty, division 2 - War Office, division 3 - Air Ministry, division 4 - Ministry of Pensions and LCC, division 5 - Air Ministry II. The 'fighting services' took a lot of trophies. Education and Patent Office II won the knockout competitions. GPO North finished 3rd in both division 1 and 2 and the two teams from Air Ministry had a marvellous season, playing 20 matches and only conceding a loss and two draws.

The *Times* reported that 'interest was well-maintained' in 1931/32.

Division 1 – GPO North 10/12, Ministry of Health and Patent Office 9 each, Customs 8½, Admiralty 7½, PO Savings Bank 7, Board of Trade and Ministry of Pensions 5½ each, Metropolitan Water Board and Somerset House 4 each, London County Council 3½, War Office 2½, Woolwich Arsenal 2.

Division 2 – Admiralty II 8/10, Denman and Office of Works 6 each, Paymaster-General's Office 5½, Air Ministry and Patent Office II 5 each, Ministry of Health II, Ministry of Agriculture and Fisheries, and Crown Agents 4½ each, London County Council II 3½, GPO North II 2½.

Division 3 – Centels 8/9, Ministry of Labour (Kew) 7, Stationery Office 6, Customs II 5½, London County

Council III 4½, Ministry of Labour (Headquarters) and Ministry of Health III 3½ each, Ministry of Pensions II 3, Savings Bank II 2½, Board of Trade II ½.

Division 4 – Somerset House II 8/10, Ministry of Agriculture and Fisheries II 7, Denman and London County Council IV 6 each, Woolwich Arsenal II, Office of Works II, Ministry of Labour (Headquarters) II, Air Ministry II, and Middlesex County Council 5 each, War Office II and Crown Agents II 1½ each.

Division 5 – Ministry of Health IV 9½/11, Metropolitan Water Board II 8, Ministry of Pensions III, Patent Office III, and Scotland Yard 7½ each, London County Council V and Board of Trade III 5½, Centels II 5, Savings Bank III 4, War Office III 3½, Customs Preventive Staff 1½, Woolwich Arsenal III 1.

Admiralty won the Bonar Law trophy, and Ministry of Labour (Kew) won the Post Annual cup, beating War Office in the final. WG Crockett (India Store Department) won the individual championship, beating GJ Webb in the final. PA Cooke won the junior individual competition. The league's adjudicators included Vera Menchik, HF Lowe and BHN Stronach.

CS lost 20-30 to Surrey on 7th January 1933, and then lost to the Commercial League 21½-18½.

59 teams entered the league and Inland Revenue won division 1 that year, after a tie with Admiralty.

Division 1 – Inland Revenue and Admiralty 11½/13 each (Inland Revenue winning the play-off), GPO North 10½, Patent Office 10, PO Savings Bank 8, Ministry of Health 7½, Ministry of Pensions 6½, Metropolitan Water Board 6, Customs and Woolwich Arsenal 5½ each, London County

Council 4, Board of Trade 3, London Postal 1½, War Office 0.

Division 2 – Air Ministry 9½/12, Patent Office II 8, Ministry of Agriculture and Fisheries 7½, Centels, GPO North II and Paymaster-General's Office 7 each, Admiralty II 6½, Ministry of Health II and Office of Works 5½ each, Ministry of Labour (Kew) 4, Crown Agents for the Colonies, Denman and London County Council II 3½ each.

Division 3 – PO Savings Bank II and Ministry of Health III 5½/8 each (PO Savings Bank II winning the play-off), Customs II 5, Board of Trade II, Inland Revenue II and Nalgo 4 each, Ministry of Labour (Headquarters) 3, London County Council III and Stationery Office 2½ each.

Division 4 – Woolwich Arsenal II 10½/12, Ministry of Agriculture and Fisheries II and Ministry of Pensions II 10 each, Denman II 9, Ministry of Health IV 7½, Ministry of Labour (Kew) II 6½, Air Ministry II 5, Office of Works II and War Office II 4½, Middlesex County Council 4, Ministry of Labour (Headquarters) II 3½, LCC IV 3, Crown Agents II 0.

Division 5 – Ministry of Transport 12/13 (in their debut season), Customs III 10, LCC V 9½, Scotland Yard 9, Metropolitan Water Board II 8½, Board of Trade III and Patent Office III 7 each, Ministry of Pensions III 6½, PO Savings Bank III 5, Inland Revenue III and War Office III 4½, Centels II and Ministry of Health V 3 each, Customs Preventive 1½.

11 teams entered the Bonar Law and GPO North beat Inland Revenue in the final on bottom board elimination. 16 teams entered the Post Annual cup and Air Ministry beat

Centels in the final. BHN Stronach (Education) beat reigning champion WG Crockett in the individual championship to win the Barstow cup. GW Henlen beat AD Church in the junior competition. A large programme of matches was announced, with CS taking on Cambridge University, Oxford University, London University, Kent, Essex, Sussex and the Commercial League. Team chess was popular then – CS had 59 teams in the league and 49 played in the Commercial League. CS beat Kent 30½-19½.

Presentation to WHM Kirk (secretary since 1904)

A meeting of the Council of the league and CSCA was held on 25 May 1933. The President, Sir George Barstow KCB, presented a radio-gramophone to WHM Kirk on behalf of the League as a mark of appreciation for his services as secretary since its formation. In making the presentation, Sir George said that the league started in 1904 with one division and now had five and that Kirk had also been secretary of the CSCA since 1927. The presentation was a mark of gratitude from hundreds of chess players to whom his work had been of help. Only those in close contact with Mr. Kirk knew of the mass of details he had had to deal with.

The Match Captain's lament

The match captain Mr Polman pointed out the difficulties which he had experienced in raising teams, particularly in mid-week matches, and wondered whether the clubs wished to continue with matches with other bodies. It seemed to him that players were not interested and that matches should cease. For the match against London Commercial Chess League he had written to all clubs in divisions 1 - 3 and indicated a quota which would provide 50 players and some reserves. Six clubs did not reply and one replied on the morning of the match that it had no players. A decision was needed now even though the question of someone else to take over the captaincy would not be decided until the AGM in the autumn. The meeting decided that matches should continue. One has to sympathise with Mr Polman as discussions like this took place in later years when only 20 or 16 or 12 players were required. It was also true in later years that clubs insisted that such matches should take place, even when the clubs were not always helpful when it came to availability of players.

At the AGM held on 20 September 1933, 11 entries were received for the Bonar Law and 16 for the Post Annual. It was decided that the elimination rule should not apply in the final round of these competitions and in the event of a draw the final must be replayed. This remained in force for many years. 18 entries had been received for the individual championship and 25 for the junior event.

Admiralty won the 1933/34 league with the magnificent score of 11/12, losing only to Patent Office. Admiralty also won the Bonar Law, narrowly defeating Patent Office in the final.

Admiralty		Patent Office
1. EG Twitchett	½-½	WO Woodfield
2. MA Sutherland	½-½	P Clarkson
3. M Robinson	0-1	JR Harman
4. G Dunn	½-½	W Langstaff
5. WB Callow	1-0	RF Whitehead
6. SE Child	1-0	H Harding
7. JJ Waudby	0-1	RJ Mumford
8. WH Bailey	1-0	SE Chisholm
9. RH Shapcott	0-1	A Burns
10. TE Denbeigh	1-0	GH Green
	5½-4½	

Division 1 – Admiralty 11/12, Patent Office 10, Ministry of Health 8½, Woolwich Arsenal and GPO North 8 each, LCC 6, Customs and Metropolitan Water Board 5 each, Board of Trade 4½, Air Ministry 4, Ministry of Pensions 3½, PO Savings Bank 3, Inland Revenue 1½.

Division 2 – War Office and Ministry of Health II 10½/13 each (War Office winning the play-off), LCC II 9½, Patent Office II 9, Admiralty II and Paymaster General's Office 8 each, Office of Works 6, Centels and Ministry of Labour (Kew) 5½, Savings Bank II, Ministry of Agriculture and Fisheries, and Denman 5, GPO North II 2½, Crown Agents 1.

Division 3 – Inland Revenue II 6½/7, NALGO 4½, Ministry of Labour HQ 4, Board of Trade II and Customs II 3½ each, Woolwich Arsenal II 3, LCC II 2½, Stationery Office ½.

Division 4 – Ministry of Transport 8½/9, Air Ministry II 7½, Ministry of Health III 7, Denman II 5, LCC IV 3½, Office of Works II and Ministry of Labour (Kew) II 3 each, Ministry of Pensions II, Ministry of Agriculture and Fisheries II, and War Office II 2½.

Division 5 – Customs III and Metropolitan Water Board 10½/12 each (Customs winning the play-off), Savings Bank III 8½, Board of Trade III 8, LCC V and Scotland Yard 7½ each, Ministry of Health IV 6½, Patent Office III 5½, Ministry of Transport II 4½, Centels II 3½, Ministry of Labour HQ II 3, War Office III 1½, Customs Preventive 1.

It is interesting to see the wide disparity in numbers of teams in divisions.

In 1934/35 the league changed the rule for adjudication fees with both fees being paid by the club whose adjudication claim was rejected. It is interesting that it took eight years after this was previously proposed for common sense to prevail.

A 50-board representative match was played on 4 November 1934 with a win 30½ –19½ against Kent and on 8th December CS beat Essex 28½-21½ at Ministry of Health. *Essex Chronicle* gives the top twenty boards as

Civil Service		Essex
1. BHN Stronach	0-1	RWB Clarke
2. WG Crockett	1-0	JG Hayes
3. WA Davidson	0-1	VB Hall
4. WO Woodfield	1-0	RH Bayley
5. GJ Webb	½-½	SD Cohen
6. WS Wallis	0-1	IR Vesselo
7. CM Cordingley	1-0	BR Nickol
8. M Robinson	1-0	RL Barnett
9. FR Belson	0-1	EJ Gibbs
10. SE Child	0-1	WA Simkins
11. HA Wyatt	0-1	E Gare
12. TE Denbeigh	0-1	RC Harvey
13. LF Fletcher	0-1	CJ Hamp
14. AJ Bates	½-½	JA Allchin
15. JL Brodie	½-½	HI Wolverton
16. FH Jerram	1-0	T Stutchbury
17. AE Baker	½-½	SC Jones
18. FW Markwick	½-½	H Polman
19. SHC Lucas	1-0	Lieut. Col. LE Fitzgerald
20. JA Johnstone	½-½	H Johnston
	9-11	

Michell drew with the talented young Russian player, Mikhail Botwinnik, at Hastings, although he did lose to former world champion Capablanca and the reigning champion Euwe. Percy B Cook, a future Inland Revenue star, shared first in the London Boys Championship of 1935, but lost to Frank Parr in the play off. The British Boys Championship took place 25-30th April and Frank Parr won again, with PB Cook 5th and Ron Fleming 10th. The latter was destined to be CS treasurer for a very long time. Ministry of Health beat Customs in the Bonar Law final, and finished level with Admiralty in the league, but lost the play-off match.

Admiralty		Health
1. RG Turtchett	1-0	WHM Kirk
2. MA Sutherland	1-0	EJ Price
3. M Robinson	½-½	CA Thorogood
4. WB Callow	1-0	HJ Pearman
5. G Dunn	½-½	R Daly
6. SE Child	0-1	CM Cordingley
7. WH Bailey	½-½	PA Cooke
8. JJ Wandby	0-1	FHO Jerram
9. TE Denbeigh	1-0	AD Biles
10. RH Shapcott	1-0	AA Greneski
	6½-3½	

Admiralty II team also won their division. Inland Revenue I finished bottom of division 1 but the members would not agree that the team should play in division 2 alongside Revenue II who won division 3 and were promoted. It seems that clubs had some choice about the division in which they played with the league committee having the final decision. The Post Annual cup was won by National Physical Laboratory (NPL).

Division 1 – Admiralty and Ministry of Health 11/12 each, Customs, GPO and Patent Office 9, Inland Revenue, LCC and Woolwich Arsenal 5½, Board of Trade 3½, Metropolitan Water Board 3, Air Ministry, Ministry of Pensions, Savings Bank 2.

Division 2 – Admiralty II 11/12, Paymaster General's Office 10½, GPO II 9, Ministry of Health II 7½, Centels and LCC II 6 each, Office of Works 5½, War Office 5 (1 point deducted for winning the previous year), Patent Office II 4½, Denman 4, Inland Revenue II 3½, Savings Bank II 3, Ministry of Agriculture and Fisheries 1½.

Division 3 – Customs II 8/9, NALGO and Ministry of Transport 6 each, Crown Agents, Ministry of Labour (HQ), Ministry of Labour (Kew) 5½, Woolwich Arsenal II 5, LCC III 2½, Air Ministry and Board of Trade II ½ each.

Division 4 – Customs III and Metropolitan Water Board II 7½/9 each, (Customs III won the play-off), Ministry of Health III 6, Scotland Yard 5½, Admiralty III 4½, Woolwich Arsenal III 4, LCC IV and Ministry of Agriculture and Fisheries II 3½ each, Denman II 2½, War Office II ½.

Division 5 – LCC V 11½/12, Customs IV and Savings Bank III 8½ each, Ministry of Labour II, Ministry of Pensions II, Ministry of Transport II 7, Board of Trade III 6½, Air Ministry III and Centels II 5 each, Ministry of Health IV and Office of Works II 4 each, Patent Office III 3, Customs Preventive 1.

There were still 59 teams in the league and some clubs were running a good number of teams. The individual title went to

JC Thompson (Customs, and later Government Chemists), a notable eccentric. He devised the opening system called the Hippopotamus, where most of the pawns are on the third rank. Earlier, Alapin's 3... Bb4 in the Ruy Lopez had been christened the Hippopotamus, but the name (and the move) fell into disuse. Admiralty had a further success with W.H. Bailey winning the junior championship.

The rather strong Ludlow Congress (August 12th – 17th) was won by EGR Cordingley (6/7), ahead of BH Wood and FGT Collins 4½. Collins became a strong CS player. *Chess* in October 1935 featured an article by WH Watts about the London Chess League, which contained the extraordinary comment, 'When it started, and for a great many years afterwards, the London Chess League had the field to itself, but now there is competition. We have the North London League, the South London League, the Commercial League, the Banks and Insurance League and probably others.' There is of course a startling omission there, but Watts continues that as the LCL started first, it claims pre-eminence. 'All these other leagues do more for their members. I doubt if any of them would have come into existence had the London League been progressive...' He thought all these leagues should be represented at BCF meetings. The Secretary of LCL (JH van Meurs) responded in the next edition, pointing out that the South London League no longer existed and that some of the other leagues were not open to all. 'The suggestion that all these leagues be represented on the BCF is a rather comic one. Why not have every league in the country represented there?' It happened eventually.

The division 1 clubs for 1935/36 were: Inland Revenue, P O Savings Bank, Royal Arsenal, Admiralty, Customs & Excise, Ministry of Health, Air Ministry, Metropolitan Water Board,

London County Council, Patent Office, General Post Office (HQ), Board of Trade. Division II had 2nd teams from Inland Revenue, Admiralty, Customs, London County Council, Patent Office and GPO (HQ) plus 1st teams from Centels, War Office, Ministry of Pensions, Office of Works, Paymaster General, Denman and Ministry of Agriculture and Fisheries.

CS had had a busy season in representative matches, beating Essex 28½-21½, Cambridge University 11½-3½, London University 13-8, drawing 7½-7½ with Oxford University, and losing 24½-25½ to Kent, and 19½-25½ to Surrey.

In late 1935, Cambridge University lost 2½-12½ to Civil Service, with F Kitto beating JC Thompson on top board, but CS struck back on board 2, where BHN Stronach beat Schultz. CS also beat Surrey 34½-15½, where JC Thompson lost to Frank Parr, and BHN Stronach drew with HC Griffith. Essex beat CS 29½-20½ on 18th January 1936 at the Ministry of Health. The *Essex Chronicle* reported the match on 24th January, but it seems reasonable to doubt the name of the Essex Board 14.

Essex   Civil Service

1. TH George   1-0   JC Thompson
2. WO Woodfield ½-½   R Coman
3. VB Hall   0-1   GJ Webb
4. RH Bayley   ½-½   FB Belson
5. IR Vesselo   1-0   S Child
6. JG Hayes   ½-½   GPS Coy
7. FN Jameson   ½-½   GJ Craddock
8. GF Hawkins   ½-½   TE Denbeigh
9. G Booth   0-1   GP Kitchener
10. ER Nickol   1-0   EF Vivian
11. CT Quinn   0-1   DO Peach

12. EJ Randall	½-½	EV Beeton
13. SC Jones	0-1	TH Fish
14. AN Other	0-1	CE Gaugh
15. RC Harvey	1-0	WS Westwood
16. EJ Gibbs	1-0	HJ Sheryer
17. FW Markwick	½-½	H Polman
18. J Mason	1-0	EG Johnson
19. HJ Wolverton	1-0	GP Barnard
20. SJ Roope	0-1	W Wakeham
	10½-9½ (top 20 boards)	

Ministry of Health won the league, but the Bonar Law trophy went to Patent Office who beat Ministry of Health 6-4 after the first match was drawn 5-5. Even the 6-4 win relied on 6 adjudications. The individual trophy was won by GPS Coy in 1936, the start of a very long and distinguished career in CS chess – he was still doing adjudications and playing correspondence chess over 70 years later! The junior champion was EG Fenelon.

LCC staged a simultaneous display on 26th March 1936, by Sir George Thomas, who won 24, drew 2 (against AD Wheeler and J Foley) and lost 3 games, to WP Willis, T Pearce and CK Blyth. One of his opponents, W Hughes, was a retired LCC official, aged over 80. The next day, Sir George visited the Ministry of Health to play 25 members of the Civil Service League. He won 20, conceding draws to HJ Pearman, PA Cooke and A Morton, and losing to TF Maher and CT Kelk. These simultaneous displays were part of a tour to raise money for the Nottingham Congress Fund.

LCC also had an internal team tournament, run by the LCC Staff Association, who apparently did not welcome advice or input from the chess club on how to run the event, an attitude which is not uncommon.

Civil Service played Kent at the Ministry of Health on Saturday 28th March 1936, losing 28½-21½. Top 20 boards were as follows

Kent		Civil Service
1. RC Noel-Johnson	1-0	JC Thompson
2. HH Cole	0-1	WO Woodfield
3. W Skillicorn	½-½	W Henderson
4. CV Podger	1-0	WS Wallis
5. H Watkins	0-1	M Robinson
6. EA Coad-Pryor	1-0	FR Belson
7. FW Chambers	1-0	SE Child
8. Dr Lloyd Storr Best	½-½	EF Vivian
9. G Hanson	½-½	GJ Craddock
10. AJ Duke	½-½	DG Gould
11. EV Beeton	1-0	TE Denbeigh
12. A Flynn	0-1	GP Kitchener
13. EL Gardner	1-0	JA Ford
14. JE Povey	1-0	JL Brodie
15. Mrs Wheelwright	0-1	FH Jerram
16. RJ Potter	1-0	DO Peach
17. JJ Moore	1-0	TH Fish
18. CH Goldman	0-1	HJ Sheryer
19. FJ Dennis	1-0	FW Daniel
20. J Stuart Hodgson	½-½	EG Johnson
	12½-7½	

Civil Service travelled to Cambridge to play the University on Saturday 17th October 1936.

Cambridge University		Civil Service
1. FEA Kitto (King's)	1-0	GPS Coy
2. DB Schultz (Magdalene)	0-1	BHN Stronach
3. J Dean (St. Catherine's)	1-0	GJ Webb
4. RG Stansfield (Clare)	0-1	JM Craddock
5. EW Brocklesby (Christ's)	½-½	JC Thompson
6. HM Close (St. John's)	½-½	WS Wallis
7. DW Greenwood (Christ's)	½-½	BC Gould
8. JF O'Donovan (Jesus)	½-½	PA Cooke
9. ME Wise (Pembroke)	0-1	JL Brodie
10. A Morrison (Pembroke)	1-0	T Stutchbury
11. AF Devonshire (Trinity Hall)	1-0	D Peach
12. JS Abraham (Downing)	1-0	H Polman
13. AL Mascall (Sidney Sussex)	1-0	D Silverton
14. ER Woodcock (Clare)	1-0	AC Walker
15. IJ Good (Jesus)	1-0	LE Fletcher
16. PB Sarson (Magdalene)	1-0	JC Hamer
17. RK Guy (Caius)	½-½	WJ Gillies
18. AJ Peters (Pembroke)	0-1	GG Homan
	11½-6½	

We will hear more of IJ Good. He and PB Sarson were to change sides later!

CS beat Kent 30-20 on 31st October 1936 and then lost to Essex (23½-26½) on 6th February 1937 at Ministry of Health. Top board results in the latter match were

Civil Service		Essex
1. GPS Coy	½-½	TH George
2. GJ Webb	½-½	JR Vesselo
3. JM Craddock	1-0	RH Bayley

4.	W Henderson	1-0	JG Hayes
5.	JC Thompson	0-1	VB Hall
6.	WS Wallis	1-0	EJ Randall
7.	FR Belson	1-0	EW Osler
8.	NA Perkins	1-0	RC Harvey
9.	S Child	½-½	HI Woolverton
10.	GP Kitchener	1-0	AR Duff
11.	JL Brodie	0-1	J Mason
12.	SHC Lucas	½-½	AD Church
13.	FHO Jerram	0-1	G Booth
14.	JA Ford	½-½	Miss Poupard
15.	TE Denbeigh	1-0	JC McKelvey
16.	JP Morgan	½-½	AE Anderson
17.	H Hoskin	0-1	H Love
18.	TH Fish	1-0	L Mullen
19.	EV Becton	½-½	E Gare
20.	SGR Champ	0-1	WA Simpkins
		11½-8½	

Mr George was Essex Champion, and later wrote a column in the *Ilford Recorder*. The author met him in 1967 and found Mr George very helpful and approachable. RJ Broadbent showed the shape of things to come as he won the Northern Counties Chess Union championship and also scored 12/12 in the Manchester Club championship.

It is interesting to see different approaches from clubs to prizes. The LCC treasurer was unhappy that the AGM had agreed to present silver spoons instead of cash prizes for the best percentage performance in each team and for the winners of internal events, as the cost was too great. The Committee made the not unreasonable point that the AGM had made the decision and they had to comply. The Committee did agree that home players should contribute 2/6 (12½ p) for refreshments at home matches.

Edinburgh CS made their first appearance in the 1937 Richardson cup final (Scottish national team KO competition), but lost to their local rivals. The loss was even more decisive than the score suggests, as one Civil Servant lost in 12 moves and another in 13. George Page was a former Scottish champion and played for each of the clubs as top board for many years.

Edinburgh		Edinburgh Civil Service
1. JM Aitken (w)	1-0	G Page
2. P Reid	1-0	DS Clunie
3. D Simpson	½-½	Ian Hamilton
4. AA Foster	1-0	F Crombie
5. AJD Lothian	1-0	AG Burnett
6. DW Robertson	1-0	R Laing
7. G Romanes	½-½	WC McMurtrie
	6-1	

Mr Lothian was very aptly named for the location!

CS played Kent on 9th October 1937 and some fine players were on show. Kent won 30-20.

Civil Service		Kent
1. EG Sergeant	1-0	RC Noel-Johnson
2. GPS Coy	0-1	WJE Yeely
3. WO Woodfield	0-1	HH Cole

A week later and CS travelled to Cambridge University for a 10½-9½ defeat. The individual championship was won by FGT Collins, whose career was to be cut short tragically, like so many others, in the forthcoming conflict. The British Championship was won by Alexander 8/11, ahead of Golombek and Sergeant on 7.5, Vera Menchik (by then Stevenson) and Milner-Barry 6.5, Aitken was 8th on 5. This was a retrospective triumph for the Civil Service as only Sergeant had CS connections at that time, although Mrs Stevenson was an adjudicator for the league. Early September saw the Plymouth Jubilee Congress. World Champion Alekhine and the veteran Sir George Thomas shared first on 6/7, with Milner-Barry 3[rd]= on 3.5 Alekhine toured the country giving simultaneous displays, including a 27½ – ½ victory over Ministry of Health.

Alexander wrote to *Chess* in October 1937 proposing that the challenger for the World Championship match should come from an assessment of leading players' results against each other over the last two or three years. This was before the days of rating systems.

In 1937, the House of Commons was undergoing redecoration and it was proposed to move the chess room. Sir John Simon (Chancellor of the Exchequer) led calls that the chess room should remain close to the dining-room and the smoking room, and this was agreed. The size of the dining room was reduced slightly to accommodate the players. Chess remained the only official game in the House and billiards players remained disappointed. The Minister of Transport, Dr Burgin, gave a speech where he referred to Sir John's love of chess and commented, 'Of chess it has been said that life is not long enough for it – but that is the fault of life, not chess'. Sir John had been home secretary earlier in the year and when opening the Margate Congress quoted Bonar Law as saying, 'I find chess acts like a cold bath to my mind.'

Hastings was not a great success for British players, Milner-Barry scoring 4½/9, Golombek 4, and EG Sergeant was last on

1½, but he did draw with Max Euwe, who had recently been World Champion. Premier Reserves 'C', saw a good score by WHM Kirk, 6½/9 undefeated to share second place.

Edinburgh CS were narrowly defeated in the semi-final of the Richardson cup, and also finished second in the Edinburgh League.

Edinburgh CS		Glasgow CC
1. G Page	1-0	WA Fairhurst
2. DS Clunie	0-1	UM Inverarity
3. NA Perkins	1-0	A Murray
4. E Schacke	0-1	J McGrouther
5. AG Burnett	1-0	J Andrews
6. R Laing	0-1	RP Smeaton
7. TH Shapley	0-1	DG Nicolson
	4-3	

The 1937/38 Hastings Congress Premier was won by Sammy Reshevsky, but Alexander was undefeated and only half a point behind, sharing second with Keres. Flohr and Fine were a further half-point back. World Champion Alekhine commented that Alexander would have won if he had had more luck. EG Sergeant of Inland Revenue shared third with Koltanowski in the Premier Reserves behind Konig and Luckis, but ahead of such talented players as Prins. RP Michell played in Premier Reserves II. LCC again took on Sir George Thomas in a simultaneous display, this time losing 24 games, but Mr A Banks had the pleasure of winning his game.

Margate Easter Congress in 1938 featured ten players including a good Civil Service contingent. It was won by Alekhine, Milner-Barry was 4th equal, Golombek 6th, Alexander (who drew with the World Champion) 7th, EG Sergeant 8th, ahead of Vera (Menchik) Stevenson.

The *Star* newspaper (not to be confused with the current *Daily Star*) presented the 'Star Trophy', which was won by Civil Service with 4/4, ahead of United Banks 3/4, United Insurances 2/4, the National Liberal Club 1/4, and Municipal Authorities 0/4. The newspaper had intended the Stock Exchange to play as well, but that did not happen. The trophy was to be 'presented at the Carnival Dance to be held on the 14th October 1938.'

On 15th October, 1938 Civil Service travelled to Cambridge to play the University.

Cambridge University			Civil Service
1. FEA Kitto	(black)	0-1	BHN Stronach
2. ME Wise		½-½	GJ Webb
3. PC Hoad		½-½	GPS Coy
		7½-12½	

Ron Fleming recalled, 'When I joined the Estate Duty Office in November 1938 I and my colleague Eric Peel used to attend Law lectures at King's College which was next door to Somerset House. We were approached by someone – I cannot recall whom – to play for the Inland Revenue chess team, and turned out for this team on several occasions. Eric was stronger than I was and played one board higher. I suppose we turned out in some six matches during the season. With the outbreak of War this ceased and, after the War, Eric abandoned chess in favour of bridge as he said he did not want to play chess at a lower standard than he had previously attained while he recovered his past prowess. So he drops out of Revenue chess history.'

Many CS chess clubs were affiliated to their department's Sports and Social Club, and could apply for a financial grant to reduce costs to the players, who were generally members of the Sports and Social Club anyway. LCC got a shock in 1937, when their application for £5 was turned down as the chess club had £15 in their account so 'did not need' the grant. The CS League fees for the club were only 1/12/6 (£1-62½), which may have influenced the LCC Staff Association, but there were surely other costs.

CSCA had a number of other matches during the season, losing 23-27 to Surrey, beating London University 10½-9½, beating Oxford University 6½-5½, beating Middlesex 50½-49½(!) and losing 24½-25½ to Essex. CSCA had some entertaining matches that season, with 5 of the 7 being won or lost by the narrowest possible margin. The Annual Report (1937-38) of the 'Civil Service Chess Association and Civil Service and Municipal Chess League' revealed that Sir George Barstow, KCB was president, with Sir G Chrystal KCB, Sir TR Gardiner KBE and JY Bell CB as vice-presidents. WO Woodfield was chairman, HG Poor was treasurer, H Hoskin (Admiralty) was match captain, G Page (Health) was assistant secretary, who strangely got higher billing than the secretary, H Polman (also Health).

Patent Office defeated GPO in the Bonar Law final. Admiralty II beat Patent Office II in the Post Annual final. FGT Collins (Board of Trade) won the individual championship (President's Cup, later to be called the Barstow cup) at the first attempt. BHN Stronach, WO Woodfield and FE Allen reached the semi-finals, which gives some idea of the quality of the field. The junior individual competition was won by WJ Gillies (Customs), who defeated J Rowbotham (Patent Office) in the final. GPO HQ won the league with some comfort, and Customs were completely dominant in division 2.

Division 1

		1	2	3	4	5	6	7	8	9	10	11	12	Tot	Pos
1	GPO (HQ)	X	0	1	1	1	1	1	1	1	1	1	1	10	1
2	Patent Office	1	X	0	1	1	1	1	0	½	1	1	1	8½	2
3	Admiralty	0	1	X	0	1	1	½	½	0	1	1	1	7	3=
4	Customs	0	0	1	X	1	0	1	0	1	1	1	1	7	3=
5	LCC	0	0	0	0	X	1	1	1	1	½	1	1	6½	5
6	Met. Water Board	0	0	0	1	0	X	0	1	1	1	0	1	5	6=
7	Ministry of Health	0	0	½	0	0	1	X	1	1	½	0	1	5	6=
8	Inland Revenue	0	1	½	1	0	0	0	X	0	1	0	1	4½	8=
9	PO Savings Bank	0	½	1	0	0	0	0	1	X	0	1	1	4½	8=
10	Board of Trade	0	0	0	0	½	0	½	0	1	X	1	1	4	10
11	Royal Arsenal	0	0	0	0	0	1	1	1	0	0	X	0	3	11
12	Air Ministry	0	0	0	0	0	0	0	0	0	0	1	X	1	12

Division 2

		1	2	3	4	5	6	7	8	9	10	11	12	Tot	Pos
1	Customs and Excise	X	1	1	1	1	1	1	1	1	1	1	1	11	1
2	Admiralty II	0	X	0	1	½	1	1	1	1	1	1	1	8½	2
3	Paymaster General	0	1	X	1	0	½	0	0	1	1	1	1	6½	3=
4	War Office	0	0	0	X	1	0	1	1	1	½	1	1	6½	3=
5	Min of Transport	0	½	1	0	X	0	1	½	0	1	1	1	6	5=
6	Patent Office II	0	0	½	1	1	X	0	½	0	1	1	1	6	5=
7	Min of Health II	0	0	1	0	0	1	X	0	1	½	1	1	5½	7
8	Centels	0	0	1	0	½	½	1	X	0	½	½	1	5	8=
9	Denman	0	0	0	0	1	1	0	1	X	1	1	0	5	8=
10	Inland Revenue II	0	0	0	½	0	0	½	½	0	X	0	1	2½	10=
11	LCC II	0	0	0	0	0	0	0	½	0	1	X	1	2½	10=
12	Min of Agric and Fish	0	0	0	0	0	0	0	0	1	0	0	X	1	12

Division 3

		1	2	3	4	5	6	7	8	9	10	11	Tot	Pos
1	Min of Labour (Kew)	X	0	1	1	1	1	1	0	1	½	1	7½	1
2	Office of Works	1	X	½	0	½	1	1	1	1	0	1	7	2
3	Customs and Excise III	0	½	X	½	0	1	1	½	1	1	1	6½	3
4	Crown Agents	0	1	½	X	1	0	0	1	½	1	½	5½	4
5	Min of Labour HQ	0	½	1	0	X	0	½	0	1	1	1	5	5=
6	Royal Arsenal II	0	0	0	1	1	X	1	1	1	0	0	5	5=
7	NALGO	0	0	0	1	½	0	X	1	0	1	1	4½	7=
8	Board of Trade II	1	0	½	0	1	0	0	X	0	1	1	4½	7=
9	Min of Pensions	0	0	0	½	0	0	1	1	X	1	0	3½	9
10	PO Savings Bank II	½	1	0	0	0	1	0	0	0	X	½	3	10=
11	LCC III	0	0	0	½	0	1	0	0	1	½	X	3	10=

Division 4

		1	2	3	4	5	6	7	8	9	10	Tot	Pos
1	Board of Trade III	X	1	0	1	1	1	1	1	1	½	7½	1
2	LCC IV	0	X	1	0	0	1	1	1	½	1	5½	2=
3	Scotland Yard	1	0	X	1	0	1	0	1	1	½	5½	2=
4	Unemployment Assist. Board	0	1	0	X	½	1	0	1	1	1	5½	2=
5	Denman II	0	1	1	½	X	0	1	0	1	0	4½	5
6	Air Ministry II	0	0	0	0	1	X	1	1	0	1	4	6=
7	Admiralty III	0	0	1	1	0	0	X	0	1	1	4	6=
8	Min of Labour HQ II	0	0	0	0	1	0	1	X	0	1	3	8=
9	Met Water Board II	0	½	0	0	0	1	0	1	X	½	3	8=
10	Ministry of Health III	½	0	½	0	1	0	0	0	½	X	2½	10

Division 5

		1	2	3	4	5	6	7	8	Tot	Pos
1	Stationery Office	X	1	0	1	1	1	1	1	6	1
2	LCC V	0	X	1	1	1	1	1	1	5*	2=
3	Customs IV	1	0	X	0	1	1	1	1	5	2=
4	Office of Works II	0	0	1	X	½	1	0	1	3½	4
5	PO Savings Bank III	0	0	0	½	X	1	1	0	2½	5
6	Board of Trade IV	0	0	0	0	0	X	1	1	2	6
7	Centels II	0	0	0	1	0	0	X	½	1½	7=
8	Min of Transport II	0	0	0	0	1	0	½	X	1½	7=

* LCC V were penalized a point for winning the previous year. LCC V could not be promoted then as LCC IV were in the higher division.

The 1938 British Championship was a CS (present and future) triumph as it was won by CHO'D Alexander (8/11), with H Golombek and EG Sergeant equal 2nd on 7½, PS Milner-Barry 4th on 6½, and JM Aitken 8th on 5.

It was reported in early April that EG Sergeant could not get time off work for the 1939 Olympiad in Buenos Aires, as including travelling, he would need ten weeks off! The England team now comprised, CHO'D Alexander, Sir George Thomas, PS Milner-Barry, H Golombek and BH Wood. This did allow Sergeant to play at Margate, which does not seem much of a consolation. As it happened, the Olympiad was curtailed anyway.

CS defeated Surrey 26-24 on 3rd December 1938, Essex 29½-20½, and Middlesex 36½-33½ both in April. CS also won against Kent, so managed a clean sweep against the Metropolitan counties.

Civil Service turned out some good players against London University in 1939.

Civil Service		London University
1. FGT Collins	1-0	EJ Scrimgeour
2. GPS Coy	1-0	H Jacobs
3. WO Woodfield	0-1	RG Armstrong
4. P Robinson	½-½	S Black
5. WS Wallis	½-½	AD Renson
6. P Riley	½-½	HL Bennister
7. PB Botcherby	0-1	GH Govas
8. GA Shoobridge	1-0	HR Claff
9. HF Gook	½-½	LW Massey
10. SE Child	0-1	AR Gordon
11. EE Holiday	0-1	RJ Harris
12. JC Thompson	1-0	DH Halfpenny
13. WH Bailey	½-½	W Wolf

14. EC Marriot	½-½	LOJ Matthews
15. AC Ridlington	1-0	NN Tereschenko
16. JL Brodie	½-½	L Ardern
17. TH Fish	1-0	JB Wyman
18. WJ Gillies	1-0	E Laphier
19. JH Garner	½-½	C Fishwick
20. SGR Champ	1-0	BJ Gross
	12-8	

The team against Essex was even stronger

Civil Service **Essex 1st April 1939**

1. EG Sergeant (B)	1-0	TH George
2. D Miller	½-½	Dr E Zepler
3. JM Craddock	1-0	HA Melvin
4. BHN Stronach	1-0	EJ Randall
5. GJ Webb	½-½	JR Vesselo
6. GPS Coy	½-½	HI Woolverton
7. M Robinson	½-½	EH Flear
8. GM Hodgson	0-1	JG Hayes
9. GA Shoobridge	1-0	VB Hall
10. PB Botcherby	0-1	RH Bayley
11. GP Kitchener	0-1	JV Skilleter
12. W Wakeham	0-1	EW Fryd
13. SE Child	1-0	P Riley
14. WS Wallis	1-0	D Love
15. EE Holliday	½-½	CJ Hamp
16. W Henderson	½-½	Miss Poupard
17. WH Bailey	½-½	G Booth
18. FR Belson	1-0	RC Harvey
19. JC Thompson	1-0	AF Stammwitz
20. HF Gook	0-1	ER Nickol
	11½-8½	

Edinburgh CS gained revenge for their defeat two years earlier, with a close victory in the Richardson cup. This was the only time they ever won the competition. The first match was a draw and this replay stood CS 1½-2½ Edinburgh, with three games for adjudication. A draw would favour CS, as they would win on bottom board elimination (which presumably did not apply in the first match). However, CS were awarded wins on boards 2 and 3, with a draw on board 4, and had no need of the favourable tie-break.

Edinburgh Civil Service		**Edinburgh**
1. AG Burnett (W)	½-½	JM Aitken, Colle system
2. G Page	1-0	AJD Lothian, Ruy Lopez
3. DS Clunie	1-0	RTR Serjeant, Albin Counter Gambit
4. NA Perkins	½-½	AA Foster, English Opening
5. F Crombie	½-½	V Rush, Queen's Gambit Declined
6. E Schacke	0-1	EG Beckingham, Ruy Lopez
7. R Laing	½-½	TR Harvey, Queen's Gambit
	4-3	

The 1939 City of London Club championship was a 20-player all-play-all, with strong CS participation. CHO'D Alexander was 2nd (14/19), FGT Collins 5th (12½), PS Milner-Barry 6th (12), EG Sergeant 10[th] = (10), and RH Newman 15th (8).

Margate congress was won by Keres, a point ahead of Capablanca and Flohr, Milner-Barry finished 5th on 50 %, drawing with all three of them. Golombek, Sergeant and Mrs Stevenson (Vera Menchik) also played. England drew with

Holland, Alexander beating Euwe on top board, with Milner-Barry, Broadbent, Golombek and Sergeant part of the 10-player team.

Surrey were leading Kent 50-46 in a county match, with 4 adjudications to come, with Surrey the likely winners of the championship and the full match. The top 20 boards counted for the championship, the top 50 for the Amboyna Shield and all 100 for the Ebony Shield. Some familiar names participated. Vera Menchik was Board 2 for Kent, BHN Stronach was Board 7 for Surrey, and GAC Ashcroft (S) drew with GPS Coy on Board 11. Shoobridge, Coad Pryor, Felce, Hoskin and Fish were also playing.

War clouds were gathering again, and Patent Office were the 1939 league champions, in the last CS season for several years. Some chess was taking place elsewhere. The 1939-40 Hastings tournament was down to eight players and obviously nobody travelled from another country to play. Frank Parr won with WHM Kirk finishing 4th, two points behind 3rd placed Golombek, but with the satisfaction of a draw against the winner.

CHAPTER 3

1939 – 1946 Espionage, World War II and the Advent of Computers

The Government Code and Cypher School (GC&CS) was formed in 1919 and Alan Turing joined it in 1938. GC&CS was based in Broadway Buildings opposite St. James Tube station, but much of the work transferred to Bletchley Park, known as BP, in the 30s. Turing moved to BP at the start of the war. Some humourist labelled GC&CS as the 'Golf Club and Chess Society'. The 1939 Olympiad was taking place in Buenos Aires at the start of the war and the English team immediately returned home. Of the team members, Stuart Milner-Barry was recruited to work at Bletchley Park and he recruited Hugh Alexander (February 1940) and Harry Golombek (late 1941). Golombek had particular reason to be grateful. He was about to board ship with his battalion that morning. Only a handful of his former colleagues survived. *Chess* reported that Alexander and Milner-Barry had probably withdrawn from all chess for the duration of the war as, 'They have entered a Government office'.

Gordon Welchman was also at Bletchley, as were IJ (Jack) Good (joined May 1941), and mathematician Peter Hilton (January 1942). John Gilbert of Inland Revenue was also there, famous historian Asa Briggs, and doubtless many other people with an interest in chess. Good caused some confusion as he introduced himself as, 'I'm Good.' The work they did there was of immense importance and has been well-documented elsewhere. When people had been recruited, they were told to carry a 10/- note (50 p) at all times and if they got a telephone message saying, 'Aunt Flo is not so well', they should immediately head for BP. Accommodation varied, but Milner-Barry and Alexander were lucky enough to stay at a pub about a mile from the gate.

Turing worked in Hut 8, and Alexander said, 'He was always impatient of pompousness or officialdom of any kind – indeed it was incomprehensible to him; authority to him was based solely on reason and the only grounds for being in charge was that you had a better grasp of the subject involved than anyone else. He found unreasonableness in others very hard to cope with because he found it very hard to believe that other people weren't all prepared to listen to reason; thus a practical weakness in him in the office was that he wouldn't suffer fools or humbugs as gladly as one sometimes has to.'

Another colleague said, 'He naively expected (authority) to maintain literal truth-telling and constancy of policy.' There were frustrations associated with the work, as not everyone acted on the information. One code-breaker says he sent reports that German warships were on the move, he was ignored, and several British ships were sunk as a result. The Ministry of Defence denies to this day that the messages were received.

Alexander commented that Turing thought naval Enigma could be broken because it would be so interesting to break it! In October 1941, protocol was outraged when Turing, Welchman, Alexander, and Milner-Barry wrote direct to Churchill, requesting extra staff that had been promised. Milner-Barry delivered the letter by hand to Downing Street, but there was some delay as he had forgotten to take appropriate identification with him. He then had an argument with Churchill's principal private secretary, Brigadier Harvie-Walker, who did not appreciate being told that he was not authorized to know what the letter contained. Eventually, he promised to deliver the letter unopened to Churchill. Immediately Churchill read the letter, he annotated it with 'ACTION THIS DAY – Make sure they have all they want on extreme priority and report to me that this has been done', and sent it to General Ismay, his principal staff officer. Working for Churchill must have been a novel experience for a general, who was presumably quite unused to receiving such peremptory messages. In 1992, in an echo of history, Sir Stuart hand delivered a letter to Prime Minister John Major to plead for the preservation of Bletchley Park.

Alexander was a much better organizer than Turing, so gradually replaced him as head of section in 1942. He was described as, 'a model manager who treated us cryptographers as colleagues and was remarkably tolerant of our foibles.' Alexander decided they needed more typists, but requests were blocked by the administration and finance sections. His practical solution was to visit a friend at John Lewis, who immediately supplied a large team from the typing pool. He arrived at Bletchley with the large group of young women and delivered them to the Administration section, saying, 'I want these girls at work tomorrow. Settle the paperwork any way you can.'

Alexander later worked on the Japanese navy codes and did liaison work with USA. This was not without difficulties, as throughout the war, the US Navy did not seem to cooperate with anybody (even other US agencies), which caused frustration. Donald Michie also joined BP. He was not a strong chess player, but shared Turing's interest in computer chess. All these great minds were doing everything they could to win the war, sometimes working 72 hour shifts, but with such a gathering of talent, any spare time could be used to bounce ideas off each other. BP's electronic engineers were puzzled by such discussions, but did not understand that Turing wanted to build a machine which could think and learn. Tommy Flowers of General Post Office (GPO) had made a massive contribution to building the first computer as we would understand the term, and never received the recognition he deserved, but Turing and others wanted much more from computers. Colossus, the first computer, was destroyed in 1960, but a replica has since been built and may be found at the BP museum. Peter Wright (of *Spycatcher* fame) much later described GPO as, 'a British Government instrumentality for intercepting mail and tapping telephones. Tapping telephones has since been privatized. BT bug telephones and supply copies of other people's faxes at market rates.'

Turing was enthusiastic about chess but not very good, particularly compared to the strong players who had been recruited. Golombek used to give him queen odds, or turn the board round when Turing resigned and win from that position. Turing was good enough to beat fellow recruit Peter Twinn. Twinn was the first professional mathematician to be recruited by GC&CS and was later awarded a CBE. Jack Good thought Turing was too intelligent to play the obvious move and tried to work everything out from first principles. Turing did continue to think about computer chess at BP, as did Good, who played for Cambridge City, and had been Cambridgeshire champion in 1939. Good had published an article on computer chess in 1938. Turing and Good played Go as well. Good and Turing talked about chess-playing machines in 1941, and Turing and Michie discussed mathematical problems that computers could solve, as well as code breaking. Good left Hut 8 to join Michie in the 'Newmanry' in 1943, where they were using machine methods to decrypt the German cipher called 'Fish'. The first machine, christened 'Heath Robinson' worked well enough, and helped improve Colossus.

Gordon Welchman headed Hut 6, but he moved on to other duties, and was succeeded by Milner-Barry, who proved a very successful and popular manager. BP was a strange mix of military and civilian, with nobody really worrying about the respective hierarchies. The military tended to wear uniform only if they expected important visitors.

Security was paramount. One female academic started to get drunk at London parties and boast about her work and suddenly disappeared without trace. Even MI5 (British Security Service) and MI6 (Secret Intelligence Service) were not told about BP activities. A player named Jim Adams wrote to the *Daily Telegraph* to say that he played correspondence chess with a naval officer in the early 40s, with all the letters being checked by the censor, to ensure that the officer did not give away the location of the ship etc. Mr Adams was slightly surprised to find the annotation, 'Why not 14.e5?' signed by the censor.

When the war ended in 1945, many people at BP moved on to other work. There were 10000 staff in early 1945, but only 2000 moved to Eastcote in 1946. Government Communications Head Quarters (GCHQ) was formed that year, and many BP staff arrived there. GCHQ was a covert operation run by the Foreign Office, which moved to Cheltenham in 1951. Other Communications Departments came under GCHQ as well. GCHQ had a monopoly on SIGINT (Signals Intelligence), which isolated MI5, who only met the GCHQ twice a year. Alexander moved to GCHQ in 1946 and became Head of Section H (cryptanalysis) in 1949, where he remained until retirement in 1971. He actually declined promotion and a job offer from NSA, the US equivalent of GCHQ. GCHQ's building is quite spectacular. Despite the secret nature of the work, the building is somewhat obvious, and made more so by the massive road signs as you approach it, although you are forbidden to take photographs in the area.

Alexander and Milner-Barry managed to interest a cabinet minister in chess in Hastings. The cabinet minister became Prime Minister James Callaghan, later Lord Callaghan and he attended the tournament several times to present prizes. The Central Training School stayed in Bletchley until 1987. Bletchley Park was later turned into a college, but subsequently hosted a museum commemorating the code-breakers. UK kept quiet about the success at breaking Enigma as certain countries were still using it, until the news broke in 1974. One can imagine the consternation in foreign parts when they realized their secret messages had been decoded for the previous 30 years.

In June 1945, JR Womersley of National Physical Laboratory (NPL) contacted Turing and the latter joined NPL in October to build a computer. The two did not get on, and Turing said that Womersley's sole contribution to the project was to come up with the title, 'Automatic Computing Engine' (ACE), which was rather more catchy than the titles formerly proposed. This was a bit unfair as Womersley had done the necessary politicking to gain approval for the project in the first place. Turing produced an early report on what ACE should achieve, which he completed remarkably quickly, by the end of 1945! He emphasized that proper storage was crucial for a thinking computer, and said in passing that binary was the best way of operating the machine. It was obvious to him, but maybe not others. He also said that the ACE could be made to play chess and that such computers could be operated remotely, for example at the end of a telephone line. The reader may imagine how the chess-playing suggestion went down with the management. Nowadays, we take it for granted that computers play chess and can be operated remotely. Turing was not able to talk about the work at Bletchley for security reasons, so could not say that some of his proposals had been achieved already. Womersley passed an annotated copy of the report to the head of NPL and to Department of Scientific and Industrial Research (DSIR), which was the parent department at that time, and tried to paraphrase the report so that the management would understand it. Turing attended a later meeting with the administrators, but his approach proved too technical for them. A somewhat diluted ACE was approved, but then there were problems as it was difficult to find people capable of building such a complicated device. Gone were the days of just demanding staff and equipment. He did try, but now the war was over, traditional Civil Service procedures applied. Turing was astounded when someone in Stores said that a requisition had to be authorized by a senior officer. The Stores official reacted similarly when Turing told him to stop wasting time and just supply what had been ordered. Meanwhile, rival bodies were also building prototype computers, so the expertise was spread somewhat thinly. ACE was also becoming even more distant from Turing's vision, and he became disillusioned. NPL management felt the same way about him and in July 1947, he was granted a sabbatical, just before construction of ACE started. The next year he left NPL. We do not know if he played chess for NPL, but he won athletics events there, and was good enough to run the marathon in 2 hours, 46 minutes, a very respectable time. In 1950, ACE was operational, but the NPL report omitted Turing's name.

Meanwhile, Turing had worked with David Champernowne to create a primitive chess computer, called Turochamp. George Koltanowski reported in the February 1946 issue of *Chess* that Arthur Fey (of Hazleton, PA) had invented a self-recording chess board, which was demonstrated to Koltanowski the previous October. The idea was that you made the moves normally and a strip of paper emerged from the board containing the moves! Koltanowski said it might take many years before the board became common in clubs. Lord Louis Mountbatten gave a speech at the British Institute of Engineers Dinner, where he said, 'Machines are being designed to exercise those hitherto human prerogatives of choice and judgment. One of them can even be made to play a rather mediocre game of chess'.

Turing worked with Good and Max Newman (another good player) at the University of Manchester in 1947. Turing joined GCHQ as a consultant in 1949, and was later offered £5000, an enormous amount in those days, for a year's work by Hugh Alexander, who was head of cryptanalysis. Alexander had been awarded the OBE in 1946 for 'confidential work during the war', according to 'Chess'. But in 1950, the US Senate decided that 'homosexuals and other sex perverts' were a security risk. It was thought that they could be blackmailed into giving away secrets. In 1952 GCHQ banned homosexuals from being members of staff. (This was repealed in 1991.) It is a sobering thought that had such a policy operated in 1938, Turing would not have been recruited to BP, and German ciphers, such as Enigma, would not have been broken as early as they were. Maybe they would never have been broken, and the war would have been lost. Unfortunately for Turing, it was about the time of the start of GCHQ's ban that he was prosecuted for sex offences. He had naively reported a burglary and named one of his pick-ups as the likely suspect. The police wondered why the young man had been at Turing's house, so the burglar and Turing both ended up in the dock. Alexander acted as a character witness, quite a brave stance in view of GCHQ's policy, although obviously the war work could not be mentioned. Whether it would have helped is another matter. Turing was given chemical treatment (estrogen injections), rather than a prison sentence. Two years later he was dead. The inquest decided that he had coated an apple with cyanide and eaten it as he was ashamed of his homosexuality, although the authorities never tested the remainder of the apple for cyanide, and those who knew him could have said completely honestly he was not ashamed. The authorities locked down the scene for some hours, immediately after his death, possibly to remove any sensitive information. The suicide verdict was generally accepted, but one wonders if it would be nowadays. An 'open' verdict seems more appropriate than suicide. The ban on homosexuality was not terribly successful, as Sir Maurice Oldfield (head of MI6 1973-1978) admitted, shortly before his death, that he was a practising homosexual.

Turing's name was subsequently rehabilitated at NPL, after the work at Bletchley was given wide publicity. ACE had been situated in Glazebrook Hall, later the home of the staff canteen and meeting rooms, (where NPL Chess Club played), and much later NPL designated one room in the Hall the 'Turing Room'. Glazebrook Hall was demolished later, and replaced with expensive houses.

Chess players continued to work at GCHQ and for other security services. Some people with chess connections attracted unwelcome attention. Roger Hollis (father of the very strong player Adrian Hollis) was Director of MI5 from 1956-1963, and Graham Mitchell (a renowned postal chess player) was Deputy Director from 1956-1963. Peter Wright was convinced

Roger Hollis was a Russian agent. Jonathan Aitken MP wrote to the Prime Minister (Margaret Thatcher) on 31st January 1980, saying that Hollis and Mitchell were being accused of being Soviet agents, and that these allegations would soon be published. He suggested not only that a full enquiry be carried out into Hollis and Mitchell, but also into anyone they had recruited over the years. It became clear that Sir Robert Armstrong (Head of the Civil Service) and MI5 did not want any such enquiry. Peter Wright presented his evidence to Mrs Thatcher, but she passed it on to MI5, who quickly decided everyone was innocent. Wright investigated Mitchell first, as Hollis was more likely to authorize that than an investigation of himself! Sir Anthony Blunt was unmasked at much the same time, so authorities announced he was the sole spy, although many of the leaks appeared to have happened after he was off the scene. Aitken also urged the Prime Minister to be properly briefed before the news came out. Aitken later attracted unwanted attention from the courts himself. The UK Government attempted to block the publication of *Spycatcher* in a highly-expensive court case in Australia. At the *Spycatcher* trial, Armstrong made his notorious statement that he had been 'economical with the truth', which some people took to be an admission of perjury. No concrete evidence against Hollis and Mitchell has ever been published. Nigel West reported (*A Matter of Trust*) that the agents following Mitchell were suspicious, as he tried to avoid being followed, which hardly seems a surprising thing for a member of the Security Services to do.

More recently, an applicant for a job at MI5 thought he had performed well at the interview, and was disappointed to receive a letter of rejection. He subsequently received a telephone call from MI5, saying he had been rejected as he had 'been receiving coded messages from Bulgaria'. After he had overcome his initial shock, he pointed out that he was playing postal chess against a Bulgarian opponent and that 5254 5755 meant '1.e4 e5'!

World War II

By the end of 1939, over 16000 civil servants had been evacuated from London. Inland Revenue Head Office staff began their evacuation to Llandudno in February 1940. One folk legend from 1940 has it that after the disastrous defeat at Dunkirk, and invasion was expected daily, volunteers remaining at Somerset House were asked to occupy the rooms above the Strand entrance. The plan was to drop petrol bombs on tanks as they entered the quadrangle. It is highly unlikely that the story is true. Unless the staff wore military uniforms, such action would be regarded as a war crime. The Londoners descended on Llandudno and immediately set up a social club, which attracted some 800 members. This catered for various sports, dancing, photography, music and of course chess and bridge, all for 2d (under 1p) a week. They even ran a magazine until war-time strictures on newsprint spelt the end. Inland Revenue gradually returned to London after the war, but still had a presence in Llandudno in 1948. There was still chess in London. EG Sergeant won a blitz tournament at the Chess Centre with 6½/7 ahead of Tartakower on 5½ and König on 5.

The August 1941 edition of *Chess* included this humorous article by GPS Coy on 'The Playe of Ye Chesse'.

'Chess is a very ancient game – older it is rumoured, even than golf, 'Monopoly', or postman's knock, although opinions vary on this latter point. Below are reproduced a few hints to match-players from 'Chess – How to Win, Lose or Draw, As the Case May Be', from a rare and ancient manuscript.

1. Chess must be played in the right atmosphere. This can be produced with little trouble, given a dozen or so smokers of cheap shag, decaying vegetables, and woolen comforters. When arranging a home match, the club secretary must select a small room carefully and eliminate any form of ventilation (except, of course draughts). (He should also procure a double-headed coin to ensure that he gets white, but this is mentioned purely for personal convenience.) Having selected his room, accessible only via four flights of stairs, he should shut his smoking members therein at least half-an-hour before the match is due to start – actually this gives them a good hour in which to work. So long as they smoke hard, these valuable pioneers may occupy themselves as they please, provided they make no attempt to mend the chess clocks. When the opposing team begins to trickle in, smoking should be redoubled, and a confusing babel of conversation produced, and on no account should the visitors be permitted to rest in comfort after their journey. When at length the home secretary has used his coin to advantage, or has been forestalled, the players should be led carefully and tenderly to their places – this has to be done tactfully, as they will not appear to be very quick at grasping the layout.

2. When the match commences, it is advisable to know a little of the principles of the game, since otherwise one's opponent might win before the tea-interval, which is considered far more degrading than when he wins afterwards. In important matches, an 'adjudicator' is provided so that you can get away before they close; this is an excellent arrangement, too, because it relieves you of the

necessity of disclosing the result to your match captain.

3. It is advisable to cry 'j'adoube' in the following circumstances :-

   3a. If discovered attempting to rearrange the position whilst your opponent is drinking his tea or talking to the treasurer about his subscription.

   3b. At the commencement of the game, after touching each of your own and your opponent's men. This cannot fail to have an effect upon his morale. If the effect is not as great as desired, repeat the procedure at critical stages throughout the game.

   3c. When a whole rook down, edge your board up to the next pair's and nonchalantly castle with the nearest rook from their board.

4. When playing with a wobbly board, it is illegal to strike one corner of it sharply, causing a pawn prematurely to reach the back rank and become a queen (ch).

5. Do not take the chess clock too seriously, except when your opponent's clock says 5 minutes for more than a quarter of an hour on end. Such an occurrence entitles you to pick the thing up and shake it, and as neither clock will then work at all, you may continue the game untroubled by the 'time factor'.

6. At the end of a game with a complete stranger, you must say how very much you enjoyed it, and that you hope to play him again, but you may cross your fingers under the table to preserve your self-respect.

7. If your game finishes quickly, you and your opponent should at once commence an animated conversation, and

start banging the pieces down on the board for as long as the other players can stand it. This is known as a 'post mortem'.

8. If the result of the match depends on one game, everyone should crowd around the two players concerned, and silently condemn, pityingly, each move they make.

9. If your side loses the match, do not fall into the grievous error of asking your captain the score, unless you have both won your game and paid your subscription.

10. If chess is too hard, try dominoes.

11. If chess is too easy, try the Ministry of Information.

BH Wood gave a simultaneous display at Trentham, Staffordshire in 1942 against 33 members of 'Victory' and 'Outcasts' (evacuated civil servants), losing to TA Grant, JH Holdcroft, AA Archer, GF Walker and H Costello. Proceeds went to the Red Cross. In December of that year, the Trade Union Club in London saw a 20-board match between British Trade Unionists and Refugee Associations. GAC Ashcroft defeated the Czechoslovakian player Forbeath (whose name has presumably been anglicized) on Board 4, and Lewis Silkin MP lost on board 10. The latter reported that chess was now in cold storage in the House. Lord Brabazon, the distinguished aviation pioneer, was very keen on chess. He did raise BH Wood's ire by suggesting that opening theory was damaging chess and that the queen and king could be swapped round. When players had got used to that, another small change could be made. The Germans were also involved in chess. The Luftwaffe distributed chess sets where the German coast was one side of the board and the English coast on the other. The white pieces were

German aircraft, the black pieces English aircraft. The German Air Ministry recommended this as a means of teaching aircraft recognition.

A rather high-quality London Area Civil Defence chess tournament was run in 1943. RW Gosling defeated TH Acton 3-2 after several lengthy playing sessions. Eventually, AW Bowen beat H Evans in the final. Civil Defence encompassed both military (e.g. Home Guard) and civilian (e.g. Air Raid Precaution) volunteers. The Air Ministry defeated the College for the Blind at Worcester 12-2, but Air Ministry lost a later match against the same opponents at Redhill by 7-4. A Civil Defence League was started in Glasgow, containing ten teams. Civil Service chess was continuing in Fylde, where Mr Biles (Ministry of Health), Mr Hopkinson (Ministry of War Transport), Mr GA Kershaw (Ministry of Pensions) and Mr HT Goodman (War Services Grants) were prominent. Apart from inter-departmental matches, there were matches with other local clubs. National Fire Service (NFS) and Auxiliary Fire Service (AFS) teams and individual competitions were organized.

FG Tims Collins was reported missing from a bombing raid. *Chess* commented, 'How we hope that this genial and universally popular chess congress-ite managed to bale out!' Unfortunately, a subsequent report confirmed that he had died on 27th November 1943 in a Lancaster bomber over Heuchelheim, aged just 28. His name appears on a memorial in Balliol College, Oxford. His widow Derah gave birth to their only child (Christina) in mid-1944.

London Fire Force lost to Metropolitan Essex 7.5-12.5. Crayford Civil Defence lost 4.5-6.5 to Army Pay Corps. The Blackpool District League attracted six teams, Heyhouses CS Club shared first place, a half-point ahead of Ministry of Health. AD Biles was secretary of the latter, and formerly secretary of Surrey. Vera Menchik, her mother and sister were killed by a V1 'Flying Bomb' on 27th June 1944. She had been the women's world champion since 1927. Her death at such a young age (38) was tragic, what makes it even more so was that she had recently moved from Bayswater in central London to Clapham in South London, where she should have been safer. Even worse was that the Menchik family took shelter in the basement, but the house took a direct hit. The Anderson shelter in the back garden was unscathed. Vera Menchik had taught chess to individuals in the 1930s for 3/6 (17½ p) an hour, delivered talks on chess, as well as doing adjudications for the league.

Some clubs were struggling for numbers during the war, and some interesting mergers took place, one being the Crayford Civil Defence and Barnehurst Golf Club, which lost 5-3 to a Royal Army Pay Corps team, 'somewhere in Kent'. A NALGO club was formed in Luton. Alexander was in Washington DC late in 1944. Postal chess between USA and Australia was stopped by the censors as the moves could be a code.

A match between Oxford University and Bletchley was played at Balliol College on 2nd December 1944.

Oxford University		Bletchley
1. TH Tylor	½-½	CHO'D Alexander
2. Dr JW Cornforth	1-0	H Golombek
3. Dr HG Schenk	0-1	Dr JM Aitken
4. Sir Robert Robinson	0-1	Dr IJ Good
5. Dr MJS Dewar	0-1	NA Perkins
6. Dr I Berenblum	0-1	Sgt. Jacobs (US Army)
7. V Grieve	1-0	Sgt. JR Gilbert
8. RCO Matthews	0-1	MA Chamberlain

9. S Ardeshir	1-0	PJ Hilton
10. JOL Roberts	0-1	WR Cox
11. ADH Bivar	½-½	D Rees
12. EC Crossfield	0-1	Lt. A Levinson (US Army)
	4-8	

One wonders what the reaction was, when this was published. People must have been curious as to why a small place like Bletchley had such a massively strong chess club. The prevailing attitude then was to realize they were engaged in secret work and not to ask questions.

CHAPTER 4

1946 – 1967 Hitting the Heights

Although the war had caused the league to be suspended, some clubs had been playing chess. Patent Office had played matches against Insurance, for example. CS chess clubs in London were asked to contact Mr HG Poor, 20 Midholm Close, Barnet, NW11, with a view to restarting the league. Ulster CS Chess Club was back in action. The Civil Service Chess Association celebrated its Silver Jubilee in great style on 20 July 1946 in the Pump Room at Bath with a 100-board match against the West of England. Interested CS players were requested to contact the hon. secretary, CSCA, 16 Rockliffe Road, Bath. The Secretary H Hoskin deserved every credit for his courage and organizing powers. The Civil Service team was headed by the British Champion CHO'D Alexander and EG Sergeant. The West of England had a good win by 71½–26½ due to the absence of many strong players from London. *British Chess Magazine* reported, 'While the Civil Service Chess Association do not offer any excuses, but readily admit they were defeated by superior forces, it must be borne in mind that at the outbreak of hostilities all organized Civil Service sport was disbanded. Service chess clubs are, however, now re-forming, and during the coming season the Civil Service and Municipal League will be revived, thus enabling the Service to turn out a much stronger team for their return match with

West of England during Whitsun Week next year.' The match was organized by FJ Hill, Hon. Secretary for West of England and Messrs FM Norman (match captain), HG Poor (Hon. Treasurer) and H Hoskin (Hon. Secretary) for the Civil Service Chess Association.

Civil Service		West of England
1. CHO'D Alexander(B)	1-0	HV Trevenen
2. EG Sergeant	½-½	PD Bolland
3. CG Butcher	0-1*	ARB Thomas
4. GPS Coy	0-1*	HV Mallinson
5. MA Sutherland	0-1	DV Hooper
6. H Hoskin	0-1	RM Bruce
7. J Mahood	0-1	RA Slade
8. NA Perkins	0-1	JC Waterman
9. JY Bell	½-½	C Sullivan
10. GP Kitchener	1-0	H Pugh
11. M Robinson	½-½	F Mathers
12. CM Cordingley	0-1	JWF Greenleaf
13. RG Stansfield	½-½	CB Pepler
14. AC Lynch	1-0	D Price
15. AK Neale	1-0	GAM Wilkins
16. J Rowbotham	1-0	Dr HV Jones
17. RFG Wright	0-1	C Welch
18. RE Robinson	0-1	AF Devonshire
19. EC Baker	0-1	HD Wells
20. WH Bailey	0-1	HEG Courtney
21. HH Ellmers	0-1*	WH Regan
22. TE Denbeigh	1-0	AB Treloar
23. JH Garner	0-1	WH Cozens
24. W Henderson	½-½	HJ Chapman
25. GD Gillies	0-1	DA Thomas

26. WH Law	1-0	GW Powell
27. WA Sutcliffe	½-½	H Mann
28. AC Hopkinson	0-1	AP Shorney
29. H Gook	1-0	GM Robertson
30. G Roberts	0-1	Mrs RM Bruce
31. WJ Gillies	½-½	GD Crowther
32. CJ Stokes	½-½	JL Palmer
33. EJ Tibbs	0-1	CE Dickson
34. WTE Taylor	½-½	D Foster
35. HJ Phillips	½-½	WJ Williams
36. AS La Lond	0-1	HH Johnson
37. RG Edwards	0-1	C Soper
38. J Longden	0-1	G Tupper
39. AG Seeley	½-½	GF Spencer
40. EA Musto	0-1	RF Bowles
41. RW Billington	0-1	MT Todd
42. JT Curtis	0-1	TH Wallis
43. FS McRostie	1-0	FH Senneck
44. LE Fitzgerald	0-1	TJ Hart
45. R Gedling	0-1	CE Scutt
46. G Wernick	1-0	FG Ormond
47. R McCall	1-0	HC Playne
48. B Gill	0-1	EB Bishop
49. TF Forward	0-1	AS Perkins
50. JA Buggs	½-½	Dr CA Marsh
51. ACS Pindar	1-0	CH Taylor
52. Cunningham	0-1	J Aspden
53. A Nash	0-1	RB Copleston
54. T Hall	0-1	WB Iles
55. R Phillips	0-1	AS Griffiths
56. E Read	0-1	CH Snow
57. NH Powell	0-1	Budgen

58. A Gilbey	0-1	AG Edwards
59. RHL Huntley	0-1	M Staer
60. W Morse	0-1	Dr BA Crook
61. CC Percival	½-½	AE Pitt
62. OJ Smith	1-0	A Terrett
63. W Redhall	0-1	RE Smith
64. JR Brown	1-0	G Gordon
65. FM Norman	1-0	F Greenleaf
66. JS Vowles	0-1	L Winter
67. LC Allen	½-½	K Attridge
68. NL Brown	½-½	GR Cottew
69. TJ Relph	0-1	CS Louch
70. SV Hurrell	0-1	HP Nangle
71. TW Quick	0-1	KEC Budge
72. EW White	0-1	E Dewfall
73. BHN Stronach	1-0	SH Brocklesby
74. H Luce	0-1	B White
75. C Cale	0-1	W Brodribb
76. HR Coare	0-1	Bryant Eliot
77. ER Lear	0-1	EA Whiteford
78. N Atherton	0-1	EA Jones
79. LJ Gibbons	0-1	AIH Wasser
80. L Salt	1-0	Dr Ryder
81. AE Wall	0-1	RT Jones
82. RW Mitchell	0-1	FE Burgess
83. PC Moss	0-1	Mrs Dewfall
84. LGS Hedgeland	0-1	Mrs McKeng
85. G Griffin	0-1	Col. Browne
86. RO Smith	0-1	HE Sutton
87. EA Francis	1-0	W Blathway
88. ACW Glover	0-1	HG Jones
89. HC Parsons	0-1	J Carter

90. E Bedford	1-0	R Mapson
91. Cdr. ELJ Howell	0-1	W Salman
92. HG Lord	0-1	R Brereton
93. M Kielbig	0-1	R Preedy
94. PV Steer	0-1	W Padfield
95. AS Edwards	0-1	A Whitty
96. GA Sadler	0-1	L Walter
97. LF Phillips	0-1	RJ Rymer
98. JA Dean	0-1	SE Passmore
	26½-71½	

* = Games adjudicated.

Alexander's opponent was an interesting character. He subsequently spent some time in a mental hospital, and in due course one of his nurses was a keen and talented chess player. Mr Trevenen (1921-1982) decided he would like to enter the Paignton Congress, and this was approved on condition the nurse accompanied him. The first round started, but Trevenen was absent. A frantic nurse decided to play his game and then hope that his charge would arrive, which he did. Noticing that Trevenen's game had finished, he assumed the worst and duly finished his game and tracked down the patient, only to discover that Trevenen had rapidly defeated one of England's leading players, despite not having played competitively for some time. 'But why were you late?' asked the nurse. 'Oh, the hotel serves a very good breakfast – I am not rushing that.' Trevenen duly turned up late every day, but did well in the tournament.

At much the same time, latest scores in the West London Club championship saw EG Sergeant in front with 5/5, ahead of Sir George Thomas (4/4), PS Milner-Barry (3½/4) and I König (3/4).

Friendly chess had been active since the war ended and it was hoped that the league would re-commence the following season. Telephone matches were also planned and clubs were invited to contact the local telephone manager. On June 19th and 20th 1946, a radio match was held between USSR and Great Britain, several CS players appearing. Lewis Silkin, a Government Minister who was very keen on chess, opened proceedings in UK and, 'welcomed the players with a magnificent speech that the English players will remember forever. Emphasizing the development of chess in his country, he said that Members of Parliament used to play much more than in the past. He concluded by wishing that Messrs Bevin and Molotov could solve their different points of view on a chessboard!'

Nowadays some of the team might be a bit miffed at being called 'English'. USSR won heavily, but must have been worried as Ragozin complained that the British team had not played many published games, so it was difficult for USSR to prepare properly. But he did conclude that, 'The art of Soviet chess has won a prestigious victory in the radio match.' Ragozin also pointed out one of the drawbacks of radio chess, that the Flohr vs Fairhurst games lasted a total of 22 hours over the two days! A lot of time was expended in waiting for the transmission of moves. The highlight from the British point of view was that Alexander won a game against Botwinnik. Klein lost ½-1½ to Keres on Board 2, Golombek drew 1-1 with Boleslavsky on Board 5, and Aitken lost to Bondarevsky 0-2 on Board 8. Any team that has Bronstein on Board 7 is going to be tough to beat. USSR won 18-6. Great Britain did marginally better than USA had done (a 4½-15½ loss), but USSR were happy.

The Minutes of the first post-war AGM, held on Friday 6th September 1946, at Treasury Chambers, Whitehall, London,

SW1, Item 10 said, 'The formation of a Headquarters club was agreed to in principle, and the matter was left to the Executive Committee to explore the possibility of forming such a club.'. The EC duly met at Berkeley Square House on Friday 18th October and discussed the, 'formation of a chess club for retired civil servants and civil servants from departments with no club.' Peter Bond provided an extract from the Minutes in a communication with a later EC,

'This proposal had been approved in principle at the AGM, and remitted to the Committee for further consideration.

The Committee felt that the object of the Association should be to foster the formation and development of departmental clubs and that the proposed club should not therefore be regarded as a central Civil Service Club but as a subsidiary or supplementary Club. With this object in view, they agreed the attached draft rules [NOT attached – PA Bond] for submission to the next meeting of the Chess Association and suggest that the meeting might consider as a title for the new club either 'The Civil Servants (unattached) Chess Club' or 'the UNATS Chess Club'.'

Item 7 of the Minutes dealt with unattached members, 'The assistant secretary raised the question of unattached chess players and suggested for the present season or until the new chess club had become a practical proposition, unattached members should be permitted to join active Civil Service clubs.

It was pointed out that the rules of the Civil Service and Municipal Chess League limited players to members serving in the department represented by the club. In the circumstances, it was agreed that unattached members could only be invited to join the Association in that capacity and they would then be eligible for the individual and trophy events.' It was also the case that players were not allowed to represent the CS in matches unless their department played in the league.

There is no mention of the Post Office in the name of the league, but it is not clear if this were deliberate or an oversight. In October, Bristol YMCA lost 2-8 to Bath and Admiralty, H Hoskin winning on Board 3 for the visitors.

The Minutes of the General Meeting held in Room 43, Ministry of Labour, 12-13, St James' Square, SW1 on Friday 16th May, 1947, Item 7, stated,

'UNATS Chess Club. The proposed Draft Rules for the club were agreed subject to the addition to paragraph 3 of the words 'affiliated to the Civil Service Chess Association'. It was agreed to suggest to the new club that the name UNATS might be adopted but the Association would be prepared to consider any alternative suggestion. It was decided to ask Mr B Dennis of Ministry of Agriculture and Fisheries to undertake to form the new club, and the matter was left in the hands of the assistant secretary to arrange.' Subsequently, there were amendments made to the Rules of the London Civil Service and Municipal League and the Civil Service Chess Association at the Autumn GM held on Friday 5th September 1947 at 6 pm at the Treasury Chambers, Whitehall, SW1. The eligibility rule for UNATS members read, 'Full membership shall be limited to Retired Civil Servants, and to serving Civil Servants whose department has no organized chess club not affiliated to the CSCA.' (This also appeared as Rule 3 in the UNATS constitution.) Peter Bond commented that the rule only made sense, if a comma appeared before the 'not', but the rule makes more sense in its 1968 version, 'Membership shall be limited to Retired Civil Servants, and to serving Civil Servants whose department has no organized chess club affiliated to the CSCA.' In addition, Rule 10 of UNATS constitution said that 'Rule 3 shall not be altered without the approval of the CSCA.' It is probably the only occasion that a member club suffered the indignity of allowing its own rules to be dictated by another body. Rule 3 was completely unnecessary anyway as the league rules would overrule it.

The inaugural meeting was held on 7 October 1947 and was hosted by the Ministry of Supply Chess Club (Adelphi). Mr Dennis was not secretary, but FJ Dadd had taken on the job.

In the representative matches, the Civil Service won against Essex 27-23 despite the absence of such notable players as CHO'D Alexander, Dr JM Aitken, CG Butcher, RH Newman, NA Perkins, AY Green and Miss Elaine Saunders. A win v Insurance and a draw v Kent was counterbalanced by losses against Surrey and Middlesex.

The passing of WH Hipkiss (aged 90) was reported. He was the first treasurer of the CSCA and was appointed Auditor in 1929 on relinquishing the post of treasurer. On 12 December 1946 WA Fairhurst gave a simultaneous display on 25 boards against NPL and LPTB clubs winning 20, and drawing 4. His only loss was a brevity to JW Head.

The 1946/7 season ended in a blaze of glory for GPO Headquarters who not only won the division 1 championship, but defeated Health in the final of the Bonar Law. Their strong team was headed by none other than the British master RJ Broadbent whose style was said to be reminiscent of Capablanca. On board 2 they had the ex-Midlands champion CG Butcher, and several other strong players such as NA Perkins who reached the last eight of the 1946 London championship, J Neale, AC Lynch – the well-known Hampstead player who won a premier tournament at Margate in 1939, and the ex-Civil Service champion G Wernick. CG Butcher added to their trophies by winning the CS individual championship. LCC finished second in the league, winning 25/- (£1-25).

The division 2 champions were Stationery Office, who lost in the final of the Post Annual to National Physical Laboratory, but only after a replay. Transport II were division 3 champions. WH Law added to the Stationery Office trophies by winning the junior individual title. The pre-war league competitions were played over ten boards, but in this season division 1 was played over 8 boards and the other two divisions over 6 boards. League matches ended by 9 pm.

Ron Fleming recalled, 'In 1947 the EDO returned to London (from Llandudno) and I resumed playing chess for it. My recollections are hazy after all this time but I recall E G Sergeant playing on top board, Miller playing on second board (he would never play below anyone other than Sergeant!), W S Walters playing on 3, Gilchrist on 4 and then people such as Glaze and Primett. Percy Cook was a later acquisition – he was transferred to London from some provincial office – and so were those reputable warriors Barford and Gordon. As you say, the numbers expanded and we fielded IR II and then IR III and finally IR IV. To a certain extent we were restricted by the ruling that no club could have more than one team in any division of the league. So when we wanted to field a fifth team we had to create IR IV (London) and IR IV (Outer Offices) and keep them studiously separate in the nominations. Both, of course, were able to supplement IR III. GPO got round a similar problem by creating a Ladies team of six and these six ladies – with the occasional reserve – played solidly if not too spectacularly in a low division.' Bernard Glaze related that EDO returned at Easter, although other HQ departments did not. He organized a meeting at Somerset House and it was decided they could not field the ten players required for a division 1 team, but could manage eight, so would enter division 2 if it ran. A league AGM was held and it was decided to resume the league, and hope it would expand in due course.'

Despite the impressive work by Messrs Poor and Hoskin, it was felt that continuing with ten boards would cause too many difficulties for clubs. The league officials also had to contend with the fact that the contact details for clubs were likely to be out of date. Many players were no longer available for various reasons, and bomb damage meant that staff had moved to other office accommodation. This was the last season that clubs arranged their own fixtures. From the 1947/48 season onwards, the league compiled the fixture programme. Edward C Baker said that he 'persuaded PM Shaw to plan our first printed fixtures for 1947-48.' LCC abandoned the presentation of silver spoons to prize-winners in view of the cost.

Aitken did a simultaneous display at Bletchley scoring +11=2-0. Imre König won 24 games against LCC and drew with Fardon, losing only to the Treasurer, HE Hammond. BH Wood's excellent magazine '*Chess*' experimented with figurine algebraic notation around this time! A Czechoslovakian team visited Great Britain in 1947 and their schedule included (at their request!) a visit to Lords to watch cricket. They also visited the Houses of Parliament as a guest of Julius Silverman MP. Great Britain lost the match decisively (12-8), Alexander drew both games with Pachman on top board, Golombek played on board 2, Milner-Barry on 8, and Broadbent on 10. GPO won the first league title since the war.

The great excitement of the year for British chess was the visit of a USSR team. Great Britain was thoroughly outclassed, losing the double-round match 15-5. It could have been worse – Botwinnik did not play! The GB team included Alexander (Foreign Office), Milner-Barry (Treasury), RH Newman

(Transport) and Aitken (Foreign Office). For 'Foreign Office', read GCHQ. Alexander scored ½/2 against Keres, Aitken 0/2 against Ragosin, Milner-Barry ½/2 against Lilienthal and Newman ½/2 against Tolush. Golombek no longer had CS connections, but he scored ½/2 against Smyslov.

EG Sergeant won the Middlesex championship at his first attempt, although he had been playing for Middlesex for nearly 40 years. Alexander played at the Zonal tournament for the World Championship, finishing well short of qualification, but with the consolation that he won the first brilliancy prize. The British Championship in Harrogate ended in a tie between RJ Broadbent and Golombek on 8/11, Milner-Barry was 4th on 6.5 and RH Newman 5th on 6. Golombek won the play-off 4-2. The September *Chess* contained a letter from an unhappy Alexander, complaining that BH Wood had criticized the original selection for the British Championship. A late reserve (18 year-old Gordon Crown, who tragically died following an operation later that year) had finished third, and Wood suggested this was evidence he should have been in the original 12. Alexander suggested it was easy to be wise after the event. He also alluded to a friendly challenge from Dilworth. Alexander had said white was much better in the Dilworth variation of the Ruy Lopez, and Dilworth had offered to play a postal match of three games, where he would take the black pieces in all games. Alexander politely declined, saying, 'I never play correspondence chess (a) because I hate it (b) because I am very bad at it.' One assumes that this is a case of (a) following (b). He then says that Broadbent – Milner-Barry was a good example of white's play, but he accepted that black's position was not as bad as he had said. Milner-Barry himself wrote to the magazine complaining about Wood criticizing the organization of the British Championship at Harrogate. Wood had reported that play was starting even as boards were being set out and that the programme demanded adherence to rule 5 and 5a without publishing the rules anywhere! Milner-Barry makes a general point about the undesirability of people criticizing anybody else, before saying, 'But I beg him (Wood) to believe that the strong pull which he gives to his oar within the BCF is in danger of being rendered valueless by the rocking of the boat in which he indulges outside it.' Milner-Barry goes on to say, 'At the most critical time in its history the BCF needs every ounce of sympathy, understanding and practical help that it can get...' Similar laments continue to this day.

A well-attended CS AGM was held on 5 September 1947 and the match captain F (Freddie) M Norman reported that 22 Civil Service clubs had entered the competitions plus LCC and Metropolitan Water Board. HG Poor, a well-known figure in the Sports Association, was made a vice-president in recognition of his services to chess. EC Baker was elected secretary.

Civil Service played the National Liberal Club for the Star cup, which had been presented in 1939, by *The Star* newspaper. The first match was drawn 6-6 in 1939, but CS won the replay on 25th September 1947. After this, the cup was used for individual tournaments.

Civil Service		National Liberal Club
1. EG Sergeant	½-½	PM List (white)
2. NA Perkins	0-1	I Konig
3. JS Parker	½-½	SG Howell-Smith
4. BHN Stronach	1-0	FW Tanner
5. J Mahood	½-½	JET Bunston
6. WEC Richards	1-0	JE Lucas
7. WH Law	1-0	S Steinhart
8. H Cook	1-0	F Bach

9. J Ansell	1-0	B Grad
10. WS Wallis	½-½	S Merlin
11. PA Cooke	1-0	TL Humberstone
12. H Hoskin	0-1	WL Hardie
	8-4	

Civil Service also played strong University opposition in late 1947. They lost to London University 11-9, where the top board clash was a draw between Oliver Penrose and EG Sergeant, but defeated Cambridge 13½-10½ at Emmanuel College. Top boards were:-

Cambridge University — Civil Service

1. J.Harwood	1-0	NA Perkins
2. F Swinnerton-Dyer	1-0	JS Parker
3. FHC Marriot	adj	J Neale
4. M. Glauert	0-1	BHN Stronach
5. I Edelson	½-½	J Mahood
6. E.R.Reifenberg	1-0	PB Cook

CS beat Oxford University 13½-11½, with top boards being as follows:-

Oxford University — Civil Service

1. DM Horne	0-1	RH Newman
2. AF Truscott	1-0	CG Butcher
3. HF Moxon	0-1	J Gilchrist
4. L Lewis	0-1	JS Parker
5. JD Niblett	½-½	WEC Richards
6. GW Lives	0-1	BHN Stronach
7. SR Howell	1-0	J Mahood
8. P Quertier	0-1	AC Sutcliffe
	11½-13½	

Later that year, Oxford Past lost 5-6 to Cambridge Past, the former including Aitken, Newman and Cornforth and the latter Gilbert. GPO won the league and Bonar Law. CG Butcher (GPO) won the CS championship (Barstow cup) and reached the final of the London championship, a very strong event. J Gilchrist (Inland Revenue) and A Bernfield (LCC) were joint champions of the Metropolitan Chess Club. The 1947 London champion William Winter gave a simultaneous display at the Ministry of Supply, winning 18 games and drawing 2 of the 26 games.

Royal Arsenal Chess Club celebrated its 25th anniversary with a dinner held on 25 October 1947 at which the chairman mentioned that all the club's chess equipment had been destroyed in a 1941 air raid. But with the generous help of the Eltham Chess Club it had been able to replace the loss. Mrs Murges, wife of the club's first team captain, said that the wives owed a great deal to the club for it taught their husbands patience and self-control. But she found it to be the most aggravating game in the world and confessed to throwing the pieces at her husband. How he could sit at a game hour after hour she didn't know!

On 31st January 1948 Essex beat CS 21-18, courtesy of the Penrose family. On top board, O Penrose drew with EG Sergeant, board 5 saw J Penrose beat Dr Jacob Bronowski, and Professor Penrose beat J Ansell on board 8. Milner-Barry was on the warpath again, as the BCF's new capitation scheme was attracting criticism. Critics said that BCF expected people to pay up when the ordinary players had not been consulted, and that they got nothing in return, (that argument also continues now), but Milner-Barry made the entirely reasonable point that the Unions had been consulted, and if the BCF tried to speak to every county secretary individually, they would not make much progress. Milner-Barry said that it was clear that the BCF should have at least one paid official and should fund international matches. Edinburgh CS finished second in the Edinburgh Chess League, and it was interesting to see that the Oxford League included two Atomic Energy teams and one from Ministry of Food. NA Perkins finished =1st with WA Fairhurst in the Scottish championship with 7½/9, ahead of Aitken on 6. Aitken commented that the standard of chess was higher, but the publicity poorer than in England. Perkins beat Aitken in 120 moves. The London championship finalists included RH Newman, J Ansell and WEC Richards. Supply won their first CS League championship. There was welcome news of CS chess activity outside London. Lancaster PO Telephone Area had 22 members, including the manager and all other grades. They had played matches against a local industrial company (Williamsons Ltd) and Morecambe Chess Club.

The CSCA AGM in June 1948 made dramatic changes to the running of the league. For 1948/49 the league would run five divisions, restricting each to ten teams and introducing automatic promotion and relegation. There would also be a competition for women and it was agreed that the Association's bronze medal be awarded to the best-played game in each division. A fee of 1/- would be charged for each game entered. A panel would make an initial selection and RJ Broadbent kindly offered to judge the winners. More than 70 members had entered a summer tournament which Freddie Norman (match captain) would organize in groups of six or seven. The league also introduced a *Handbook* containing contact details of clubs and their officials, results, fixtures and rules. This was priced at 9d (roughly 4 p) and most clubs ensured that all their players had a copy.

EG Sergeant was eliminated from the Middlesex championship which he won in 1947 but NA Perkins (GPO) reached the final six. Imre König was described as the country's leading exponent of simultaneous play and at the Ministry of Supply (league champions) he gave a three-hour display against 20 opponents, winning 18 and drawing the other two. CG Butcher, the Civil Service champion, gave a display against 17 members of the PO Factory Club and in 2½ hours had won every game.

The summer of 1948 saw the inauguration of the Battle of Britain tournament which attracted 200 entrants. This was run as a knockout on a regional basis, which meant entrants frequently played a club colleague. Once regional winners had been found, the travelling became a bit more arduous. After 6 months, the entrants had been whittled down to 6 players and these played an all-play-all final at a central venue. The winner was appropriately RF Boxall (Supply), who had learned the game during the war whilst serving in the RAF.

The 1948 British Championship was exciting. This was the last 12-player all-play-all. Presumably, BH Wood's criticism of selections had caused a change of heart. With one round to go, Broadbent led with 7½, ahead of BH Wood on 7, Sir G Thomas and Milner-Barry on 6½, Golombek on 6. The two leaders were playing each other, and Wood, who had been a point clear on 6½/7, was probably regretting throwing away half a point against Milner-Barry in the penultimate round. Wood was struggling, but Broadbent erred and Wood could have won the exchange. Sadly for him, he saw a mate that was not there (and who can say he has not done that) and Broadbent won quickly. It is reported that Alexander and Milner-Barry were quite agitated at the prospect of a Wood victory. It is unclear whether this was because of the perceived establishment bias that permeated the British chess hierarchy for many years or merely that they disliked him personally. Certainly, Wood seemed to have got under their skins judging from the letters page in *Chess*. So Broadbent finished on 8½/11, Golombek, Milner-Barry, Thomas and Wood on 7. Alexander was back on 5½, Newman on 4½, and Aitken on 4, so Civil Service was well-represented. The London Bohemians Club (founded by Blackburne) had taken a direct hit from a bomb and the venue and equipment were destroyed. The Secretary (HR Jupp) submitted a claim and the Board of Trade paid £50. Mr Jupp called a General Meeting, but nobody else turned up. One player was interested but had moved to Liverpool. Mr Jupp now found himself with £50 belonging to a club which seemed defunct, so wrote to the Board of Trade seeking advice, who (not surprisingly) wanted the money back.

Royal Arsenal Woolwich Club were continuing to be active and arranged 50 matches. Not only did they give a good account of themselves in the Civil Service League, they also played in three Kent cup competitions and the Woolwich Business Houses League.

Big matches were once again the fashion and Civil Service entertained the British Correspondence Chess Association in an over-the-board match on 29th January 1949, losing 34½-36½, and also lost to Essex 26-24, EG Sergeant drawing on top board. In other matches, CS beat Insurance 14-6 and London University 13-7. EG Sergeant was awarded the OBE for 39 years' service in the office of Solicitor to Board of Inland Revenue. The 70th anniversary of Bath chess club was celebrated with a match ending Bath CS 8½-11½ Bristol CS.

GPO took the league title back from Supply, after the latter made a nightmare start with three consecutive losses. In the last of these, J Ansell (Supply) lost to British Champion RJ

Broadbent (GPO) on top board in a brilliant game, which CHO'D Alexander annotated for *BCM* (January 1949). Inland Revenue recruited Miss Jean Craker, who came from a well-known chess-playing family and who had just won the British U18 Girl's Championship. There was a proposal to increase the number of players in a team to ten, as it had been pre-war. LCC was approached by Sir Edward Bligh (Chief Officer of the Welfare Department of LCC) seeking a donation of some sets and a chess teacher for the Ratcliffe Settlement. This was a deprived area of London.

The Ministry of Labour club had two blind players. It was reported, 'They use a small chess board with the pieces pegged into holes and the pieces can be distinguished because there are small points on the top of the black pieces and the black squares are raised. Frank Henshaw trained as a shorthand typist. He often reported large conferences and has won several medals for ballroom dancing. The other player, JR Collacott, trained as a musician at Worcester College and later became a telephone operator. He is a difficult opponent to beat.' One has to be extremely impressed with a blind ballroom dancer.

Hastings Silver Jubilee Christmas Chess Congress 1949

The Congress was opened on 29 December 1949 by Lord Simon who described chess as the greatest indoor game and perhaps the only activity under the same rules on both sides of the 'iron curtain'. He regarded the game as one of the unifying forces for humanity and a great contribution towards international goodwill. He believed its increasing popularity in this country among young people as well as old, to be all to the good. In chess no advantage was gained by anything except the honourable struggle of keen minds, and it was the only game in which there was no cheating. Lord Simon was being unduly optimistic with his last sentence. Competitors were present from ten countries and although Civil Service had no players in the premier competitions there were many members in the graded competitions. CS prize winners were PB Cook (Inland Revenue), HF Gook (Customs & Excise), GA Peck (PO) and HB Howard (Supply). The distinguished visitors included CHO'D Alexander and EG Sergeant who were respectively the winner and runner-up in the last competition to be held before the war.

An enterprising local confectioner displayed in his shop window a large cake on which he set a two move chess problem in icing which had been composed by GM Norman of the Hastings Club. In Forsyth notation it was 8, 8, 4P2p, 4N2R, K3pkPB, 4n2R, 4P2b, 8. The purists might complain that there are a number of 'cooks' (other solutions) to the problem but, said the player who won it, you can't have a cake without a cook. A cake would have been much-prized then, as rationing was still in force.

Supply won the league in 1950, continuing their alternation with GPO, but the latter took individual honours, as NA Perkins won the championship and EA Taylor the junior cup. The league prepared to have a division 6 for the first time, matches being played over ten boards in the top three divisions, eight in division 4, and six in lower divisions. This practice was to continue for some years.

The league started a *Bulletin* for the next season. This was yet another good idea in the immediate post-war years. The editorial stated,

'In accordance with the wishes of members present at the Annual General Meeting held on Friday 28th April 1950, efforts are to be made to circulate a *Bulletin* at frequent intervals containing the latest information available relating to Civil Service Chess, and other matters which are considered to be of interest to Service chess players.

The success of this venture depends entirely on the cooperation of club secretaries and/or match captains in reporting results of matches promptly to the Hon. Assistant Secretary and CS Match Captain Mr. F M Norman.

Correspondence and articles for inclusion in the *Bulletin* will be welcomed and should be addressed to the Editor, Mr. H Hoskin. Subscribers should state whether names or initials are to be published.

The annual subscription for copies of the *Bulletin* is 2/2d (about 11 p) and should be paid to the Hon. treasurer as soon as possible. Retired Civil Servants can have copies sent to them on the same terms.'

There were reduced rates for multiple copies, supplied to clubs at the modest charge of 10/- (50p) for 6 copies a season, or 16/- (80p) for 12 copies. The editor was soon having problems, as the editorial in *Bulletin* Number 3 reveals, 'By the time Secretaries receive this copy of the *Bulletin* they will have had notice of the Autumn General Meeting which incorporates a resolution suggesting members should vest the Executive Committee with censorial and suppressive powers.

Firstly I would remind members that at the Annual General Meeting it was decided that as little publicity of Civil Service activities and matters of interest to Service chess players was accorded by the various printed publications, the Chess Association should have its own *Bulletin* which would contain results of matches and items of general interest, and to this end it was pointed out to club secretaries that the success of the *Bulletin* depended largely on their cooperation in reporting results of matches and supplying data for publication.

Secondly, I would point out that any Editor worthy of the name would insist on his prerogative of deciding what 'copy' should be published, and on his right to an 'Editorial' not necessarily representing the views of any Committee or Board of Directors. This is my attitude towards the resolution, and if by any chance the members should decide to support the resolution then I must ask them to come prepared with the name of a successor to myself.'

Mr Hoskin clearly disagreed with the resolution, which probably originated from the Chairman, Pockett, who seemed to be very unpopular with his colleagues. When the author became editor of the *Bulletin*, he encountered the same attempts at censorship and ultimately resigned over the issue.

Civil Service lost 9-8 to Combined Universities in March, with Broadbent losing to a young Leonard Barden.

Inland Revenue's PB Cook finished 2nd = in the Major Open at the British Championship, and 4th in the Premier Reserves at Hastings, just two places behind EG Sergeant. Denis Mardle scored 8/9 in Premier Reserves A, which was only good enough for second place!

The Staunton Centenary international tournament was staged at Cheltenham, Leamington and Birmingham and was won by Gligoric on 10/15, losing only once, to Alexander, who finished 5th= on 8½, Golombek was on 6, just ahead of Broadbent on 5½. Alexander's score was particularly impressive as he also did much of the organization – he was now working at GCHQ in Cheltenham. It is noticeable how Alexander seemed to get much better results in strong international events, whereas his record in British Championships was frequently disappointing. Lord Brabazon of Tara (the former Minister of Aircraft Production), opened Hastings with a speech suggesting that chess was ideal for television, and that not enough people played. He continued, 'Are we so satiated with easy entertainment that our brains are becoming atrophied?' Luckily for him, he did not see today's television. He clearly had interesting ideas, as it is reported that he made the first cargo flight in November 1909, when he attached a waste-paper basket to his Voisin biplane and used it to transport a small pig.

Inland Revenue scored 8½/9 to win the league. Originally formed in 1887, they were re-formed in 1912 as Somerset House, and the 1950-51 winning team included three members of the 1912 team, EG Sergeant, D Miller and WS Wallis. Ron Fleming was now the secretary and later was CS treasurer for many years. Division 2 was won by 'Labour and National Service', another rather transient club. AY Green won the Barstow, WTE Taylor the junior cup and P Henley 'Group III', later to be known as the James Curtis.

Ron Fleming remembered, 'My recollections of the CSCA as such span well over 50 years. In the summer of 1951 when I was with the Estate Duty Office at Rayners Lane, Harrow, I was approached by the Association with a desperate plea: their existing Treasurer, Jesse Garner, had recently had to go in to hospital for surgery – three quarters of his stomach had had to be removed, and he was unable to continue as treasurer. Would I take over the job immediately? I agreed – and continued in post until 1984. In those days the CSCA was still working in primitive conditions and had to rely on the hospitality of individual departments for housing its functions. We held committee meetings in St. James' Square under the auspices of our Chairman A G Pockett, and I seem to recall AGMs being held in County Hall by arrangement with the LCC (as it then was). Our secretary was E C Baker (GPO), our match captain was F M (Freddie) Norman, and we also had Jimmy Curtis (Admiralty) as a committee member. One of our early problems was the dissemination of information: Clubs liked during the season to know how they and their opposition were doing in league matches and who their next opponents were in cup matches, and the job of the divisional recorders was made more difficult as a result. So we decided to set up a monthly *Bulletin* to meet this need and PB (Pip) Sarson of Air Ministry became the first editor. Pip had been a keen oarsman while he was at, I think, Cambridge, and kept an oar over his mantelpiece at his home. But he had been stricken with some form of paralysis and was no longer fully active. This job was well within his capabilities and we were delighted to have his services. That the *Bulletin* later became an organ for its Editor's own character and contained specimen games etc. is historic and well outside the intentions or purposes of its founders.'

Actually Harry Hoskin was the first editor. *Bulletin* Number 6 (July 1951) reported, 'We are pleased to announce that Sir Harold Wiles, KBE, CB, has accepted the position of President of the Association in succession to Sir William Scott Douglas, GCB, KBE, who has retired from active service but has consented to become a vice-president.

Sir Harold Wiles, KBE, CB, is an active playing member of the Ministry of Labour and National Service Club, and has entered for the summer tournament.'

So the President was sacked, when he retired! In those days the President was the highest-ranking civil servant with some sort of connection to chess. At a later date, it was reported that the secretary had persuaded a divisional recorder to resign as that individual 'had found the work quite beyond him'.

Ernest Klein (Admiralty Dockyard Chatham) won the British Championship in 1951, with 8½/11, ahead of the reigning Champion, RJ Broadbent, who was 2nd on 8. Other CS players also did well – PS Milner-Barry (Treasury) 6th with 6½, AY Green (Supply) 13th with 5½, RH Newman (Supply)

19th with 5 points and J Ansell (Supply) 25th with 4½. RF Boxall (Supply) won the Major with 8½ points and thus automatically qualified for the 1952 British Championship. The results demonstrate the strength in depth of the Ministry of Supply Chess Club.

D Le B Jones, 'a young Civil Service player', performed well in a section at Paignton. Britain played Yugoslavia on 12th – 13th September and again had a strong CS contingent, Alexander, Golombek, Broadbent, Milner-Barry occupying boards 2 – 5 and Aitken on board 8.

A very strong CS team lost a close match on 28 March 1952 against the Combined Universities of Oxford and Cambridge 9½–10½

Civil Service		Combined Universities
1. RJ Broadbent	½-½	DV Mardle (C)
2. AY Green	0-1	AW Bowen (O)
3. CG Butcher	0-1	N McElvie (C)
4. NA Perkins	0-1	JW Cornforth (O)
5. JS Parker	1-0	Sir Robert Robinson (O)
6. RF Boxall	0-1	Dr HG Schenck (O)
7. EL Stuart	1-0	HA Samuels (C)
8. AH Challis	1-0	Prof LS Penrose (C)
9. WEC Richards	1-0	Dr J Dean (C)
10. BHN Stronach	½-½	JA Wall (O)
11. Dr IJ Good	1-0	RJ Taylor (C)
12. P Tillson	½-½	D.J. Youston (O)
13. D Le B Jones	0-1	H Morton (O)
14. NA McLeod	0-1	AJ Willson (C)
15. DG Mackay	1-0	DG Horseman (O)
16. PA Cooke	0-1	Rev WR Greenhalgh (O)
17. GE Wernick	½-½	V Tarnovsky (C)

18. SG Hill	½-½	GDE Soar (C)
19. P Henley	1-0	MD Penn (O)
20. R Gedling	0-1	CR Worthing (O)
	9½-10½	

This was perhaps the strongest team fielded by the Civil Service for many years. The opposition fielded future Nobel Prize winners on Boards 4 and 5. A week later CS lost to the British Correspondence Chess Association but with only eight of the strong team listed above.

CS beat Thames Valley League 14-11 on 24th May and later had wins over Cambridge University (20½-17½), London University (13½-12½) and Insurance 12½-7½.

Ron Fleming reported, 'The CSCA played up to six representative matches a year, home and away against Oxford, Cambridge, and London Universities, and an annual friendly match against Hastings Chess Club which involved a very pleasant seaside trip around Easter. The matches tended to be rather informal, and Freddie Norman had a team of assorted players on whom he called as he needed them. For the away match at Oxford, he tended to call on some strong players from GCHQ at Cheltenham, and a carload of them made the return trip from Cheltenham to Oxford. As I recall the trips were made by coach and the team met, say, outside Liverpool Street station and were transported to Cambridge. I recall going to Oxford by rail from Paddington but I also recall going to Oxford by coach and stopping for an hour or so on the way back for a pub visit so clearly the transport system varied. On arrival at our destination, we would be told to attend at a specified College at 2 pm and then would scatter. We would have a reassembly time for the return coach journey and this was necessarily fairly late because of the duration of the individual games and the following ceremonials of, say, adjudication, etc. On the way back the air would be full of analyses and general technical chatter which (to be honest) bored me sick!

The CS Sports Council funded one of the University matches each year – 2 away and 1 home or vice versa, alternately, and paid for 25 players plus 2 officials. The tariff was based on a formula and I gradually worked on this formula getting it to reflect the cost of travel from a player's home up to London as well as the coach from London to the University city, where, that is, the player had incurred extra expense not covered by his season ticket. I also pointed out to the Sports Council that we sometimes played two matches against the same University in the same season, one technically 'representative' and the other a friendly. As far as the University was concerned, they were both against the CSCA and so it behove us to put out strong teams on both occasions! I cannot recall now whether I induced the Sports Council to increase the Grant accordingly but at least it was an arguing point.

I remarked above that Freddie tended to have a regular team for these matches and, of course, this aroused complaints from players who would have liked to be included and were not. So Freddie had to listen to these voices and vary his selection. His point was that this was a representative team and not the strongest available as our objective was a literally friendly fixture and so we would not want to swamp the opposition by only fielding stars. Or at least I think that was his point!'

A National Chess Centre opened on 22nd September 1952 in Fleming's Restaurant, 307 Oxford Street, from noon – 10.30 pm, with a Civil Service Chess Association representative on the Committee. Presumably, the restaurant was not related to Ron Fleming. Alexander was complaining politely about the Hastings tournament, saying it should have either strong foreign players or good up and coming players. He also appeared on television doing a simultaneous display in support of BCF's National Chess Week. Several other events were organized by clubs and associations, and it was reported that, 'outstanding amongst these were the 100-board match arranged by Civil Service Chess Association (against Metropolitan Counties) and the lightning team tournament of the Insurance League'. 'Lightning' chess refers to an event (usually only in Britain) where a buzzer sounds every ten seconds and the player is compelled to move as it sounds. The CS League ended in victory for Patent Office, with AH Challis winning the Barstow, JR Greening the junior cup, and EW Godly (later to be chairman of CSCA) won Group III.

CHO'D Alexander did a simultaneous display against CSCA on 23rd September 1952. EW Godly reports that he was proceeding down the main line of the Sicilian Dragon, when Alexander deviated, saying, 'You won't find that in any ruddy book!' Alexander went on to win the game.

LCC paid £16 for four clocks, and happily the Staff Association contributed the bulk of that. A member of the LCC Committee was concerned about registration fees in the league. 'At present, every club has to pay a registration fee for every player who plays in any of the league matches, whether he plays once or a dozen times during the season.' It was suggested that only players who played three or more games should be charged. After some discussion, it was decided to raise the matter informally with the league committee. The 'capitation' charge was to remain for many years.

Roland Smith (Inland Revenue) won his postal chess game in 1952 playing for Northumberland against G Wernick (Surrey). When Roland was transferred to London in 1953, Wernick invited him to join his club (Battersea) and Roland played a season for them in the London League.

Civil Service beat Insurance 32½-27½, but the return match was an exciting 13½-13½ draw. The strength of Civil Service chess was again shown when they only lost to the Combined Counties by the narrowest of margins over 94 boards. LCC ran some most successful internal tournaments, but of course problems can arise wherever chess is played. The Minutes of the LCC Chess Club Committee Meeting for 21st May 1953 relating to a dispute over a sealed move are interesting, 'The Committee considered this matter very carefully and arrived at an unanimous decision, after considering statements from both persons concerned. The decision was satisfactorily accepted.' What is more interesting is that this page has been glued into the minute book, on top of a more detailed report! The names of the players are not given in the new version, so possibly the change was made to protect them. Presumably, one of the players had accused the opponent of cheating, so anonymity was a wise precaution. Perhaps the matter should remain a mystery, although modern scientific techniques could no doubt provide an answer. On a more positive note, Tom Fish had scored 9/9 for LCC in 1952/53 – a magnificent result. A later meeting reported that, 'Mr Bernfield and Mr Camroux attended the CSCA AGM and there was nothing raised at the meeting of interest to the club.' Doubtless, other delegates felt the same... The LCC AGM had decided to run their club championship as a 9-round Swiss. Although such events are common-place now, they did not become popular in Britain until the early 70s, despite being first run in Switzerland (of course) in the late 19th century. At the next Committee meeting, the organizer of the tournament objected and insisted he would only run 8 rounds. The chairman pointed out that as the AGM had decided on 9 rounds, the Committee had no choice but to run 9 rounds. After a vote, the Committee agreed that the tournament would be run over 9 rounds, and that they would find another organizer for the last round. As it happened, the original organizer resigned, so the replacement ran the whole event. The number of rounds has always been controversial. An even number of rounds seems attractive, on the basis that players may get an equal number of games with the white and black pieces, in this case four. In practice, players tend to get an uneven split, which is all right if you get five whites and three blacks, but complaints happen if a player gets three whites and five blacks. A 9-round tournament means that it is almost inevitable that there will be a five-four split, one way or the other. The tournament was clearly popular, as the championship had 28 players and there was also a Knockout event, played at odds, for the Martin Trophy.

There was no league rule about playing with clocks and clubs bought clocks as and when finances permitted. It was not until 1953 that the Inland Revenue had 10 clocks. There was an amusing incident concerning clocks that year in a Bonar Law match between Inland Revenue 1 and Admiralty who played in division 2. Prior to this match Admiralty had played Revenue 2 in a division 2 league match and there was an unpleasant dispute between the captains. Because of this dispute Admiralty threatened that Revenue I would not be admitted to their building for the Bonar Law match. They eventually relented as they would have lost the match by default. But rather mysteriously the match had to be played without clocks as all their clocks were away being repaired. The Revenue team assumed that Admiralty had done this so that their players could play slowly and draw the match. In fact the opposite happened and they played so quickly that the match was over in record time and Revenue won 9½-½.

By now PS Milner-Barry was Chief of the Organisation and Methods Division at the Treasury. CS chess continued outside London as Lancaster and Morecambe CS beat Trimpell 5½-2½.

The *Bulletin* was pleased to report in July 1953, 'That ubiquitous pair of Government Chemists, Mr. Godly and Miss Cresswell, were mated in one on the 18th July. Mr. Battersby was present and Mr. Symes was at the organ. We offer our congratulations and wish that the only checks they receive will be those we administer over the board.' The *Bulletin* of August 1953 reported that, 'Mr. Garner has been told by his doctor that his health will not permit of his carrying on the duties of treasurer. All of us will extend our sympathy at the present, our thanks for his work in the past, and our hope that, even if he is no longer our stern treasurer (or because of that) we shall see him as often as before.

His place has been taken for the time being by Mr. Fleming, who will seek relaxation from extracting our money from us in his official capacity in Inland Revenue, by extracting our money from us as our treasurer.

An election for treasurer will be held at the September 1953 General Meeting to be held on the 11th.'

The 'for the time being' turned into more than 30 years. Sadly, Mr Garner died the following year.

Honours in 1953/54 went to Inland Revenue, who won division 1, and Inland Revenue II won division 2, after a three-way tie with LCC II and UNATS, all on 6½/9. A three-way play-off was organized. Strangely, this still did not encourage the league to adopt a tie-break system which would avoid play-off matches. GPO were winners of the Bonar Law and the Post Annual cup was won by UNATS. By now 68 teams were playing in the league. Individual champion was AY Green and junior champion J Eyre.

This year saw the publication of the first BCF grading list. It was based on games played over the period 1950 – 1953 and several civil servants featured at the top end.

1a CHO'D Alexander, RBroadbent, E Klein (and the non-CS player Yanovsky.)

1b H Golombek etc

2a PS Milner-Barry etc

2b DV Mardle, EG Sergeant etc

3b PB Cook etc

1a is roughly equivalent to 233 – 240 on the grading system that was used more recently, 1b is 225-232, 2a is 217-224 etc. It should be noted that the number one player in the country was the equivalent of 240 at most, whereas now the top player is about 270, so the conversion is not necessarily exact. It was thought that the middle of one grade would be expected (on the performance in the period) to beat a player in the middle of the next grade below by 7-5 (approximately). This system was created by Sir Richard Clarke (Treasury), who had a strong statistical background. His words on the grading system should be considered carefully,

'A warning should be sounded about the significance of these gradings. Firstly, the gradings do not purport to measure the intrinsic strength of the players. They measure the performance in the period shown.'

Unfortunately, few people heed that warning, as it was not unknown for players graded 151 to claim they are better than a 150! Clarke was saying a 1a might not be stronger than a 1b. The grading system did not go down very far, unlike the current system which attempts to contain everybody.

CS gave the Universities a hard time in representative matches, beating Cambridge 20½-15½, Oxford 8-5 and London 15½-8½, although there was less success in the return matches, with losses to Oxford 9-16 and Cambridge 13½-15½. A trip to Essex ended in a 26½-15½ defeat, and Surrey won 35½-14½.

Players from seven Employment Exchanges (later to be called Job Centres) in Norfolk and Suffolk formed a Ministry of Labour (Eastern Region) Postal Chess Club. The league in London was thriving, as there were now 72 teams, and a seventh division appeared for the first time. GPO won the Bonar Law trophy, beating Board of Trade 6-4 in the final, and UNATS won the Post Annual cup, beating Air Ministry 7-3.

In 1955, CS lost 13½-11½ to Insurance, with Broadbent losing to Ron Blow on top board, and RF Boxall losing to W Veitch on the next board. There was more success elsewhere, with CS beating Oxford U 15-10 and London U 16½-8½. CS lost narrowly to Combined Universities 8½-9½, but Broadbent beat the talented Israeli player Raaphy Persitz. The previous year, Persitz had won his game in the varsity match then went off to play a county match the same day, where he defeated Alexander! Ministry of Supply won the Bonar Law trophy with a 6½-3½ win over Customs and Excise, whilst the Post Annual cup went to Cable and Wireless after a 5½-4½ victory over Patent Office II. The CS individual competition (Barstow cup) was won by EC Hughes, who beat RF Boxall in a play-off. Oxford University got their revenge over CS with a 13½-11½ win, but this time Persitz lost to Aitken. The return match against Insurance ended in a 9½-13½ loss, and even London Schoolboys beat the CS 10½-9½. The LCC AGM proposed that Abram Bernfield should be the official delegate to the CSCA meetings. Someone else proposed that the Hon

Secretary (John Gorton) should be the delegate. Mr Gorton was eagerly seconded by Mr Bernfield! However, the latter won the vote by 9-6, with one abstention.

The new Grading List had Alexander as 1a, Golombek at 1b, Broadbent and Milner-Barry at 2a, Aitken and AY Green at 2b, J Ansell, RF Boxall and EG Sergeant at 3a, all of whom would be regarded as over 200 on the later grading system. The CS League grew even more and a division 8 started. Broadbent took on the North Thames Gas Board and won +20=3-1.

UNATS had a home venue in Room 240, Home Office, Whitehall, and subscriptions were 7/6 (37½ p) a year, but only 2/6 (12½ p) for retired members of the Civil Service.

CSSC's *Handbook* listed departmental Associations with chess clubs. These were :-

Admiralty, Air Ministry, Cabinet Office and Ministry of Defence, Commonwealth Offices, Customs and Excise, Exchequer and Audit, Credex (Export Credits Guarantee Department), Ministry of Fuel and Power, General Register Office, Government Communications (entry says 'all sports', which is perhaps their habitual secrecy), Ministry of Health, Inland Revenue, Ministry of Labour and National Service, Natural History Museum, New Scotland Yard (Civil Staff) (Comets), Paymaster General's Office, Ministry of Pensions and National Insurance, Department of Scientific and Industrial Research, HM Stationery Office, Ministry of Supply, Supreme Court, Board of Trade, Ministry of Transport and Civil Aviation.

Other clubs mentioned were

Bristol Civil Service, Crown Agents & Colonial Office, GPO HQ, Government Chemists Department, Lancaster and Morecambe (GPO), London County Council, LTR (GPO), Metropolitan Water Board, Ministry of Labour and National

Service – Leeds, Ministry of Housing and Local Government, Ministry of Works, Mount Pleasant (GPO), National Physical Laboratory, New Scotland Yard, Norwich Post Office, Patent Office, PO NE Region HQ, Leeds, PO Savings Bank Division, PO Savings Certificates Division, PO Supplies Department, UNATS, West Telephone Area (GPO)

In 1956, England played Scotland, with the top board being Golombek vs Aitken. Any unfinished games would be adjudicated by Dr Euwe, the former World Champion. It had long been the custom that matches would have an adjudicator present to deal with unfinished games, but it does rather suggest that not much time was spent analyzing the final position. Presumably a few minutes of thought by Euwe would come up with the right decision. NA Perkins was board 5 for Scotland. Roger Stockwell finished 4th in the London Boys championship, and was to go on to be a strong player and adjudicator for many years. PB 'Pip' Sarson became the secretary of the National Chess Week Committee. During this week the Teenagers defeated the Old Stagers by 841 – 497. The annual Battle of Britain tournament reached its final stages, the finalists being M Franklin, J Fuller, JB Howson and KC Messere (Customs and Excise), Messere finishing third in rather strong company. Sadly, the Battle of Britain tournament no longer takes place.

LCC were seeking someone to repair some defective chess clocks, and the Secretary (John Gorton) had written to a Mr Fardon (also of LCC), but received no reply. The Chairman (C Howard) said that Mr Fardon, 'on the strength of his prowess with a rifle, was being considered for entry as a competitor into the Olympic Games at Melbourne, and as a consequence would probably be devoting the greater part of his leisure time to practice.' It was agreed to approach the LCC Staff Association watch-repairer. Presumably, this was an official post. There was discussion about LCC Staff Association ties, with the appropriate emblem, coming 'in two shades, 'silk' and 'silk and brown'.' Mr J Eyre asked the entirely reasonable question, 'What colour was pure silk?' Mr Gorton said he was somewhat confused as well, and offered to enquire. However, nobody was interested in buying said ties anyway.

Civil Service lost 22½-23½ to Kent, and by 19-25 to Essex. Broadbent gave a simultaneous display at North Thames Gas Board, scoring +20=3-1.

The *Bulletin* (Volume IV, Number 9) of February 1956 had strong words,

'UNFAIR TO ADJUDICATORS!

There has recently been an increase in the number of diagrams submitted for adjudication with absurdly optimistic claims by one side or the other. During the last few weeks these have provoked the following unsolicited testimonials from adjudicators,

'On the face of it, White's claim seems unreasonable.'

'Black must have been exercising his sense of humour when he made this claim.'

'It is quite impossible to award anything but a draw here. There is no attack and there is far too much play. In fact the game has not really started.'

'I must comment on the claims. In each case the side with the weaker force is claiming a win with no attacking prospects that I can see to justify it. The adjudicator cannot work wonders, and if one side's only hope of saving a match was to get wins from two lost or at best drawn positions then it is time that someone had a word with the match captain to instil a dose of realism into his hopes. Adjudications like these really seem to me a waste of time and money.'

To invite an adjudicator, whose services are given voluntarily, to devote himself seriously to the consideration of a position the verdict on which must be painfully obvious from the outset is to waste his time and insult his expert knowledge. Will match captains please ensure that the adjudication system is not abused.'

This was still an issue 50 years later.

Customs and Excise won division 1, with Inland Revenue taking the Bonar Law trophy. Other winners were Crown Agents (Div.2), Cable and Wireless, and LCC II (Div. 3), Patent Office II (Div. 4), Housing and Local Government II (Div. 5), Exchequer and Audit (Div. 6), PO Supplies II (Div. 7), Exchequer and Audit II (Div. 8), and Cable Wireless won the Post Annual cup.

The *Bulletin* (Volume V, Number 1) in summer 1956 reported,

'Doughty doings in Division 3!

Spare a thought, dear reader, for the valiant warriors of London County Council II and Cable & Wireless who, whilst you have been recuperating from the season's labours, were fighting one another to a standstill in the struggle for championship honours in division 3!

It will be recalled that on the season's play LCC II and Cable & Wireless emerged as joint holders of the top position in division 3; Rule 16 was accordingly invoked and a 'play-off' duly held. When the dust of battle subsided, it was found that the score stood at 2½ all with five games for adjudication. Even on the adjudicated games the two sides demonstrated their equality by both claiming four points out of five possible! The adjudicators, not to be outdone, awarded a win to each side and three draws, with the result that the match stood drawn at 5 all. No arrangements for 'breaking' a draw having been agreed before the match, deadlock was reached.

The situation was desperate. Already the senior recorder (who at this season of the year goes into purdah for a fortnight in order that he may, in modest solitude, perform his annual function of hatching out the new season's fixture list) was growing snappish and beginning to moult. The Executive Committee, having looked all over (and underneath) the Rules without finding anything useful, made an ad hoc decision. The two sides were given three weeks in which, if they so desired, to hold another play-off; no adjudications were allowed – all games to be played out or the result agreed. If the match could not be played, or did not lead to a decisive result, the two teams would be held as joint champions of the division and the question of promotion would be resolved by the drawing of lots.

Accordingly, at 6pm on June 5th, the two teams lined up once more with clocks on all boards ticking to a fight to the finish rhythm. At 11pm (!) the struggle was adjourned with the score 4½-3½ (two games unfinished) in favour of LCC II and the spectre of yet another draw sniggering hopefully in the corridor and preparing to demand admission!

Finally, on June 12th, four players (having surrendered all weapons to the door keeper) sat down once again to complete the two unfinished games. After another session of grim struggling the marathon was brought to a conclusion: LCC II were home by the narrowest of margins (match result: LCC II 5½ - 4½ Cable & Wireless). Let us hope that the players concerned have a restful summer holiday and that their energies are restored before the new season's operations begin!'

This rather nice report was written by the Senior Recorder of the day, G Briddon. Yet it was many more years before a suitable means of breaking ties was brought into the league. The December 1956 *Bulletin* (Volume V, Number 5) carried this greeting, 'May we offer our good friend Harry Poor much belated best wishes on the occasion of his 80th birthday on October 4th. Harry Poor has been and is a pillar of strength to the Association. He called the association together again after the War in 1946. He was treasurer for a great many years before the War, and is now our most active vice-president – despite his great age. During the War he continually urged the Civil Service Sports Council to set up an indoor sports headquarters. Through lack of money this could not be done, and the scheme has suffered many changes eventually to emerge as the Civil Service Club in Great Scotland Yard. It was in this club which he helped to set up that, at the invitation of Sir Arthur Watson, Harry Poor celebrated his birthday and many of his friends drank his health.'

The 1957 Grading List featured Alexander as 1b, Broadbent, Green and Milner-Barry as 2b, Aitken, Ansell, Cornforth, Mardle as 3a and Hughes, DE Lloyd, NA Perkins, WEC Richards and Sergeant as 3b. Many other CS players were in the next few groups. Exchequer and Audit became the first winners of the Jesse Garner cup, the new Knockout Competition for divisions 5-8. There was a proposal to limit the Civil Service championships to civil servants, which did not please clubs like LCC, which had been members of the CSCA for a very long time. The secretary of LCC reported the loss of two files of club records, 'The papers were contained in a suitcase and were taken from the luggage rack of a railway train.' This must have been very annoying for the club and the secretary, but probably equally annoying to the thief, when he came to examine his swag.

LCC clearly read their insurance policy very carefully as the insurers had referred to a '54 oz silver cup', when it should have been 5¼ oz. LCC hosted the Civil Service jamboree match on

21st March 1958. Inland Revenue won, the prize being 100 cigarettes. Ironically, this was just after LCC's Staff Association had complained to the chess club about the excessive amount of cigarette ash found on the floor. The chess club had denied responsibility.

CS were largely successful in matches against Universities, beating London 12½-10½, Oxford 15½-9½, 14-10 and 16-9, but losing to Cambridge 14½-15½. CS beat Cambridge U in the return match 15-12. The famous Gambit Rooms closed 18th January 1958 after 60 years. The Gloucestershire championship was dominated by CS players, reflecting the presence of GCHQ, J Ansell winning, ahead of JM Aitken, C Braunholtz and DV Mardle. The Ladies championship was won by Mrs Mardle. Meanwhile, Chris Carew (later Home Office) won the U14 London championship. JM Aitken won the Scottish Championship with 10/11, NA Perkins finishing 3rd= on 7½. Ken Messere managed 2nd place in the Battle of Britain tournament. Remarkably, the CS League started a division 9. 78 teams participated in all.

1959 saw CS narrowly beat Insurance 13-12, and Oxford University by the same score, but lose to London University 11½-13½ and 9-16, and Cambridge University by 14-16 and 12½-16½. Another loss by 8½-11½ came against Oxford and Cambridge Universities. Denis Mardle won the Postal Chess championship (with 6/8) of 'The Infantile Paralysis Fellowship'. This was formed in 1939 and is now called the British Polio Fellowship. Mardle was also in action at the Stevenson Memorial at Bognor Regis from 1st – 11th April, and he shared 1st place with the Swiss (originally Hungarian) IM Erno Gereben with 8/10, Mardle winning their individual game. AY Green and DE Lloyd were two points behind. GPO won the Bonar Law trophy, beating Crown Agents, the Post Annual cup was won by Board of Trade, who beat Post Office Savings Department II, and the Jesse Garner cup went to British Museum, who beat Air Ministry II. Inland Revenue V became the inaugural winners of division 9. The CSCA AGM decided that for adjudications which did not affect the result of the match, the team making the incorrect claim would be charged 7/6 (37½p) instead of 5/- (25p). There was also a proposal to change the time limit for matches from 36 moves in 90 minutes, then 6 moves per 15 minutes, to 42 moves in 90 minutes, then 7 in 15 minutes. The proposal lost 'almost unanimously'. 50 years were to elapse before the change was approved. Divisions 1 – 3 would be played over 10 boards, 4 – 6 over 8 boards, and 7 – 9 over 6 boards. There was also discussion about the individual competitions. LCC made a proposal, seconded by MWB, that all players in the league (not just the civil servants), be allowed to enter the competitions. The Chairman of CSCA (EC Baker) explained that the competition was run by CSCA on behalf of the Civil Service Sports Council, who awarded medals to the winners. For this reason it would be better not to draw attention to the participation of municipal club members. However, he did undertake that if a non-member of CSSC won, the committee would give careful consideration as to the possible award of a title or trophy to that player. Following this undertaking the resolution was withdrawn.

The Ilford tournament held at Whitsun 1960 was a triumph for Denis Mardle, who won with the remarkable score of 4½/5, ahead of Milner-Barry on 3, and AY Green was 6th and last with 1. Percy Cook of Inland Revenue came second in the Major Open at the British Championship, a mere half-point behind the winner. The Grading List featured more CS players. JR Cooke (Government Chemists), DJ McCue (Ministry of Supply), LS Perry (Patent Office) and EL Stuart (Ministry of Labour) were all 4a (185 – 192) and JR Gilbert, BE Glaze, D Miller (all Inland Revenue) and LAJ Glyde (Ministry of Housing) were all 4b (177 – 184). LAJ Glyde became well-known for his organizational work at Hastings. The 1960 Autumn GM of the CSCA was attended by 80 people.

The 1962 West of England championship was won by Denis Mardle on 5½/7, ahead of ARB Thomas and JM Aitken. LCC Chess Club celebrated its 75th anniversary. The November *Bulletin* (Volume XI, Number 3) reported that, 'The ivory chess set left to the Association by Jimmy Curtis will be held each year by the individual champion. The ivory set left by Harry Poor is to become a trophy for Group III of the individual championship.' Unfortunately, both these ivory sets 'disappeared' sooner or later. 84 teams played in the league.

The 1964 West of England championship ended in a four-way tie for first, with considerable CS presence. JM Aitken, J Ansell, DV Mardle and D Gray all scored 4½. The Battle of Britain final tournament was won by Mike Basman (later to play for Treasury) with 3/3, ahead of NA Perkins 2, WF Coles 1 and A Bernfield (GLC) 0.

The CSCA Executive Committee met on 1st July 1964 and the Secretary (T McDade) wrote 'Presentation to Mr F.M.Norman - Mr F.M. Norman had retired from the Civil Service. Through the years he had given much time to the Association's affairs in his capacity as match captain. The committee voted that a sum in the region of 5 guineas (£5-25) should be used to buy Mr. Norman a gift as a token of the Association's appreciation. It was agreed that the secretary should write to Mr. Norman for his suggestions and report back at the next committee meeting.' It seems that the match captain was also the senior recorder in those days. The EC were also seeking a *Bulletin* editor, as Mr Soutar had resigned. They decided to contact

CSSC to see if the latter would do the typing and stencilling. An amendment to League Rule 16 was discussed. Three teams had tied for promotion in division 4. After an indecisive play-off, promotion had been decided by ballot. The Council had felt it desirable that the rule be amended to cover such an occurrence but had remitted the problem to the EC, their findings to be reported to the Autumn General Meeting. No one could suggest a wholly suitable alternative to the existing rule. The EC decided to report that the current rule should stand 'as it was unlikely that the problem would arise again'. The EC frequently suffered from such misplaced optimism. The EC also frequently tried to get club proposals remitted to the EC, so they could forget about them. They would invoke Rule 16 if necessary. At this stage, Rule 16 stated that a play-off should take place and bottom board elimination would apply to split a tie. However, that might be difficult in a three-way tie. The EC were rather unwise to think that a multiple tie would not happen again. It was agreed that grading should be extended as far as possible beyond the first four divisions only. The graders were to be approached to ascertain 'if they were willing and able to extend their field of operations.' The Minutes therefore imply that there was more than one grader, and that the EC was so scared of upsetting them, that they were going to politely enquire about more grading, instead of telling them the decision. But the EC meeting of 16th September provides clarification. No results from division 1 and 3 had been graded and Mr Perry was unwilling to continue in post. So it appears that the league recorders doubled up as graders. This would be easy nowadays, using appropriate software, but then it was by no means easy to organize the grading. The suggestion at the previous meeting to extend grading was rejected. It was also agreed, 'that the winner of division 1 be given a bye in the first round of the Bonar Law trophy.' This is a rather poorly worded decision as it might just happen that the competition attracted 8 entries, when giving a bye would cause difficulties. It was this year that the Bronowski Trophy started. According to Ron Fleming, 'Dr. Bronowski presented a cup to be competed for by the champion clubs of the Civil Service Chess League, the Insurance Chess League, the Banks Chess League and the Commercial Chess League. Originally this went smoothly and I can recall going to the Prudential Building, to the home of Chiswick Products. To Hangar Sports, etc. to play games on behalf of IR as chess league champions. But this arrangement soured and the competition became between representative teams of the various leagues and not between champion clubs. And there my recollection ceases.' Inland Revenue won the inaugural event and on five other occasions, including the final club event in 1972. In a match v Shell one of their players lost on time but when this was pointed out, he grabbed the clock and wound the pointer back 15 minutes. His captain professed that he hadn't seen the incident even though he was watching his player's flag. Later the Bronowski Committee restored peace by declaring the result a draw!

The EC meeting in November revealed that Eric Croker had done the missing grading, albeit too late for inclusion in that year's BCF grading list. Obviously the delay was not his fault. There was a proposal to have EC meetings on the first Wednesday of each month, which seems rather a lot of meetings. The missing James Curtis Chess Set (presented by his widow) was discussed as was a proposal to try to enter a team in the SCCU championships, which was restricted to counties.

86 teams participated in the league.

Denis Mardle found the 1964-65 Hastings tournament rather heavy going, (scoring 1/9), but won the West of England championship again. LCC Chess Club changed its name to GLC (Staff) Chess Club. The EC met on 7th April 1965. There was concern that RG Wade had given a Simultaneous Display and several players failed to arrive. There was a brief discussion of competitions for non-London players or teams. There was also news that CSSC had acquired premises in London for use as a Recreation Centre. The EC had been invited to attend a meeting relating to this. After some discussion, the EC agreed to attend and ask for accommodation for chess activities. This was the Monck Street venue. Ron Fleming recalled, 'I mentioned above that the Association originally held its events courtesy of some constituent club but when Bernard Sunley got round to building the vast structure in Marsham Street the two basement floors – called the Rotunda – were occupied by the Sports Council for recreational purposes and the CSCA had the occasional use of rooms there. This was fine as long as it was informal but then a problem arose over Saturday representative matches and the reluctance of the security staff to open up the entire Rotunda for our benefit. Another example of a pleasant working arrangement going sour.'

The two floors which he mentioned were at ground level or lower, but it is said that there were more floors lower yet, although not accessible to the public. The Monck Street venue used was the 'South Rotunda'. The spaces occupied by the two rotundas were originally gasholders, built in 1877, but demolished in 1937. The Government wanted secure buildings during World War II, so built the rotundas in the holes left by the gasholders. The rotundas had to withstand the blast of a 500 lb bomb, so the roof was 12 feet thick! It was also reinforced with metal bars. Higgs Ltd built the South Rotunda. Work started in late 1940 and was completed in mid-1941. A V1 flying bomb landed in Monck Street and barely disturbed the rotundas although there was considerable damage and loss of life outside. Churchill and his staff worked and slept in the other rotunda. The buildings were linked by tunnel with other Government buildings. A work colleague of the author found an old book about London, which said that there was a huge number of tunnels for Government use. After the war the Ministry of Information occupied the South Rotunda. Both buildings became less important, hence the use of the South Rotunda as a centre for the Civil Service Sports Council. The centre included a rifle range, cricket nets, snooker and table-tennis tables, a bar and a restaurant area. The centre was certainly a somewhat bleak place, but was heavily used. Users were puzzled at large square holes in the internal walls. It transpired that the post was delivered by a large model railway, which passed through these holes. One drawback was that there were steps up to the front door, then more down to the 'ground floor' level in the centre, (which was slightly below ground level), and also steps up to the toilets then down the other side. In one of John Sargent's Rapidplay events, a player in a wheelchair entered and had to be carried into the venue. When we asked the caretaker (who appeared to live in the centre) about the existence of toilets for the disabled, he said rather angrily there were none, and the person in question should not have entered the tournament. It was no surprise when the Centre closed. John staged several tournaments there and some of the visitors (perhaps affectionately) called the venue the 'Dungeon', which is how it is known to this day. Some of us toured it before closure and were intrigued to encounter very solid security doors some three levels down. We were told that a 'plant room' was contained therein. The centre later became a haunt of the homeless, and numerous rats, and Security guards operated in pairs when touring the building. In the early 21st century attempts were made to demolish the buildings. Not surprisingly, the reinforced concrete caused problems and explosives were used to remove the top two levels. The author passed the centre en route to a meeting, after the roof had gone, and it was fascinating to see the very thick walls with metal bars sticking out of them. Demolition continued and apparently the lower levels were filled with concrete and used as solid foundations.

Ron Fleming continued, 'Sometime in, I think the 1960's the CSCA acquired a stadium on the banks of the Thames at, I think, Chiswick and it was formally opened by the then Duchess of Gloucester. The Sports Association invited the various affiliated organisations to put on a display to commemorate this opening, and the CSCA mounted a living chess game, i.e. two of our young chess playing ladies sat at a table with a chess board between them and solidly played a series of games until such time as the Duchess had made her tour of inspection. I cannot recall the names of the two ladies concerned, but a good time was had by all.'

CSSC had owned the Chiswick ground for some 40 years, so doubtless he refers to a new building that was added to the ground. The pavilion appears to be typical of 60s architecture.

Some discussion took place about extending interests by introducing competitions for provincial players and teams. The Ministry of Labour ran a regional competition, and the secretary agreed to make contact. Another EC meeting took place on 12th May, where there was concern that the James Curtis trophy was missing. A board and set were presented to the winner Mr JD Berry. It was agreed to set-up a Sub-Committee consisting of J Loften (*Bulletin* editor), E Croker and T McDade (Secretary) to formulate arrangements for a national chess tournament to be played by civil servants throughout Britain. This sub-committee met quickly, but nothing concrete had happened by the time of the next EC meeting at the end of June. But the 38th AGM had been held on Friday 28th May 1965. The Chairman (Dr Calvert) opened the meeting by apologising for the loss of the 1964 AGM minutes caused by the change of secretary and the absence of the chairman overseas. But the secretary was re-elected, so the chairman's comment seems strange. The CSCA presented the sum of 5 guineas to Mr. FM Norman. Of the officers elected, it was specifically mentioned that Mr. FJ Dadd had been an auditor since 1922. He was to go on to establish a record 55 years of service to CSCA. 11 adjudicators were elected, namely Dr. JM Aitken, J Ansell, A Bernfield, RJ Broadbent, PB Cook, NG Hammond, GB Lewis, DV Mardle, NA Perkins, WEC Richards, and RA Slade. Mr. RE Lawrence (Defence Central) explained the present relationship between the Admiralty and Defence (Central) Clubs. These two clubs had now amalgamated to form the new Ministry of Defence (Central) and Navy Department Chess Club. The chairman thanked Mr. J Loften for arranging the hall and the refreshments for the meeting. It is interesting to see that the EC provided refreshments for the meeting. More recent meetings have taken place in CSRC, so refreshments were generally available then.

G Maskell was instructed to draw up a set of rules for the individual tournaments. For reasons that remain unclear, he offered his resignation, stating this would allow him to continue as tournament controller although outside the Executive. Dr. Calvert asked him to reconsider, and after further discussion Mr Maskell withdrew his offer. It would be unusual for someone to hold such a post and yet not be a member of the EC, and if he had an aversion to being on the EC, he could decline all the invitations to meetings. The annual match against Hastings was discussed. It was suggested that the venue should alternate between London and Hastings rather than playing all matches in Hastings. The CSCA tended to turn out weak teams in Hastings whereas Hastings turned out strong teams. Obviously, prestige was at stake! It appears that the match in June 1965 produced an adverse report in the local Hastings press and the CSCA were offended (or at least someone on the EC was). The EC agreed to leave the matter in the hands of the match captain. This again sounds an over-reaction. Why should anyone care that much about the result of friendly matches? The James Curtis trophy consisted of a set and a board and as it had still failed to appear, the EC decided to write it off. At a meeting on the 17th November, the EC agreed that early in 1966 the secretary should find zone organizers in the twelve Treasury regions. Meanwhile, the National Sub-Committee would meet and discuss conditions of entry. SCCU had agreed that CSCA could play in the SCCU Jamboree event.

The EC met on 6th April 1966 and the secretary reported that he had been unable to pursue arrangements for the national Civil Service individual tournament because of increasing personal commitments elsewhere. The Chairman, Dr. Calvert, said that planning should go ahead as soon as possible. It was noted that the CSSC's *Handbook* provided a valuable source of contacts which could overcome the issue of finding zone organizers. The secretary also asked for the 1966 AGM to be postponed from 3rd May 1966 to later that month. No reason was given but the EC agreed, and it took place on Wednesday 25th May. By now there were 34 clubs in the league, entering 86 teams in 9 divisions. They managed to generate only 65 adjudications. The CSCA match captain had arranged 15 matches. Numerically, this period must be regarded as the zenith of CS chess. Sadly, FM Norman had died in the preceding year, but it appears that the customary period of silence was not observed, which is strange given the high regard in which he was held. Comment was passed by an unnamed person about the occasional delay in processing adjudications. It was agreed that the fault did not lie with the adjudicators. The chairman spoke of the new Indoor Sports Centre due for completion at the end of the year. The Minutes also record that, 'Mr Foley proposed a note of thanks to the chairman for the official manner in which he had carried out his duties and for the considerable amount of time that Dr Calvert had spent on his duties. Dr Calvert replied that he did not think he gave sufficient of his time to the CSCA but was more than pleased if the Association thought his work had been of some value.' The wording is slightly odd, possibly the secretary misheard 'efficient' as 'official', the former appearing to make more sense. The EC met on 14th September, where Mr Gould submitted draft rules for the individual tournaments which were approved with some amendments. It was agreed that the new secretary should write to Mr S Butley (CSSC) to obtain the addresses of regional secretaries. The chairman thanked the retiring Secretary (T McDade) for his work. The secretary resigned because of a posting to Washington DC. The Ministry of Housing played in the Business Houses championship, rather than the CS League.

The SCCU jamboree on 19th November 1966 was impressive. Twenty teams participated and Kent won on tie-break from Middlesex, narrowly ahead of Essex, Surrey Juniors and Civil Service. The CSCA EC met on 23rd November and discussion of the national individual tournament continued. Mr Fleming agreed to write to all regional Secretaries inviting them to have a tournament. The regional winners would meet in a Final competition in London. Eric Croker suggested it could be played at the Ilford Congress. The next meeting of the

EC (25th January 1967) heard Mr Fleming report little response to his invitations, but he said he would send out reminders. It was also noted that Leonard Barford (President) had been knighted in the New Year's Honours List. The EC agreed for the National Final to be included in the Ilford Congress after Mr Croker reported that the Ilford Congress organizer was willing to host it. The EC agreed that if 6 regional champions were unavailable this year the necessary players would be available from the London area. The further letter seemed to be to no avail as Mr Fleming had only received four replies by April, and subsequent withdrawals led the EC to request approval from CSSC to postpone the tournament. It has been a recurring problem for CS chess that there appears to be little interest outside London. Mr. Fleming reported that he still could not collect dues from Aviation and Ministry of Defence Chess Clubs. CSSC were to be informed. The last two notes show that CSSC appeared to be the overall governing body.

The Hastings tournament at Christmas 1966 had featured ex-world champion Mikhail Botwinnik, and it was announced by BH Wood that the Russian would tour the country giving simultaneous displays after Hastings finished. The author's father, Ivan Thurlow, worked for Customs and sought permission from the Board of HM Customs and Excise for the great man to perform a simultaneous display at the Customs venue. The reply was not long in coming, 'Under no circumstances may a Russian national be permitted on official premises'. How the Board thought he was a threat is a mystery.

CHAPTER 5

1967 – 1983 Modernization

The 40th AGM of CSCA was held on Wednesday 24th May 1967 and the rules were amended to include extra officers on the Committee, these being the grader, tournament controllers and up to five committee members. Also, EC Baker was elected as a vice-president. By now, vice-presidents were generally elected on the basis of service to CS chess. British Museum proposed that the Rule which said that no club may have more than one team in a division be deleted. Mr Gould pointed out that if this proposal were accepted other changes would be necessary which were not up for discussion. The proposal was withdrawn, and it was agreed a Sub-Committee be set up to investigate the Rule and make proposals if considered necessary. The Sub-Committee put forward many proposals at the Autumn General Meeting later in the year. The motions were lost 18-20. The accounts showed a balance of £528/14/10½. The sum of £5/9/5 (roughly £5-47) had been spent on 'Hospitality at Cup Finals'. Given the prices at the time, this may look a little high, but they were probably catering for about 60 people. The EC met on 9th August 1967 and the chairman decided that, as the Autumn General Meeting was of a social nature, he would limit discussions on the Sub-Committee's proposals to 20 minutes after which the discussions would be adjourned until the following AGM. The

Autumn General Meeting was primarily to award prizes, hand out results sheets, handbooks, adjudication forms etc., then there would be some sort of event, for example, a lightning tournament. The EC met on 11th October and Mr Fleming again reported difficulties in getting the national individual tournament started. It was agreed that the tournament would be abandoned until such time as the EC were approached by the CSSC. There was to be a long wait. According to the Minutes, 'Mr Foley suggested that in future all motions for an AGM should be fully discussed and considered by the EC before being presented to an AGM.' It is not clear if this is the entirely sensible suggestion that the EC should have some sort of view to present to the AGM, or the more sinister one that the EC could block any motion it disliked. One chairman of the CSCA subsequently stated that he could just remove an item from the agenda if he felt like it.

The next EC meeting was on 1st May 1968, where the EC agreed that a lightning tournament would be held annually. The President, Sir Leonard Barford, wished to present a trophy to the CSCA. Hence the Barford trophy was presented to the winners of the Team Lightning event. Two new adjudicators were appointed, GPS Coy (who only stopped doing them a few years ago) and RJ Stockwell. RJ Broadbent retired as an adjudicator because as he was also an adjudicator for other bodies, he was doing over 100 adjudications per year which he thought (reasonably) was too many. London University refused to have adjudications done by JM Aitken. A disputed position was referred to the BCF who overruled Aitken, and charged 30 shillings (£1-50) for doing so. Honoraria for adjudicators had risen from a packet of cigarettes to one guinea (£1-05). Dr Calvert, the retiring Chairman, was to be nominated as a vice-president in recognition of his services. Mr Foley (GLC) proposed that all games should be played to a finish, adjourning if necessary. Interestingly, division 5 had seen a three-way tie for first place, so the EC view in 1964 that such an event would not happen again was very quickly proved wrong.

On 21st September 1968, the UNATS secretary wrote to CSCA saying, 'The Committee of this club have recently been considering number 3 (covering eligibility - ed) of the enclosed rules. They are concerned about the possibility that someone who had been a member for many years might be transferred to another department of the Civil Service which had its own organized chess club or that such a club might be started in his original department. In either of these events such a member would cease (possibly much against his will) to be a full member of UNATS.' He then asked informally if the CSCA in General Meeting or the Executive Committee would have to decide if UNATS applied to change Rule 3. CSCA did not seem to know either, but there was a suggestion within the EC that Rule 3 could be amended to, 'Membership shall be limited to past and serving Civil and Municipal Servants whose department has (or had, at the date of the member's application for membership) no organized chess club affiliated to the CSCA.' Ultimately, the EC decided that members of UNATS must leave the club if their department set up a club of its own. For example Aviation members had to now play for the Board of Trade. This issue was to surface again some years later.

The EC had another knotty problem. Sir Harold Emmerson resigned as a vice-president as it was many years since he retired from the Civil Service. Though the secretary pointed out this was a life appointment, Sir Harold insisted the EC must accept his resignation. The EC decided that neither it nor the AGM had the power to do so, but would remove his name from the *Handbook*. This seems an eminently practical solution. A copy of the 1967/68 Civil Service grading list appeared in the Minute book. The Grader, Ralph Hulme, thanked Mr Felce (best known for his Surrey activities), for his sterling work in analysing around 3,000 match results to enable the list to be produced. The minutes also reveal that CS representative matches were usually contested over 25 boards and friendly matches were still over as many as 80 boards. There were about 40 clubs in the league, with a total of almost 2000 affiliated players, about ten times the number of players 40 years later. The figure 2000 looks wrong as a couple of years later, the league had 830 players and such a huge drop would presumably have attracted comment.

The 41st AGM was held on Wednesday 29th May 1968 and it was agreed to award the Barford trophy annually. It was announced that Sir Archibald Carter, Sir Harold Wiles and WO Woodfield had died. The meeting noted that CHO'D Alexander, EC Baker, Sir Harold Emmerson and AG Pockett were still alive. This must have been reassuring for the individuals concerned but it seems a strange discussion. It was explained that the position of vice-president was permanent and that formal re-election of these Officers was not necessary. Joe Xuereb (Cable and Wireless) was retiring as secretary as he found the position very strenuous after a year or two. Doubtless it was, so one must admire even more those individuals who held the post for decades. EW Godly (Government Chemists) was suggested as being keen to be deputy match captain. The Ministry of Technology, formerly Aviation, wished to amalgamate with Government Chemists with the club known as Government Chemists (Ministry of Technology). By this time, the Laboratory of the Government Chemist was part of the Ministry of Technology. Labour changed its name to 'Employment and Productivity'. The EC met on 31st July and Sir Leonard Barford expressed a wish to pay £40-£50 for his trophy which would consist of a silver Queen mounted on a plinth. The original James Curtis trophy was a set and board initially intended for presentation to PR Vivian (Stationery Office) and subsequently lost. It was replaced later. Joe Watson (Inland Revenue) was appointed as a divisional recorder for divisions 7 and 8, and Peter Bond received from Joe Xuereb six volumes of minutes of the CSCA excluding those from 1957-1964. EC Baker was thought to have started compiling a history of the Association. The secretary had no notes of this but the early Minute Books incorporated much literature on the founding of the Association. Sadly, the early Minutes Books were lost some years later, or to be more accurate, someone threw them in the bin, without telling anybody that he had done so. This action caused considerable difficulties in the preparation of this book. The CSSC stated that the EC must gain their permission before they hold representative matches if CSCA were to continue to receive financial support. The limit would be 3 matches per year. This restriction still applied 40 years later, although there were sporadic arguments about the decision. POCOMPS had become National Data Processing Service. Only one divisional recorder had sent in results to the grader meaning that around 100 members normally in the grading list would not have their league games included this year. This would affect one member in the National Grading List. It was the custom up until fairly recently to have a National Grading List for higher graded players only, whereas the various 'Unions' would provide lists for players within their borders. So a player living in Surrey could be graded 170 and play in an event in Lancashire (or vice versa), where the organizers would have no idea how strong the player was.

The British Championship saw several CS or future CS players in the top ten, including AH Perkins (Post Office), Craig Pritchett (DHSS), MJ Basman (Treasury) and AH Williams (IR). The following year, the Welsh Howard Williams was Board 1 of the England Junior Team in the European Championships. There was a proposal at a GLC Committee Meeting that Miss GLC, Patricia Collyer, be invited to present prizes at the AGM. This proposal 'caused some lively discussion', (this is where one would really like more detailed minutes!), before being carried 5 – 1, with 4 abstentions. Miss Collyer duly presented the prizes. The order of the agenda was changed so she did not have to sit through a 'boring meeting, but she stayed to the end and joined some members afterwards at a well-known establishment close to County Hall for (liquid) refreshments.'

The 4th International Post Office Championship took place in Canterbury from August 30th to September 3rd, 1968. Harry Golombek was Controller and wrote an entertaining report in BCM about it. Six teams participated and reigning champions Switzerland were firm favourites. They lived up to this with three straight 4-0 victories, ahead of Germany and Netherlands on two wins and a loss. Britain then beat Switzerland 3-1 to throw the competition wide open. In the last round Germany also beat Switzerland 3-1 to finish on 8 points, ahead of Netherlands on tie-break, Switzerland were two points further back, level with Britain but with the better tie-break. France and Belgium scored 2 and 0 respectively. Of course, 4-board matches tend to be volatile, one little mistake can turn an entire match. In board order, the British team scored, M Firth +2=3-0, JS Emsley +1=0-2, RJ Stockwell +2=1-1, PC Griffiths +1=2-0, NA Perkins +1=2-0, GFO Barnard +1=0-1. Golombek finished his report with the somewhat poetic, 'I cannot help adding how touched I was at the warmth of the ovation I myself received as controller. Clearly, my efforts had been welcomed by the players in the spirit in which I made them and this made me even more happy at having been part of an historic event at an historic milieu.'

At an EC meeting on 14th October, EC Baker denied making a history of the Association. The Recreation Centre (Monck Street) secretary refused to make Rooms 19 and 20 available for a match because it was alleged the CSCA had not been replacing the furniture to its normal Committee room position. The meeting 'considered the Association to have been in existence in about 1884, whereas the Minute books only began around 1918', although no evidence to support either statement appears in the Minutes. Mr Fleming reported that the CSSC was exerting pressure for the representative matches to be representative of all localities and all grades. The EC agreed that team selection was entirely up to the match captain. It has to be added that the CSSC attitude was wholly unrealistic. Anyone who has been a match captain for any sport will know that it is difficult enough finding a team of any kind, without further obstacles being imposed. And how do you tell an eager volunteer he is not allowed to play as it is necessary to persuade some unwilling individual from another part of the country to take part? You just lose your willing volunteer and the unwilling player is still unwilling!

With the setting–up of the Post Office as a non-Civil Service State Corporation, the future of the GPO, Fortels, Cable & Wireless, Savings Bank Division, etc., Clubs was causing natural concern and foreboding. Ron Fleming thought a few basic facts might help clarify the situation.

'The Civil Service Sports Council Limited is the parent Body of all Civil Service recreational activity. The Sports Council gives grants for the representative matches, and a grant of £10 per annum towards the cost of running the Bonar Law trophy, the Post Annual cup, the Barstow trophy and the Star trophy. These four trophies were all originally presented to the CSSC for competition in CS chess. They cannot therefore be awarded to a non-civil servant.

Postmen cannot play in events run by the CSSC.'

Mr Fleming was using the term 'Postmen' to mean any employee of the Post Office. CSSC changed its rules since then to include Post Office employees, and more recently to include military personnel, teachers and any friends or relatives of an existing member. The EC met on 14th January 1969. Dr RHS Phillips requested clarification on the use of franked envelopes. Mr Fleming considered it was proper to use the IDS (Inter Dispatch Service) rather than franked envelopes. Similarly, telephone calls should be paid for by the individual. 'This problem arose from a complaint made by the GPO to the CSSC.' But how did they know? Did a GPO employee illegally open envelopes to see what was in them, or did a recipient complain to GPO about what he had received? Some years later, the league instructed team captains not to use IDS as it became increasingly unreliable. Auditing expenses were discussed, and it was stated that Mr Dadd had been auditor since 1926, although other sources suggest it was 1922. Mrs Rogers (nee Craker) and Miss D Colmer had frequently won the Ladies Challenge cup. The EC was informed that the GPO would shortly become a Corporation, and the members of the 8 cubs who had GPO membership would not be eligible for CSSC representative matches. The Ministry of Health had now combined with the Ministry of Social Security. The Office of the Paymaster General moved to Crawley (Sussex) in 1968, although the Paymaster General himself stayed in London. There was chess activity, but eventually the office was absorbed by Royal Bank of Scotland some 40 years later. The Office was very active in mid-Sussex and Sussex leagues, with some high-graded players.

The EC met on 31st March 1969 and Mr Fleming reported that the Ladies championship trophy had been traced to Mrs Rogers whose father had originated the award. The EC considered putting a motion to the AGM which would split ties for the purposes of final positions by the number of game points scored. However, there was insufficient support in the EC. This was a matter that came up for discussion every so often and the tie-break system changed from time to time. The EC noted it only had 4 vice-presidents. Messrs. Milner-Barry, Broadbent and Richards were considered for addition to the ranks. Some of the EC thought they may be suitable but the majority of EC members thought a vice-presidency was awarded more in recognition of long service to the Association on a person's retirement than as a token of his chess playing ability. Of course, the named individuals had made significant contributions to CS chess. The CSSC had asked the CSCA to make a case for having a larger grant. At the 42nd AGM, held 20th May 1969, it was reported that 33 clubs had fielded 69 teams in the league. No fewer than 830 players had participated. There was some discussion about the three-way play-off that was needed to decide division 5. Presumably this was the catalyst for discussions on tie-break systems at the recent EC meeting. The senior recorder had nothing to say on the matter, which is slightly surprising, (after all he was running the competitions!) and Ron Fleming was prominent in the discussion. There has been speculation that higher rank in the Civil Service might take precedence at these meetings. RHS Phillips presented his report as match captain and added that he deplored the increase in the number of players who depended on adjudication. The secretary protested, pointing out that was nothing to do with association matches! Discussions on the merits or otherwise of adjudications continue to this day. An ivory chess set had previously been bequeathed by Harry Poor to the CS Sports Council, who passed it on to the CSCA. According to Ron Fleming, 'It was delegated to a nationwide contest for female players and was won by a girl from Manchester. She took it to Manchester with her and I cannot recall it being played for since or ever returned by her!' The *Bulletin* for September 1969 reported, 'The CSSC, in recognition of the sterling efforts of Miss Lesley Turpin and Miss Joan Burrell at the Chiswick Opening on May 28th 1969, has approved the award of the Harry Poor Memorial trophy – an ivory chess set insured for £100 – as a prize for the annual Ladies' individual championship.' It was not quite clear who held the trophy, and it was valued at nearly £600 in the early 70s, so the insurance value quoted here seems a little strange. What is even stranger is that the EC made so little effort to track down the trophy. Nobody seems to have reported seeing it since the comment in the *Bulletin*.

The treasurer's report was read by Ron Fleming who reported it was the first time there had been proper accounts at the Annual General Meeting for four years! This observation seemed to pass without comment. It was reported that James Curtis, a former member of the Association, had bequeathed a chess set on his death. This had been presented to the winner of Group 3 of the individual tournament one year and never seen again. The EC met again on 26th August 1969. The Ordnance Survey office in Southampton had given the CSCA free permission to publish a map of our 'home ground' in the *Handbook*.

Many organisations would just publish without concerning themselves with the legalities. A number of advertisements had been received, and those for such things as cheap charter planes and Christmas beer had been disposed of because they were regarded as 'unlikely Association matters'. But the Association did have members who might be interested in either offer. The next EC meeting was on 20th November 1969, where Ron Fleming reported 6 entries for the Ladies tournament. The EC agreed to pay the expenses of Miss Sharon Walls (later Sharon Furlong) to travel to London to play the other 5 entries. The CSSC had noticed the Association had two shields which were not being competed for and that the Association should therefore do something about it. The CSSC had asked the Association to consider making a donation to one of the CSSC officers, a Miss Bentley, who was retiring after 44 years. The Association declined in view of its precarious financial situation, partly caused by CSSC being unwilling to increase its grant. The EC agreed to sell ties with a chess motif for £1 each. This would produce additional income as each tie cost only 13/8 (about 68p) to produce.

UNATS were having venue problems, but a letter from Ministry of Agriculture, Fisheries and Food (MAFF) brought good news. It apparently was not plain sailing, as B Dennis wrote:-

'I am now pleased to be able to be able to say that the Ministry has agreed to provide accommodation for the club in Room 460, Great Westminster House. (Horseferry Road, SW1 – ed.) Tables can be provided and the club's cupboard can be kept in the room. There is a nearby point for tea making.

Access to the building has proved a difficulty. The Ministry is naturally sensitive about this following the recent raid on the cashier's office.'

Already, members and visitors were required to show proof of identification and a team list had to be submitted to Security in advance of the match.

GLC complained to CSCA that they had been away to SBD for three consecutive seasons, but were told that it was 'the luck of the draw'. Not surprisingly, GLC were somewhat unhappy at this response. They complained later that Health's Board 1 was graded only 138, much lower than his team-mates. Someone pointed out that the player in question was the chairman of the club. Some board orders seemed to bear little relationship to the strength of the players at this time and for the next decade or so. There was very much an attitude that players who were higher in the Civil Service, or were long-standing committee members, should play above younger players, whatever the difference in ability. Several clubs did exactly the same as Health. Gradings are not everything, but should be of some use as a guide to playing strength.

The EC meeting on 9th April 1970 agreed to Peter Bond's proposal to set up a correspondence tournament or league. There was also heated discussion over the time taken for adjudications.

The English team for the 7th Correspondence Chess Olympiad in 1970 reached the final, with an impressive team, comprising A Hollis (son of ex-MI5 head, Roger), CHO'D Alexander (who had obviously forgotten his 1947 statement, 'I never play correspondence chess (a) because I hate it (b) because I am very bad at it.' He did later say that, 'two things I enjoy about correspondence chess are that one can experiment with unfamiliar defences and that with the long time available for analysis one can get to the bottom of complex positions and perhaps contribute in a small way to theory.'), J Littlewood,

KB Richardson, C Hunter and K Messere. Great Britain went on to win the bronze medals for finishing 3rd out of 10 in the Final (1972-1976). That team consisted of Hollis 6, Alexander/Messere 5, Richardson 7½, Hunter 4½, Littlewood 4, Cafferty 2½. Alexander died in early 1974, so Ken Messere replaced him. Allowing substitutes mid-game is normal in team postal chess events.

The 43rd Annual General Meeting was held on 14th May 1970. The ivory set donated by Harry Poor was to be used as the prize for the Ladies tournament in place of the prize retained by its custodian when the tournament had last been held many years previously. The treasurer reported dwindling finances and proposed an increase in capitation (CSCA membership) fee from 2/6 (12.5p) to 4/- (20p). The chairman and match captain thought that 5/- (25p) was more sensible. Geoff Ashelford (GLC) strongly objected to the suggestion of 5/- because GLC subscriptions would need to increase from 7/6 (37.5p) to 10/- (50p). Roland Smith said the GLC subscription was low by Revenue standards. Revenue members had been paying 15/- (75p) for the last 10 years. Eric Hammond (Government Chemists) thought decimalisation suited 4/- rather than 5/-. Mr P. Neal (Credex) was not in favour of steep increases. The sum of 4/- was approved by the AGM. The treasurer announced that the Officers not only rendered their services free of charge but also subsidized the Association by not claiming their expenses in full. This was rather generous of the officers concerned. The match captain did not think the match results mattered provided CSCA kept up its good name. A correspondence match against the RAF was won 15½-14½. Geoff Ashelford complained about some adjudications being slow. He also asked why Mr Bernfield (also GLC) was no longer an adjudicator. The chairman replied that Mr Bernfield had been ill and that there were sufficient adjudicators anyway. EW Godly suggested that if adjudicators actually gave analysis to support their decisions, it should be passed on to the players. The AGM unanimously approved an EC motion 'that the name 'London Civil Service & Municipal Chess League' be changed to 'London Civil Service, Post Office and Municipal Chess League'. The chairman explained this was a natural result of the Post Office becoming a Corporation.

The league had hitherto prohibited two teams from the same club from being in the same division, but this changed now. In the past, a failing high team in a club could come last without being relegated or a successful lower team could win the division by a mile and then play in it again, as that club had a team in the higher division. This was somewhat unfair to the opposition. The league had an existing rule that each team except the lowest in a club had to have a number of nominated players, who could not play for lower teams. If players made too many appearances for higher teams, they became barred from the lower team(s). GLC V and GLC VI were both placed in division 6 for the 1970/71 season. But CSCA did amend the rules, and told the clubs that, 'no member of the sixth team would be allowed to play for the fifth team, and of course, under existing rules the reverse procedure was already precluded.' GLC were told they would have to nominate players for both the fifth and sixth teams. Unfortunately, some confusion arose, and the GLC Minutes reveal that the secretary had not got the impression, 'the ruling given by CSCA in May 1970 would be extended to other non-nominated players of GLC and he considered it most reprehensible of Mr Bond, Secretary of CSCA, to raise this issue so late (in a letter dated 19/2/1971) in the season and to state that 'games of players who had so 'transgressed' would be declared void'. It is clear that the CSCA thought they had said the teams must be mutually exclusive, and GLC thought CSCA had said that GLC must use players for the fifth team and different players for the sixth team. In the normal scheme of things, you can use reserves or new members for any teams. So, an eager reserve could play for all the different teams, until becoming ineligible for lower ones due to too many appearances for higher teams. GLC had used such reserves for both fifth and sixth teams and were eventually penalized. The wording of the CSCA ruling looks ambiguous, and GLC's confusion is understandable. When a similar rule was brought in for cup competitions much later, the words 'mutually exclusive' were used to make it absolutely clear – or so one would think, but some clubs still used players for two teams.

Ron Fleming commented on this issue,

'Each year at the AGM we had the problem of arranging the number of divisions in the league and the number of players in a team in each division. This was inevitably the subject of some controversy for clubs in the lower divisions were reluctant to contest more boards in case it stretched their membership capacity too far. The basic requirement that no club should have more than one team in any one division was applied rigorously until it became an embarrassment! When IR II became too strong for division 2 we had to fiddle the rules so that both the first and second team could play in division 1 but on terms that they did not overlap when it came to reserves. Nominations were another source of difficulty. I have touched above on the inclusion by some clubs of 'deadwood players' in order to strengthen their second teams. We also had the problem of a London posting mid-season of some club's strong provincial player: if a highly graded player was posted from HMIT Cardiff to HMIT Willesden in January could he turn out at will for IR IV, IR III, IR II and IR I until such time as he had completed the specified number of appearances to lead to disqualification? I have dealt above with transfers from one Ministry to another and the problems it caused. I have also dealt with the transfer of Ministries from one department to another. We had the problem as with Surgeon Commander Holford of whether a member of H M Forces could turn out for the civilian department which ran his branch of the Armed Forces. We had a separate club called UNATS (i.e. unattached players) which was meant to cater for small departments which could not raise enough players to form a competitive team, and the question arose inevitably on whether these players could, if they chose, turn out for a department in which they had been historically. Dr Calvert was with the Science Museum and Fred Dadd was with the Home Office but both played for UNATS. AG Pockett was our chairman for some time but was with the Ministry of Transport. When Admiralty and the Air Ministry were incorporated into the Ministry of Defence we had strained allegiances. National Physical Laboratory was located in Teddington and so played all of its matches away.'

GLC Minutes report the death of a former Secretary, WP Willis, who had died aged 85, having played for GLC as early as 1912. This particular meeting seems to have been fairly heated, as there was even a complaint that losing too many friendly matches reflected badly on the club. This was the complete opposite of the CSCA attitude.

The EC met on 22nd April 1971. The DOE Chess Club comprising Housing & Local Government Chess Club, Ministry of Public Buildings and Works Chess Club, and the Ministry of Transport Chess Club had been advised by the 'powers that be' that they must only have one club between them. Subsequently, members represented one centre only, Marsham Street, Elizabeth House or St. Christopher House.

A proposed weekend tournament was cancelled due to lack of support. Insurers had paid for the replacement of the (second) James Curtis trophy box and men lost when the previous year's holder moved. The origin of the Post Annual cup had been determined by HM Whitfield (Post Office). The EC reported that 60 teams from 26 clubs entered the league. There were 766 players, down from 830 two years earlier. The fact that clubs were advised of adjudication results very late was in no way due to the adjudicators. It was reported that the *Bulletin* was not well managed as, 'The Editor had an attack of marriage!' An audit of equipment revealed 78 boards, 72 sets, 31 clocks and 'a host of odds and ends'. Certainly the equipment seemed to diminish over the following years, which is not surprising especially with clocks. The 44th Annual General Meeting was held on 26th May 1971. Mr Ashelford (GLC) objected to the item relating to adjudication results in the EC Report for 1970/71. The senior recorder expected clubs to contact him for results. Mr Ashelford disagreed, stating that he expected the vast resources of the Association to provide secretarial assistance. The chairman objected to Mr Ashelford's remarks. CSCA later adopted a system of only supplying results to clubs if they had supplied a stamped addressed envelope for the purpose. Mr H Buchan (Works) deplored adjudications caused by grading conscious players. Mr Ashelford disagreed as he was very concerned with the effect on players' gradings. Roland Smith (Inland Revenue) pointed out the effects of adjudications on match captains' batting orders were more important.

Craig Pritchett (later DHSS) and Howard Williams (later Inland Revenue) shared 3rd place at the British Championships.

The EC met on 20th March 1972. DOE Croydon were admitted to the league, with all matches to be played away from home. CSCA rules had changed over the years. At one stage, all matches had to be played within 12 miles of Charing Cross, and later this changed to six miles. There was a dispute between UNATS II and DOE Marsham Street II. UNATS had changed the room within the building. Three DOE players waited until 6.45pm (the default time) and then went home. UNATS claimed the three wins by default. DOE disagreed. The EC decided that if the change in room had been notified in the *Bulletin* then UNATS would receive three wins. If the change had not been notified, then the specific boards would be played at a later date, and if anyone disagreed they would be defaulted! This is another slightly puzzling decision. The EC Report for 1971/72 revealed that 28 clubs supplied 60 teams and a total of 768 players. So the number of teams and players remained stable, but there were two extra clubs. The 45th Annual General Meeting was held on 17th May 1972. Mr Foley (GLC) proposed that Mr CB Stronach, the outgoing chairman be made a vice-president. This was accepted unanimously. The affiliation of the Australian High Commission to the Association was accepted, they being within the Commonwealth and there being no UK restriction in the Rules. This seemed to imply that the CSCA represented the whole of Civil Service chess in the Commonwealth! Perhaps it meant that any civil servant, of any nationality, was eligible if (s)he worked in the UK. Mr Foley suggested that resumption of games should be permitted. Mr Stronach said such a system would be complicated. Adjudication fees were increased to 40p.

Inland Revenue won the London Business Houses League, ahead of King and King (who played in the Commercial League) and Midland Bank. Howard Williams was now board 1 for Cambridge University. GLC was clearly a thriving club with 117 members!

It was in the early 70s that DHSS played some matches

against patients at Broadmoor, the well-known high-security psychiatric hospital. Rumours circulated that the matches ceased as the home side included the 'Moors Murderer' Ian Brady and nobody wanted to shake hands with him. DHSS players dispute that and it seems that Brady had never been a patient in that institution. Apparently, the home side were identified by first name only and made encouraging starts to the games, before losing later as they appeared to be falling asleep. The visiting players assumed that medication was responsible, and this was confirmed by one of the Broadmoor staff. A few years later, DHSS again asked if Broadmoor wanted a match and received a terse reply declining the offer and said there was no shortage of teams wanting to play there! Another attempt was made 15 years later but to no avail.

The EC met on 24th August 1972 and EC considered introducing adjudication after move 42, but decided to put it to the next AGM. This possibility was finally implemented some 40 years later. The treasurer said he would enquire whether Mr Purdy wished to continue as auditor as he was now stationed at Bath, and it was suggested in an entry in the Minutes that 'Mr Purdy was held responsible for unnamed problems.' The treasurer agreed that accounts should be made up to 30th April each year.

The EC met on 20th March 1973, one item being,

Proposals (a) to play matches to a finish, (b) to play matches 42 moves in 105 minutes, (c) to play matches 42 moves in 90 minutes, were discussed and rejected as each had difficulties.' It is not clear who proposed the changes. Interestingly, DHSS proposed a national individual tournament for departmental champions to enter. The Committee was broadly in favour, but decided to wait for CSSC to set up regions, so as to align the event on those.

RC Pentecost had volunteered to be an auditor. It was noted that the Barstow and Bonar Law Trophies were property for national competitions. A rather strange decision was that in division 5, if one team had 8 players and the other 6, then it should count as a 6-board match. BML rearranged another match for semi-final day and was therefore defaulted in the Post Annual cup.

Teams raised objections to playing cup finals in Room 20 at Monck Street in view of the noise and the dim lighting. The AGM preferred Room 20 to the Cinema. The EC approved of affiliation to the British Postal Chess Federation (BPCF). Inland Revenue and GLC finished equal first in division 1, and the senior recorder decided after a lengthy delay that the title should be shared, rather than using existing procedures to split ties. At a GLC meeting, some Committee members pointed out that Inland Revenue had a superior game point score, so they could easily have been declared winners. WL Bush (GLC) said he would raise it at the next CSCA Committee meeting. At this stage, the meeting discovered that John Foley had already appealed against the decision. The next meeting voted to delete this reference to an appeal. GLC still regularly had simultaneous displays with prizes for the most successful players, with the rather nice addition of 'mystery' prizes, which were donated by club members and awarded for such esoteric achievements as being the first to have their queen captured, or being the first to get a pawn in the other half of the board. The criteria were decided before the event, but only announced afterwards. There was again some discussion on tie-breaks and it was proposed that game points should be used to split ties for the league championship. This was defeated 4-5. There was a counter proposal that all ties for the championship, or promotion or relegation should have a play-off match. If this were drawn, bottom board elimination would apply. That was carried 9-1 and put forward to CSCA, where it became the rule for the 1974-75 season. It is surprising that such an old-fashioned idea was brought in at that time. The special case for having two teams in a division was relaxed and it now became standard practice to allow that eventuality, and there was now no need for these teams to be mutually exclusive.

Civil Service CA won the 1972/73 Bronowski trophy, with the aid of a default, which cannot have pleased LCCL. Admittedly, any win would have gained CS or United Banks the title, and only a draw would have given LCCL victory. This was the first year that leagues had competed for the trophy, hitherto the champion clubs of the leagues contested it.

		CSCA	LCCL	Insu	UniB	G	Pts
1	Civil Service	X	8	12	20	40	2
2	London Commercial CL	12	X	10½	7	29½	2
3	Insurance	8	9½	X	10½	28	1
4	United Banks	0def	13	9½	X	22½	1

London Commercial Chess League   **Civil Service Chess Association**

At Shell Centre 11th April 1973

1.	JI Century	1-0	MJ Basman
2.	T Wickens	1-0	JS Emsley
3.	RF Harman	1-0	PA Bond
4.	JF Wheeler	0-1	J Kirk O'Grady
5.	FE Tinworth	½-½	JT Pascoe
6.	FL Start	0-1	M Bissell
7.	AJ Roycroft	1-0	R Smith
8.	M Hall	0-1	RC Lawrance

9. RG Bellinger	½-½	NA Perkins
10. SM Kalinsky	½-½	WEC Richards
11. GH Govas	½-½	PB Cook
12. M Szyszkin	½-½	A Heaton
13. JA McDonnell	1-0	AP Primett
14. D Smith	1-0	P Tillson
15. RL Turnham	½-½	WF Hartman
16. G Spittle	1-0	M Kiernan
17. LC Kuiken	½-½	RK Lowen
18. MJ Rose	1-0	RF Shephard
19. P Edwards	½-½	TB West
20. PM Shaw	0-1	EC Baker
	12-8	

Presumably, Peter Bond played as a reserve, as board 3 would not be his natural home in the team.

Hexagonal Chess made an appearance, being recommended by AJ Roycroft and 'Mr Day of the Civil Service'. The author has played this variant and it is somewhat entertaining and frequently confusing. The league had seven divisions in 1974. The EC considered that supporting analysis should be submitted by both captains with each position for adjudication, and that such a proposal would be put to the AGM. There was a dispute in the Patent Office v Government Chemists match where apparently a Government Chemists player wrongly informed his opponent of the rate of play and his opponent thus lost on time. The EC found in favour of Government Chemists as it was the responsibility of the Patent Office player to know the Rules.

GLC had another exciting committee meeting, where John Foley complained bitterly about GLC fielding a weak team in a friendly match against a junior team and losing 5-14.

According to Mr Foley, this was 'very bad for the club's image'. Geoff Ashelford (who captained the team) explained that the team was selected to try to produce a good match against new opposition, but doubtless the club could put a better team out the next time. However, in view of Mr Foley's remarks, he would not again raise a team for such a friendly match and certainly would not captain it. Many people would regard a loss in a friendly match as relatively unimportant, but Mr Foley was clearly not of the number as then raised exactly the same issue at the next two committee meetings. Committee members were probably pleased that he missed the next meeting, so was unable to bring the matter up yet again as a 'matter arising'. On a more positive note, GLC ran a highly successful weekend congress, sponsored by the Lambeth Arts and Recreation Association (LARA). 441 players entered the first tournament, a number that tournament organizers could only dream about these days.

The EC met on 10th September. Patent Office had complained that Government Chemists II had fielded ineligible players in the Post Annual cup final. The claim was dismissed by the EC. Patent Office played two divisions higher in the league, so one can understand their disappointment. What was interesting was that a senior member of the EC demanded the complaint be thrown out without discussion, leaving other EC members to wonder if his club had used ineligible players. It did help that Government Chemists had received permission from CSCA to use the players in 1960, and as the GC chairman pointed out, 'some of them have been playing for us for five years or so. In such cases, I must say this objection comes rather late in the day'. Metropolitan Police complained about the lightning tournament. It was agreed that the Recreation Centre was not an ideal place for such events. Metropolitan Police also complained about how Peter Bond ran the event. The EC backed Peter and told the Metropolitan Police that if they thought they could do it better they should try! The accounts had not been audited because Mr Dadd had been ill for a long time. Mr Fleming proposed that Mr Dadd be made a vice-president as he had been an auditor for 50 years. The EC inexplicably decided to delay the decision. The 47th AGM was held on 15th May. It was decided to no longer print names of club members to reduce printing costs of the *Handbook*. The *Handbook* also revealed a number of clubs from outside London as 'other affiliated clubs'. These included 'Belfast Taxes', 'Business Statistics Office' (based in Cwmbran) and 'Glasgow Telephones Recreational Chess Club Section'. The last name makes you wonder if there were a 'Glasgow Telephones Deadly Serious Chess Club Section', but presumably they were making the reasonable point that the game is supposed to be enjoyable.

The 1973/74 Bronowski trophy was closely contested.

		LCCL	CSCA	UB	Ins	G	Pts
1	London Commercial CL	X	10	10	10½	30½	2
2	Civil Service	10	X	9	11	30	1½
3	United Banks	10	11	X	8½	29½	1½
4	Insurance	9½	9	11½	X	30	1

With the exception of the Insurance win over United Banks, every match result could have been changed by just one game going a different way. Indeed, if Insurance had drawn 10-10 with LCCL, they would have been first instead of last.

10th April 1974, at Monck Street

Civil Service Chess Association		London Commercial Chess League
1. JK O'Grady	1-0	Default
2. GD Lee	1-0	JI Century
3. D Vaughan	0-1	JF Wheeler
4. R Myers	1-0	AJ Roycroft
5. M Bissell	½-½	R Harman
6. WEC Richards	0-1	P Hutchinson
7. D Groffman	½-½	JV Skilleter
8. P Rosman	½-½	M Szyszkin
9. PB Cook	½-½	JM Soesan
10. JS Emsley	1-0	GH Govas
11. AP Primett	0-1	SM Kalinsky
12. AC Ashby	½-½	J Hobbs
13. RR Greenfield	0-1	MC Harris
14. JT Pascoe	0-1	RL Turnham
15. RC Lawrance	1-0	G Spittle
16. J Horrocks	1-0	SH Band
17. P Tillson	½-½	JA Yeo
18. JM Allain	0-1	MJ Rose
19. RJ Shephard	1-0	PM Shaw
20. RJ Pomeroy	0-1	R Blake
	10-10	

RL Turnham and JM Allain played for Metropolitan Police, who played in both leagues, so they could represent either side. MJ Rose and PM Shaw could also have played for either side.

The February 1975 *Bulletin* reported an amusing episode, 'One of our clubs appointed an ex-regular soldier as its equipment officer. Mindful of the precepts inculcated by numerous Quartermasters, he promptly acquired a security cabinet (which happened to be in a small room on the Ministry's main conference floor) and firmly locked away all the sets, boards and clocks he could find. Then someone bumped into the cabinet. Later that day a security man on a routine inspection found himself faced with a safe loudly ticking!

When the ministers, permanent secretary and other chief officers were eventually allowed back into their conference rooms...'

We can now reveal that the club was DHSS. A leading member of the club was summoned by the permanent secretary (Sir Patrick Nairne), who angrily ordered the removal of the cabinet. The departmental minister was Barbara Castle. The security staff (perhaps unwisely – or perhaps they were skilled enough to know that modern bombs did not tick) broke into the cabinet to discover that the ticking was caused by a large collection of chess clocks.

The EC met on 22nd April. There was a dispute that DOE Croydon had not played their players in grading order in a match against Inland Revenue. It was agreed that the EC could not legislate on this matter as board order was something of a gentlemen's agreement. This further hammers home the point that some members of the EC were quite unfit to hold their posts. Government Chemists complained about the refusal of the senior recorder and the EC to change the date of the Bonar Law trophy final against UNATS. It was stated that Government Chemists knew the date of the Final when they entered the competition and should not have sought a postponement because they could only field a weak team. The EC confirmed UNATS win by default. This was clearly the right decision, although it is unlikely that the date of the final was published before teams entered the competition. Ian Pheby suggested that appeals should be permitted against adjudication decisions. The EC disagreed. GLC proposed that adjudications should be replaced by adjournments (within one week) in the league. However, this was heavily defeated at the CSCA AGM. EW Godly (Government Chemists) raised the issue of the Bonar Law final, and the AGM instructed the EC to review the rules. The EC duly met on 13th August and decided the rules did not need amendment! Well, that is a 'review'. CS was celebrating winning the Bronowski trophy again. There were still seven divisions in the league, with 29 clubs and 67 teams.

The 2nd LARA congress had 555 entries! 211 played in the Open, (30 of them graded over 200, and a further 40 graded between 180 and 200), and there were so many entries in the Major that it was split into two sections.

The EC met on 30th April 1976 and now thought that adjudication appeals should be permitted. It was agreed that Mr Godly would take over as chairman, Mr Sefton as grader, and Mr Pheby as Ladies tournament controller. The EC also agreed that a default in a match between Cable & Wireless and British Museum due to a bomb incident must stand. The 49th AGM of the CSCA took place on 26th May, where a vote of thanks was proposed to the retiring Chairman, Tom West. It is rather surprising that he was not made a vice-president. There was one embarrassing rule change, where an entry fee had to be changed from 'four shillings' (20p) to '30p'. Most of the changes had been made at the time of decimalization (five years earlier), but that had slipped through the net. The EC met on 6th July and decided that appeals against adjudication would be permitted and that there would be no referral back to the adjudicator if his decision were disputed. Ron Fleming was not impressed, 'We were constantly having problems with our self-styled prima donnas. At first we never bothered about gradings and each match result was reported to the appropriate recorder so that he could keep his records. But then the mood changed and the concept of grading was forced on us and we appointed a Civil Service grader who produced annual lists. This, of course, introduced more problems for when a match was unfinished as time was called the match captain's ability to 'trade' unfinished games or, if the result of the match was already settled, to abandon all unfinished games as draws was prejudiced by prima donnas who were conscious of their grading points and wanted to be given a win on adjudication. Sometimes an adjudicator would complain about being asked to spend his time on a lost cause i.e. a ridiculous claim and so we introduced a tariff whereby an adjudication where the result of the match was already settled cost the club concerned more than where the result depended on this game. We had disgruntled prima donnas who challenged the adjudicators' competence. Our general attitude was that the adjudicator's decision was final and binding but this was weakened when we got prima donnas on the Executive Committee and their voices had to be heard. My own feeling was that the identity of the adjudicator concerned should not be divulged and that the complainant should merely be told 'the oracle has spoken!' However, the Executive Committee were too keen to lean over backwards to accommodate complainants and so appeals were accepted if backed up with logical analysis.

The basic trouble was, of course, too much success. When the CSCA was small it ran fairly smoothly with plenty of goodwill. As it expanded and the total membership exceeded 1000 the odd sore spot emerged. With more adjudications we needed more adjudicators and whereas Freddie (Norman) had been in the habit of giving the original panel a packet of 20 cigarettes a year as a token of appreciation, we had to give them a cash honorarium and work them harder as their burden increased. With the advent of more competitive cup matches we had to introduce strict regulations on when and where they were played; no longer did it suffice to tell a club 'you are drawn against X in the next round. Fix a date and tell us who won.' But we had to fix a week during which the match must be played and on the day in that week when the home team had its club night, and the senior recorder had to so arrange the league fixtures that that week was left free from commitments. We still had the problem of clubs which wanted to rearrange its fixture on the grounds that its best players were not available on the day specified. Alas, the foul fiend Gamesmanship reared its ugly head and courtesy and accommodation went out of the window!'

Mr Fleming's views on adjudication appeals reflect the changes in society. In past times, the proletariat would just have to accept the master's decision. Now, they were standing up for themselves, and players had a more professional attitude. It was clear that some adjudication decisions were wrong – nobody gets every decision right. So why shouldn't there be the possibility of an appeal? Sometimes it allowed the adjudicator to show the players that the original decision was right. NALGO quite justifiably complained about one position where the adjudicator commented that he had received the position submitted by one club, which identified the players. This put pressure on the adjudicator as it could appear he had been influenced by this information.

The 3rd LARA congress took place in October 1976, and just beat the previous year's total entry, with 556 players. 194 played in the Open, which was won by Mike Basman (Treasury) with 6/6, winning £300, ahead of David Rumens (DHSS) on 5½

(£150), and NR Benjamin, BJ Denman, AP Law (Post Office), HJ Plaskett and J Speelman finished on 5, winning £35 each. The Major (Under 160 grade) was again split into two and GLC's own Emil Semm-Skrzypecki won his half with 5½/6, taking home £88.35, much to his delight and the club's as well. The congress made a very healthy profit as well, as one would expect with such a huge entry. The prizes were somewhat higher than you would expect at most modern weekend events. The EC met on 13th December and rescinded their decision on adjudication appeals made at the previous meeting. Ian Pheby suggested that recorders should check team lists against nominations, but it was agreed that this would be 'impracticable and unnecessary'. Again, one wonders why some of the EC members thought that. Teams did (and do) make mistakes, and some would deliberately break the rules, so some sort of check needed to be carried out.

Rather proving the last point, the EC met on 18th April 1977. A serious dispute had arisen. One player had greeted a member of the opposing team and expressed surprise that he was there. The reason for his surprise became apparent when he noticed that the opposing player was playing under an assumed name. The EC agreed that all games played during the season by the individual (still graded over 170) playing under the assumed name of Peter Hart should be forfeited and that the secretary should convey this decision and the EC's displeasure to the club concerned (DOE Marsham Street). This caused great embarrassment to the then senior recorder as he was a member of that club, although there is no suggestion that he knew what his club was doing in this matter. The 50th CSCA AGM took place on 19th May 1977. It was announced that Mr Dadd had died in February of that year.

The Chairman (EW Godly of Government Chemists) made

the following statement:-

'I would be failing in my duty if I did not comment on some of the things which have happened this past season. We, your Committee, have had to consider some extraordinary cases of irregularity of behaviour, to use polite terminology, including the following:

a game abandoned because a player touched a piece and moved another;

players fielded well below their established position in the team-order;

the playing of two games at once by a single player;

blatant disregard of Rule 4;

impersonation or use of a false name in a series of league matches.

I would hope that most of you here this evening would deplore certain aspects of this behaviour as I do and my purpose in delivering this homily is not to preach to the converted but to follow the modern practice of delivering a prepared text for reproduction in the *Bulletin* so that the message reaches all our members.

It is this: Cheating is despicable and sharp practice is scarcely better. I leave it to you to work out where on this scale comes fiddling around the letter of a rule in order to override its spirit. There is a widely held view that in many sports and games that winning is all-important and the methods of achieving victory are merely incidental. There is also a seductive theory that behaviour normally regarded as outrageous when indulged in for oneself is somehow redeemed and justified when perpetrated on behalf of the team or the club. I would like to stamp on that notion. I speak for your committee and, I hope, the vast majority of our members, in condemning the contamination of Civil Service chess by such approaches to the game. Personally, I think it no coincidence that incidents of the sort I have described were unheard of in the days before the institution of the present grading system. As far as many of us in Civil Service chess are concerned, I feel justified in saying that the numerical grading is a very rough and untrustworthy index of ability. It is vain and self-deceiving to set too much store in it.

A word about the *Handbook*: pp 2-7 contains Rules for the conduct of the leagues, competitions and individual tournaments. They do not constitute a legal document and they cannot hope to cover every eventuality - any more than the MCC Laws for cricket, as any experienced player will testify. If clubs are deliberately going to search for areas of unfair and improper behaviour to try out on their opponents in order to take advantage of supposed inadequacy in our Rules or to initiate test cases, then I fear we shall be embarking on a period of battle between our drafting experts and these loophole-hounds which can only have the result of souring the atmosphere and generating more prolonged texts in the book - an exercise which will grow more and more expensive and one that must ultimately be paid for by you, the members.

Confirmation of matches: Many of our buildings now have strict security arrangements and it is no longer reasonable to expect to turn up on the night without prior ceremony and expect admittance. Recently the committee was asked to rule on the case of two opposing teams who spent the evening of their match in different parts of London, because, although the captains conversed on the 'phone, they did not touch on the subject of the venue. Following this and other cases of what might be called insouciance, I propose to lay down a protocol for your guidance, viz. that the duty of the home team is to provide a suitable venue, adequately lit and equipped, with the traditional, frugal refreshments.

It is the duty of the visiting captain or his agent to contact the home captain in good time - a few days - before the match and confirm the venue, time, security arrangements, etc. I do not propose to clutter the rule book with such stuff. It should not really need stating but recent events appear to warrant it.

I am sorry to have spent time on what must be a tiny minority. I hope most of us love the game and play it for its own sake but it is the minorities that often cause all the trouble. There is of course a great deal, as you have heard, to applaud in our activity, and to be grateful for. I hope you enjoy the coming season and that you all play on your best form throughout. May the best man and the best team win - though not, I hope, at all costs.'

Strong words – but just what was needed. Ted Godly made a major contribution to CS chess with these words. The league was paying the price for past weakness in various disputes. If there are no punishments for 'cheating and sharp practice', there will be more and more transgressions. It is arguable whether playing for two teams at once is a terrible offence, and certainly the chairman was unaware that a member of his own club had done this. Government Chemists had two home matches at once, but in separate rooms. One player (Chris Woollam – one of the league recorders!) went for a walk to the other room to see how the match was going and noticed the club was a player short. He stepped in as reserve and then had a healthy evening making his move and rushing back to his other game. Luckily he won one game quite quickly and then was able to concentrate on the other and won that as well. Hardly anyone knew what had happened. His opponents raised no complaint that he made a move and then disappeared. It is sure that the senior recorder did not notice. The 'touch-move' dispute was extraordinary. There were several witnesses and even the player's team-mates stated openly that they had seen him touch the piece and then move another. The same player was obsessed with his grading and always complained that it was not high enough, on one occasion sending his results to the grader to prove his case, only to omit a couple of losses. The grader noticed.

Ron Fleming commented on the problem as well, 'Before I leave the subject of the annual list of nominations I had better mention a 'problem arising'. Certain clubs had members who had retired or passed on and (the clubs) had the practice of listing those members in their annual list of nominations so as to push down into second or even third teams their regular players. At the end of the season the divisional recorders would make a list of the players who had actually turned out for each club and I, as treasurer, would collect retrospective capitation fees for the excess of this number over the number in the original nominations list. This meant the 'dead wood' players were now caught and so served their purpose of franking the actual practising players. We had to alter the Rules to provide that capitation fees should be paid for all players nominated for or actually turning out for a club. We found in practice that a club might call on its strong but retired members to augment a team in a cup semi-final or final so there was a general feeling of underlying fairness.

You will always find individuals or clubs who will try to manipulate the Rules for their own benefit even if a little unscrupulously, and the Executive Committee of the CSCA was constantly having to deal with such sharp practice.'

When Ian Pheby took over as senior recorder, he noticed that one club in particular had nominated several players of whom he had never heard. After he made a few discreet enquiries, he discovered that some of the players were dead and others did not exist.

Ron Fleming continued, 'I feel and felt that the Executive Committee was too keen to lean over backwards and accommodate the mavericks but it was conscious of its position of trust and was reluctant to be firm. My own professional experience was that firmness never came amiss and that people functioned better if they knew clearly where they stood. There is a legal maxim to the effect that it is better for the law to be certain than fair in all circumstances and the best 'rule' is that the arbiter's decision is final. But this is paddling in water that has long since flowed away.'

Rule changes were discussed. Trade proposed that adjournment be mandatory, and GLC proposed that adjournment should be allowed as an option. Both motions were defeated. There were successful proposals. It was agreed that clubs should be allowed to appeal against adjudication results. Some players were amazed that this was not already the case. The lack of the option to appeal against adjudication decisions might explain the proposals for adjournments. Admittedly, the system introduced was faulty. Analysis should be invited from both clubs, and the positions referred back to the original adjudicator, and then the appeal adjudicators could consider all the evidence. But the league system was that the appellant's analysis was simply sent to a separate adjudicator. The following season, one adjudicator had his completely correct decision overthrown, as the appeal adjudicator failed to find the original adjudicator's brilliant idea.

Whatever the merits of adjournments might be, there were practical difficulties in the league. Most clubs played in Government buildings and visitors were not allowed in without security clearance. For a league or cup match, the visiting captain would have to supply a team list a few days before the match, so that the home captain could present it to Security. When players arrived for the match, their names would be checked against the list and they were normally allowed in the building, and would be escorted to the playing venue. This generally ran fairly smoothly. However, for an adjournment session, Security would need a list (maybe of one name), as supplied by the two captains, and the home side would need to book a room, and supply someone with a key to the equipment cupboard. The home captain might not be entirely happy about spending an evening sitting around whilst two players continued their game.

The league was well aware that there were issues with adjudications too. There were a lot of them for one thing and some teams were submitting games for adjudication where a player was a piece down in the hope that the opposition would forget to make a claim. The team or teams making an incorrect claim paid a fee, but obviously this was not large enough to discourage hopeless claims. Accordingly, a new rule was passed saying that if an adjudicator declared a claim 'frivolous', the team that had made that claim would be charged double the usual fee. The CSCA Committee had also leapt into action, writing to one club to instruct them to play their teams in order of descending strength, and also that their first team had to be stronger than their second team. It was fairly common then for board orders to be fairly random. Some of the older members refused to use the BCF grades as a guide, as they were 'only based on ten games'. This might have applied to those who played solely in the league, who admittedly were in the majority, but it came as a bit of a shock to players who joined the Civil Service and discovered that their high grade, based on 70 or more games a year, was just ignored in favour of the grade of somebody who had played in the league for 20 years and was therefore 'more experienced', even if he had only played in the CS League. The author was faced with this attitude when he joined Government Chemists. Certainly, the comment, 'I have played more games in the last five years than you have in your entire career! I am much more experienced than you.' did not seem to go down well with one club official.

The league was still getting things wrong. The first division had two teams from Inland Revenue in it, and they were unaccountably scheduled to meet late in the season. Other clubs complained. Normally such teams would play the first match of the season, to stop any accusations that they had arranged a result that would suit both of them. If the teams play last in the season and one needs a draw to win the title and the other needs a draw to avoid relegation and it finishes 5-5, questions might be asked. So it is fairer to everybody, including the club concerned, to arrange such matches to take place before any other fixtures involving the club. However, the league had not introduced such a rule when it had finally allowed two teams from a club to play in the same division. The EC met on 4th July and appointed John Sargent as match captain.

The 1976/77 Bronowski trophy resulted in a triumph for CSCA, the 10½-9½ win over Banks being crucial.

		CSCA	LonB	LCCL	Insu	G	Pts
1	Civil Service	X	10½	13	13½	37	3
2	London Banks	9½	X	12½	12½	34½	2
3	London Commercial CL	7	7½	X	11	25½	1
4	Insurance	6½	7½	9	X	23	0

London Commercial Chess League   Civil Service Chess
                                       Association

At Shell Centre 27th April 1977

1. TW Pelling   ½-½   DO Vaughan
2. W Broome   0-1   A Brameld
3. JV Skilleter   1-0   Default
4. LC Kuiken   0-1   D Banks
5. JA Yeo   0-1   CD Gilliam
6. RA Faint   ½-½   WEC Richards
7. GT Carter   ½-½   R Smith
8. GH Govas   ½-½   L Moullin
9. CHJ Orton   ½-½   JT Pascoe
10. TJ Wheeler   ½-½   P Tillson
11. FE Tinworth   0-1   R Sefton
12. MC Harris   0-1   D Barasi
13. D Grange   0-1   B Glaze
14. WH Partridge   0-1   M Rose
15. H Gripaios   ½-½   M Breslin
16. LC Cardy   ½-½   R Bauld
17. SH Band   0-1   D Robinson
18. JM Allain   1-0   R Cleave
19. RJ Reddin   ½-½   A Bernfield
20. JP Law   ½-½   TB Packham
                       7-13

The 7th Union Internationale Sportive des Postes, Télégraphes et Télécommunications (UISPTT) Chess Championship was held in the Netherlands in May 1977. Hungary (15/16, 22 Game Points) won, ahead of Great Britain (12, 23 GP) and Austria (12, 19 GP), nine teams played. This was an excellent result by the GB team, which largely comprised the players representing them in the London CS League. AP Law scored 5/8, M Firth 3½/6, GD Lee 7/8(!), RJ Stockwell 4/6. KM Weinhold 1½/2 and WJ Bailey 2/2. GB lost 1½-2½ to Hungary in the final match, when a GB win would have given them the gold medals. The Civil Servants were a bit jealous of the event and wished that there could be an analogous CS championship.

The 4th LARA congress took place in October, again with over 550 players. The EC met on 21st November and agreed that no Ladies tournament would be held. It was announced that the secretary and the individual tournaments controller would be stepping down.

The EC met on 27th February 1978. The secretary withdrew his resignation. However, Mr Pomeroy said he intended to resign as correspondence tournament controller. Mr Stronach had complained about playing conditions at NALGO. A letter from NALGO in reply to the secretary's request for comments on Mr Stronach's letter was read. The EC considered the tone of the NALGO reply was offensive and rejected the allegations made that the EC had acted improperly. The EC considered that the playing conditions at Camden Town Hall were not satisfactory and that NALGO ought to ensure that matches were played in conditions which did not cause distraction and also ought to provide at least a hot drink. Mr Stronach was a former chairman of CSCA and therefore not without influence. Ron Fleming's view on the matter is illuminating, 'For one season, and one season only, we admitted a team from NALGO into league matches but we found that their ethos differed from ours so we excluded them as being ineligible!' That was not true, NALGO chose not to enter again as they were angered by an adjudication claim that had failed and they were told there was no right of appeal. Also, they had played more than one season. NALGO had staged two matches in the same room (in different leagues) at the same time. As they were short of players, three players had played in both matches. This raised Mr Stronach's ire. Strangely, this very issue had been raised at the 1977 AGM, and it was agreed that playing in two matches simultaneously was perfectly acceptable. Also, the lack of refreshments was regarded as unacceptable in the CS League, and continued to be viewed in that manner. Some people feel the CS League is behind the times, but in this aspect at least, the league's approach would appear to be correct. It has to be said though that the league was wrong to reject NALGO's complaint out of hand, and it seems that they were more interested in placating Mr Stronach than actually looking at the facts. There is no evidence that members of the EC had actually seen the playing conditions. The league continued to act in that manner for a number of years.

The 51st AGM agreed to a proposal from the match captain to hold a Selected Openings tournament. This was an interesting event, where players would be assigned opponents and then select a card from a box at random. This card would give the first few moves, which the players would play on the board and then start a rapid or blitz game from there. This was very entertaining and also beneficial for players who only played one or two systems. Someone who played 1.d4 might flounder a bit if presented with the position after an obscure 1.e4 line. Unfortunately, some of the lines did lead to rapid losses if one player knew the line and the other did not. The idea was used at the end of the 1993 Kasparov - Short match, when the former was unhappy at being given a line that was known to be bad. The 5th LARA congress had over 600 players and naturally made an impressive profit.

The EC met on 27th April 1979, when PS Morton was

appointed as correspondence tournament controller. The EC were in favour of the senior recorder's suggestion that CSCA would pay for refreshments on cup final night. It also considered that the post of vice-chairman which had been vacant for many years should be filled. The senior recorder pointed out a case of sharp practice where of the 10 nominated players for one team only 4 had played during the season. The EC sought explanations for why the others had not played. This probably followed from the chairman's comments two years before. The 52nd AGM was held on 22nd May. The author made four proposals. The chairman stated he could not accept these as motions since they had been received too late to be included in the agenda. The proposals were still discussed however! The EC met on 7th September 1979, where John Sargent reported the equipment cupboard had been broken open and 4 sets, boards and clocks seemed to be missing. 'He undertook to enquire from DOE whether they had borrowed this equipment.' Some would think that 'borrowed' would not be the word to use if the equipment were removed this way. Happily, the missing equipment was found later. John Sargent ran a CS weekend tournament at the CS Recreation Centre at Monck Street, London SW1. John Nunn won the Open on tie-break ahead of L Blackstock, M Chandler and MM Silva. The Major was won by P Tickner and G Hutchinson. John had the bright idea of running a table-tennis event alongside the chess, and this was won by the author. This idea was repeated the following year, where Ian Pheby won the table-tennis. This led John to the even more interesting idea of a 'Superstars' tournament, including chess, draughts, cribbage, snooker, darts, table-tennis etc. He was full of good ideas and ran various CS Lightning or Blitz events, including Selected Openings and Selected Endings, where entrants were given the starting position and went from there. In the endings event, players met the same opponent twice in the same ending, so that entrants played both sides of the ending. It was important to win the toss for such endings as bishop and knight against king, so you could choose to defend first, thereby not demonstrating to the opponent how to win it, or alternatively you got the opponent to teach you how to win. Perhaps the most interesting John Sargent event was the All-Play-All simultaneous. If there were five players, ten boards placed in a circle would be required. There were gaps, so that the players could run in from either side to play a move. The boards would be labelled with 'A', 'B', 'C', 'D' and 'E' (each signifying one player) so the players knew where they were playing and with which colour. So one board would be A v B, then C v D, then E v A, B v C etc. Cards were supplied on each board, labelled 'Draw?' and 'Draw Agreed', so that these could be left on the board, as it was rare for the opponent to be there at the same time. Normally the players had 30 minutes each, which seemed like a lot at first. The most important things to remember were where your boards were, as you did not want to search for them when short of time, and which code letter designated which opponent, in case you wanted to avoid a specific opening for an opponent. Getting ahead on the clock was a good tactic, and if a game were looking doomed, it was quite a good idea to concentrate on the other games. There were occasions that players had four promising positions but no time. It was definitely for the quick-moving, fit player! The idea was brought back as a side event for the 2013 British Championships and was well-received. The 6th LARA congress had a record 642 players.

Post Office chess was still going strong and Hungary again won the European Post Office event in 1980, ahead of Great Britain. Although the Post Office League had fallen by the wayside, there was a national teams event, and Post Office HQ finished first of 14 teams with 18½, ahead of London Telephone Region and South West Post Office on 14. The POHQ team was GD Lee, RJ Stockwell, KM Weinhold and NA Perkins, so their success was hardly surprising.

There were more problems in the league. The EC met on 22nd February 1980. Government Chemists complained that GLC II had defaulted on board 2, whilst a late arrival had played on a lower board. Government Chemists said that defaults should be as low as possible in the team. 'Mr Bush (GLC) explained the reasons for this and the CS committee decided no further action was necessary.' Mr Bush had been involved in CS chess for a long time, which probably influenced the EC. It was decided that Mr Fleming would be nominated as vice-chairman if Mr. Sefton were unable to take a more active part in CS chess.

GLC had another heated committee meeting. Mr Jewell was very unhappy that the usual GLC board 1 had played on board 10 in the GLC I v GLC II match, and had also played table-tennis at the same time (presumably not in the same room). Mr Jewell said, 'Such action could only be seen as a drop in the standards of the club and that it could also be interpreted in many ways by the CSCA'. According to the Minutes, it was agreed that CSCA might take action, but there was no need for the club to do anything, and there was 'little support for Mr Jewell's attitude'. The CSCA committee of the day took no action as usual, despite this blatant breach of the rules. Possibly, they felt that as it was an all GLC contest, it did not matter. The 53rd CSCA AGM on 28th May 1980 decided to abandon play-off matches to split ties, and use Game Points as tie-break. This was quite good timing as another three-way tie happened shortly afterwards.

The EC met on 15th February 1981, where the secretary announced he had no record of the address or telephone number of EC member A Beech. Consequently, the latter had received no invitations to EC meetings, and explained his poor attendance record. John Sargent reported that the Association only had 15 good clocks. The recent purchase of ten clocks had clearly been just in time. The 2nd Civil Service weekend tournament had made a profit of £85. Government Chemists complained that a GLC captain had given advice to one of his players. The Government Chemist player had a bad position and was playing quickly to encourage his opponent to play on and blunder, when the GLC captain approached, studied the position carefully, looked at the score sheet, and said, 'You don't have to make any more moves.' The complaint made its way to the CSCA Committee who decided it was a 'technical offence against BCF Laws of Chess'. However, they would not award the game to Government Chemists as it was 'not the opposing player's fault', but deliver a reprimand to the club. The GLC Committee felt that the rules were open to interpretation. In fairness to the captain concerned, he did admit what he had done. Mr Bush instructed the GLC Committee that captains must ensure they and their teams knew the rules. Government Chemists asked the CSCA Committee if they had any plans to enforce the Laws of Chess. The EC met again on 14th May 1981. Eight motions for the AGM were considered by the EC. The majority were not supported by the EC. The 54th AGM was held on 26th May 1981. There were clearly problems with the finances, probably due to the fact that clubs' accounts were not collected on time. A motion proposing fines for late payment of fees was adopted. The treasurer negotiated a loan of £800 from the CSSC, and also made a personal loan of £500. This came as a quite a shock to everyone, even the EC, as it had not been discussed at any of their meetings. The treasurer's actions seem surprising. There was a proposal to change the number of boards in various divisions but this was defeated. Metropolitan Police proposed that if a club had two teams in one division, that the teams be mutually exclusive, as previously, but lost the vote heavily. There were a number of proposals regarding adjudications. It was agreed that all positions should be sent to two adjudicators, and if they disagreed, the position was sent to a third adjudicator. Any appeals would be sent to an adjudicator outside the league. A proposal that any nominated player not playing during the season had to be an addition the following season was rejected. A proposal that the cup draw be made at the Autumn General Meeting did not even receive a seconder. The EC felt it was impractical to do the draw for the cup competitions at this stage, although the Surrey League had been doing exactly that for many years.

The 1980/81 Bronowski trophy was won by London Banks. CS were last by some way and it was clear that the team was not competitive. It is notable that nine of the LCCL team against CSCA could have played for CSCA instead.

		LonB	Insu	LCCL	CSCA	G	Pts
1	London Banks	X	16	10	15½	41½	2½
2	Insurance	4	X	12½	14	30½	2
3	London Commercial CL	10	7½	X	11	28½	1½
4	Civil Service	4½	6	9	X	19½	0

London Commercial Chess League   Civil Service Chess Association

At Vincent Street 21st April 1981

1.	RJ Pearce	0-1	CD Leach
2.	TW Pelling	1-0	R Smith
3.	CR Cope	0-1	KJ Thurlow

4.	DR Macdonald	½-½	A Stimson
5.	SJ Rodericks	1-0	WEC Richards
6.	N Skinner	½-½	MJ Rose
7.	NA Perkins	½-½	PB Cook
8.	KM Weinhold	½-½	AP Primett
9.	RS Guha	0-1	RC Lawrence
10.	GH Govas	½-½	BE Glaze
11.	W Broome	½-½	TB Packham
12.	DR Jarmain	0-1	D Gleave
13.	RS Walker	½-½	L Boxall
14.	M Duncan	1-0	Default
15.	RA Chapman	1-0	E Hazell
16.	D Smith	1-0	JM Xuereb
17.	AJ Mant	½-½	K Lovel
18.	Default	½-½	Default
19.	PA Statham	1-0	M Coles
20.	JC Valente	½-½	A Gallagher
		11-9	

At the time it appears that double defaults wrongly counted as a draw, rather than a double loss.

The EC met on 5th March 1982. CSD/Treasury were instructed to improve their arrangements for visiting players to reach the playing room after Government Chemists defaulted on board 1. The Security Guard gave the wrong directions! Government Chemists II were due to play GLC IV but owing to the rail strike due the following day were unable to field a team. GLC IV claimed the match by default. The EC instructed the match to be played. There was a great example of sportsmanship in the match between British Museum II and Government Chemists II. The home side's board 6 was missing, and their captain said he was willing to step in as reserve, but as he usually played higher in the team he would just concede the default if desired. The Government Chemists captain rather less sportingly accepted the default win and the match was drawn 4-4! PS Morton tendered his resignation as Correspondence Controller.

The EC met on 12th August 1982. By now the league had 10 boards in division 1 and 2, 8 in divisions 3 and 4, and 6 in the other divisions. The Senior Recorder (Ian Pheby) informed the EC that double defaults would now be properly scored as 0-0 rather than ½-½. League Rules would be enforced. The EC thought there should be no appeals against adjudication decisions in cup matches.

The CS weekend tournament was another strong event and there was a close finish. The 1981 congress had been financed entirely from money borrowed from the CSSC. More than 200 players attended. CM Cooley won on tie-break, ahead of G Flear, C Pritchett and SJ Rodericks on 4½/5. The event was most memorable for a dispute, which became known as 'The Rogers Affair'. DJ Rogers entered the Minor section (for players graded under 120) and swept all the opposition away. Tournament Controller John Sargent decided that Mr Rogers was too strong for the section and should not have any prize money. The player in question was somewhat unhappy (to put it mildly) at this and said that he had explained his grading history when he entered. He also pointed out that rumours were circulating at the Congress that he 'had been kicked out', and had 'falsified his name', etc., and it was now of importance that he should clear his name. The EC upheld John Sargent's decision, but it is clear that the Minutes of the meeting are incomplete. Mr Rogers had been graded over 200 in the recent past, but now had an estimated grade of 117 based on three games. He stated he was 117 on the entry form. Furthermore, he was a grader so it was felt that he should have been well-aware that the 117 was unreliable. Players at the weekend event were certainly complaining about him well before the end of the event. The fact that he was winning in an average of fewer than 20 moves a game suggested he was too good. It is quite possible that John Sargent was unaware that 'DJ Rogers' and 'John Rogers' were the same person, and reliable grading information was very difficult to acquire in a hurry in those days. The EC met on 20th April 1982, and the Minutes report:-

'A letter from the BCF regarding the Rogers issue was read out. A senior BCF official thought that the CSCA could send Rogers an open letter exonerating him from any intention to cheat, and send him £10 to cover his expenses. After some discussion it was decided that the chairman would write to Mr. Rogers informing him that the decision of the congress tournament controller in disqualifying him from receiving any prize was unanimously upheld by the EC and that no further correspondence on the matter would be entered into. A copy of this letter would be sent to BCF.' The EC communicated their final decision to Mr Rogers and BCF. If the EC thought that was the end of matters, they were wrong.

The following letter appeared in *Chess* magazine, Volume 47, Nos. 883-4, September 1982.

'HE ALLEGES ROUGH TREATMENT

I write this letter in the hope that it will prompt the Civil Service Chess Association into initiating much-needed improvements in their annual congress, if they hold one this autumn.

Last year their entry form implied that the congress was run under the auspices of the British Chess Federation, because games would be submitted for grading and the Open was expected to qualify for Leigh Grand Prix points. Unfortunately this was not true because it was not a BCF event; games were not eligible for grading (owing to non-payment of the 10p per game fee) and the event was certainly not part of the Leigh Grand Prix.

And worse yet, because if prize money was withheld from any player, on any pretext, he had no right of appeal to any chess authority, as I found out to my cost. Briefly, my experience was as follows. Civil Service lost trace of my entry form and covering letter, but they managed to bank my entry fee cheque which had been enclosed with the other documents. The letter explained my special circumstances, i.e. formerly a very strong player who had not played for several years and currently had a very low estimated grade based on no games. When I arrived for the first round, I had to explain this again verbally and pay another entry fee. The Congress Controller, in full possession of all the facts (twice) decided entirely on his own to put me in a low section.

At the end of the congress, when I had won the section, they disqualified me for playing too low down and withheld the prize money. The Controller, Mr Sargent, offered only to return my entry fee, but I have never even received that. Also, a rumour was allowed to circulate that I had 'cheated' in some undefined way.

I appealed to BCF, and it was then that I learned they have no jurisdiction over the Civil Service congress. However, Mr Buswell kindly forwarded my appeal to Stewart Reuben for unofficial arbitration. Mr Reuben's findings were, in essence, that 'the whole business has been slanderous', that Civil Service C. A. should return my entry fee and pay me £10 expenses as well, and they should send me an open letter exonerating me from any intention to cheat. Unfortunately, the Civil Service C. A. Chairman E. W. Godly has rejected all Mr Reuben's recommendations and they 'intend no further action in this matter and can enter into no further correspondence on it.'.

That, for me, is the end of the road – unless I decide to turn to the due processes of the legal system.

(Documentary evidence of all above statements has been enclosed with this letter to the editor.)

JOHN ROGERS

London W3, 9 August 1982

(This letter was certainly well documented. We have tried in vain to contact Civil Services C. A. officials but should be happy to give space to a reply from them – Editor.)'

BH Wood was being a bit mischievous with the italicized part as when the author enquired whom Mr Wood had attempted to contact and when, he was somewhat evasive, and then admitted he had not tried to contact anybody. John Sargent did write to *Chess* in November 1982 giving his side of the story. But the EC decided to ignore the article in the hope it would go away. Some committee members felt this was very unsatisfactory. A serious complaint had been made against John Sargent and the CSCA and basically it had been ignored. This is fairly typical of chess organizations, who too often think, 'If we ignore a problem, it will go away.' This tends not to work, as anyone hearing about the dispute will probably think that the organization does not have an answer to the complaint and the silence is an admission of guilt. But many committees (whether or not involved in chess) have a habit of sweeping things under the carpet.

Now that nearly 40 years have elapsed, it is clear that Mr Rogers should not have been allowed to play in the Under 120 section, but also he should never have considered entering any section but the Open. Even the Major at under 160 grading would be too low for someone recently graded over 200. All in all, the whole situation was a mess. The BCF secretary tried to make it worse by complaining that the CSCA *Bulletin* should not have reported the dispute, as 'Mr Rogers quotes Mr Reuben out of context, as will be clear to anyone who saw the entire text of Mr Reuben's letter to Mr Rogers.' As nobody at CSCA had seen the letter, it was suggested that BCF should aim their ire at Mr Rogers.

RHS (Hugh) Phillips, the BCF Adjudication Secretary, wrote to say the Rogers Affair highlighted problems with gradings. At the time, national grades only existed for elite players, after that the different 'Unions', like Northern, Southern, Western etc. issued their own lists, so someone with a Southern Union grade could be unknown in the North. He went on to say that a grade based on a few games was not much use, yet people seemed to take grades 'so terribly seriously that one feels they are taking over from chess…'

A £1200 loan from the CSSC helped finance the 1982 Congress. At the next meeting of the EC on 17th March 1983, 'Mr Sargent thought that CSCA should take no further action in respect of matters related to Mr Rogers. The EC agreed.'

Sir Richard Clarke attributed the decline in British chess to the formation of the British Chess Federation. The effect of this, he said, was to diminish the amount of initiative on the part of voluntary workers and outside bodies on the grounds that they believed, 'It is the Federation's task to do this, not ours'. This is certainly not the case now, as the staging of World Championships and strong tournaments, as well as the formation of the 4NCL, a very strong British league, have all been achieved due to people working outside the Federation. Another BCF official commented that gradings were taken far too seriously.

GLC had a somewhat perplexing problem to sort out as LARA had ceased to exist and had been replaced by the Lambeth Arts Council, which refused to let GLC affiliate. This left GLC Chess Club with nearly £2000 in profits from the congresses and no sponsors, but also nobody to whom they could return the money. They took the practical view and decided to use it to keep running what were clearly very popular and successful events, although it must have been tempting to just use the money in the club's account for other matters. GLC did an excellent job with those tournaments.

CSCA had problems with the CSSC Recreation Centre at Monck Street. The venue had been booked well in advance for the Knockout Finals, which were staged at the end of March. The correct room was duly available, but none of the requested furniture necessary for three matches. The Monck Street staff were thoroughly unhelpful, so the distinctly annoyed senior recorder had to wander round the building gathering tables and chairs and set them up, as well as set up 28 sets and clocks, all in the space of an hour. Luckily, the senior recorder was sufficiently well-organized to get there very early. The next CSCA committee meeting (12th May 1983), chaired by Ian Pheby in the absence of Messrs Godly and Fleming, agreed that this was unacceptable, and luckily GLC agreed to host the subsequent finals. They provided a very fine venue and everything ran smoothly thereafter. The EC were not happy that two EC members had not attended meetings for 2 years. The 56th AGM was held on 26th May 1983, where the chairman presented an obituary for Mr Bernfield (GLC). Ray Pomeroy reported that CSCA had won the British Correspondence Chess League (BCCL) and the Postal Chess League (PCL). A ballot took place to elect five Officers without portfolio, as six people made themselves available. This was most unusual as normally it was a struggle to entice five people to join the committee, even when they had no specific duties. Each club with more than one team in the league was required to nominate a set of players that would only play in the first team, and so on down to the penultimate team. The new senior recorder had noticed that some clubs were repeatedly nominating players who never participated, so he proposed a rule that any such players would be additions the following year. Adjudication appeals were now allowed, but the system changed. It was now proposed to send any appeal to the original adjudicator for comment, then send the appeal and his comments to two more adjudicators to decide. If they came up with three different results, it would go to a fourth adjudicator.

British Chess Magazine noted that the Minutes of the 1982 AGM stated that the treasurer, Ron Fleming, had 'presented his 31st report, preceded by a request that a younger member should now stand for the post.' The editor of *BCM* offered sympathy! *BCM* also commented on a lament by David Mills (Hull) in a book review of '*Romantic Chess Openings*' by Vladimir Zagorovsky (Batsford), in the *Bulletin*, 'Eric Schiller has translated the text and frequently lapses into reverse English, unfortunately a common fault in chess books generally nowadays; e.g. 'Bad is 9....Qe7', 'No better is 7....d5', 'Fully possible is...' Not pleased am I with this method of expression and possible is it that Batsford may rectify the error in future!' The author was then *Bulletin* editor and commented that the formation was normal Russian. Bernard Cafferty (editor of *BCM*) said, 'Your editor can afford to smile apologetically. He has perpetrated the fault frequently enough himself. In mitigation one should say that the 'strait-jacket' of Russian syntax does make such difficulties for a translator. Just reversing the word order does not always fit the bill, but merely transfers the difficulty to later on in the sentence. In recasting the sentence more fundamentally the translator sometimes has the awkward feeling that he is bringing in a nuance or emphasis not intended by the author.' *BCM* often published extracts from the *Bulletin* then.

CHAPTER 6

1983 – 1998 Drama follows Drama

The EC met on 6th September 1983. David Mills proposed a national individual championship and provided detail. No decision was recorded. Mr Sefton resigned as grader following the SCCU failure to include Civil Service grades in the 1983 Grading list. It was around about now that clocks were finally made compulsory in the league.

GLC Chess Club had the good news that Lambeth Sports Council had decided that chess was a sport and had offered £2500 to run a tournament as long as the club paid any 'portion of the grant which may be constrained to be working as profit'. The club still had the profit from the LARA events. The 7th Lambeth Congress duly took place, with 383 competitors and actually made a loss, due to the generous prize fund, and good playing conditions. GLC's chess club was again having problems with the GLC Sports Club, which was refusing to give any sort of grant. After some discussion, the chess club voted 16-0 to disaffiliate from its parent sports club. Apparently the GLC Sports Club was 'horrified and shocked that any club would want to disaffiliate'. But there was to be no rapprochement. GLC lost a friendly match with the British Intelligence Services by 4-2. Sadly, detailed results of the match were not published, which is perhaps not surprising. The first prize for the CS weekend tournament was shared by S Taulbut, J Gallagher and PG Large on 4½/5.

There was a most interesting match at Hastings this year, between four veterans of the original British Boys' Championship in 1923 and Grove School, all junior members of the Hastings Club. Here are the results, with ages in brackets.

Old Boys		Younger Boys
1. Sir Stuart Milner-Barry (76)	0-1	S Conquest (16)
2. WA Winser (76)	1-0	R Brooks (17)
3. LAJ Glyde (77)	0-1	M Rich (15)
4. RE James (77)	½-½	I Pierson (16)
	1½-2½	

Grove School reached the last four of the *Sunday Times* school tournament that year, but finished fourth. Unfortunately they were missing Stuart Conquest (later a grandmaster), who was away winning the World U16 Championship, despite a broken arm! Mark Rich went on to be graded over 200 and his two colleagues achieved grades in the 170s. Mr Glyde (formerly Ministry of Housing) sadly died a few weeks after the match.

The EC met on 9th February 1984. Mr Sefton had been persuaded to continue as grader. David Mills had informed the secretary of regional interest for a national individual championship. Ron Fleming recalled previous attempts to run such a tournament and continued by saying that the Barstow cup was technically awarded to the Civil Service individual champion but was in fact awarded to the London champion as there was 'no interest from elsewhere'. (That was clearly no longer the case.) The EC remained doubtful of the viability of the event. The senior recorder announced the cup finals would be held at County Hall as the conditions at Monck Street the previous year had been disgraceful. The EC agreed to a fee of £10 for

GLC. The EC met on 27th April 1984. It was announced that PB 'Pip' Sarson had died. He was a former *Bulletin* editor and represented Air Ministry chess club. The 57th AGM was held on 31st May 1984. The chairman presented obituaries for Messrs Aitken and Sarson. The treasurer presented his 33rd and final report. The 1983 Congress had made a loss of over £200, and expenses were continuing to rise. The chairman expressed the deep gratitude of CSCA for Ron Fleming's dedicated service, pointing out that Jesse Garner was Ron's predecessor in 1951. The chairman presented Mr. Fleming with an engraved tray. Ron said he was very happy to receive the tray but was still unwilling to serve another year! A proposal to make Ron Fleming a vice-president was carried with acclamation. Ron Fleming later spoke of his years as treasurer, 'In my capacity as treasurer I had various odd experiences from some of which I learned wisdom. At the September Autumn General Meeting I produced bills for the clubs, and one item was to charge a club for its adjudications in the previous season. If it did not owe anything for adjudications I wrote 'NIL' across the three columns – in the days of LSD, of course, but found that when the Club came to tot its bill and found '1' in the shillings column it would regard this as 1/- and add up its total accordingly! So in future I entered '- - -'across the three columns instead.

Annually I had to go to audit, and my first two auditors were James Curtis and Fred Dadd. Dadd was a MVO (Member of the Royal Victorian Order) as an acknowledgement of his work in arranging the 1930's Jubilee. We had a little contretemps on one occasion when he queried my charge in my account for postage. I explained that these were postage stamps and he must take these on trust. He said that an organisation to which he belonged privately demanded empty stamp books to be produced by its treasurer. Fortunately, Jimmy Curtis jumped on this suggestion and said that an empty stamp book did not prove that all the stamps had been used legitimately on official business! So Dadd abandoned his suggestion.

When I moved away from London in 1980 the CSCA asked me to continue as treasurer on the understanding that I would not attend EC meetings but travel up to London for the AGMs, etc. I parcelled up my accounts and supporting ledgers and sent them by post to my auditors together with a 'flow chart' to guide them through their audit and then received back the duly audited accounts. Finally, a successor as treasurer was found and I effected a formal handing over.'

'Every year the EC collected together all of the shields and trophies and they were taken to the 'Army and Navy' for the appropriate engraving. As treasurer I used from time to time to visit Mr Hitchins of Awards and Trophies in Craven Passage by Charing Cross Station. I mentioned this engraving drill to him and he laughed. 'We actually do the engraving here, and the 'Army and Navy' merely act as agents and add on their commission!' So we cut them out and had the trophies taken direct to Craven Passage.

When Barford became president of CSCA he wanted to donate a trophy and asked me to arrange it. So I went to Craven Passage and asked Hitchins to produce one. He designed and executed a very acceptable object and Barford was delighted.'

Ron Fleming was later to say, 'My general impression of over fifty years of Civil Service chess is that the whole attitude has deteriorated and that what was originally enjoyable has been spoilt by a change of attitude. When I first joined the CSCA it was a number of clubs who had gathered together into a league and spent their time putting out teams to play each other over the winter months and visiting each other's club rooms in turn. In addition to these league fixtures the various Civil Service departments played each other for the Bonar Law trophy and the Post Annual cup and then, when their numbers grew sufficiently, for the Jesse Garner trophy as well. The two municipal clubs (LCC and Metropolitan Water Board) who had historically formed part of the league were not, as I recall, barred from these competitive cups and their teams were accepted for fixtures. But I cannot recall them ever being allowed to win a cup!'

A final memory from Ron Fleming, 'At times the AGM in May or the September AGM for distribution of *Handbooks* and payment of capitation fees would command an attendance of well over one hundred members, and the room would be packed with enthusiasts. Those were the days!'

Back at the 1984 AGM, Simon Gillam (Treasury) proposed that adjudicators should come from outside of the league because on many occasions, adjudicators were weaker than the players involved. The senior recorder replied that his panel of adjudicators was much stronger now, and that grading is not necessarily the best indicator of adjudicating ability. The chairman said that adjudicators should be thanked for their voluntary work not criticized. The motion lost 1-18. There was also a proposal to have adjournments in the league, but the proposer withdrew the motion.

At this stage there were 20 clubs in the league, fielding 58 teams in 6 divisions. 610 players took part. But a sign of the problems was that there were 18 match defaults, 216 individual defaults, 40 (!) ineligible players and 77 fines for late submission of results. The *Bulletin* commented at the start of the 1984-85 season, 'Towards the end of last season, one captain was asked why he had not sent in a single match result, to which he replied 'We have not sent results in as we have had a poor season and through unavailability of players.' To say the senior recorder was not impressed with this attitude would be a considerable understatement. This was not the only problem. Rule 8 stated that matches would begin at 6.15 pm, unless mutually agreed otherwise. One experienced captain was indignant when his opposite number claimed the toss at 6.35 pm, and stated he had never heard of the rule. This sort of issue happens throughout chess leagues!

It was shortly after this that Civil Service Department/Treasury changed their name to COMPOST. Somebody said he hoped they would organize a match with Mushrooms Chess Club in Surrey. COMPOST stood for 'Cabinet Office, Management & Personnel Office, Central Statistical Office and Treasury.'

The EC met on 5th February 1985. Government Chemists II complained that Treasury II announced two defaults against them a week before the match but that these defaults were not below the lowest contested board. The EC agreed that the result would stand and that the divisional recorder would write to Treasury II about the ethics of chess and with a warning about their future conduct. Metropolitan Police II accused Inland Revenue III of cheating by playing their board 2 on board 8 and board 5 on board 7. The EC found in favour of Metropolitan Police II. The result was reversed and this had the effect of fining Inland Revenue III a ½ match point, as the boards were treated as defaults. It is mysterious that the two disputes were treated completely differently. The EC met on 22nd April 1985. The EC agreed to sack two of its members for non-attendance at meetings. After years of pussyfooting around, the EC was getting a taste for blood! However, EC members in later years missed meetings as well and were not removed. The 58th AGM was held on 31st May 1985. The chairman presented an obituary for PB Cook.

Ian Pheby's campaign to improve the organization of the league continued with a proposal that teams must be fielded in order of strength, which provoked 41 minutes of argument at the AGM. Some clubs were placing senior members of the club on high boards out of respect and some were sacrificing a weak player on board 1 to improve their chances elsewhere, and this was causing some ill-feeling.

GLC Chess Club had the misfortune to receive (from GLC management) a circular requiring staff clubs to 'provide information relating to equal opportunities within their respective club/society'. The circular stated that failure to provide such information could result in withdrawal of facilities. The Hon Secretary, Mr Field, completed a questionnaire which asked about 'the objectives of the club, means of election to its membership, any limitations of membership and the nature of facilities used'. Apparently the Equal Opportunities Branch was satisfied with the reply. The Lambeth Congress was held 16-18/8/1985, attracting 113 entries in the Open, 113 in the Major and 100 in the Minor. These were still very healthy figures, although nearly 60 down on the previous year, but a large loss occurred, owing to the expense of running the event. John Nunn was not complaining – he took home £500 for scoring 6/6. GLC Chess Club sent out a questionnaire to its members relating to the abolition of GLC, receiving 30 replies out of 90. The club was disappointed that so few people seemed to be showing an interest, but an answer rate of 33 % is quite respectable.

Ray Pomeroy had run CS postal chess teams for many years (and continues to do so) and rarely had problems, but did find himself in a couple of acrimonious disputes. He complained that the Controller of a British Correspondence Chess League

(BCCL) division (Peter Bond, ironically of CSCA) had declared CSCA's adjudication claims lost, as they had not arrived before the deadline of 10th October. Games were due to finish on 30th September. The BCCA (British Correspondence Chess Association) Tournament Controller (David Blair) informed Ray that the decision must stand, and, 'Should you wish to appeal further, please reply to myself, and I will remit the details to Mr J Allain'. John Allain was ironically another CSCA member as he worked for Metropolitan Police. Ray responded, saying that he sent eleven adjudication claims and fees to various controllers by first class post on the 7th October and everything arrived safely and on time, except the letter to Peter Bond. Ray thought it unfair that CSCA were being penalized for postal delays. He further commented that the 'A' team had only two adjudications, gaining 1½ points, but the opposing captains had resigned both games. The 'C' team had sent in claims for a win and 4 draws, but had been given 5 losses, apparently without adjudication. He also thought giving seven days for adjudications to be collated was unreasonably short. On 15th November, John Allain wrote, making a number of points. Firstly, he made the reasonable point that Ray's letter was undated, so he did not know if it had been made in time to comply with BCCA rules, but he would assume that it was. Secondly, he complained that Ray should have written directly to him. Presumably he did not know that Ray was following Mr Blair's request. He rejected Ray's comments about the deadlines as they were known in advance, and it was up to CSCA to appoint more captains if they had trouble meeting the deadlines. John Allain said that the 'A' team dispute was confusing. He said CSCA had claimed two wins (on 4th August) but had not sent the appropriate fees, and the resignations from the opponent were not received until mid-October, 'after he had closed the books', so Peter Bond could have scored the games 0-0, instead of 1½-½. Therefore, he rejected the appeal as Peter Bond's decision was 'if anything generous to CSCA'. Some might think it was more generous to the opponents, who had made no claim whatsoever, and resigned both games, but still drawn one of them! The claims relating to the 'C' team were also rejected, as three of the games had already finished, including two losses on time, and the other two claims were received late. He also said that it was difficult to make decisions when evidence was sketchy, but he had read the correspondence between Ray Pomeroy and David Blair. Ray pointed out that much of what Mr Allain said was not correct, and the latter did now concede that was the case. He now accepted that Peter Bond had received the two win claims for CSCA 'A' and two resignations from the opposition on the same day. Peter Bond decided to score the games 1½-½, which Mr Allain found, 'arbitrary but it could have been less favourable to the Civil Service. There is no reason now to interfere with it.' He said that in the 'C' team dispute, Peter Bond had assumed that Ray Pomeroy knew about the losses on time. He concluded, 'It is now too late to change any of the results even if that was desirable, but we can hope for better things in 1985/6.'

The February 1986 edition of the *Bulletin* reported the dispute, and pointed out that as the game is over when a player resigns that it was just wrong to score such a game as a draw. Mr Allain sent a rather angry letter complaining about this, and claiming that,

'The article was written and published before the dispute was finally settled and before the BCCA Executive Committee had decided its final action.'

This contradicted his last sentence in the previous letter. The *Bulletin* Editor queried this and other points and received an evasive reply. Another issue was the means of doing adjudications in BCCL. Peter Bond wrote at some length, and felt that the BCCA should improve its rules, rather than worry about the contents of the CSCA *Bulletin*. He added that he used a computer program, 'White Knight Mk III', on a BBC computer, analysing for ten half moves. He then sent the 'best' line to a leading CSCA player for confirmation of the result. This was actually an improvement on the previous year, where he had used an even weaker computer program and run it for a short time, without checking the lines. So the hard working players thought hard for many months, and then had their games adjudicated by a weak computer. BCCA insisted that Peter Bond had acted correctly throughout, then immediately wrote to him to say he would be replaced as soon as possible! Peter sent all his paperwork back by return of post. The argument rumbled on for about a year, and well over 50 pages of writing. Mr Allain was a Commander in the Metropolitan Police and was doubtless unused to anyone disagreeing with him. In a letter to the author (8th July 1986), the British Postal Chess Federation stated they could not intervene as it was not one of their events, although they could deal with adjudication appeals. About a year later, Norman Blake (DTI) became editor of the BCCA magazine and asked the author to write some book reviews. Having cautiously agreed to do this as long as Mr Allain did not object, some articles were published and peace broke out a bit later when Mr Allain congratulated the author on the quality of the articles.

The abolition of GLC caused severe problems for the chess club. They contacted the head of the London Residuary Body (LRB) to seek permission to carry on staging matches in County Hall, but had trouble extracting a reply. In view of the uncertainty over playing rooms, they warned CSCA that it might not be possible to stage the Knockout Finals. Happily, a reply did eventually arrive from LRB and the matches carried on as before. There was also the vexed question of what to call the club once GLC ceased to exist. Discussion on this was somewhat time-consuming and a number of different proposals were made. Eventually, 'Greater London Chess Club' was the majority verdict, and eligibility rules were established. The club also had issues with another club (not in the CS League) which had started to use County Hall for home matches and had been rather disruptive and noisy, which had annoyed players in GLC's club championship. Worse still, GLC equipment appeared to be somewhat depleted after such visits. The committee was rather puzzled that the other club was there at all, and it transpired that two of the committee members had given permission for the visiting club to play one match there, and they were unaware that it had turned into a regular occurrence. The visiting club also caused problems for CSCA a few years later. The CS Recreation Centre (based in Monck Street) sent CSCA several sizeable bills for rent and refreshments, causing the treasurer some concern. He asked CSRC for the dates concerned and then asked the CSCA match captain for his match dates. It transpired that the dates (the ones with food and drink bills) were not for CSCA events. After some fairly heated argument between CSCA and CSRC, someone discovered that the club that had made such cavalier use of GLC's facilities was doing the same with CSCA, and one of their officials, (PM Shaw), a former Civil Servant, and President of the BCF(!), when asked to pay the refreshment bill, had said, 'Charge it to CSCA'. When he was BCF President he survived a 'Motion of No Confidence' by a single vote, although this fact was never published in the Minutes.

The EC met on 18th April 1986. Western District Office

(WDO) had been the subject of several serious complaints from GLC Chess Club. The senior recorder had requested an explanation from WDO but had received no reply. The EC expelled WDO from the CSCA. They would have to reapply giving a guarantee of proper future behaviour at matches. There were also issues relating to non-payment of fees. Bob Turnham and John Allain proposed (on behalf of Metropolitan Police Chess Club) sacking all the adjudicators and replacing them with adjudicators from the BCF panel or abolishing adjudications and having Quickplay finishes. The EC would put these proposals to the AGM. Home Office Chess Club had re-joined the Association. This caused some excitement as the *Bulletin* casually remarked that half of the current UNATS first team would now play for Home Office, which would damage the former club, although the players were of course acting completely correctly by now playing for their parent department (now there was one).

The 59th AGM took place on 19th May 1986. An excitable Home Office official complained loudly to the editor before the meeting about the comments in the *Bulletin*. The editor agreed to look at what was said and clarify it if necessary (which it very clearly was not). The Home Office official repeated the complaint in the meeting. The *Bulletin* editor commented that he had already been asked the same question, but he would repeat the answer for everyone's benefit. The treasurer was ill and therefore the chairman appealed for a replacement. Mr Allain complained that the names of adjudicators were no longer being published in the *Handbook* and then withdrew the proposals referred to above. There was a good reason for not publishing adjudicators' names. The senior recorder had heard that some adjudicators were being approached by players who complained about results they had received. This was unfair to the adjudicators, especially if it were just before or during a match, hence the decision to stop publication of their names. LTR (London Telephone Region) objected to Dave Scuffam playing for Government Chemists II when he was 1st team captain. It was pointed out that Mr. Scuffam was not a 1st team nominee and therefore he could play for a lower team if he wished. Inland Revenue won the league with 8½/9, ahead of Government Chemists on 6, a somewhat crushing victory. Inland Revenue have since merged with Customs, Government Chemists were exiled to Teddington and withdrew from the league, and other clubs playing then but not 25 years later were, Employment, Treasury, Patent Office, Environment, LTR, BML (British Museum Library), WDO (Western District Office), Education, Energy, NWPSC (North-West Postal Sports Club).

PR Vivian died aged 60, after retiring early from the Stationery Office.

The EC met on 9th February 1987. The EC agreed that the new Treasurer, Brian Smith (Trade) should balance the accounts the best he could in view of his predecessor's poor accounting. The BCF Master (Grading) list had been issued 8 months late. No CSCA grading work had been done for two years. Mr Pheby (having been Essex county grader) agreed to grade those games not processed so far. The EC thought this was an onerous task which needed to be completed in a very short period of time and therefore agreed to make a one-off payment to compensate Mr Pheby. The EC were concerned that the match captain had organized a rapidplay grand prix event without their knowledge. It was agreed that the secretary would write to the match captain informing him that the EC must be notified in advance and be given the chance to discuss and authorize any new ventures. The EC met on 27th

April 1987. The EC confirmed the acceptance of Mr Sefton as grader. The Treasurer (Brian Smith) reported that £600 of the CSSC loan still had to be repaid. Mr Scuffam announced he was retiring from the post of secretary due to work pressures. One club had complained that they had lost an appeal on adjudication, despite the fact that their chess computer said they were winning. It was gently explained that chess computers were still fairly primitive and it might be some years before they were usable for adjudications. The Chairman (EW Godly) had written to John Allain about the Correspondence Chess dispute and was informed that BCCA considered the matter closed. This was presumably acceptance that they were in the wrong and wanted to avoid further discussion. The 60th AGM was held on 27th May 1987. Metropolitan Police proposed that adjudications should be abolished, and a time limit be 30 moves in 75 minutes, followed by 15 minutes Quickplay finish. If that failed, they proposed the time limit be 42 moves in 90 minutes. Both motions were lost.

The June 1987 edition of *Chess* carried a late report from the British Ladies Correspondence Chess championship of 1985/86. Keith Escott reported that Laura Cohen (Secretary of the British Women's Chess Association) had suspicions that Leigh Strange, the winner of the 1985/86 championship was not a woman, but Nick Down, the British Junior Correspondence Chess champion. 'After extensive detective work ..., I had sufficient evidence on March 4 to confront Nick Down with the accusation and he immediately admitted the deception.' 'It was an elaborate conspiracy involving other Cambridge students, two forwarding addresses, specially printed stationery and well-disguised handwriting.' It was accepted that it was a student prank that had got out of control, but had caused great damage to 'women's chess and postal chess'. Nick returned the trophy, apologized to all opponents and sent £50 to the BPCF to cover expenses. He was banned for two years from BPCF events. The trophy was then awarded to Doreen Helbig, who had scored a win and a loss against Nick (everyone else got two losses), and finished on 9/12, second was Lynn Spencer on 8½. Of course, if the organizer had deleted all records, he would have got a different winner, so perhaps it would have been better to share the title. Nick Down went on to play for Inland Revenue. He certainly had a sense of humour – his home in Devon was named 'Hartston Bill'! The news of the event hit the national press, and Postal Chess got even more unwelcome publicity. The author spoke to Nick shortly afterwards and was surprised to find that Leigh Strange was a real person, having assumed like everyone else, she was invented. Nick also revealed that after the event he had spoken quite openly about the prank, and that the 'extensive detective work' was an exaggeration. As soon as Keith Escott asked the question, Nick immediately said what happened. Nick's actions were intended as a joke, and he was not looking for financial gain or glory. Obviously, there was a serious effect on his opponents, and one of them dropped out of postal chess as soon as the news broke, although she did resume playing later. The trouble with postal chess is that it relies a lot on trust. Nick did comment afterwards that one international postal chess team had actually consisted of one player playing all the games under eight names. One correspondence chess world champion wrote (and was not sued!) that another correspondence chess world champion employed a team of grandmasters to play his games, and other players have undoubtedly done what Nick Down did, but with darker motives.

The *FDA News* (FDA was originally the 'Association of First

Division Civil Servants', i.e. senior CS) published a diatribe about advertisements seeking recruits for the Inland Revenue. The advertisement sought bridge and chess players, which the FDA article claimed was racist, as only white people played chess. Two members of IR chess club had letters published explaining in some detail the foolishness of the comments. Ian Hunter finished by saying, 'I will be very grateful if Ms Pickering would confine herself in future to strictures on subjects which she understands. If this reduces her output, this might not be a bad thing. Certainly we have suffered a great deal in the past from the recruitment of bridge players of which Ms Pickering also complains. This abomination should cease.'

The EC met on 14th December 1987. The auction of old equipment (particularly broken clocks) after the AGM had been abandoned due to lack of interest, which is not surprising. The treasurer reported that the CSCA had very little funds available because money was still owed to various parties and he did not have the time to approach clubs for their dues. Mr. Turnham announced that as he had not taken over as secretary until the autumn of 1987, it had not been possible to organize an Autumn AGM. The EC agreed that we should support a national championship otherwise our CSSC grant might be reduced. The secretary would write to David Mills suggesting a maximum of four players per Region to compete at a central venue e.g. Birmingham. Jerry Jordan and Brian Smith would resign as members of the Committee at the AGM.

A meeting took place on 12th January 1988 between two representatives of CSSC (both called Smith) and selected CSCA officers (EW Godly, RL Turnham, Brian Smith, JM Sargent, PA Bond). This seems straightforward enough, but the rest of the committee were kept in the dark about the meeting, even to the extent that they did not know the meeting had taken place. Those who did attend have remained tight-lipped about the meeting. It appeared to go smoothly enough, but it seems CSSC were excited that the CSCA weekend chess tournament had included a table tennis tournament to amuse people who had finished their chess games early. Apparently CSSC's table tennis club might be annoyed, although there is no evidence they were. In fact, when they were told about the event, they merely said that they hoped it had gone well. So, the CSCA committee members went home fairly happy, after what appears from the minutes to be a low-key meeting.

The EC met on 17th March 1988. The treasurer had repaid the money owed to the previous treasurer. A long and heated discussion took place about the Congress, which made a loss of £242.71. It was agreed that the CSCA would not hold another Congress. Problems also existed regarding the financing of the Rapidplay events. The EC agreed that any such future event would no longer come under the auspices of the CSCA. The EC agreed that Mr. Sargent and Mr. Bond as organizers of the 'Westminster Quick Play Congress' could use CSCA equipment on the strict understanding that the CSCA was reimbursed for any loss or damage howsoever caused. It was thought that a national championship would be held in 1989 with David Mills as organizer.

GLCC still had 70 members, despite the fact that GLC no longer existed, but of course they were having problems finding new players. People working for the GLC's replacement were eligible, but chess players appeared to be thin on the ground. The 61st AGM was held on 26th May 1988. Allocation of prize money at Special Events had been discontinued at the CSSC's behest. This disagreement continued for twenty years, with CSSC insisting that prize money was not appropriate for chess events, and with CS chess representatives repeatedly explaining that prize money is normal. CSSC officials were shown entry forms for weekend tournaments and still refused to accept that cash prizes were normal. This continued even after other CSSC events featured cash prizes, when CSSC at last accepted that it might be possible to give vouchers for chess events. The meeting agreed to the restructuring of the league. Ian Pheby produced a plan, to be implemented two seasons later, where each division except the lowest would be formed of six teams, meeting each other twice during the season. Numbers of teams were falling off, so divisions of ten teams were unwieldy and producing more mismatches, which were not enjoyable for anyone. The meeting accepted the plans with little argument. It was necessary to delay the implementation, so that teams would start the following season knowing they needed a top six finish in the top division to remain there the following season. It would have been unfair to inform a team after the event that they had been relegated when they thought they were safe. Teams winning lower divisions might find they had not won promotion, owing to the reorganization. A few people did not like the idea, as they played only in the CS League and liked to play nine different players in a season, instead of five players twice. Even players who played other leagues as well preferred to play a variety of opposition. But it made the league more competitive and any 'Home' advantage was nullified. Most of the meeting was devoted to proposed Rule changes. CS won the Bronowski trophy for the first time since 1976.

CSCA had major problems this year. An apparently routine meeting (although the minutes seem to be missing from the records) with CSSC officials (again both called Smith) on 27th July had not started well, when said officials had complained that CSCA's secretary and treasurer were serving police officers. It was explained that the league rules had been written before

CSSC existed and it had always been accepted by CSSC that (for example) Metropolitan Police and GLC teams and individuals were welcome to be members of CSCA. The meeting continued, with the CSSC officials apparently accepting the point, but then CSSC wrote to CSCA on 29th July 1988, with the following demands.

'It is an immediate requirement that steps be taken, possibly by calling an Extraordinary General meeting, to elect Officers and a Committee wholly comprised of CSSC members. Please let me know if this cannot be achieved by the end of September'

'Steps should be taken to ensure that only CSSC members form your representative match team.'

'Affiliation should only be accepted from clubs containing CSSC members, all of whom should be treated equally without giving emphasis to those forming the London League.'

(London League in this case means the London CS League.)

For once, the CSCA Committee was united in its anger. Bob Turnham (Secretary CSCA) replied on 4th August 1988, explaining the situation and inviting the CSSC to reconsider. The letter pointed out a couple of omissions, including, 'you also stated that you would overlook the fact that Mick Wiles and I are serving police officers'. The secretary also pointed out that several issues in the letter from CSSC had already been explained at the meeting. CSCA's letter finished, 'I am very surprised that you chose to put these radical demands in a letter and not to have mentioned them during our meeting. It is for the elected representatives of the clubs to decide how they wish to deal with your demands and I shall notify you of their decision after our Special A.G.M.' He also stated that the date for the SGM would be 22nd September 1988.

CSSC just repeated its demands. The EC met on 18th August 1988. It was agreed that the CSSC demands were unacceptable.

After much discussion, it was proposed that CSCA would cease affiliation to CSSC. This was agreed unanimously by the EC, a remarkable show of solidarity. A Special General Meeting was held on 22nd September 1988 with 39 members attending. The Chairman (EW Godly) was absent due to ill-health. The meeting instructed the secretary to write to the general secretary of the CSSC to inform them of the CSCA's decision to withdraw from the CSSC, but to express a desire to reaffiliate if the terms and conditions were acceptable to the CSCA. The meeting recognized that this meant fees would increase. Many clubs ran on a shoestring, as they did not need to pay rent for a club venue, so their major expense was entry to the league. Clearly the CSCA had expenses and these would need to be met somehow.

On the 27th September, one Mr Smith (CSSC) wrote again, responding to CSCA's letter of early August, backtracking and saying the complete opposite of what he had said on 29th July and later,

'Nor was I intending to debar clubs containing non-civil servant members from affiliation – we are well aware that Municipal Bodies have played a full and active part in CSCA affairs for many years.'

Unfortunately, this was too little, too late. Bob Turnham (Hon. Sec CSCA) wrote to CSSC announcing CSCA's decision. It would be fair to say that CSSC was somewhat startled by the communication from the CSCA secretary, which provoked a rapid response from Frank Krinks (General Secretary, CSSC), who replied on 7th October, saying,

'I was sorry to receive your letter of 28 September notifying me that a resolution had been passed at a Special General meeting of the CSCA to disaffiliate from the Council.

I will take up the points you have made with Officers of

the Council and will reply to you as soon as possible. In the meantime I hope no irrevocable action has been taken.'

Mr Krinks wrote again on 21st October,

'It is evident to me that the Council's position has been misunderstood or misrepresented and it is a pity that our request to be informed of the time and place of the SGM, so that we could be represented at the meeting, was not answered.'

This was typical of the attitude of CSSC officials. However, Mr Krinks did suggest a meeting between CSSC and CSCA to try to resolve the issue.

Bob Turnham responded on 1st November,

'I had informed Mr Smith of the date of the SGM, acknowledged by him in his letter dated 8/8/88.'

Mr Krinks completely ignored this clarification and clearly felt that he had no need to apologize for his false accusations. However, in his eventual reply on 26th January, he accepted that CSCA could continue to accept municipal clubs and have police offers on the Committee. He did also say that, 'It is unfortunate that your letters have represented the CSSC as an unsympathetic, interfering, organization. That picture is far from the truth.' The recipients took a different view. Mr Krinks did state that ex-civil servants could not be members of CSSC, although retired members could be.

The meeting between CSSC and CSCA took place on 4th April 1989. Following this, Frank Krinks, Margaret Grainger and David Burford from the CSSC attended the CSCA Executive Committee meeting on 17th April 1989. There was a wide-ranging discussion of the CSCA's activities and how the CSSC might be able to assist. Margaret Grainger complained about the *Bulletin*, but was shut down by Ian Pheby and Frank Krinks. Mr. Krinks thought the best course of action was for the CSCA and the CSSC to have a 'relaxed relationship' rather than formal affiliation. The matter would be discussed by the CSSC General Purposes Committee. Under the terms of the new relationship the CSSC would continue some financial support for the CSCA, paying for the *Handbook* and a contribution towards postal chess expenditure. The CSCA would actively encourage players to join the CSSC. Both Mr Smiths of CSSC, who had caused the problem, disappeared without trace. Enquiries as to their fate went unanswered.

The EC agreed to propose to the AGM that the Autumn General Meeting be abolished. The Autumn meeting was used for prize-giving and distribution of Handbooks, result forms, adjudication forms etc. It was decided it was easier to post the paperwork, and trophies were more properly distributed at the AGM. The 62nd AGM was held on 18th May 1989. The meeting was in favour of resuming links with the CSSC on an informal basis after the CSSC had accepted that earlier correspondence had not been very tactful. This may not have been a very enthusiastic apology, (or even any sort of apology), but probably the best that CSCA could hope for. Mr. Pheby, the new chairman, proposed that Mr Godly become a vice-president of the CSCA which was carried, and then he presented Mr Godly with a gift in appreciation of his work for the CSCA. It was agreed to abolish the Autumn General Meeting but that the 1989 meeting would be held as it would create too many difficulties to cancel it with such short notice. It was also decided to reduce the size of division 1 – 3 teams from 10 boards to 8.

Frank Krinks wrote again to Bob Turnham (11th May 1989) suggesting a new national competition, interestingly adding, 'You were sceptical, though, that good players would not enter unless, as in most chess tournaments – cash prizes were on offer.' This is a rare example of CSSC admitting that prize-money was normal.

GLCC discussed eligibilities of players at a committee meeting. One member pointed out that new members were recruited to play in other leagues, but were not eligible to play in the CS League, and he was worried that they might be used in the CS League as well. It was decided to try to amend CS league rules, by allowing anyone to play in the CS League, not just past or present civil or municipal servants.

GLCC had their last meeting at County Hall on 12th March 1990 and moved to Monck Street. One team had a dispute over an adjudication. Both sides had claimed a draw on one game, so the league recorder had scored this as a draw, as there is obviously no need to adjudicate the position. One captain then tried to appeal against the result, only to be told that the result agreed with his claim, so could not appeal. The captain then explained that he had confused the colours, and had he got the colours right he would have claimed a win. He felt this was obvious, and that the league recorder should have told him he had made a mistake. The league recorder said that teams frequently claimed draws or even wins when it was completely obvious they were losing and he did not consider it his job to tell captains what to claim. The captain approached his club and invented some tale that the appeal had been declined on an unspecified technicality, so the club complained to the league. The EC met on 17th April 1990. The league committee threw the complaint out by three votes to one. (What the one in the minority was thinking about is not clear.) The league committee's reply enlightened the club as to what had really happened, and they subsided. Strangely enough, a very similar argument occurred with another club a few months later. It was agreed that the match captain could purchase 10 new clocks. The CSSC had honoured their agreement and paid for the production of the *Handbook* and contributed to the costs of running the Correspondence teams. The 63rd AGM was held on 24th May 1990. The CSSC proposed a national championship *and the rules* in their letter of 3rd April 1990. This letter again showed the problem in relationships between CSCA and CSSC. The latter kept presuming to enforce their rules and ideology, when they clearly had no understanding of the sport. It was akin to them proposing a cricket tournament, which would be played on a pitch of a different length from usual.

CSSC's rules were,

All competitors to be Civil Service Sports Council members.

FIDE rules of chess as amended by the BCF to apply.

The Championship Final to be arranged as a round Swiss Tournament. Round 1 to be staged on the first day of the event, rounds 2-4 to be staged on the second day of the event, and round 5 to be staged on the third and final day of the event.

Regions to provide two representatives by way of a winner and runner up of their Regional Competition. Representatives to be notified to the National Championship Organizer by the end of March 31 1991.

Time control: 30 moves in 1¼ hours. After Black's 30th move both clocks will be put back 15 minutes and the game completed in the time remaining.

Tied scores to be broken by the following methods in turn:-

i) Sum of progressive scores

ii) Sum of opponent's scores

iii) Result of the individual game(s) between the players concerned

The arbiter's decision to be final in all matters

The Final will be held in April/May 1991.

Nobody could object to rule 1, but other rules featured poor

English and rather sloppy presentation. The covering letter started, 'Dear collegue'! The AGM thought the time limit was unsatisfactory and the secretary agreed to approach the CSSC with a proposal of the time limit being 40 moves in 1¾ hours followed by a quickplay finish. John Sargent agreed to organize the London qualifying event. Most of the meeting was devoted to proposed Rule changes. A proposal to allow adjournments in the league (by mutual agreement) was carried 10-1. The membership sportingly agreed to this just in case anybody wanted to adjourn games. As it happened, the idea did not seem to be popular and the number of games adjourned over the following years only just exceeded zero. There were of course the practical difficulties mentioned earlier. You also needed access to the equipment cupboard, which usually had a limited number of key-holders. CS again won the Bronowski trophy. As some clubs were inclined to pay their entry and affiliation fees late (or not at all), an escalating system of 'fines' had been introduced to encourage prompt payment. Employment fell foul of this as they owed £40 at the 1989 AGM which had risen to £69 by the next AGM. Employment's sports club refused to pay as they thought this was unreasonable. The CS treasurer suggested cancelling the debt as the only way to get the money might be to take Employment to court, even assuming CS won, and expelling them from the league would just reduce the number of teams. Accordingly, the debt was cancelled, which surprisingly did not lead to wholesale refusal to pay the next year!

The senior recorder reported that 12 matches were defaulted in the league and there were 133 individual defaults, 9 % of the scheduled games. There were now only 427 players in the league. There were 50 fines for late submission of results and eight instances of ineligible players being used.

GLCC's stay at Monck Street looked to be short-lived, when it was announced that CSRC would close in March 1991. This move was delayed several times and it was eventually announced that there would be a temporary move ('twelve to eighteen months') of CSRC to nearby Chadwick Street in spring 1992. This temporary move was to last nearly 20 years. The Civil Service has an unusual definition of 'temporary'. It was pointed out again at a GLCC committee meeting that GLCC's membership rules did not match those of the CSCA, and this might be a problem. Some members were surprised at the comment, as the change in rules had happened some years earlier. Nevertheless, it was decided to propose that the league change its rules to avoid any problems.

CSCA got slightly excited when seeing that David Mills' magazine *Time Trouble* was advertising a team event, so asked him what he was doing and why he had not consulted the CSCA. David explained it was regional, not national, and was aimed at Yorkshire and Humberside.

The EC met on 11th April 1991. The EC agreed to fund the 'Sir Stuart Milner-Barry' trophy for the national championship when CSSC declined to do so, up to a value of £125. Naturally, Sir Stuart was asked for his views before the trophy was named, and he wrote a nice letter in which he said what a great honour it was, and (surprisingly) saying that nobody had named a trophy after him before. Mr Sargent reported that one of the cupboards had been broken into at Monck Street resulting in the loss of Mr Godly's trophy. John Sargent agreed to replace it and to ascertain the position regarding insurance. The chairman proposed that any individual should be allowed to play for the parent department or UNATS as he/she thinks fit. This was carried 3-1. The author offered to organize an individual national Postal Chess championship. The 64th AGM was held on 9th May 1991. Roland Smith and Peter Bond (both Inland Revenue) were elected vice-presidents of the Association. CS won the Bronowski trophy for the second year in a row. Eight years after David Mills suggested it, (and at least 25 years after CSSC had!) the first CSSC national individual championship was held at York University, with the proposer running it, and CSSC generously funding accommodation, food and travel. It was a nice venue, with a stream running through the grounds near the accommodation. This was less appealing when the geese and ducks awoke at dawn and decided to announce the fact! 16 players participated, with the relatively lowly-graded (at the time) Charlie Storey scoring a magnificent 5/5, beating all the theoretically leading players. Sir Stuart Milner-Barry attended and presented his trophy. Sadly, the trophy 'disappeared' a few years ago. All the players received mementos, and there was special applause for Barkat Ali, who scored zero, but kept a smile on his face throughout. Sir Stuart kept us entertained with reminiscences, like, 'I drew my last game with Capablanca.' That was at Margate in 1939. He also reported that he played in a tournament with Alekhine and Capablanca, when these two met on Capablanca's birthday. A cake was presented to Capablanca before the game, then Alekhine won (instead of agreeing a quick draw as is customary). On the bus back to the hotel, Alekhine turned to Sir Stuart and said, 'Did you see how I beat him? Ha ha ha!'

It was in 1991 that the Royal Gunpowder Mills in Essex closed down. Powdermill Chess Club continued in Essex. Previously, some staff had played for Government Chemists. The Civil Service team usually played in the Eastman cup, for London-based teams. It was normal for the CS team to lose an early round, then try to win a few matches in the 'Plate' competition for teams that had been eliminated. It was different this year.

Eastman Cup Round 2
Civil Service CA   **Charlton**
(16th January 1992)

1.	G Moore (199) (B)	1-0	A Hanreck (203)
2.	AC Ashby (190)	½-½	A Stebbings (206)
3.	KJ Thurlow (185)	½-½	J Wager (191)
4.	JJ McDonnell (176)	½-½	N Donovan (184)
5.	PS Milner-Barry (173)	½-½	R Hyde (167)
6.	S Dickinson (156)	½-½	A Sherriff (150)
7.	TB Packham (154)	1-0	TJ Lloyd (151)
8.	KJ Hurst (150)	1-0	S Watson (131)
9.	HJ Williams (155)	1-0	JE Smith (-)
10.	EW Godly (138)	1-0	T Jefferies (113)
		7½-2½	

Ted Godly set the ball rolling with a 15-move win and CSCA never looked back. A couple of weeks later, there was a friendly match with RAF.

Civil Service CA   **Royal Air Force**
(1st February 1992)

1.	KJ Thurlow (185) (B)	1-0	DB Pritchard (188)
2.	PS Milner-Barry (173)	1-0	G Sage (173)
3.	MJ Rose (153)	0-1	AJ Toll (187)
4.	DI Calvert (148)	½-½	P Doye (158)
5.	L Aris (148)	1-0	W Barkworth (U)
6.	EW Godly (138)	0-1	A Nelder (128)
7.	PM Shaw (139)	0-1	A Foulds (126)
8.	K Lovel (132)	0-1	P Ball (125)
9.	D Cooper (U)	0-1	K Bawbridge (U)
10.	E Hazell (115)	1-0	M Morrison (U)

11. D Scuffam (106)	0-1	M Carbin (78)
12. J Spencer (U)	½-½	A Ball (88)
13. C Cooper (U)	1-0	M Adamson (U)
	6-7	

The author was delighted to defeat his well-known opponent in a very tough game, but was stunned to watch the miniature on board 2, which started 1.e4 e5, 2.f4 exf4, 3.Qf3. It should be added that the RAF players frequently have somewhat unreliable gradings, (as they do not play all that regularly) so their board order was not as strange as it might look.

The EC met on 10th February 1992. Mr Sargent confirmed a replacement trophy for Mr Godly had been purchased and presented. The Post Annual cup had been valued at £820 and the Bonar Law trophy at £3000 for insurance purposes. It was agreed that Employment be expelled from the league and only allowed to re-enter if all outstanding monies had been paid and they reapplied to be league members. There were several complaints about teams defaulting on high boards. It was also mentioned that the Recreation Centre in Monck Street was due to close that month, and that the temporary move to Chadwick Street site would then happen. Eligibility for clubs was clarified, with new wording, 'Any individual should be allowed to play for the parent department or UNATS as he/she thinks fit.' This was partly as one player was in dispute with his club and this meant he could actually play CS chess, as he was unable to play for his own department. Another player had firstly worked for a department without a club, then his second department's club had folded, but had historically been linked with three other departments, which did have clubs. He felt it was fairer to play for UNATS than to provoke outrage by trying to argue that he qualified for any of the other clubs.

Victory over Charlton in the Eastman cup meant that CS had to face the mighty Wood Green in the quarter-final, who had reached the last eight of the European Club cup that season. Obviously, this would be completely one-sided.

Eastman Cup Round 2

Civil Service CA (26th February 1992)		Wood Green
1. G Moore (199) (B)	1-0	P Littlewood (230)
2. Default	0-1	AD Martin (228)
3. KJ Thurlow (185)	1-0	GD Lee (226)
4. JMG Toon (181)	½-½	T Farrand (216)
5. M Coogan (185)	0-1	PJ Sowray (209)
6. PS Milner-Barry (173)	0-1	J Friedland (188)
7. JJ McDonnell (176)	0-1	RL Turnham (163)
8. RW Bauld (155)	0-1	M McCall (170)
9. MJ Rose (153)	1-0	B Kerr (177)
10. DI Calvert (148)	1-0	J Ellis (-)
	4½-5½	

This was a really impressive performance and the CS players that lost all put up a strong fight, with the outcome in doubt until the end of the match.

It was reported in March that Eric Croker (of Education) was one of the 1991 recipients of the BCF President's Award for services to chess. 'He has carried out an immense amount of administration at local, County, Union, and National level. He is a BCF Senior Arbiter and FIDE Arbiter, and initiated grading in the Middlesex League.' This is a synopsis of the report in BCF's 'ChessMoves', but the last paragraph needs to be quoted in full. 'Like many other dedicated chess administrators, Eric

Croker does not claim to have a distinguished playing record. He started playing postal chess in the late 1940's before he joined Hendon. His contribution to other players' enjoyment of the game has been considerable and he is a worthy recipient of this Award.'

In early 1992, one club was not happy with a couple of its opponents. In one match, the complainant (a match captain) was playing an opponent that kept forgetting to press his clock. As time-control loomed, the opposing captain allegedly picked up the clock and pointed at it until his player pressed the clock. The opposing captain was told not to interfere, but the damage was done and the complainant blundered into a draw.

The senior recorder invited the opposing club to comment. The opposing captain said he had not picked up the clock, but he had pointed out that his player had forgotten to press the clock. He added that his player insisted this was the only occasion in the game that he had forgotten to press the clock. Many years later, one has to think if he had forgotten to press the clock, he might still be unaware of the fact at the end of the game! The league committee bizarrely decided to warn the opposing captain as to his future conduct, and that the game's result would stand, although it would not be graded.

In another match an opponent had exceeded the time limit many moves short, but the captain felt he could not tell his player, and his player then lost on time as well. 'I hoped his opponent would do the decent thing and resign but he claimed his entitlement to the draw as both flags had now fallen.' The league committee pointed out that if both flags fall, the game continues, (actually only one member of the committee knew this), but the result of the game would not be changed. This dispute was actually quite useful as it was one of the events which led to a document outlining guidance for match captains, and saying what they could and could not do.

Another postal chess dispute occurred in a British Postal Chess Federation team event. An opponent offered a draw in Game 2, but it appeared the '2' had been written on top of the '1'. The CS player decided to accept the draw, whereupon his opponent said that he had meant to offer a draw in Game 1. The CS player was happy with a draw in Game 1, so suggested they agree two draws. The opponent refused. The Controller decided to award a draw in Game 1 but instructed the CS player to continue Game 2. As it was near the end of the session, Ray Pomeroy suggested just sending the position for adjudication. At this stage, the Controller said that the opposing player had claimed the game and he had so awarded it (without talking to the CS player or captain), as the CS player had 'refused to play'. In fact the last move from the opponent had not arrived and the opponent had not repeated the move, as the rules demand. At this stage the opposing team tried to claim two wins! This was rejected. Ray protested the decision and was informed the result did not matter as it did not affect the destination of the league title. CS were infuriated by this attitude and considered withdrawing from the competition. The Controller said this would be 'spiteful'. It was made clear to the controller that his treatment of the CS player was unacceptable.

The controller of the event published in the results report, 'There remains one disputed result in a game between BCCS and CSCA (Board 3), owing to a misunderstanding between the players. Rather than sort it out between captains the CSCA captain referred the matter directly to me, resulting in a lot of correspondence (and telephone calls) all routed through me and thus taking twice as long. Ultimately, while one game was agreed drawn, for a number of reasons I awarded the other game to BCCS by default. The CSCA captain is unhappy with this decision and I suggested that I would at least add this note of dissent to the results sheet. It can in any case be seen from the table above that even if the game had been awarded a draw (as CSCA wanted) it would have made no difference whatsoever to either team's final placing. For the record the result shown above stands, but the fact of the dispute and the CSCA's unwillingness to accept the decision has been recorded.' The controller's attitude seems extraordinary.

CS did decide to continue in the tournament, but the player who was unfairly treated and two of his colleagues refused to play. Chess is supposed to be fun, but it does require good will of players and organizers, and why waste a year playing a game, only to be robbed of it by a poor decision? Another argument occurred with the same controller shortly afterwards and CSCA appealed the decisions. CSCA had claimed two wins on adjudication for one player, the opposition had claimed two draws and the Controller awarded the opposition two wins as he said CSCA had not sent the fee for adjudications, although CSCA said the fees had been sent. After several months, the BPCF said they had no power to overturn the Controller's decisions, despite the fact that BPCF had said CSCA was entitled to appeal. CSCA decided not to enter the competition until the controller was replaced. Many people were particularly outraged that a man of the cloth could be so dishonest. Some years later the competition was run by a new controller and CSCA and two of the three players returned to the fray.

Another league dispute followed a default on top board. The defaulting club had two extra players in the room, who were not approached to step in as reserve. The player who got the default win protested to the opposing club, saying they should have put in one player as a reserve, to fulfil the fixture, and should pay his travelling expenses. When he received no reply, he complained to the league. The opposing club then replied, somewhat dismissively, saying that the two people present were not reserves, had refused to play, and were not strong enough to play anyway. The league committee pointed out that clubs should fulfil fixtures, but decided not to force the defaulting club to pay expenses, although the league would pay expenses on this occasion.

Another dispute over defaults occurred when a player defaulted as the home side's security guards gave the wrong directions to the playing room. This was a recurring problem.

One club complained about an opposing team playing their team in the wrong order. About a month later, the league recorder noticed that the complaining team had used the fourth highest-graded player in the club in the fourth team! They explained that he was a friend of the captain's and they did not see the problem. They also complained that the senior recorder's letter had said, 'It has been brought to my attention...' and demanded to know who had complained. The senior recorder responded that the appropriate league recorder was doing his job and had noticed the infringement.

The EC met on 23rd April 1992. The chairman announced with regret the death of Sir Leonard Barford. A letter would be sent to his widow offering a cheque to her nominated charity. Unfortunately, Employment Chess Club were expelled from the Association for paying their fees some 16 months late. The appropriate rule stated that expulsion was compulsory, but the club was informed that if it paid the following season's fees and paid a deposit for the forthcoming season. They would be admitted to the league. They rapidly complied.

There were not many serious disputes, but one incident a few years earlier had caused some problems. At one league match, the visitors were somewhat embarrassed and perplexed that their top board did not arrive for the match. They apologized profusely to the opponents and the match proceeded. The next morning the visiting captain telephoned his delinquent player and was horrified to learn that the player had indeed reached the venue, but had failed to gain entry to the building as the door had been slammed in his face repeatedly. Eventually he gave up and went away. The visiting captain now rang his opposite number, who was equally horrified, and went to talk to his club colleague who had been on door duty. This individual reported that he had barred the way to one person as he did not like the look of him. The home captain telephoned the visiting captain with a very heartfelt apology and said that obviously they would concede board one, and would write apologetically to the player concerned and pay his travelling expenses. Both captains contacted the league recorder who thanked them for sorting the problem out so sensibly. The league recorder then telephoned the visiting player who was incredibly calm about the whole matter, and insisted he did not want to pursue a complaint against the opposing club or the person who had stopped him entering the building. The player had a reputation for being extremely pleasant, but to decline to complain in such circumstances showed he was a quite remarkable individual. The entire committee was relieved that they did not have to discuss such a matter, which appeared to be racially motivated.

The second CSSC championship was held in April. York University was unavailable, so the event moved to Devonshire Hall, Leeds University, where it was to remain until 2013. This venue was just as good as York and became even better when Leeds suggested a few years later that if we moved the event to summer, we could use en-suite accommodation, which was being supplied as academic-year-long lets to students. CSSC immediately agreed to this, and the venue became absolutely first class. David Mills originally thought we should move the event round the country, but every time the players were asked, they voted to stay at Leeds. At that time, Beverley Kenny was the manager of the Hall and she did a fantastic job, and set the standard for those who followed her. She was awarded a well-deserved MBE in 2011.

The 65th AGM was held on 21st May 1992. It was announced that the EC would not tolerate cheating, two instances having been reported during the year. 'Guidance for Captains' would be published in subsequent *Handbooks*. Some adjudicators felt underpaid, so it was agreed to pay a £10 retainer and £1-50 a position. CS also won the Bronowski trophy, completing the hat-trick. Sadly, it was the last time CS won the trophy. The league rule regarding defaults was clarified. Hitherto, the rule had stated that a player must be 'present' within half an hour of the start of the match, which was ambiguous – it could just mean in the building. This was changed to 'having arrived at the chessboard'.

Sir Stuart Milner-Barry was elected as president. He replied to the chairman on 9th June, in a most charming manner,

'Dear Mr Pheby,

Thank you very much for your kind letter of 1st June. I am much honoured by my election as President of the CSCA and I thank you for your personal congratulations. I will do my best, but at my age one cannot of course rely on a long tenure!

With all good wishes,

Yours sincerely,
Stuart Milner-Barry'

The EC met on 4th March 1993. The CSCA had agreed to supply 18 players for a 50-board match to celebrate the Centenary of the Insurance League. There was another major problem in the league. A member of the EC played against GLCC and in a friendly chat with his opponent afterwards, said he was unaware that his opponent was eligible to play in the CS League. The opponent cheerfully said he was not eligible. This was reported to the senior recorder, who started an investigation. GLCC failed to answer the first letter. He gave GLCC seven weeks to confirm or otherwise the eligibility of their players. GLCC asked for an extra week, which was granted. It then became clear that they had asked for this as they had a Committee meeting scheduled just after the deadline and thought the matter should be discussed there. Some members of the league EC felt that the matter was sufficiently important for GLCC to have an extra meeting. GLCC admitted that a number of their players were ineligible. This matter provoked considerable discussion and ill feeling. It was agreed not to expel GLC from the league but to fine the club £10 per ineligible player (total £110 for 11 ineligible players), and that past employees of GLC, LCC and ILEA (Inner London Education Authority) were eligible. The total number of appearances made by these players was over 150 over the preceding five years, and GLCC teams had formerly won the league, and gained promotion from lower divisions using such players. The EC decided that there was no sensible way of retrospectively awarding trophies to other teams, or changing the composition of the league. Members of the EC were not amused when the GLCC President (Geoff Ashelford), who was an EC member, commented, 'Your league needs GLCC more than GLCC needs the League.' Anybody wavering over the need to punish GLCC probably stopped wavering at that point! The EC also did not know that eligibility of players had been discussed at GLCC meetings, so the use of ineligible players was deliberate .

There was a dispute between Emil Semm (GLCC) and Alan Sands (UNATS). The chairman declared an interest as he was a member of UNATS. James Toon (Vice-Chairman) therefore took the Chair. Alan Sands had been very short of time (a not infrequent state of affairs), and Emil Semm's score sheet was not entirely up to date (also a not infrequent state of affairs). The latter was rather absent-minded in that respect. The author counts both players as former team-mates. There was some confusion as time control approached and Alan lost, but protested he had been distracted by Emil, who should have been recording the game properly. Alan had one minute to play ten moves, Emil had an hour. It was agreed by casting vote that the result Semm 1-0 Sands would stand but that the secretary would write to Mr. Semm warning him as to his future conduct. The author was also a member of UNATS, so was also barred from taking part in the discussion. Perhaps, annulling the game would have been preferable. It does show the difficulty of running a league. In a tournament, the arbiter should pounce and (nowadays) award Alan Sands more time, whilst warning Emil.

Ray Pomeroy reported a challenge match against the European Commission at correspondence chess had started, with Owen Philips (Trade) as opposing captain. The EC met on 15th April 1993. GLCC appealed against the fines imposed at the previous meeting. The fine was reduced from £110 to £50, and two of the members previously declared ineligible were reinstated. One of the banned players had played again since his ban, and he had been selected by Mr Ashelford, who was an EC member and had been present at the previous meeting, and therefore was well-aware of the EC's decision. The EC considered that Mr Ashelford had committed a blatant breach of the Rules as well as totally disregarding the authority of the EC. One member proposed a 3-year ban from league activities, another proposed a 5-year ban. The ban was for 5 years by a 4-2 vote. The chairman pointed out that a motion to ban him for 5 years would need to be presented to the AGM otherwise he would be eligible to participate in non-league activities. This was agreed. The CS Recreation Centre had demanded £320 back rent at the rate of £80 per year. It was agreed with varying degrees of outrage that we were not liable for previous years, and that there was no evidence that the bills had been sent before. The author suggested that if they insisted on payment, we should offer £20 only. The chairman agreed to write saying that all the bills were retrospective and we were willing to negotiate suitable rates in the future. The 66th AGM was held on 20th May 1993. The chairman announced the death of Dr HR Calvert. The meeting was informed that the CS Recreation centre at Monck Street was due to close in January 1994. BTHQ asked for proxy votes to be accepted. This was rejected 2-9. It was agreed to participate in the Game Fee scheme. Game Fee was originally announced by BCF as 'Payment for Grading', but it was thought 'Game Fee' sounded better. It also made it more difficult to sue BCF if games were not graded for any reason. The proposal to expel Mr Ashelford from the CSCA was defeated 7-9 after much heated discussion. GLCC produced Bill Bush, who had been a member of the league for many years, and he delivered a speech, explaining that it was all a misunderstanding and that GLCC had accidentally used ineligible players on a few occasions. Your author commented that over 150 appearances had been made by ineligible players, and in his opinion, this did not constitute 'a few'. The look on Mr Bush's face suggested that he was totally shocked by this revelation. As he had signed the Minutes Book when GLCC had debated the issue in 1991, his shock is difficult to explain. Richard Fries and Brian Smith then proposed that the new Executive Committee rescind the ban on Mr Ashelford from 20th May 1993. This was carried 11-1. As soon as the AGM ended, the EC met and in accordance with the motion carried at the AGM, the EC reconsidered the ban and decided unanimously to rescind the ban with immediate effect. His ban therefore only lasted from 15th April 1993 until 20th May 1993. Ironically, within twenty years, any club could use whomever they liked in league matches. It also turned out that the player who had originally cheerfully said he was not eligible to play in the league was wrong! He inadvertently caused a lot of ill-feeling and annoyance.

CSSC had apparently downgraded CSCA to a 'local' body in 1990, although they did not tell anybody. CSSC were apparently willing to consider a national body and David Mills sought support to create it. He had spoken to Margaret Grainger (CSSC) over many years and said she agreed. CSCA were a bit startled to see such ideas in print and spoke to CSSC, who had obviously remembered the problems that had happened a few years earlier, so they proposed a meeting of the parties.

On 30th September, Ian Pheby and the author represented CSCA at a meeting with Frank Krinks (CSSC) and David Mills, to discuss CS chess. It would be fair to say that the CSCA representatives were expecting a difficult time. Mr Krinks started by saying that the CSSC recognized CSCA as the only CS body which represented chess at a national level.

David Mills took offence and said that CSCA was only a local body. Mr Krinks firmly stated that the point was not for discussion. David was extremely unhappy, as he had been told by Margaret Grainger that this would be discussed (although it was not on the agenda). It has to be said that CSSC has a long history of saying different things to different people over the same subject, and this continued into the 21st Century. It has always been difficult to assess if CSSC did this by accident or design. The CSCA representatives were asked to list its activities, which included the London-based league. Mr Krinks noted that all participants were eligible for membership of the CSSC except some GLCC and Metropolitan Police players. He accepted that it would be unfair to exclude them. He was also happy with the Postal Chess activity, both individual and team events. Representative matches were more problematic, as most of the players came from the London area and CSSC wanted a wider base of players to be used. CSCA pointed out that getting players to travel a long way would be too expensive. David said he had plans for matches but Margaret Grainger had told him to keep them secret. He then revealed that a tournament could be set up between Army, RAF, Navy and CS, and sponsorship could be sought. It was agreed that this was an interesting idea, but difficult to arrange quickly. CSCA were asked to propose suggested opposition. At some stage, David Mills set off for a comfort break, and as soon as he left the room, Mr Krinks said, 'Don't worry. We're on your side. This meeting is just to keep David quiet.' The CSCA delegation was startled. The national individual championship was discussed. This had started in 1991, under the aegis of CSSC and run by David Mills, who had suggested such an event years earlier, and had continued suggesting it with great determination until it actually happened. Mr Krinks outlined the history of the event, and asked if CSCA would like to take it over, preferably as soon as possible. Before the startled (again) CSCA representatives could react, David complained bitterly about the request, saying he had done all the work and was now being discarded. By now, Ian and the author were feeling really sorry for David, as it appeared he was being hung out to dry. Everyone present attempted to placate David by saying he had done a great job, which he clearly had. Ian said that CSCA could take it over, but the EC would have to agree to it. The format of the event was then discussed. Mr Krinks wanted one qualifier a region, as in some other CSSC events. Everyone else said that would not work as you needed more players, and the second player from London (e.g.) might be better than other regions' best player. Mr Krinks said it did not matter if you were eliminated regionally or at the finals. It was agreed that CSCA would make proposals to CSSC. The knotty problem of the controller of the event was raised. The controller was an experienced organizer, but was not a BCF Arbiter and there had been a number of complaints about his decisions and pairings. In the most recent event, both players on one board pointed out they had the wrong colours, and suggested changing the pairing. The controller insisted it was right, and then said afterwards, 'Actually I know it's wrong, but it would look bad to change it now.' Unfortunately, that looked worse. He also refused to publish the draw until immediately before the round, as players might have time to prepare for their opponents, which he thought was a bad thing, although it was entirely normal tournament practice. David felt very strongly that the controller should continue and it was agreed to discuss the matter later.

David also felt that it was wrong for all CSCA AGMs to be held in London. Mr Krinks thought that CSCA should consider holding a meeting at the weekend and in another location, like Birmingham. CSCA agreed to discuss this, and pointed out that its officials did not get time off work to attend meetings, and that we were both taking leave to attend the current meeting. Ian did comment that he doubted a Birmingham AGM would be quorate. Ian asked about the letter from Margaret Grainger which said chess was only a local organization, and Mr Krinks said the entry was incorrect and had been deleted. He added that CSCA's constitution needed to be updated, as it was out of date. CSSC would not help pay for Game Fee for league grading, but would pay for the national individual games to be graded. Ian pointed out that the Grainger letter had referred to an important meeting, but CSCA had not been invited. Mr Krinks said he would arrange an invitation, and requested that CSCA attend the meeting.

He subsequently wrote to the CSCA, saying (inter alia), 'I am sure the GPSC will be pleased with the advances represented in the record and I am grateful to you for your forbearance in the changing – and, sometimes trying – circumstances.'

(GPSC was the CSSC's General Purposes Sub-Committee.)

The EC met on 9th November 1993. The belated rent demand from the CS Recreation Centre was agreed at £80. Some members were unhappy with the contents of the *Bulletin* in relation to the GLCC dispute. Discussion was deferred so that the editor could consider the comments. The chairman made it clear that neither he nor anyone on the EC had the right of censorship. The auditors were unhappy with the 1992/93 accounts, and raised several issues. In 1990/91 the EC had agreed that old equipment could be written off, but this had not been included in the Minutes. There was a discussion relating to the 30th September meeting between CSSC and CSCA. It would divide the CSCA into two bodies, a new 'national' CSCA, and London-based activities coming under the London Civil Service, Post Office and Municipal League. Roland Smith prepared the appropriate constitutional and rule changes.

The EC agreed to undertake the running of the national championship with two qualifiers per Region. David Mills would organize the Finals but the CSCA would select the arbiter as David could not use an unqualified controller. This referred to Sir John Lawson, who had controlled events for many years, but the BCF had recently decided that all people designated as 'arbiter' had to have passed the appropriate examination, or they could not call themselves an 'arbiter'. For people like Sir John, this was a bit of a kick in the teeth as he was very experienced, and he refused to take the test. He also pointed out that some rather senior BCF 'Arbiters' had not taken the test either, and he would take his test the day the others took theirs. All of them carried on at the events they had traditionally organized.

The EC met on 23rd February 1994. An application for a rent reduction based upon maximum usage of 8 occasions per year of the Chadwick Street facilities was agreed. Chadwick Street would be the 'temporary' new home of the CS Recreation Centre, following the eventual closure of Monck Street. An EC member again voiced concerns about some of the views expressed in the *Bulletin*. The editor made it clear that he was not subject to censorship and that those views expressed were those of himself and not necessarily of the EC. There was lengthy discussion on the draft Constitution which was prepared by Roland Smith for the separation of the new CSCA from the old CSCA which would become the London Civil Service Post Office and Municipal Chess League. David Mills refused to organize the National Finals, as he objected to his controller being sacked, so the author would run the event with Richard Furness as Arbiter. The author took over with very short notice and ran the event for the next ten years. There was a suggestion to hold the Barstow cup as an invitation event at a weekend, possibly with prize money. Traditionally, the Barstow cup was awarded to the CS champion, but as there was now a national CS championship for the Milner-Barry cup, the Barstow cup continued in London, although it was open to players from anywhere in the country. There were of course practical difficulties as the games were played mid-week in the evenings.

The EC met on 13th April 1994. The EC agreed that A. Gallagher could only play for DHSS 4 if DHSS obtained prior approval from the opposing match captain before the date of the match. The author resigned as divisional recorder, and the chairman proposed a vote of thanks which was endorsed by the EC.

The 67th AGM was held on 19th May 1994, still in Monck Street. The meeting observed a minute's silence for Mr. W L Bush (GLCC). Roland Smith's constitutional drafts were accepted. He put a great deal of effort into these and really did a marvellous job. Those for the new CSCA were based upon the CSSC model, and amendments were approved by the CSSC, after some discussion. CSSC were eager to insert some phrases that CSCA could not accept, but it was sorted out amicably. The treasurer commented that he could remain treasurer of the league but not treasurer of the new CSCA which would be formed in September 1994, as he did not qualify for membership of the CSSC. New CSCA's financial year was the same as the calendar year, unlike the 'old' CSCA which ran April to March. This was the last AGM of the traditional CSCA and the first of the League alone. The

League officials became the temporary committee of the new CSCA. The author was elected as vice-president for his 'considerable service'. The combined CSCA and London CS League lasted from 1927 – 1994. In view of previous problems, it was made clear to captains that they must insert a reserve if one were available, to avoid defaults. There were issues with the CS Recreation Centre again, as staff insisted on charging non-CSSC members 50 p admission to the centre, even for CSCA meetings. As the toilet cubicles were largely without locks on the doors and also without toilet paper, there was some adverse comment. Chadwick Street was a great improvement in that respect, although the standard and variety of food offered in the canteen suffered a considerable drop in quality. A very cheery woman prepared and served the food at Monck Street and two days before its closure was saying how much she was looking forward to working at Chadwick Street. When the new centre opened, outside caterers were introduced and the cheery woman was never seen again. Visitors to the Chadwick Street canteen asked for a menu and were told, 'It's on that board.' 'But there are only three items!' The general conditions at Chadwick Street were good, and it had previously housed the 'Property Services Agency' (which had originally been part of the Ministry of Works). PSA's role was to 'provide, manage, maintain, and furnish the property used by the government, including defence establishments, offices, courts, research laboratories, training centres and land'. Naturally they ensured their own accommodation was of the highest quality.

The league now had 15 clubs and 38 teams, so participation had roughly halved in the previous 20 years.

The 68th Annual General Meeting was held on 15th September 1994, but this was also the inaugural meeting of the 'new' Civil Service Chess Association. The Acting Chairman, Ian

Pheby, welcomed those who attended this meeting of the new Association. Frank Krinks, General Secretary CSSC, had been unable to attend but had sent a letter wishing the Association every success. He had included a 'special vote of thanks to Ian M Pheby and Kevin Thurlow for their work on Civil Service chess'. Ian also placed on record the thanks of the CSCA to Roland Smith for his work on the new Constitution. The new treasurer would need to compile an estimate for financial support from the CSSC. The programme of activities was discussed and included the national championship, correspondence chess and representative matches. The former holders of the posts of president and vice-presidents were elected en bloc. The officers would be chairman, secretary and treasurer. The additional members of the EC would be representative match captain, CSSC national championship organizer, grader, correspondence captain, *Bulletin* editor, and two others without portfolio. The league AGM heard that the Senior Recorder (Ian Pheby) would be solely responsible for the league and cup organization. Hitherto, divisional recorders had assisted by compiling the results for the league. What caused some confusion was that the senior officers of the league and the 'new' CSCA were mainly the same people. The future was to bring instances of people saying, 'Haven't we discussed this before?', only to be told that it had been at the league meeting, rather than the CSCA one.

The CSCA committee met on 17th November 1994. The treasurer thought the grant from CSSC for 1995 would be approximately £4250 but he was yet to receive sufficient detail from some Committee members. One confusing issue was that the money and trophies had to be shared properly between CSCA and CSCL. On 19th September 1996, Jan McLean (CSSC) telephoned to tell Roland Smith that the CS League could use the trophies in perpetuity. This welcome clarification was also agreed in a meeting with CSSC.

It was thought that David Mills could take over from John Sargent as representative match captain. The time and travelling problems associated with David Mills were considered but no possible solution was acceptable to the majority of the Committee. The problem was that whilst David lived in Hull and Ray Pomeroy (correspondence chess captain) in the North-West, the rest of the Committee resided in London and the South-East. Ray was frequently unable to attend owing to work commitments. It made sense to have meetings in London and that way only one person had to travel a significant distance. David was also the only person who got time off from his employer to attend meetings.

The CSCA Committee met on 9th March 1995. It was agreed to change the accounting period to be in line with the CSSC (calendar year instead of April – March). The treasurer was due to prepare the first accounts for the period ending 31st December 1995 with CSSC approval. There was discussion about the publication of the minutes by David Mills in his magazine, 'Time Trouble'. It was eventually agreed that David could do so providing he omitted any item of a confidential nature as designated by the chairman or secretary. The *Bulletin* editor had briefly reported disputes at a tournament in Surrey, and an official of Surrey County Chess Association (SCCA), had written to CSCA to complain. The Surrey official acted independently and did not seek approval from any other SCCA Officers. It later became clear that the SCCA Committee never met. Jeremy Burrows (Treasurer) commented on the law of libel and drafted a reply which would provide the recipient with no satisfaction. The treasurer would discuss with CSSC whether occasional meetings could be held outside London. The league EC met on 11th April 1995. The chairman announced the death of our president, Sir Stuart Milner-Barry. Ian proposed to write to Ron Fleming, who had been our treasurer for 31 years, to offer him the post of president. The EC agreed. A CSSC official had written a letter which the *Bulletin* editor considered libellous. After a letter of complaint was sent, the CSSC official refused to apologize and even denied that he had made the comments, which was surprising as the *Bulletin* editor had a copy of the letter.

This season saw an incredibly close battle for the league title. GLCC, Home Office or Inland Revenue were all in contention, but IR beat Home Office 4.5-3.5 to take the title. The Bonar Law was equally exciting. Trade (division 3) knocked out Eastern Knights and Home Office from division 1 and were beating UNATS until a last-move blunder cost them victory in the semi-final. Revenue were leading UNATS 3-2 with 10 minutes to go in the final, but it looked likely that the final score would be 4-4, with UNATS winning on board count. As so often, it all changed dramatically and Revenue were (apparently) comfortable winners by 5.5-2.5

Revenue also collected the Barford trophy for team lightning chess. Paul Hare scored 10/10 on Board 1 and had previously finished fifth in the British lightning chess championship. Nick Down scored 8/10 on Board 2, and then won the Civil Service individual lightning tournament the following week. Steve Tovey and Nigel Fleming completed the team, so a Revenue victory was no surprise.

David Mills had asked at a CSCA committee meeting why they were held in the evening, whereas an afternoon start would allow him to travel to the meeting and back home in a day. He was told that that nobody else got special leave (i.e. time off with pay) to attend the meetings. One committee member related that a colleague had been refused time off to represent Great Britain in the Olympic Games, another had been refused time off to participate in the national chess finals, and another was not even allowed to take annual leave for sport and recreational purposes. David had initially been refused time off to attend the meeting, but CSSC wrote to his management to request it and it had been agreed. CSSC later said they would have even raised it with the Head of David's department. David represented CSCA at the CSSC Annual Conference on 22nd and 23rd May 1995, and raised this issue of official time off to play and organize chess events. CSSC responded that up until 1992, Treasury controlled the matter, so could instruct departments to allow time off for CSSC events and meetings, but subsequently it was delegated to individual departments. The Head of the CSSC had written to the top people in CS departments and asked for their cooperation. The letter said that the rules for special leave were being devolved and this 'should make it easier for those who work voluntarily for Civil Service Sport to arrange short absences from work.' This new 'freedom' was an improvement and would allow employers to be more generous. In practice, this did not happen. Not surprisingly, employers were not keen on giving time off to staff to play sport. In many cases it caused ill feeling. The author's father complained to his boss that the office was nearly empty on every Wednesday as staff were either playing or watching football or cricket depending on the time of the year. 'Why can't I have an afternoon off to throw boomerangs?' he said. His boss took the pragmatic view and authorized the request.

Times were changing. Some Civil Service departments were becoming agencies to make it look as if they cost less money and some parts were even being privatized. The author's own employer, Laboratory of the Government Chemist, was about to become LGC Limited. This caused membership problems for CSSC. They reacted to this by saying that staff that were privatized or left CS could retain their membership, and even new employees at former CS departments could join CSSC. This contradicted their previous eligibility requirements, but at least showed a willingness to move with the times.

The CSSC individual championship continued. When it had started, meal times dictated that we play one game on Wednesday, three on Thursday and one on Friday. There was only a fifteen-minute gap between the end of round three and start of round four. The author felt that a two, two, one split was better, and the players agreed. Devonshire Hall, Leeds obliged by slightly moving a meal time and we had a more relaxing schedule. It also left Thursday evening free for a Blitz event and other social activities. The author had forgotten that CSSC had originally insisted on the one, three, one split, but CSSC happily agreed to the change, or more likely, did not notice it.

The 1st Annual General Meeting of the league was held on 25th May 1995. The chairman announced the death of Sir Stuart Milner-Barry, our President. Geoff White (UNATS) paid a fitting tribute to Sir Stuart, and also to Pat O'Shea, a long serving member of UNATS. The Constitution was amended to bring the accounting period in line with that of CSSC. The new league treasurer was asked to propose an apportionment of funds between the league and CSCA. Ronald Fleming was elected as our new President, and then addressed the meeting, thanking them for the honour bestowed upon him. The author retired as *Bulletin* editor after 14 years of service. He wrongly assumed that one of the many critics would take over the post.

Inland Revenue won the league with 9/10, with GLCC some way behind on 7. Division 2 was very close.

		1	2	3	4	5	6	W	D	L	P	Bd
1	Treasury	X	5½-2½	4½-3½	5½-2½	4-4	7-1	6	2	2	7	47½
2	Met Police	5-3	X	7-1	2½-5½	5-3	5-3	7	0	3	7	47
3	GLCC II	4-4	5½-2½	X	4½-3½	5½-2½	4½-3½	6	2	2	7	42½
4	DHSS I	3-5	3½-4½	3-5	X	6-2	4½-3½	5	0	5	5	42½
5	Environment	4½-3½	3-5	3-5	3-5	X	2½-5½	2	1	7	2	33
6	DHSS II	2½-5½	0-8	4-4	2-6	2½-5½	X	1	1	8	1½	27½

Environment were deducted ½ point for too many defaults above contested boards. Clubs were fined ½ point for each 4 such defaults. The senior recorder was relieved that the league had a tie-break system (game points) as a three-way play-off would have taken some organisation. The teams played each other twice, and the home side is the one on the left. Treasury were promoted by a very narrow margin. Metropolitan Police succeeded the following year. Interestingly, it was round about now that the Metropolitan Police players stopped being treated as if they were on duty. Before this, an on-duty police officer could play chess for Metropolitan Police, or if he were off-duty, he got paid overtime for playing chess! Metropolitan Police also had different sports clubs for officers and for civilian staff, the latter being members of a sports club called 'Comets'.

Division 4

		1	2	3	4	5	6	W	D	L	P	Bd
1	BTHQ II	X	4-2	4-2	3-2+	4-2	5-0+	7	0	3	7	35
2	Treasury II	3½-2½	X	3-3	4-2	3½-2½	2-4	6	2	2	7	34½
3	Education	5½-½	3-3	X	3-3	2½-3½	5½-½	5	3	2	6½	39
4	DHSS III	3-2+	1½-4½	1½-4½	X	3-3	3½-2½a	4	2	4	5	27
5	Environment II	1-5	1½-4½	2-4	2-3+	X	4-2	3	1	6	3½	25½
6	GLCC IV	0-5+	1½-4½	0-6	1½-4½	2-4	X	1	0	9	1	14

'+' means double default; 'a' means amended score.

BTHQ had a similarly narrow victory. Education had three

3-3 draws and a 3½-2½ loss – an extra half point in any of them would have put them first, not third.

The Committee met on 24th September 1995 in Devonshire Hall, University of Leeds. The Constitution amendments had been agreed by the CSSC. Apportionment of old CSCA funds was still not complete as the league Treasurer, Brian Smith, was very ill. John Sargent had confirmed that all the CSCA equipment was at Chadwick Street. This comprised 24 boards, 20 sets and 18 clocks. It was decided that no equipment was permitted to be taken from Chadwick Street, and the agreement with John that the CSCA equipment could be used by Westminster Chess was rescinded. One unfortunate part of the move to Chadwick Street was that it did not open at weekends. Also, the 50p charge for entry for non-members continued and nearly £20 was charged for tea/coffee for an 8-board match which caused GLCC some problems. The eligibility of one player to participate in the National Finals was questioned. It was decided that in future, any participant had to quote his/her CSSC membership number. David Mills would have sole responsibility for representative matches. The chairman would ensure that the author was nominated for a CSSC Merit Award. It was agreed that the author could dispose of the old photocopier for the best price obtainable. This had been obtained when the CSSC had decided not to continue copying the *Bulletin*, and it was considered more cost effective to buy a photocopier than pay commercial copying rates. Owen Phillips was confirmed as new *Bulletin* editor.

The league EC met on 18th October 1995. The chairman had written to Lady Milner-Barry with an offer of a donation to the charity of her choice. She declined the offer, much to the surprise of those present at the meeting. Apportionment of funds (between 'old' and 'new' CSCA) had not been carried out due to the death of the Treasurer (Brian Smith). It was decided to carry out the apportionment of funds as soon as possible. The secretary was going to write to Mr. Sargent regarding a lightning buzzer he was authorized to purchase which was not present when the chairman and secretary carried out an audit. The Bond individual lightning trophy had not been traced despite extensive efforts. Future recipients of all trophies would need to sign a receipt.

CSSC helpfully provided a breakdown of entry in its regional competitions. Players attempting to qualify for the chess championship numbered 120, broken down by region as Eastern 8, London 6, Southern 7, South East 9, South West 19, Wales 0, Midlands 12, Yorkshire/Humberside 10, Northern 26, North West 17, Scotland 6 and Northern Ireland 0. The CSSC General Purposes Subcommittee felt that a qualifying event needed four entries to justify its continuation. This later changed to a requirement for six entries for it to count as a qualifying event. It may seem surprising that London, with its thriving league, only had six entries but the players were generally quite strong and even some other strong players would not enter as they did not think they would qualify. Three players graded over 170 failed to qualify one year from London, whilst two players graded under 100 qualified from another region. CSSC thought this was entirely reasonable as it made the event 'national' to have qualifiers from many regions. CSCA wanted the strongest possible final. A suggestion that London should have more qualifiers in view of the strength of players was firmly rebuffed. North's magnificent turn-out of 26 players fell away to virtually nothing over the next few years. It is interesting to compare chess entries with other activities.

There were 42 entries for team bridge, but apparently only two regional competitions. Only 72 male squash players entered CSSC championships, but 1239 five-a-side football teams participated. Bowls attracted 48 entries in Eastern region and none whatsoever in London, Southern and South East. CSSC not unreasonably thought that if entries were low overall that finals should not take place.

The CSCA Committee met on 17th January 1996. Colin Cheek had replaced Owen Phillips as *Bulletin* editor. The nomination for a CSSC Merit Award for the author was not successful. The photocopier was sold for £50. '£200 in relation to apportionment of funds between the old and new CSCA was agreed.' The league EC met on 28th February 1996 and heard that Mr. Sargent had not purchased a buzzer. The EC agreed to the proposal of £200 to be transferred from league funds to the CSCA. The chairman announced that Sharon Furlong had sadly died, Sharon being the last Ladies champion of the Civil Service.

The 69th CSCA AGM was held on 28th March 1996. The chairman announced the passing of Brian Smith. David Mills would raise the matter of automatic qualification of the national champion for the following year's event at CSSC Conference. When he did so, there was quite a discussion on the matter. Eventually, Conference agreed to refer the matter to the CSSC General Purposes Sub-Committee, who would report back in a year's time. Not surprisingly, they felt that no change was necessary. This argument continued for many years and was never resolved to the satisfaction of CSCA. CSSC said it was their policy that entrants had to qualify for the finals every year, and that the reigning champion could not qualify automatically. It was pointed out that the reigning champion did qualify automatically in several other sports, which CSSC denied. It was almost certainly the case that CSSC did not realize that other sports broke their rules. CSSC were funding the event, so CSCA had to accept that CSSC could impose any rules they liked. CSCA could try to persuade CSSC to make changes, but it was not really possible to complain too much, without risking termination of the tournament.

The league EC met on 9th April 1996. The secretary was instructed to advise Environment that a motion for their expulsion would be placed before the AGM if they failed to pay their fees by 30th April 1996. There had been no support for the Selected Openings tournament or the Ten-Minute tournament, and it was agreed these would not be held in the future. The 2nd AGM of the league was held on 23rd May 1996. It was agreed that matches be limited to Bronowski trophy and Eastman cup. There were to be no individual tournaments as the Controller had resigned and had not been replaced.

1995/96 Division 1

		1	2	3	4	5	6	W	D	L	P	Bd
1	Home Office	X	4½-3½	3½-4½	5-3	3-5	6½-1½	6	0	4	6	45½
2	E Knights	4½-3½	X	5½-2½	3-5	3½-4½	7-1	6	0	4	6	45½
3	UNATS	3½-4½	5½-2½	X	3½-4½	4½-3½	4½-3½	6	0	4	6	45
4	Inland Revenue	1½-6½	3-5	4½-3½	X	7-1	4-4	5	2	3	6	43
5	GLCC	5½-2½	3-5	1½-6½	4-4	X	5-3	4	2	4	5	37
6	Treasury	2-6	2-6	1½-6½	1½-6½	4-4	X	0	2	8	1	24

Incredibly, four teams finished on 6 points, and the senior recorder was even more grateful for a tie-break system. However, even this failed, but luckily it happened in the top division, so it was decided to share the title between Eastern Knights and Home Office. It was really amazing that none of the top three teams drew a match. UNATS had six matches which finished 4½-3½, three wins and three losses. The last round of matches was decisive. Eastern Knights surprisingly lost 3½-4½ at home to GLCC on the 12th March. Two days later, Home Office fell (also at home) 3½-4½ to UNATS, and probably thought Inland Revenue would add to their impressive total of championships the same night. But in a final twist, Inland Revenue could only draw 4-4 at home to already relegated Treasury, who perhaps regretted their narrow victory in division 2 the previous year. The Committee then got to work on more detailed tie-break rules, and the AGM duly accepted that after match-points and game-points, the next tie-break would be the board score in the matches between the teams that tied. If still level, the teams would have a play-off match, and if that were drawn, board count, then bottom board elimination would be used to split the tie, as in cup matches. If all games were drawn, the team with the lower average grade would win. This last rule was changed later, as there would be a problem if players were ungraded, so the winning team would be the one that had black on the odd boards. Nobody thought that would ever be needed, but sure enough a cup match ended 4-4, all draws, a year later!

The CSCA Committee met on 6th November 1996. The chairman welcomed Chris Goulden as the new grader. David Mills announced a representative match against the RAF to be held in December 1996. One player failed to turn up for the national finals. The Committee would consider imposing a ban if he failed to respond to enquiries. David Mills complained about the sparse nature of meal portions and that only salad was available at the CSSC Conference. He was not the only one. The Northern Ireland delegate enquired if the 'Potato Famine' had now reached the mainland, and this became a standing joke at subsequent meetings. There was discussion about the awarding of 'colours' to players representing CSCA in matches. It was agreed that a tie would be preferable to a blazer badge when 'colours' were awarded. The league EC met on 4th December 1996. Brian Skinner (DHSS) had volunteered to be individual tournaments controller. The chairman and secretary reported the audit of equipment. The secretary was authorized to purchase 3 clocks and 5 plastic sets.

The league EC meeting of 29th January 1997 heard that the equipment had been purchased. Mr Sargent proposed the purchase of 2 clocks, 5 hard boards and a buzzer. It was agreed that this would require approval by the AGM.

The CSCA Committee met on 12th February 1997. The player who had failed to arrive at the National Finals had apologized, and it was agreed no further action be taken on this occasion. If there were a repetition, the CSSC considered a ban to be reasonable. As expected, the CSSC would not accept automatic entry to the Finals for the previous year's National Champion. The CSSC was asked to consider prize money for the National Finals in order to attract top Civil Service players. David Mills would attend the Finals to recruit for representative matches. It was agreed that the organizer of the National Finals could make a charge for conveying the equipment to Leeds. Grading for the National Finals would be paid for by the CSSC. The CSSC also agreed to fund Correspondence Chess costs. The 70th AGM was held on 19th March 1997. The chairman announced the death of CB Stronach who had been chairman 1968-1971.

The CSSC and the CSCA would continue to insure the Bonar Law trophy, The Post Annual cup and the Barstow cup. This led to the CS league acquiring valuations for the trophies. The magnificent Bonar Law trophy was valued at £3000 five years earlier, and everyone assumed it was the most valuable trophy. The league was in for a shock. One of the old and battered wooden shields awarded to a team winning a division was valued at £6000. The secret lay in the engraving. The winning team had its name engraved on a small metal shield which was then attached to the large shield. Many of these small shields were silver, hence the surprisingly high value. This left the league in something of a quandary. Should all the trophies be insured, at quite a high cost, or should the league take the view that if a trophy disappeared, it could be replaced by a cheaper version? There was considerable discussion at Committee and AGM level, with conflicting views expressed with some vigour.

The CSSC contacted CSCA to say that Frank Krinks was retiring and that they expected a donation to be made by member organisations. It was agreed with one Committee member dissenting that £10 should be donated from the CSCA and the league. The league EC met on 9th April 1997. It was agreed not to enter a team in the Ralph Barnett Memorial (a jamboree event for leagues in the Greater London area) in the future. Mike Keohane (Treasury) offered to stand as treasurer. The EC agreed to take no action against Inland Revenue for defaulting both matches against Eastern Knights. The 3rd AGM of the league was held on 15th May 1997. Roland Smith as Treasurer presented a detailed set of accounts and a financial projection to include engraving, valuation fees and insurance. It was agreed we would not renew the insurance for trophies and equipment. Bob Turnham retired as auditor. The league was unhappy with the conduct of certain captains. Despite the fact that there was a £2.50 fine for submitting a match result late (or not at all), several captains offended repeatedly. Five clubs were fined additional amounts, one of them a further £30 for frequent non-compliance with the rules. Additionally, defaults were running at more than 10 % of the available boards. There were proposals to reduce the size of teams in the hope that this would solve the problem. There were also issues with adjudications. There had been 62 adjudications in the 1996/97 season, of which six had been declared 'frivolous'.

Colin Cheek resigned as *Bulletin* editor as he had no access to a computer. CSSC were asked if they would provide one, but they understandably declined to help. This signalled the end of the *Bulletin*. But the electronic age was upon us, so it was possible to provide information, without being concerned with formatting or lengths of pages. CSSC provided their rules for representative matches. They would fund three such matches a year, but insisted that the best available team would be fielded. This was at odds with their attitude to national championships, where they were more concerned with the number of people playing, rather than the quality of the event. CSSC said that 'special leave with pay is normally available', but this was devolved to departments and agencies, so CSSC needed a team list three weeks before the match, to give them time to ask departments to give the players time off. It would be quite rare for a chess captain to know his team that far before the match. There was some concern that the same document talked about running combined finals, with different sports held at the same venue at the same time, but CSSC were quick to reassure CSCA that this was not intended for chess. The document also said that organizers should ensure that all the players had the same playing kit. This did not apply to chess either.

Division 1 could never be as exciting as the previous season, could it? Well, it was not as close.

1996/97 Division 1

		1	2	3	4	5	6	W	D	L	P	Bd
1	Eastern Knights	X	5-3	5-3	8-0	5½-2½	8-0*	10	0	0	10	62
2	UNATS	2-6	X	5-3	5½-2½	3½-4½	4-4	4	1	5	4½	39½
3	Met Police	3½-4½	5-3	X	4½-3½	1½-6½	4-4	4	1	5	4½	38½
4	Home Office	2½-5½	4½-3½	4½-3½	X	5-3	5½-2½	4	1	5	4½	34½
5	GLCC	1½-6½	2½-5½	2½-5½	4-4	X	4½-3½	3	1	6	3½	33½
6	Inland Revenue	0-8*	3½-4½	3-5	5½-2½	6-2	X	2	2	6	3	32

'*' means by default

Eastern Knights were the only team to exceed 50 % and had won the league with three matches still to go, a truly magnificent performance. This included a rare 8-0 victory over the board, as well as the two default wins. The other teams were fairly evenly matched. Inland Revenue made a surprise exit from the top division. Even here, if they had scored an extra half game point in the away match to GLCC, Revenue would have survived. Inland Revenue were lucky that they played in a league that did not penalize match defaults. Not surprisingly, Eastern Knights won the Bonar Law trophy as well. Dave Jarmain (their captain) must have been very pleased. The author cannot recall a more dominant performance in a chess league.

DHSS won division 2 by 2½ points, and Inland Revenue II won division 3 by 1½ points. Treasury II won division 4 and BML won division 5 (in their final season) in closer contests. division 6 was reduced to 4 teams owing to a pre-season withdrawal, but the writing was on the wall for the competition. Only 5 of the remaining 12 matches avoided having a double-default on any board. One team twice turned up with only three players for a six-board match and won 3-0, as the entire opposing team defaulted! Owing to withdrawals the competition shrank to five divisions the following season.

CSSC continued to fund the postal chess and were insuring some of the trophies. They were now willing to consider prize money for the national individual competition. They also decided to play participants' expenses directly. The organizer had to pay them the previous year, although CSSC did provide a float to cover the costs. CSSC funding was some £8000 per year to cover all chess activities, which was obviously a significant investment. The national final took a reasonable chunk of that. Hedley Featherstone very helpfully said that CSSC could book players' rail tickets for them, which saved qualifiers having to pay sizeable sums and then claim them back, leaving them out of pocket for a month or two. Marian Holmes became general secretary of CSSC on 27th May 1997. She turned out to be very good for CS chess, and doubtless for the CSSC in general. She attended the national finals along with Carolyn Thompson, a very enthusiastic and helpful CSSC organizer, and both showed a great deal of interest in what we were doing. Admittedly, one person there was so eager to rant about how to run CSSC that Marian and Carolyn went to hide in the 'Ladies' for a while. They kept their cheerful demeanour even after that and the chess players certainly felt that there was support from CSSC.

In June CSSC helpfully distributed a 'Sports Body Manual' which gave 'aid and advice' to those running representative matches and national championships. It said that, 'Special leave with pay including time for travelling to and from the event is normally available for Civil Servants.' It did add that, 'Special leave will be subject to the exigencies of the appropriate department.' By this time, fewer and fewer departments were allowing special leave, although there were exceptions.

The word 'normally' was certainly optimistic. There were some oddities in the 'Manual', as expenses for use of a private car were allowed, (about half the rates CSSC staff could claim), although drivers could not claim for the use of car parks. It was confirmed that prize money was not allowed, although vouchers were permitted, if authorized in advance. CSSC's policy on representative matches and national championships was clarified – teams were required to field the best players available, against good quality representative opposition. In fairness, CSSC's cricket team had played the Australian touring team in the past. National championships were supposed to encourage participation, rather than include the best players. At least CSCA now had a document explaining CSSC's rules.

There was an amusing discussion with CSSC over mileage claims for the national individual championship. They refused to pay the author's mileage claim to Leeds as it was 'excessive'. This was puzzling, so clarification was sought. CSSC gave a distance, eliciting the reply, 'That's crazy – that must be the straight-line distance – are you seriously suggesting I drive right through the middle of London?' From the stunned silence, the author realized that was exactly what they had expected. Luckily, they relented.

The proposal in the league that quickplay finish (QP) should be first choice but you could adjudicate by agreement lost 5-13, and the proposal for compulsory QP in cup competitions lost 6-9. A proposal to change the time limit to 42 moves in 90 minutes, and 7 moves per 15 minutes won 9-5, but failed as a two-thirds majority was required. Surprisingly, it took more than ten years before this change occurred. A final cup tie-break of who had black on top board was adopted. The league was now down to 383 players, and dropped to 290 the next year. The league had defaulted the first two Bronowski trophy matches through lack of players and it was agreed to default the last one out of fairness to the opposition. We heard the sad news that EC Baker, a stalwart of CSCA, had died aged 97.

The CSCA Committee met on 24th September 1997. The Treasurer, Jeremy Burrows, had resigned. CSCA felt that the Milner-Barry trophy should be insured by the CSSC. The national individual tournament organizer detailed the problems associated with two participants at the finals who were more interested in getting drunk and disturbing others at 3.30 am than playing chess. The chairman would consult the CSSC about a possible ban. The rather bizarre response from CSSC was to complain to CSCA about the behaviour of the players concerned and said it was CSCA's responsibility to sort it out, in complete contradiction of CSSC's own rules. The 1996 winner of the championship forgot to return the trophy for presentation in 1997 despite playing in the 1997 Finals. This was very embarrassing as a VIP was due to present the trophy that year.

The Committee asked CSSC to reduce the rent paid by GLCC for the Chadwick Street venue. In 1990, Monck Street had charged £160 per year, but this had increased to £60 per month at Chadwick Street in 1996, then £70 per month the following year, then £75 per month the year after that. CSSC refused as GLCC were not members of the CSSC.

The CSCA Committee met on 21st January 1998. The 1996 accounts had been audited with some reservations expressed about the state of the records. The Milner-Barry cup had still not been returned by the previous winner. The meeting was reminded that any punishment handed down by the CSCA could also result in a punishment by the CSSC and his Government department. As some people were allowed Special

Leave to play in the finals, CSSC considered that players were representing their department, and that they were effectively on duty when they attended the event. Admittedly, CSSC's lack of interest over the drunkenness issue suggested they would not worry too much about failure to return a trophy. The league EC also met on that date. The grader highlighted problems with the Grading List in respect of the listing of clubs associated with Civil Service players. There were problems with the BCF as results were not included in the grading list. The committee passed a unanimous vote of censure on BCF. CSCA also complained to the British Postal Chess Federation about the unacceptable behaviour of the organizer of the BPCF club championship, and resolved not to enter the competition again.

The 71st CSCA AGM was held on 31st March 1998. Roland Smith had taken over as treasurer when Jeremy Burrows had resigned, and had done a splendid job. The Constitution had been amended in relation to the number of auditors. It was agreed a written and verbal warning would be given to everyone at the National Finals in future in an attempt to avoid possible disciplinary action being taken by the CSCA, the CSSC and the appropriate Government department. The great majority of players behaved well, but it was necessary to deal with the handful that did not. The league EC met on 8th April 1998. Geoff Ashelford (GLCC) was willing to stand as auditor. The EC fully supported GLCC's decision not to provide the customary refreshments because of excessive charges at Chadwick Street. It was written into the league guidance that teams should provide 'tea and biscuits' as a minimum at home matches, but the Recreation Centre at Chadwick Street was charging £18 for a not particularly large flask of coffee. A dispute arose when a player turned up for an away match slightly late, but the home team's Security staff apparently did not know where the match was being played and nobody went to look for the visitor.

The 4th league AGM was held on 28th May 1998. The chairman paid tribute to Vice-President E C Baker MBE who had prepared the first CSCA Handbook in 1948, and had given long and distinguished service to CSCA. EC Baker corresponded with the author for some years and produced entertaining and helpful information. Staff at the Civil Service Recreation Centre had moved the league's cupboard without consulting CSCA, causing damage to equipment estimated to be £100-£200. It was agreed to renew insurance cover for equipment because the CSRC required an indemnity from the league for damage to the league's equipment howsoever caused. Some felt that the CSRC could not insist on such a condition if it could be shown that CSRC had been negligent. CSRC sent an extraordinary letter to CSCA suggesting that it was CSCA's fault that expensive or delicate equipment was stored in the cupboard. The league had written to the organizers of the Bronowski trophy, proposing that the number of boards be reduced from 20 to 12, but it was clear that this would be rejected by the Bronowski Committee, who had recently reviewed the number of boards and decided upon 16. Civil Service were struggling to find 20 players, a sign of the changing times. It was decided to elect BE Glaze and AP Primett (both Inland Revenue) as vice-presidents. David Mills represented CSCA at CSSC's Annual Conference, seconding a proposal that organizers should be permitted to claim mileage rates at the same level as CSSC staff did, and that some allowance should be made for transport of equipment. Conference decided to pass the matter to CSSC's GPSC, who again decided not to change anything. They did however accept that some payment for transport of equipment might be allowed in special circumstances, and took the trouble to write to CSCA to explain the decision. CSSC had badgered the organizer of the national finals for a full report and photographs to be sent immediately after the event. Sadly, none of this information was published by CSSC and chess was as usual omitted from the forthcoming events section.

CHAPTER 7

1999 – 2016 Decline and Fall

The CSCA Committee met on 10th February 1999. Roland Smith had announced he would not continue as treasurer prior to the meeting. As nobody had volunteered except Chris Reeve whom the CSSC deemed to be ineligible, the chairman visited Marian Holmes and Hedley Featherstone at High Wycombe to discuss the way forward. Ian gave the CSSC three options:-

Chris Reeve be allowed to rejoin the CSSC and become CSCA treasurer;

CSSC provide a treasurer;

The CSCA ceases to exist.

After some discussion, Marian Holmes volunteered Hedley Featherstone to be the treasurer (much to his surprise). The Committee approved this course of action and said it would come into effect after the 1999 Annual General Meeting. Membership of the CSSC had fallen from 189 500 in 1992 to 165 000 in 1997. This trend continued, partly due to external factors, like the cut in civil servants, and longer working hours. Several years later, CSSC changed their rules, so that any former member could rejoin, and later changed them again so that existing members could recruit friends and family. However, as the rules were at the time, option 1 was clearly not possible.

The CSCA EC heard that the 1998 national individual finals had been played in a better spirit and did not have the nightly rowdiness. The league EC also met that night, as there was considerable overlap in personnel between the two committees. The EC agreed to the secretary's proposal to engrave trophies more often, in order to avoid the massive cost from the previous year. Somerfields (CSRC caterers) had placed a Notice of Proceedings in the County Court for non-payment of refreshment fees. The EC took offence at this action because the original bill had not been received, nor any reminder. The bill was now paid and Court action withdrawn. The chairman advised that a team had been entered into the Ralph Barnett Memorial tournament (a jamboree event for counties and leagues in London and surrounding areas) despite a veto by the EC. John Sargent denied this, saying that the entry was in the name of Westminster Chess. The secretary agreed to write to the organizer to ensure there would be no more confusion. CS had played in it many times before and the Ralph Barnett organizer might well have not noticed the change in the name of team. The chairman visited Marian Holmes, Chief Executive of the CSSC, at High Wycombe in another attempt to persuade the CSRC to provide special rates for the GLCC. However, Ian Pheby's attempt was rejected, again because GLCC was a non-CSSC club. The league EC met on 22nd April. The EC agreed that the creation of space on the Post Annual cup and Jesse Garner trophy for the purpose of engraving could not be justified. Contact between the secretary and Somerfields had been established, and a procedure for future bookings had been agreed. The EC agreed minimum entries for the team lightning (four teams) and individual lightning (6 individuals). Numbers had been falling off and it was illogical and expensive to run events with very few entrants. Divisional awards for the highest scoring player in each division were proposed by the chairman and agreed upon by the EC. The chairman proposed an annual match to be played as a curtain raiser to the new season between the Champions and The Rest. The EC agreed, and Richard Fries agreed to captain The Rest.

There was a close match between CSCA and RAF on 14th February 1999.

Royal Air Force		Civil Service Chess Association
1. AJC Hammond (w)	0-1	MG Shephard
2. AJ Toll	½-½	KJ Thurlow
3. PR Watson	½-½	A Maxwell
4. N McInnes	0-1	M Charter
5. P Martin	0-1	JN Fraser-Mitchell
6. M Donkin	1-0	I Lewyk
7. AJ Nelder	0-1	D Wolstencroft
8. A Foulds	1-0	IM Pheby
9. M Gilding	0-1	RP Archer
10. P Ball	1-0	D Baillie
11. M Morrison	1-0	MJ Rose
12. W Barkworth	0-1	DG Mills
13. S Fields	½-½	B Skinner
14. R Gates	½-½	SGP O'Neill
15. B Smith	1-0	A Ball
	7-8	

The match was scheduled for 16 boards, and CSCA were down to 13 players due to late withdrawals, but RAF had 17 players, and generously declined to claim the 3 defaults. They loaned us two players who appeared on boards 14 and 15 for CSCA. This is typical of the spirit in which these matches were played. RAF were out-graded on most boards so the close result was a credit to their team.

The 72nd AGM was held on 31st March 1999. CSSC (Hedley Featherstone) was confirmed as treasurer. The league EC was rather cross about failures in the BCF grading system and wrote to complain. New software had been introduced without consultation and the CS League grader had been unable to submit the results with the new software that had been imposed. As the league had already paid for the grading, it was pointed out that if the grading were not done, the league would want its money back, and that the league would no longer affiliate to BCF. BCF actually replied fairly quickly, with one letter from the office apologising profusely, and one from the chairman of the BCF saying that BCF would only grade the games if the league submitted the results correctly (!), although he conceded that the complaint from the league might be justified. Ultimately, the problem was sorted out, but near the end of the season. The author attended the BCF meeting with a mandate to propose 'motions of no confidence' in anyone associated with the system, but the matter was not discussed, as BCF had carried out their usual procedure of putting controversial matters late on the agenda so that there was no time to discuss them. An unusually poetic secretary stated in the league committee minutes that, 'Kevin attended the BCF meeting but because of filibustering tactics the meeting did not consider the motion of censure relating to the grading shambles'. The 5th league AGM took place on 27th May 1999. The author suggested that the League should have a website. The CS Recreation Centre had paid £86 compensation for the damaged clocks. The league treasurer resigned in December, and Chris Reeve (UNATS) took over on 2nd

February 2000.

CSCA had an exciting match against Insurance. CSCA's second board was the former Martin Shephard.

Insurance Chess Club		vs	Civil Service Chess Association	
(8th December 1999)				
1. DR Sedgwick	(w) 171	1-0	KJ Thurlow	179
2. AGC Paish	167	0-1	MG Walker	189
3. ID Hunnable	164	½-½	JN Fraser-Mitchell	178
4. MC Page	163	1-0	I Lewyk	168
5. DI Calvert	161	½-½	A Brusey	164
6. Default		0-1	C Bowering	164
7. AR Kent	149	0-1	P Robson	161
8. JH Aldred	149	½-½	R Archer	160
9. BW Atkinson	146	1-0	Default	
10. MR Wiltshire	145	½-½	I Thackray	132
11. GW Naldrett	126	½-½	BA Tysoe	138
12. K Parrott	109	0-1	GM Smith	136
13. DMP Burford	---	½-½	DG Mills	131
14. J MacNamara	98	1-0	AD Dalby	116
15. DSJ Shipp	96	1-0	J Barker	105
16. DJ Downing	79	1-0	M Roberts	---
		9-7		

The Committee met on 2nd February 2000. David Mills had wished to attend the national finals to recruit players for the CSCA team. The national organizer asked which day he intended to attend. It became clear that the captain wanted to attend for the whole event, but CSSC were not happy with that. David complained about the CSSC's objection to funding his stay for two nights at Devonshire Hall. The CSSC did not think three Officials were required, and it was up to the national organizer to decide who to invite. His decision as to who would be his assistant was fully justified and within CSSC Guidelines. All Sports and Recreation Bodies (SRB) would be reviewed by CSSC in view of the reduction in CSSC membership, resulting in lower income.

CS defeated a heavily outgunned RAF, who were not entirely happy with the mismatch.

Civil Service Chess Association vs Royal Air Force
(26th February 2000)

1.	AJ Ledger (w)	228	½-½	AJC Hammond	202
2.	KJ Thurlow	179	½-½	EJ Canham	153
3.	MG Walker	190	1-0	PR Watson	157
4.	AC Ashby	175	1-0	RW Kermeen	154
5.	D Wolstencroft	190	½-½	N McInnes	155
6.	AW Brusey	164	0-1	M Donkin	143
7.	IM Pheby	172	1-0	K Royce	101
8.	P Robson	161	1-0	P Ball	132
9.	R Archer	160	1-0	R Morris	---
10.	DC Baillie	149	1-0	D Johnson	---
11.	GM Smith	136	1-0	S O'Neill	74
12.	E Hazell	127	1-0	A Ball	71
13.	P Lewis	126	1-0	DI Dickson	87
14.	RE Dennington	121	1-0	P Batchford	---
15.	ID Strickland	116	½-½	DW Greentree	---
16.	B Skinner	118	1-0	T Cross	---
17.	AD Dalby	116	½-½	J Barker	105
			13½-3½		

There followed a thoroughly uninspiring match in the 'Plate' in the Eastman cup (organized by London League.)

Insurance (8th March 2000)		vs	Civil Service	
1. MCRich (b)	184	1-0	AC Ashby	175
2. DR Sedgwick	171	1-0	HJ Williams	150
3. D Malcolm	169	1-0	Default	
4. AGC Paish	167	1-0	Default	
5. I Hunnable	164	1-0	TB Packham	
6. MC Page	163	½-½	R Fries	142
7. DI Calvert	161	½-½	EW Godly	135
8. DIW Reynolds	156	0-1	AJ Mant	132
9. PR Barclay	156	1-0	E Hazell	117
10. DJE Harris	152	1-0	P Biggs	112
		8-2		

It actually got worse as both the top boards were ineligible for the competition, presumably because they had played for different teams earlier. There are so many competitions in and around London, that this is quite easy to do. Neither player would deliberately play if ineligible. The organizers decided the ineligible players cancelled each other out and took no further action. But the CS captain was obviously having trouble persuading the stronger players to participate.

The 73rd AGM was held on 16th March 2000. On the secretary's proposal, the author took the Chair as Ian Pheby was unable to attend the meeting. The CSSC took over responsibility for the financial affairs of the CSCA. The meeting noted the national individual tournament organiser's success in winning the championship. The league EC met on 6th April 2000. Chris Reeve presented a most comprehensive report of the accounts which had been produced from the unclear documentation of the previous treasurer. Chris received a vote of thanks for such an excellent job. The 6th Annual General Meeting of the league was held on 25th May 2000. Chris Reeve was formally elected as treasurer and thanked for taking on the post at such short notice. DETR apologized for the level of noise at some matches. Unfortunately, a nearby room was used for band practice! The league had 253 players (down from 290). There were 11 match defaults and 163 individual defaults, 10.6 % of the total boards. A proposal to reduce board numbers from 8 to 6 failed. UNATS dominated the season. The first team won the league and lost 4½-3½ to Eastern Knights in the Bonar Law final. UNATS II won division 3 and the Post Annual cup (which was open to Division 2 teams), and UNATS III won division 4 and the Jesse Garner trophy. All three cup finals were played on the same night, so practically the whole UNATS membership was needed.

Peter Chapman (CSSC) wrote to say how much he had enjoyed the 2000 CSSC individual tournament, and how well organized it was, which was pleasing to CSCA. He also commented, 'Apart from its relative ease of access, the large quantities of very good food provided by the Devonshire Hall chef seemed to go down well with everyone, and probably contributed to this venue's popularity.' Absolutely right.

The Committee met on 18th October 2000. This was the first joint meeting of the CSCA and the London Civil Service, Post Office and Municipal Chess League. Not only would time of the committee members be saved (most of whom were members of both committees), but also the cost of hiring the accommodation and the Game Fee affected both bodies. On the subject of Game Fee, FIDE were considering introducing a new system which would be limited to games where the minimum playing time is four hours, and a fixed fee per player would become mandatory. BCF grading problems continued with three lists published with the most recent 'only about 90% accurate' by their own admission. It was thought the Game Fee could be withheld either wholly or in part until we had confidence in the grading system. This subject was to be discussed at the next AGM. Game Fee charges totalled some £600 and the results had not been processed properly, so CS chess considered demanding its money back, and withdrawing from the BCF grading system. David Mills wished to stand for the CSSC Management Board, and it was agreed the CSCA would support him. The October *BCM* published a letter by John Allain, which noted that horses called 'Steinitz' and 'Smyslov' had run in races in early August. Having lost on both occasions, Mr Allain carefully did not back 'Schachmatt' (checkmate) a couple of weeks later, and of course it won. BCM revealed that Steinitz and Smyslov were both owned by Benny Andersson of ABBA and of course joint composer of the musical, 'Chess'.

CSCA had an interesting match with Insurance Chess Club.

Insurance Chess Club		vs	Civil Service Chess Association	
(9th December 2000)				
1. J Farrand (w)	184	0-1	A Ledger	225
2. D Sedgwick	178	½-½	KJ Thurlow	183
3. D Malcolm	171	1-0	AW Brusey	176
4. S Essen	165	½-½	D Roberts	174
5. MC Page	159	0-1	JN Fraser-Mitchell	170
6. DI Calvert	156	½-½	B O'Gorman	150
7. JH Aldred	145	½-½	MJ Rose	148
8. DG Cannan	140	½-½	B Skinner	125
9. GW Naldrett	130	1-0	E Hazell	128

10. AC Bullock	125	0-1	RE Dennington	122
11. RF Collins	109	0-1	M Coles	122
12. J MacNamara	99	0-1	M Zukunft	109
13. VJ Rosoux	75	0-1	D Green	---
		4½-8½		

The CSCA Committee met on 31st January 2001. It was agreed that David Mills should receive a float of £200. David Mills proposed a match against Hull & District League who were celebrating their 50th anniversary. However, funding could be a problem in view of the CSSC's position on the grant for representative matches. CSSC insisted that only three matches could be funded each year and they had to be against 'suitable' opposition. The league EC meeting discussed a dispute in Treasury v DHSS, where the home team was unable to provide the equipment and DHSS refused two alternative dates, 21st December and the first week of January. The EC awarded the match to DHSS. The chairman agreed to publish Civil Service grades in the *Handbook* in case there was a need to withdraw from BCF grading, which had experienced considerable problems over a significant period of time. The chairman then wrote (20/02/2001) to the BCF expressing concern with the grading shambles, mainly that results were not included and the grading list was published near the end of the season. He pointed out that the CSCA and CSCL expected the 2001 list to be published on time and to contain meaningful figures, and the organizations would seek compensation if results were omitted. The BCF director of grading sent a detailed reply, explaining that a lot of results were submitted late or incorrectly (without mentioning that the grading software frequently did not work!). He explained the 'benefits' of 'Game Fee', including, 'One of the benefits of paying Game Fee is being represented at BCF Council meetings.' Few people attending BCF Council meetings regarded it as a benefit. However, there was reassurance that the coming grading list would be much improved.

The 74th AGM was held on 22nd March 2001. The chairman paid tribute to deceased members, including Vice-President Denis Mardle CBE (GCHQ), who had been an adjudicator for many years. The treasurer's report was discussed. There were radical differences which could not be explained (at the time) for the comparative figures for 1999. Subsequently it became apparent that the CSSC favoured an unusual method of presenting accounts. The secretary suggested that future accounts contain explanatory notes. The accounts were adopted and signed. The Yorkshire Region of CSSC had provided £250 from their 'Special Needs Fund' for a coaching day given by Angus Dunnington. The term 'Special Needs' is now commonly used jargon for underperforming children. There is no reason to think that CSSC intended the term in a pejorative manner. It does show the problem with using jargon and buzzwords, instead of plain English. Richard Fries was elected to the new post of vice-chairman.

The league EC met on 11th April 2001. The team lightning had been cancelled because the controller had suffered a bereavement. There was discussion whether to apply a 'board fee' in the league, rather than a capitation fee. Clubs paid according to how many players were used, and some felt that the number of boards scheduled to be played was a better measure. It could be that teams would default a board, rather than pay for a player to make his first appearance of the season. This would be a real 'Game Fee'.

The 7th league AGM was held on 17th May 2001. It was decided to replace both the team and individual lightning tournaments with blitz events. Lightning events normally require a move every ten seconds, whereas blitz usually requires you to make all the moves in five minutes (say). Capitation fee was reduced to £3.00. John McAllister's suggestion about the introduction of a board fee was discussed, and the treasurer agreed to produce a discussion document for the next AGM. Mike Keohane (Treasury) asked the EC to reconsider insuring trophies. Ian M Pheby was elected as vice-president.

The CSCA Committee met on 11th December 2001. Following an informal meeting of the chairman with Hedley Featherstone, the grant had been increased from £8,000 to £10,000. Strict conditions applied, for example, no money could be carried over to the next year. The CSCA had not been invited to the inaugural CSSC Games because invitations were limited to sports which did not receive funding for travel and subsistence. The league EC also met on 11th December 2001 and it was agreed to scrap the 'Champions v The Rest' fixture as there was little support. The EC thanked John McAllister for setting up the league website. The EC agreed that tie-breaks for divisional awards be (a) player who played most games and (b) if still tied all players to receive full amount. The secretary proposed that all CSCA details appear in the *Handbook*, and this was agreed by the EC. GLCC asked for eligibility rules to be changed for their club, and it was agreed that members of various bodies working in traditional areas of the old GLC and LCC should be permitted to play.

A slightly unusual dispute occurred near the end of 2001. The away team arrived two players short, whilst the home side was missing its board 3. As the home board 6 did not have an opponent, he waited in Reception to escort any late arrivals to the playing room. Nobody realized he had done this, so at default time, both sides assumed he had defaulted as well, so board 6 was scored 0-0. He did return briefly to the playing area to offer to play the opposing board 3, who declined, so the board 6 headed home. When the home side realized what had happened, they claimed the default win on board 6, but the opponents demurred, saying 0-0 had been agreed. The committee voted 4-1 (1 abstention) that it was a win on default.

The February 2002 *Bulletin* reported that, 'Ian Pheby has just achieved the title of International Master (IM) in correspondence chess. Correspondence chess has some great advantages over conventional chess. You sit at home and play and you have an average of 3 days a move, not 3 minutes a move. However, it is hard work. Owing to the time available, opponents are much less likely to make stupid moves, so you have to put a lot of effort into grinding them down. If you make a mistake, you might spend several months defending a difficult position. Of course it can be expensive, and there can be long periods when you wonder if your Mexican opponent is ever going to reply, or if indeed your last move ever got there. So you need a disciplined and logical approach. The experts analyse the games whilst the moves are heading to and from the opposition.

Ian won the Social Correspondence Chess Association's (SCCA) championship and was invited to play in the Pat Thorn Memorial event, comprising 15 players from 12 countries. Pat Thorn was a former SCCA member and a Senior International Master. Postal chess has a title between IM and GM. Ian was seeded 13th out of 15, so expected a difficult time, but his first target was to score the required 9/14 to become an IM.'

The 75th AGM was held on 21st March 2002. The chairman paid tribute to Jerry Jordan (GLCC), who had died recently. It was confirmed that the CSCA could hold a maximum of 3 representative matches per year. The chairman discussed possible centennial celebrations of the CSCA, asking for an indication of possible financial support from the CSSC.

Hedley Featherstone responded by saying that the CSSC did not support anniversaries nor publishing books. However, the CSSC would provide a maximum of £3000 to fund special events which would give national publicity to CSSC. JM Sargent and DG Mills were made vice-presidents. The league EC met after the CSCA AGM and the treasurer's report on amending capitation fee to board fee was approved for submission to the AGM. The 8th AGM of the league was held on 9th May 2002. The chairman paid tribute to S. Yates, J. Jordan and Dr K Lovel. The EC had reviewed the cost of insuring trophies and found it to be prohibitive. There were only 23 teams in the league. The Jesse Garner trophy, a knockout competition for teams below division 4, was cancelled until further notice. GLCC and DHSS were level at the bottom of division 1 on match points and boards scored, but the individual match scores were GLCC 3-5 DHSS and DHSS 3½-4½ GLCC, so DHSS just survived. The AGM approved the treasurer's paper to introduce a board fee rather than continue with a capitation fee. John Sargent was elected as vice-president of the league. Centennial celebrations were discussed, including a possible jamboree, simultaneous display, book, etc. CSSC would only sponsor a congress where they were able to attract publicity for the CSSC. Of course, normal weekend congresses would be open to all, rather than restricted to civil servants. There had been plans to reclaim 'Game Fee' from BCF in view of the omission of CS results from the grading list. However, it appeared that the problems had been sorted out, so it was decided to defer the claim for another year.

Civil service chess players were sorry to hear that Roy Daines, a regular spectator and CSSC VIP at the individual championship finals, had resigned from Yorkshire Regional Council. He also announced he would resign his membership of CSSC (after more than 30 years) as he was disillusioned by 'recent headquarters policy decisions'. He was a good friend to CS chess.

The January 2003 *Bulletin* reported, 'About a year ago, I reported that Ian Pheby had achieved the International Master title (IM) for correspondence chess. This was a considerable achievement, but now he has done even better by gaining the Senior International Master title (SIM). Ian achieved his first SIM norm in the Pat Thorn Memorial event, and the second norm with a score of 10/14 (+7 =6 -1) (9½/14 required) in the 1st North American/Pacific E-Mail invitational event, where he will finish second, third or fourth depending upon outstanding games. The winner of the event scored 11/14 and was the only person to beat Ian.'

The CSCA Committee met on 6th February 2003. The chairman and secretary paid glowing tributes to Vice-President AP Primett (Inland Revenue), who had died recently. There was no representative of CSSC at the meeting. The chairman would write to CSSC explaining the importance of a CSSC representative being present at these meetings because no progress on the finances could be made in their absence. Peter Chapman (CSSC) had written a letter about the new arrangements for the regional qualifiers for the national individual tournament, i.e. a minimum of 6 players. The CSCA found the letter to be very disturbing, for it could easily exclude many regions and make the Finals a farce. The chairman agreed to write to Peter Chapman with copies to Marian Holmes and Hedley Featherstone. The treasurer proposed that the league could sponsor a centennial congress with a grant not exceeding £1500. The EC agreed to put the matter before the AGM. The EC agreed to recognize Roland Smith's service to Civil Service chess over the past 50 years. A maximum sum of £200 would be made available to Roland to purchase a suitable memento. £100 was donated to a local hospice in honour of the late AP Primett. The EC also agreed that his name should be honoured by linking his name to a memorial tournament.

David Mills was dissatisfied with the method used for listing names of those standing for election to the CSSC Committee. The CSCA gave him backing to challenge this at CSSC Conference. The election paper had carried the names of existing committee members, followed, looking like an afterthought, by anyone else wishing to stand. The CSCA Committee agreed that all names should be listed in alphabetical order.

The league EC met on 16th April 2003, where it was agreed that financial support from CSSC would be needed to support any simultaneous display. Another dispute had occurred earlier in the year. There was a massive time-scramble on one board, but both players reached time-control (move 36) safely and indeed 37 moves had been played. Then someone noticed that black had failed to get out of check on move 35. White wanted to resume the game at move 35 (the last correct position), but black pointed out that the session had finished. He offered a draw and pointed out that after the only move to get out of check, white had to establish equality of material, and after the re-capture, that was move 36 and black was slightly better. The captain of black's team said, 'White threatened black's king and black moved another piece. White did not say 'check', therefore black's king was not in check, therefore black's move was legal. On the other hand, the illegality lies with white and the present squabble flows from this. I submit that white be disqualified for illegal play.'

Incredibly, this came from an experienced captain. As white had declined the draw offer and 36 moves had not been made (the minimum required for adjudication) it was decided to score the game 0-0, and to explain the Laws of Chess to the captain. He had earlier caused problems when he had repeatedly placed himself on Board 1 in his team, when he was only in the team as he was captain, and all the other players were higher-graded. No opposing teams complained so his club escaped sanctions.

The 76th AGM was held on 16th April 2003. Ruth Bentley (CSSC) presented revised accounts but there were still a few outstanding queries. The meeting appreciated Ruth's attendance, and she agreed to send the chairman the final accounts. CSSC had shown over a period of time that they had not appreciated the need for cash prizes which were expected in chess tournaments, and that a Congress would be open to all not just CSSC members. Hedley Featherstone confirmed the CSSC position that they did not approve of cash prizes. It was agreed that 'colours' (for players representing CSCA in a number of matches) would consist of a navy-blue tie with a yellow rook. Peter Chapman's letter regarding a minimum of 6 players in a regional competition for qualification to the national individual final was raised again. Though Hedley Featherstone understood the difficulties, his hands were tied, and the minimum number would apply from the following season. The problem from the CSCA point of view was that five very strong players could play in a region and the event would not count, but twenty very weak players could play in another region and the CSSC thought this was wonderful and that players were only interested in representing their departments! On the plus side, players could now attempt to qualify in any region. David Mills complained about the inflexibility of the CSSC regarding carrying over unused grant to the following year. Kate Newbery (CSSC) did write (8th January 2004) saying, 'Please advise us if you wish to carry over funds from 2003'. Unfortunately, CSSC later said this was a mistake and that funds could not be carried over to the next year. It was noted that the author was retiring as National Championship Organizer after a period of 10 years. Upon hearing this news, Marian Holmes, Chief Executive of the CSSC, had written to the chairman indicating that a gift could be purchased to the value of £50. The meeting passed a very grateful vote of thanks 'for this valuable work'.

The 9th AGM of the league was held on 22nd May 2003. 22 teams had participated, fielding a total of 207 players. Roland Smith paid tribute to AP Primett and his obituary was published on the BCM website. The treasurer agreed to reduce the sizeable balance on the current account. The chairman made a detailed tribute to Roland Smith to honour his 50 years of service to Civil Service chess. Roland's multiplicity of offices totalled in excess of 120 years. Ian made a presentation to Roland, and the meeting showed its appreciation. The Bonar Law competition was reduced to six boards. One captain angrily complained about the board order in a division 1 match, but ended up looking rather foolish, as the opposition had two players with similar names (but vastly different grades), and the complainant wrote the wrong name down!

Combined Services Chess Association vs Civil Service Chess Association (19th July 2003.)

1.	AJC Hammond (w)	½-½	MG Walker
2.	KJ Thurlow	1-0	I Lewyk
3.	EJ Canham	½-½	F Bowers
4.	J Taylor	½-½	R Archer
5.	P Martin	1-0	P Robson
6.	P Watson	1-0	M Baker

7. D Johnston	1-0	GM Smith
8. A Nelder	0-1	G Lawrence
9. P Ball	½-½	G Yeo
10. K Emmins	½-½	M Coles
11. D. Ross	½-½	DG Mills
12. M Carbin	0-1	J McGranaghan
13. F Haynes	1-0	B Skinner
14. J Copsey	½-½	A Dalby
15. K Rigby	½-½	E Hazell
16. RM O'Harney	1-0	M Zukunft
17. T McCullough	½-½	I Strickland
18. S O'Neill	1-0	J Cattermole
19. S Bower	1-0	B Miles
20. A Ball	1-0	Default
21. F King	1-0	M Roberts
	4½-6½	

The observant reader will notice that the author played for Combined Services, courtesy of his first department, Ministry of Defence. The Civil Service did out-grade the opposition on most boards, so it was a good effort by the military team, and a 21-board match was the largest for some time between the teams. It was slightly confusing as both teams were 'CSCA'.

The national finals took place in Leeds as usual, and the chairman attended the prizegiving on 25th July 2003, rather surprising the author with a lengthy tribute for organizing the championship for ten years. This included a comment from Marian Holmes, Chief Executive of the Civil Service Sports Council, who said 'I am sorry to learn that Kevin has decided to retire. Kevin clearly deserves warmest congratulations for the time and effort he has expended on organizing the national finals.'. Ian concluded, 'I would like to present you on behalf of the Civil Service Chess Association with this gift. The inscription says 'AWARDED TO KEVIN J THURLOW FOR DEDICATED SERVICE TO THE CIVIL SERVICE CHESS ASSOCIATION 2003'.

The recipient of the award was deeply touched and somewhat embarrassed by these sentiments, as well as being unusually lost for words.

The October *Bulletin* reported another award. Ian Pheby wrote, 'Members will recall that I announced at the 2003 Annual General Meeting that I had proposed to the BCF that Roland Smith receive a BCF President's Award for services to chess. I am pleased to inform you that Roland has received this award, presented by Roy Heppinstall (BCF Chief Executive Officer) on 9 September 2003. Roland's wife and I attended the presentation. The award is fully deserved.

The proposal read (in part),

'In April 2003 Roland Smith will have completed 50 years continuous service as an officer for Civil Service chess within the Civil Service Chess Association and the London Civil Service, Post Office and Municipal Chess League. His record is quite outstanding; his record for Inland Revenue shows 23 years as first team captain, 30 years as secretary, 40 years as correspondence chess organizer, and 8 years as Inland Revenue national championship organizer.

He has been secretary of the London Civil Service, Post Office and Municipal Chess League for 10 years, and he has served the Civil Service Chess Association as secretary for 10 years and as treasurer for 2 years. Many of the above posts have been held at the same time. At the age of 72 he is still active in both of his posts as secretary for the Civil Service, together with his responsibilities for the Inland Revenue as first team captain, correspondence chess organizer, and Inland Revenue national championship organizer.'

Roland said at the presentation 'It is an honour I shall treasure'.

The league EC met on 3rd February 2004, where the chairman paid tribute to vice-president Peter Bond, who had died. There was an informal meeting between CSCA and CSSC in Beckenham, Kent on 24th February 2004. Those present were Ian Pheby (CSCA Chairman), Roland Smith (CSCA Secretary) and Kate Newberry (CSSC Event Team Manager). It had been agreed at the CSCA Committee meeting on 3 February 2004 that Ian and Roland would have an informal meeting with a representative of the CSSC to discuss ways in which Civil Service chess may be improved. The agenda for the informal discussions was as follows:-

Current CSCA activities and personnel.

CSCA needs and CSSC policy.

Future plans.

Item 1 - Current CSCA activities and personnel

Ian provided a brief history of the CSCA. He explained that prior to 1994 the CSCA was effectively the current London Civil Service, Post Office and Municipal Chess League. Since that date, two separate Bodies existed - the current CSCA and the LCSPO&MCL. It was pointed out that Roland and Ian served as secretary and chairman respectively of both Bodies.

Ian detailed the list of officers and committee members of the CSCA as follows:-

Officers - Ian M Pheby (Chairman), Roland Smith (Secretary), CSSC - Hedley Featherstone (Treasurer)

Committee members - Richard J Fries (Vice-Chairman), David G Mills (Representative Match Captain), Robert

Dennington (National Championship Organizer), Ray J Pomeroy (Correspondence Match Captain), David T Johnson (Grading Officer).

The current activities were

Three representative matches per year held in different locations in the United Kingdom incorporating all standards of play;

A national championship, the finals of which were held in Devonshire Hall, Leeds in July of each year;

Several teams entering correspondence chess tournaments run by the British Federation for Correspondence Chess (BFCC).

The CSSC provided the CSCA with a grant of around £8,000 per year in order to fund these activities. Part of the grant was allocated to funding the *Handbook* of the London Civil Service, Post Office and Municipal Chess League.

Item 2 - CSCA needs and CSSC policy

Discussions on the national championships took place. Chess players expected to win prize money if they were successful in a tournament. However, it was contrary to CSSC policy to offer prize money for any event. However, Kate did suggest the possibility of prizes *in kind* e.g. a weekend trip away as an alternative. Roland and Ian thought this was a possible solution to a long-standing problem. Kate would look further into this possibility.

The future of the national championships had been put in jeopardy by the CSSC Ruling that each Qualifying event must have at least six participants in order for two finalists to qualify. This Ruling would almost certainly mean that London Region (where so many strong players are based) would not hold a qualifying event for the 2004 Finals. Other Regions might similarly suffer. Kate was informed that for the Finals to be successful, at least six Regions would need to hold qualifying events i.e. the Finals would require a minimum of 12 participants. Kate acknowledged this to be a potential problem. She suggested that Robert Dennington (the new organizer) indicate as early as possible which Region(s) would not be holding events under the current rules in order that the number of participants required in those Regions may be relaxed for the current year. Both Roland and Ian welcomed this approach as well as Kate's further comment that the CSSC could consider a relaxation of the requirement of six participants to four for Chess if a case were forwarded to the CSSC.

Kate confirmed that a list of regional organizers had been sent to Robert Dennington by Finn Casey (CSSC). She also confirmed that the requirement to know the name of qualifiers at least three months in advance of the National Finals had been waived for Chess.

Robert Dennington had been informed that Devonshire Hall might not be able to host the National Finals after 2004. He was due to have further discussions with the venue in July. In the meantime, consideration for an alternative venue was required. Ian pointed out that any potential venue would need to be visited and arrangements made. This would be time consuming. Roland suggested Nottingham as a possibility based upon his experience of the Inland Revenue championships which were held there annually. Nottingham would certainly benefit from being a fairly central location, something which was necessary. Kate suggested that the CSCA provide her with a specification for requirements for the National Finals so that CSSC could assist.

Kate confirmed that contrary to her recent letter that any

underspend from the previous year's grant could not be carried forward to the following year.

Roland enquired about the draft accounts in view of the questions raised about them at the recent CSCA Committee meeting. Kate did not know the current position but would make enquiries. Roland and Ian provided details of the questions which were raised about the draft accounts.

Item 3 - Future plans

Centennial celebrations were again considered. It was disappointing that a Centennial Congress could not be held for various reasons. Whereas it seems that the CSSC did not previously think that a match between the CSCA and the LCSPO&MCL would be regarded as a 'representative' match, Kate thought that it would be a good idea if such a match could take place, effectively as a celebration of Civil Service chess. It is envisaged the CSSC would sponsor the event for the CSCA team members with the LCSPO&MCL sponsoring its team members. Roland and Ian thought this was an excellent idea. Kate would investigate the possibility.

The need for representative matches was discussed. Ian explained that these matches were not solely for the elite players as would be the case for some other sports but were designed for all strengths from International Master to novice. David Mills had often said that ideally, he would like a fourth representative match each year, and indeed there had been sufficient interest expressed for such a match. However, current CSSC policy stipulated a maximum of three representative matches each year. Kate suggested that if Chess were to have a fourth representative match each year the CSCA would require SLC (CSSC's Sport and Leisure Committee) backing. Kate suggested that the CSCA submitted a request to the SLC for 2005 onwards for four representative matches.

Kate suggested a way to increase membership and overall participation would be to produce an article for *Leisure Scene* (CSSC magazine). This could perhaps be a general interest story based upon representative matches, highlighting the range of abilities who play and why they enjoy participating.

Ian raised the subject common to all Committees, that there was a lack of interest within the membership to sit on Committees and the lack of an obvious successor for both Roland and Ian both of whom were likely to retire within a few years, and who probably have in excess of 250 man-years chess administrative experience between them on different Committees. Kate recognized this problem and suggested that a possible solution would be for the CSSC to act as a 'Committee' i.e. would carry out normal Committee duties but for Chess to elect a National Organizer who would decide CSCA policy. Whilst this suggestion was not dismissed out of hand, concern was raised that one individual would not necessarily represent the whole of CSCA's interests in the future, and that a proper Committee was still the preferred option if at all possible.

Ian enquired whether the CSSC had any new ideas about promoting chess in the future. Kate acknowledged that the CSCA members were the 'experts' and that CSSC would seek advice from CSCA members about what events they would like to see take place.

Conclusion

The meeting concluded with Kate and Ian expressing their appreciation to Roland and his wife for hosting the meeting and supplying a more than adequate spread for our consumption.

Kate felt that she now had a greater understanding of chess as a sport and the needs of the CSCA. Roland and Ian thought that the meeting had been worthwhile and that progress had been made on matters relating to representative chess in particular.

The 77th AGM was held at 22nd April 2004. The chairman read David Mills' letter dated 15th April 2004 and afterwards confirmed he would write to David to confirm the letter had been read. The contents of David's letter were as follows:-

Open letter to the Civil Service Chess Association Executive Committee

I wish to express my concern at the actions of the Executive Committee on 3rd February 2004 which culminated in the decision not to nominate me as delegate to CSSC Annual Conference 2004. The Executive Committee is at liberty to nominate whomsoever it wishes to represent the Civil Service Chess Association, however I believe that the ruling should be viewed in context. I suggest that the motives of those who supported this determination were questionable to say the least.

The Civil Service Chess Association Executive Committee has nominated me as its delegate to CSSC Annual Conference for about ten years. On each occasion I have tried to raise the profile and status of our Sports Body. This involved developing contacts with other delegates, liaising with officers and employees of CSSC and addressing meetings. In other words, I have taken the duties extremely seriously. After each Conference I have compiled a report for the Civil Service Chess Association Executive Committee. It was always described as a personal view and was published in *Time Trouble* and elsewhere as such with the approval of the Civil Service Chess Association chairman. Anyone who wishes to read the standard CSSC account of proceedings has that option, although I believe that by its nature the official account offers a rather bland version of events, lacking colour, passion and spice. My reports are forthright and seek to give perspective. I make no apology for calling a spade a shovel.

Prior to the last EC meeting copies of my report on the 2003 CSSC Annual Conference were forwarded for distribution to members. I anticipated that there would be discussion of the contents, my recommendations and in particular the matter on which I had been asked to address Conference – Imposition of Conditions on Governing Sports Bodies by CSSC Management Committee. This did not take place. The Civil Service Chess Association secretary made some general remarks about the report, explained what his wife thought of it – I do not know why this should be relevant – and voiced the opinion that he was not prepared to support my candidature on any future occasion as Civil Service Chess Association delegate to CSSC Annual Conference. I left the room to allow those present to discuss this matter freely but realized at that point the likely outcome and who would be voting to support the proposal.

Such events no longer come as a surprise although I had hoped that they were a thing of the past. The manoeuvrings of a certain Frank Krinks in the early 1990s regarding the Civil Service Chess Association Individual Championship spring to mind. Nevertheless, they are frustrating, given the amount of time and effort that I give to Civil Service chess at local, regional and national levels. I am of the opinion that the sentiments expressed in my report on 2003 CSSC Annual Conference are shared by a significant majority of the Civil Service Chess Association Executive Committee. They simply lack the bottle to express them in public. The Civil Service Chess Association Executive Committee has effectively dismissed an experienced delegate to CSSC Annual Conference without taking the sensible precaution of first securing a replacement! I have been asked to represent Hull Area CSSC at the 2004 CSSC Annual Conference and will make my report available should anyone wish to read it.

Yours sincerely

David G Mills.

It was reported that Peter Bond had left £1000 to Civil Service Chess and it was agreed that the legacy be equally shared between the CSCA and the London Civil Service, Post Office and Municipal Chess League. Peter had left money for CS chess and his will had not been updated since CSCA split into 'new' CSCA and the London-based league. The meeting was impressed with Peter's generosity. The informal meeting with Kate Newberry (details above) was discussed. The secretary asked Hedley Featherstone to consider increasing the number of qualifiers from a combined Region e.g. London/South-East. The 13th CSSC individual chess championship was discussed. The author reported, 'Problems arose with this event. The winner was John Wager. He quoted a CSSC reference number when he entered the London region event and when he qualified for the finals. I was also aware that Metropolitan Police had employed him as a civilian. Therefore, I did not check his membership details with CSSC. I did seek a membership number from CSSC for another player in the past, (who had lost his membership card), but was told they didn't know if he were a member (!), so again it did not seem worth asking. After the event, John informed me that he could not trace any debits against his account for CSSC membership, and subsequently CSSC declined to pay his expenses for the event, saying he was not a member. He did point out that they had continued to send him CSSC literature, even after he changed address, subsequent to leaving the CS. And as he left more than six months ago, they would not accept him as a member now. So, John is not a member of CSSC, and therefore ineligible to participate in the tournament. I am quite satisfied that this was an honest mistake on John's part - after all, he could have just kept quiet about the non-membership (and CSSC are not blameless). However, it does leave us with a problem.

John scored 4.5/5, Tony Ashby & Martin Walker 3.5, Tony finishing second on tie-break. John drew with Tony but beat Martin. He did not play any of those finishing on 3, but did beat Ken Norman in round 3 (who got 2.5), Paul Robson in round 1, and Colin Proctor in round 2 (both of whom scored 2).'

Various proposals were made about what to do, but before taking action, CSCA consulted CSCC. The latter agreed that they could have been considerably more efficient. In view of the fact that John thought he was a member and also that CSSC realized they had difficulties with their membership lists, and could not be sure he was not a member, they took the pragmatic path and allowed the result to stand. They even broke their own rules and allowed him to continue his membership from when he left the Civil Service. This seemed eminently sensible and everybody was relieved that worse problems were avoided. The author was not eager to disqualify John, (who had done nothing wrong), but assumed CSSC would insist on it.

The 10th AGM of the league was held on 20th May 2004. The chairman announced that he had nominated Roland Smith for the BCF President's Award, and that Roland had been presented with the award by Roy Heppinstall (CEO of the BCF), as above. The meeting expressed its appreciation of Roland Smith. It was agreed to hold a Simultaneous Display. Nigel Blades presented his proposal for a Centennial Congress. The meeting approved. A Sub-Committee reporting to the EC would be in charge of the Congress. This sub-committee met on 16th June 2004. The text for the Congress leaflet was agreed. The league EC met on 20th September 2004, where it was agreed to purchase a Phil Primett Memorial trophy. The chairman would invite the Rt. Hon. Charles Clarke MP (son of Sir Richard Clarke) and Marian Holmes (Chief Executive, CSSC) to present prizes at the Centennial Congress. Marian politely declined, and no reply was received from Mr Clarke. There was a long discussion about this book. Although the AGM had decided not to proceed with it, a mystery benefactor made a sizeable donation to ensure its publication. It was agreed to continue to publish Civil Service grades and those of the BCF in the Handbook despite the fact that some people felt this infringed the Data Protection Act. A simple statement that anyone playing a graded game was presumed to consent to their grading data being published solved this problem.

The Centenary Congress attracted 122 entries, 28 of whom had a connection with the Civil Service. This latter point had caused CSSC some concern, which was why they declined to support the event. CSSC initially thought the tournament would be restricted to members of CSSC, but it was always clear that there would be little point running it, if that were the case. The London CS League sponsored the event and it just about broke even, after a few late items of expense occurred. Alexander Cherniaev won the 'Open' with 4.5/5, David Ledger (UNATS) was 2= on 3.5, and won the Civil Service prize. Andrew Waters (Metropolitan Police) was one of three co-winners on 4/5 in the 'Major' and took the Civil Service prize. Sheila Dines scored a splendid 5/5 in the 'Minor' and Terry Hogan was 2= and won the Civil Service prize on 4/5. The London vs The Rest match had to be cancelled due to almost complete indifference from the London players.

Jon Speelman gave a simultaneous display on 22nd September 2005 to help celebrate the centenary. It was staged at Chadwick Street and CSSC kindly waived the booking fee of £280. Jon did a pretty effective demolition job, (29 wins and one draw), but was very friendly and chatty afterwards. London Region of CSSC decided to include chess in their annual 'Barbados Challenge'. The winner and runner-up won a heavily-sponsored week in Barbados for only £120 (partners could accompany them for the same amount) and played their opposite numbers. Sadly, the chess was cancelled as there were only five entries, which was unbelievably bad given what was at stake. Such apathy would hardly encourage CSSC to support chess. BTHQ were short of players and apologized for being unable to continue in the league. This was the year that HM Customs and Excise merged with Inland Revenue, so the league lost another club.

At the CSSC Annual Conference, Andrew Turnbull (Head of the Home Civil Service) said that, 'CSSC makes a significant contribution to CS efficiency' and:-

'Participation in activities gives a sense of inclusion

Sporting activities promote well-being and help reduce sick leave.

Relaxation makes for a happier work force'

His illustrious predecessor, Sir Warren Fisher, would doubtless agree, but senior managers a few grades lower probably would not.

The CS league website was revamped. John McAllister (BTHQ) had started it, but now handed over to James Toon (Home Office) and the site expanded significantly over the next few years. The site was nominated for 'BCF Website of the Year', but unfortunately did not win. James put a lot of work into the website.

CSCA played a few matches this year. In February, CSCA defeated Insurance 11 – 7 at Insurance's venue – the Civil

Service College in Belgrave Road, near London Victoria Station! The following month saw defeat in an away match to York and District Chess Association by 4½-11½. CSCA were only narrowly out-graded, so this was a good performance by the home side. CSCA travelled to Woolwich Barracks in June to play the Combined Services Chess Association. Civil Service emerged victorious 9½-6½, better than the grades would suggest. David Mills did a great job at getting these teams out, but it was clearly disappointing that only three players from London/South East made themselves available for the Civil Service team in the last match.

A league committee meeting was held 30th November 2005. The 2005 CS chess congress had been successful, and Nigel Blades and his wife Julia received a vote of thanks for the huge amount of work they had done. On the downside, the conduct of two players was regarded as unacceptable. It was decided to ban one of the miscreants from future events.

The CSCA AGM was held on 5th April 2006. Hedley Featherstone of CSSC explained that several sports bodies no longer had representative matches or national finals, but there might be regional activity, and that chess should go the same way. The AGM agreed that Ian Pheby, Roland Smith and Robert Dennington would meet Kate Newberry (CSSC) to discuss possible changes. The meeting took place on 16th October 2006, without Robert, who had a domestic emergency. CSCA then organized a survey of members, asking if they wanted to keep national finals, have rapid or blitz events, and if they had any other ideas. A small majority favoured a rapid event, blitz was not as popular, but classical chess was the favourite method, with a suggestion that the national finals would be better with stronger players. A question on representative matches did not attract an enthusiastic response, but it was generally agreed (by the few who offered an opinion) that two matches a year would suffice. This coincided with CSSC ideas, but CSSC also suggested that the national finals should cease in 2007. Robert Dennington had been running the National Finals for the last few years and felt sufficiently strongly about this to resign his membership of CSSC. The author stepped forward again to run what was meant to be the last National Final. CSSC were understandably very concerned over value for money, but withdrawal of support would lead to the end of the CSCA. CSSC were even willing to have cash prizes at rapid events.

CSCA played Insurance at York over two days. CSCA won 8½-1½ on the first day, and 6-4 on the second, with a number of hangover-induced short draws. One long game ended as a win for CSCA Captain David Mills against Insurance Captain Geoff Naldrett. David offered draws on moves 14 and 22, and Geoff offered draws on moves 27, 39 and 46, then went wrong and lost. If David had not been wearing earplugs, he would have accepted any of the draw offers. CSCA played the Combined Services at the splendid (but hot) venue of Whiteley Village in Surrey, with an exciting 8-8 draw the result.

Civil Service CA   Combined Services CA
(17th June 2006)

	Civil Service CA		Combined Services CA
1.	MG Walker (W)	0-1	AJC Hammond
2.	B McCague	1-0	KJ Thurlow
3.	G Harley-Yeo	½-½	P Doye
4.	FJ Bowers	0-1	SJF Walsh
5.	R Archer	½-½	JJ Kay
6.	S Appleby	1-0	S Lefevre
7.	D Baillie	1-0	D O'Byrne
8.	M Baker	0-1	A Foulds

9.	GM Smith	1-0	M Morrison
10.	M Coles	1-0	P Ball
11.	A Dalby	½-½	P Martin
12.	K Wood	1-0	S Field
13.	M Jones	0-1	AM Davies
14.	ID Strickland	½-½	H Brown
15.	J Cattermole	0-1	M Lake
16.	M Sant	0-1	A Ball
		8-8	

A trophy for the best grading performance in the London CS League was proposed in 2007 to celebrate a landmark birthday of frequent CS champion Tony Ashby. Roland Smith received a CSSC Merit Award. He had been turned down a couple of years earlier as his 50 years' service was apparently insufficient to win the award, but a sudden change of heart by CSSC ensured Roland received deserved recognition for his hard work.

A couple of years earlier, the London Commercial Chess League had approached the London CS Chess League, proposing discussion of a merger. There were a few issues to sort out. Both leagues owned trophies, so they would have to be divided somehow. CSSC provided some funding for the CS League, which would presumably cease when more non-civil servants joined the new league. Some clubs received funding from their Staff Clubs, which again involved CSSC funding, so that might cease. The composition of divisions would cause some problems, especially as some clubs played in both leagues. Some players played for different clubs in the different leagues. The leagues had different rules, and finding agreement on those would probably be problematic. LCCL and CSCL had a preliminary meeting, where all the above was pointed out by CSCL, which more or less terminated the discussion.

This year saw a change of approach by the CSCL, allowing players who had been members of clubs for three years to play in the league, even if they were not qualified in the usual manner. This was a far-reaching decision as it rather removed the point of the league if anybody could play. It might allow the league to last a little longer, but when the numbers of guest players outnumbered the traditional members, it was likely that the league would fold. The qualifying period was later changed to two years.

Insurance Chess Club V Civil Service Chess Association.
(21st April 2007)

1.	JT Farrand	0-1	C Walton
2.	ID Hunnable	0-1	R Archer
3.	DI Calvert	½-½	J Cooper
4.	DR Sedgwick	½-½	F Bowers
5.	D Malcolm	½-½	S Appleby
6.	MC Page	½-½	P Robson
7.	P Carlucci	1-0	D Baillie
8.	BW Atkinson	½-½	I Thackray
9.	GW Naldrett	0-1	DG Mills
10.	J Dowlen	0-1	M Coles
11.	J Cattermole	0-1	ID Strickland
		3½-7½	

The Insurance Chess Club had white on the even numbered boards. CSCA player J. Cattermole acted as a guest for them to balance numbers.

The 2007 national individual tournament took place, but the winner did not receive the Milner-Barry cup. The 2006 winner insisted that he had left the trophy in the venue the previous year. The then organizer insisted that the trophy had not been left there. The trophy has not been seen since. There were a few issues with a new CSSC staff member, who at least apologized for the problems, and said,

'Thanks for all your help. I do appreciate all the problems you have been having. With the changes that will be happening within chess, we hope that these will be rectified.'

This left the recipient wondering what was meant by that. We did not have to wait long.

2008 National Civil Service Correspondence Chess Championship (organized by Ian Pheby)

	IMP	WT	KJT	AD	NM	CM	Score	Place
Ian M Pheby	XX	11	1½	11	11	11	9½	1
Wilfrid Taylor	00	XX	1½	11	11	11	7½	2
Kevin J Thurlow	½0	½0	XX	11	11	11	7	3
Alan Draycott	00	00	00	XX	11	11	4	4
Nick Meekins	00·	00	00	00	XX	11	2	5
Colin Mair	00	00	00	00	00	XX	0	6

The tournament was not desperately successful. The bottom two dropped out soon after the start of the event, and Alan was somewhat outclassed, but fought bravely on to the end. The remaining triangular tournament decided the title.

2008 saw a proposal from CSSC to dissolve the CSCA and have an individual as 'National Organizer', as alluded to by Kate Newberry earlier. Ian Pheby and Roland Smith appeared to have been officers forever and both wished to step down. At the same time CSSC wanted to move away from formal organizations, especially where AGMs were poorly attended, and have an individual in charge who would seek assistance as necessary. They stressed that this individual would not be paid for his time and work, (and were affronted by the suggestion), but CSSC would send a report on him/her to their line manager! A number of people felt that having an individual in charge has its dangers. The individual might have too much power and make incorrect decisions as nobody was around to argue. However, the individual could just do things without being obstructed by committee members. You need the right individual. At the same time, CSSC advertised the post of National Individual Championship Organizer. The author held that post and initially felt the implied insult was good enough reason not to apply, but then decided that it would be amusing to send a full chess CV to CSSC. CSSC's advertisement closely followed a serious complaint from the author regarding the lack of assistance from some CSSC staff. The application was successful, but nobody else applied. The complaint was ignored. CSSC promised (letter from Kate Newberry dated 17th March 2008) that funding would be available to chess on a national and regional basis, and that all the trophies held by the London CS League could be retained by that league as long as it wished. However, no representative matches would be funded by CSSC that year. Kate Newberry was busy talking to various organizers within CSCA, but they all seemed to get different impressions about CSSC's plans.

The end of CSCA was not as easy as all that. The SGM was held on 2nd October 2008. There was strong opposition in some quarters, but a well-attended meeting (CSSC kindly paid travelling expenses for the more far-flung members) did see the motion carried, after some vigorous discussion. The cycle was complete. CSCA was formed in 1922 as part of CSSC and merged with LCSL in 1928. Apart from the short period where CSCA left CSSC in 1988, the bodies stayed together until CSCA and the London-based league separated in 1994.

Ian Pheby and Roland Smith finished their long association with CSCA. CSSC wrote to Ian Pheby (Chairman), saying in part, 'Quite apart from the many years that you have been central to the organization of chess within CSSC, I am also aware how carefully and skilfully you oversaw the process that led to the CSCA's disillusionment, first at the AGM earlier this year then at the SGM.' One hopes the reference to 'disillusionment' was supposed to read 'dissolution'! Despite other nice letters from senior members of CSSC and also the Head of the Home Civil Service, the CSSC still refused to honour Ian with a Merit Award. CSSC continued to fund some aspects of CS chess. Ihor Lewyk (Yorkshire) bravely took on the 'national organizer' job, and David Mills (Yorkshire) took on the post of match captain, so with the author running the individual tournament, a trio of Yorkshiremen was running Civil Service chess nationally. The London-based organization carried on as before. At the CSSC Annual Conference, the Chairman uttered the stirring words, 'As a unifying feature of the Civil Service, CSSC's methods of organization are altering to reflect changes within the Civil Service. We need to continue to be a leader in sports and leisure provision. The Civil Service as a whole benefits from those who volunteer their time and efforts.'

Sadly, over the next few years, sporting activities received less and less support. More emphasis was given to art and crafts (which of course are worthy activities) and discount vouchers.

2008 Individual Blitz Tournament

Nigel Blades reported,

Thirty league players took part in the annual CS Individual Blitz tournament, held at the CS Recreation Centre (Chadwick Street), on Thursday 11th September 2008, 6.45 pm – 9.30 pm. The tournament was run as a 10 – round Swiss, 5 minutes per player per game.

Arne Eilers (Metropolitan Police) was the winner on tie-break from Martin Walker (Revenue & Customs), both players finishing with 8½/10. Arne well deserved his victory, having started on ferocious form with six straight wins, before faltering in rounds 7 and 8. Arne recovered well to win his last two games. Martin also had a run of six straight wins in the latter half of the tournament, but finished with a lesser sum of progressive scores. Arne defeated Martin in their individual encounter.

The tournament was played in a competitive but friendly spirit and included several players new to the league, in one of the highest turnouts of recent years. Several league players also came to spectate. Nigel Blades controlled the tournament using a laptop running 'Swissperfect' software displayed on the plasma screen in the Greycoat Room.'

The presence of 30 players was very encouraging. In the mid-70s, entries totalled about 50, but over the next 15 years, the tournament dwindled so much that it ceased to exist.

Ian Pheby received an ECF President's Award for services to chess in 2009, having been a tireless worker for chess for about 40 years. Ian was presented with his award by Stewart Reuben (ECF Director). Highlights included

London Civil Service, Post Office and Municipal Chess League

Committee member since the early 1970s, including individual tournament organizer, grader, league recorder, then senior recorder. Production of the *Handbook*, which contained club details, fixtures and rules, which was supplied to all players in the CS League. He was vice-chairman 1984-88, chairman since 1989, and vice-president 2000 onwards.

Civil Service Chess Association (the National body)

Vice-chairman 1984-88, chairman 1989-2008, vice-president

2000 onwards. He also prepared the budget and applied for grants from Civil Service Sports Council for last few years.

International Correspondence Chess Federation

Tournament director 2006-present, member of the BFCC Committee who organized the 2009 ICCF Congress in Leeds, and presented with his International Arbiter title at the 2009 ICCF Congress.

There were numerous club credits as well.

2008-2009 showed the league was continuing to shrink. In the past 25 years the number of clubs had decreased from 21 to 11, teams from 55 to 20, and players from 613 to 196. In the 50s, there had been over 1000 players. Ian Pheby produced a consultation paper, suggesting a number of ideas for the future. These included a team grand prix blitz event, a rapid-play league, a grading-restricted minor league, and another restructuring of the league. The first three ideas were well-received at the time. Chess was included at the CSSC Games at Loughborough, with Ihor Lewyk as organizer, and these events continued in alternate years.

After some rather heated arguments over the years about eligibility, CSSC recognized that membership was declining and changed the rules, so that any CSSC member could invite three people to become CSSC members, even if they had no connection whatsoever with the Civil Service.

UNATS had problems when a security guard refused to allow visitors into the venue despite having the appropriate team lists. This was becoming an increasingly frequent occurrence. Luckily, the match was a meaningless mid-table clash, and the teams sensibly agreed a draw. Pimlico (the former Home Office) kindly stepped in and offered UNATS a venue share.

CSSC announced the closure of the Chadwick Street

Recreation Centre, which caused the CS League problems. All General and Committee meetings were held there and chess equipment was stored for the various speed chess tournaments. The CSRC staff and many users were very unhappy at this decision and CSSC called a special meeting to discuss the matter, at which they announced that the building had already been sold and the bulldozers would arrive in early summer, which largely rendered the meeting pointless. As it happened, the building was still standing three years later. There were complaints at the meeting that the accounts contained errors, for example, national chess expenses being wrongly marked as charged to regions. The Vice-Chairman of the CSSC London Management Board (Ian Hughes) wrote to the Chairman of CSSC (David Bell) complaining that CSSC was refusing to give the real reasons for the closure of Chadwick Street, adding, 'that there was a real feeling of betrayal in the meeting, and much bewilderment expressed that CSSC is riding rough-shod over so many of its members'. Many of the people attending (including Roland Smith) suggested that CSSC membership would plummet as a result. David Bell had previously written to Sir Gus O'Donnell (Head of Home Civil Service) on 21st January stating, 'The CSSC Management Board has decided to close CSRC by June 2011. This will release funds for an enhanced, and more widely distributed, programme of activities in London.' How closing the main CS venue in London could be considered an improvement mystified many people. Strangely, CSSC had emailed CSCA on 22nd February saying that the 'proposed' closure would be discussed at the special meeting. Possibly they had forgotten that the decision had already been made. Of course, CSSC would make rather a lot of money from the sale of a large building in London SW1. *Hansard* reported that the cost of running 1, Chadwick Street was £148,655 in 1996/97. The local Planning Department turned down a plan to build 46 flats on the site, but seem to have changed their minds, (or were overruled), and one of the flats sold for more than a million pounds a few years later.

The Civil Service Club agreed to store the chess equipment cupboard, and reduce subscriptions significantly (by more than 50 %) for CSSC members. Room hire was higher though. It was hoped CSSC would assist with that, but sadly that was not to be.

The 2011 AGM saw enthusiasm for the proposed minor league (intended for players graded under 120) and also the rapidplay league. Despite the theoretical enthusiasm, insufficient entries were received for either competition to take place. The author was honoured with an ECF President's Award, which was presented by CJ de Mooi (the President) before a simultaneous display by Nigel Short. Ihor Lewyk (Yorkshire) received a President's Award the following year, and Carl Portman (ex-Ministry of Defence) followed in 2015.

More problems for CS chess came when ECF re-introduced a compulsory membership scheme in 2012. Many players played only in the CS League, so the thought of paying more money just to play a handful of games upset some of them. CSSC announced that the national individual championship should be run as an open event in future. Anybody could play in the finals, but would have to apply for funding from their region, (with no guarantee of getting anything) or pay their own expenses. Ihor Lewyk and the author pointed out that there were many weekend events in the country, some with significant prize money, and it was unreasonable to expect players to pay significant expenses to attend the CSSC event, when there was no prize money. Some qualifying events had already taken place and it was a bit much to say they now did not count. Ihor explained that some players did not play in the CSSC games due to excessive cost, and he had played week-long events overseas which cost only slightly more than two nights at the CSSC games. The author commented that it was too late to organize an 'Open' event, and if we booked a large venue, and only got six entries, that would be costly and look silly. If we stuck with Leeds University, and had hundreds of entries, that would be swamped. We proposed continuing as usual for one more year. CSSC replied with a suggested compromise of running a 'hybrid' event where qualifiers would be funded as usual, but others could enter if they wished. It was agreed to do this. It did complicate matters for the organizers and Leeds University, as local players would probably commute and would only be charged a 'day rate', whereas those requiring overnight accommodation would pay a higher rate. As it happened, only the 12 qualifiers participated.

CSSC announced in late 2012 that representative matches in all sports would not be supported in future. Several members complained but received no reply. In early 2013, CSSC slashed the grant to CS chess by around 75 %, so that it became unrealistic to run the national individual finals in the usual form. CSSC discarded the qualifying events and wanted to run an 'open' competition, as outlined above. Experienced chess organizers recognized that such a system would discourage entries. The author explained again how the event had been run throughout its existence and the CSSC response was, 'Unfortunately, we are not aware of the arrangement that Kevin has outlined below and this approach would need to be approved by the SLC as it is a departure from CSSC's current policy.' The author pointed that good record-keeping was recommended. This was a regular occurrence. CSSC would claim something was 'policy' and if anyone said, 'Why not tell us if you change things?',

CSSC just denied there was a change. Admittedly, they had such an extraordinary turnover of staff, that they might genuinely not know what had happened before. The 2013 Civil Service individual championships were held, but with only eight players, some commuting, and some staying at the venue. Some of the players did receive assistance from their regions for the expenses. Only the organizer and the arbiter received expenses, and yet a CSSC official complained about the expense of the event, saying that all the expenses were still attributable to CSSC, which was not true. The organizer quietly resigned his post. Further reductions to the budget made it very likely that the event would not be run again. However, Ihor Lewyk managed to stage it in Edinburgh in 2014. Eventually, even he gave up the losing battle, although not before winning the title himself. There had been other problems with the event. CSSC had been very helpful in ordering the individual trophies for presentation to the prize-winners. The trophies were then sent by courier to the organizer's home. One year, the author got home from work and discovered a card saying a delivery had been attempted but nobody was in. The author set off on a 10-mile journey to collect the trophies. The report to the EC continued, 'The couriers turned out to be hidden in an industrial estate near Gatwick Airport. When I eventually found it, I was told that the couriers had actually left the trophies with my next-door neighbour. I expressed disappointment that the card had not actually said this. The person at the counter apologized. I went home again. Luckily, my neighbour was actually off work that day, so I got the trophies and set off somewhat late for Leeds. The following year, I got the same message that they had attempted delivery, but nobody was in. Having first asked my neighbour, I then set off on the 10-mile journey to collect the trophies. Unfortunately, the courier would not release the trophies as the name on the order form was Tom Power (CSSC). 'Yes, I know. He ordered them but arranged for them to be delivered to me.' This made no difference. Tom rang the couriers the next day, to authorize the author to collect the trophies, but they would not accept that either, so Tom drove the 60 miles from High Wycombe to Crawley, collected the trophies, left the box in the author's porch in Redhill, Surrey, (which the couriers could have done in the first place) then drove back to work. What a splendid attitude!'

The following year, the author said, 'Please use a different courier this time!' Tom agreed immediately.

90 years after CSSC welcomed chess into the fold, the last few years had seen ever-decreasing support and the final curtain fell with a resounding thud. In fairness to CSSC, their funding from Government had reduced considerably, to an extent that Sir Warren Fisher must have been spinning in his grave, but if no activities were funded, there seemed little point having the CSSC. From a Government point of view, they were reducing funding in a number of areas, and CSSC did own valuable properties, so there were obvious advantages to shutting down sports activities within CSSC. Their attitude to chess did not improve. A search of 'chess' on the CSSC website showed in order, the Hampton Court Flower Show, Chessington World of Adventures and a Rapidplay chess tournament at the CSSC Games.

The great majority of CS chess has been played in an honest sporting way, but there were occasionally humorous, unfortunate or unpleasant incidents. Some of these have been reported already, but there are some where it is better to conceal the date where they occurred, to avoid unnecessary embarrassment. Chess can be a tense affair. One fairly senior player was clearly winning his game and struggling to find the killer move.

Unfortunately for him, he then lost on time. When this was pointed out to him, he burst into tears. In an incredible act of sportsmanship, the opposing captain suggested to his player (who agreed), that as the match did not depend on the game, why not agree a draw? Security has increasingly and understandably caused problems at various venues in recent years. The author approached Scotland Yard on a showery night, clutching a furled umbrella, and was rather alarmed to see the PC on guard outside the venue reach for his gun. Luckily, he changed his mind. For a fleeting moment, the author wondered if the home team had circulated descriptions of their likely opponents and this was an attempt at intimidation. More common problems surrounded security guards at various venues denying that they had the list of players for a match, even when said list was clearly visible on their table.

One player always turned up a couple of minutes before default time, as a tactic to distract his opponent, but miscalculated once and arrived too late. For some reason, he then ranted at everyone else about his misfortune. Another player was a serial defaulter. One of his regular opponents commented that he had a -6 score against the defaulter, but if you included the defaults, he had a plus score. The same player (having been defaulted against yet again) went home and was outraged to be told that the defaulter arrived at the venue an hour or so later and accused him of being rude for not waiting for the defaulter to arrive to make a personal apology. One player became irritated by his opponent's frequent draw offers. Having politely declined the first two offers, and curtly saying 'no' to the third and ignoring the fourth, he answered the fifth draw offer with, 'No I don't want a bloody draw. I'm winning easily.' The opponent went a rather becoming shade of deep red. One player found himself playing a blind opponent. Nine boards were played in silence and occasionally someone spoke at the other board to announce a move. Play carried on for a while until the sighted player announced, 'Pawn takes queen, equals queen, double check.' The remaining players crowded round the board to have a look. One player bought a more-convincing wig every time he got promoted at work. Another cracked a whip in front of his opponent at the start of a match. The opponent complained this was intimidation. The whip-handler calmly coiled the 20-foot American bullwhip and handed over a copy of the Laws of Chess and asked the opponent to find where the Laws stated that use of whips before a match was illegal. The War Office was a popular venue in the 50s as it had a bar open at reduced rates in the venue. Many a player would have to look at his score-sheet the next day to find out how he had fared. Strange things happened at the league committee. One secretary felt that a league recorder was incompetent so instructed him to resign. One treasurer got in the habit of ordering the chairman to call 'next business' if he did not want a matter discussed. You would think chess players and civil servants would be somewhat staid. One former committee member had a near-fatal heart attack. Happily, he recovered but when we met at a tournament, he miserably explained that he was doomed to eat boiled fish and salad for the rest of his life. We met again a couple of years later and he bounded into the room clutching a burger and sporting some new tattoos. He said he would have died of boredom on the fish/salad diet, so now he enjoyed burgers, cannabis and getting new tattoos. Surprisingly, he lasted quite some time after that, although one cannot commend his lifestyle choices.

The league had been running for over a hundred years and there were many changes. At the dawn of the twentieth century, many of the country's leading players were civil servants, based in London, and the working hours were clearly defined. The London League was running already, but there were not too many other leagues, and very few tournaments, so the CS League offered chances to play competitive chess in convenient and pleasant locations. The league grew over the years, although the two global conflicts brought proceedings to a temporary halt. The league was at its height in the early 1960s, when there were nine divisions. The 1970s brought a number of changes. The number of weekend tournaments started to grow and professional players began to appear on the scene. There were now many successful county leagues and far more opportunities to play chess. Top class players were now largely absent (with a few notable exceptions) from the Civil Service. Successive Governments decided to disperse the Civil Service so that a number of Head Offices were situated far from London. Pay and working conditions deteriorated, so that a career in the CS became less desirable. Pressure was increased to foster a more 'professional' attitude, so that staff were expected to do unpaid overtime, and the numbers of those staff were reduced dramatically. Paradoxically, the growing number of labour-saving devices did not mean that people had more free time. There were many demands on what free time there was. As the new millennium approached, online chess became attractive, as people could play when they wanted. Clubs struggled to find new members, and existing members found it increasingly difficult to commit to a 6.15 and subsequently 6.30 pm start on a specific date. An eight-board team could not function if there were only about a dozen players. Teams folded when there were still enthusiastic players, just not enough of them. Over the years, the league tried to prevent the decay. Teams were reduced in size from ten boards to eight or even six. Eligibility requirements were eased, which has caused controversy. Both

CSSC and the league had stringent eligibility rules which have disappeared. Rules were changed so anyone could play in the CS League if they had been a member of a club for a short qualifying period. These and other ideas slowed the decline, but the signs were not good. Some players felt that if the CS League were completely open, it would lose its appeal. Fewer people were playing competitive chess in this country, and too many competitions were trying to attract the same players. The league needed a major injection of new players. The Committee continued to propose new rules to try to encourage more people and teams to play.

A document entitled *The Future of the Civil Service League* (dated 1st April 2014) was circulated to clubs. This commented that only 170 players and nine clubs participated in the league and numbers were likely to decline further. Additionally, there were many committee members and trophies and the rules were too complicated. Various options were suggested; (a) recruit more committee members, (b) stop the league, (c) start a new league with no committee and just a few rules. After some comments were received, the 2014 AGM decided on a completely new arrangement, and title, 'London Public Service League', with a much-simplified set of rules.

The eligibility rules were changed dramatically, for the first time in over a century, and this marked the end of the Civil Service League. The fines and penalties which were so necessary in the past were eliminated, demonstrating a rather touching faith in the present-day clubs and their officials. Evening leagues have struggled throughout the country, and opening up the league to all comers was probably the only way it could continue in some form.

The Civil Service League lasted 110 years, with breaks during the two world wars, and had good times and bad times. The glory days have long gone, but those involved will never forget them.

ANNEX

Articles by E C Baker, M.B.E.

Edward Cecil Baker, M.B.E. held various posts within the Civil Service Chess Association, namely secretary (1948-1951), additional committee member (1951-1956), vice-chairman (1956-1958), and chairman (1958-1965). Together with Harry G Poor he was instrumental in starting up the Association again after the conclusion of the Second World War. In recognition of his service to the Association he was made a vice-president in 1968. He died in 1997, aged 94.

The following text was sent to the *Bulletin* editor (Kevin Thurlow) in the 1980s and was published in the *Bulletin* as a series of articles. It provides a most illuminating informal history of the Civil Service Chess Association. Some of the recollections are very sad.

****

The human race to which so many of my readers belong – as G. K. Chesterton once wrote – has a great advantage over other mammals for, thanks to words the memory of a human being is not restricted to personal experience. He can profit from the recorded memories of others. The past is on top of us and with us all the time. An egoist who thinks that everything worth considering resides within himself is unaware of Michelet's truism, 'He who would confine his thoughts to the present time will not understand present reality.'.

What brought that on? Vague references in recent issues of our *Bulletin* such as a paucity of information on J. Ansell, a comment on WEC Richards' services as being over 'a very long time', the suggestion that I once edited our *Bulletin*, stimulates me to add to our Corporate memory. Series of fact and figures will not increase our *Bulletin's* undoubted attractions but informality and truth (so far as memory and tact will allow) should not be unpalatable.

Every member will welcome the latest additions to our vice-presidents; C. A. Roeder served as senior recorder, team competitions, from 1964 to 1982. S. N. Owen of H. M. Customs filled that post during the 1963-1964 season, when I was listed as chairman, whereas our vice-chairman ran our Executive Committee then, since I was in America. W. E. C. Richards, the Patent Office captain, undertook adjudications when we resuscitated our Association in 1946 and did so until 1984. He succumbed to C. G. Butcher (GPO) in our individual championship that year. Butcher had been transferred from Birmingham – where he was Midlands champion – to London during the War, and retained that title during the next two seasons. We did not present the Barstow cup to him for it was missing. My eventual discovery and retrieval of it proved to be a poignant experience.

One of our members wrote recently of a number of our stronger players serving in Cheltenham during the War. C. H. O'D. Alexander (formerly with the John Lewis Partnership) was appointed to the Foreign Office where he had to recruit a team to break codes; he decided that chess players were the most likely to possess the mental abilities needed. Their contribution is described in a 1984 Penguin paperback '*The Hut Six*

Story' by G. Welchman, and need not further concern us here.

Chamberlain's declaration of War in 1939 brought our activities to an abrupt close. That we got going again as early as 1946 was mainly due to Harry G. Poor. That cheerful and determined little man had retired but was full of energy which he spent on painstakingly getting in touch with 1938-1939 Club Officers, and before long he had set them to pursue the even tenor of their pre-War ways.

J. E. Neale reorganised the GPO Club, swallowing up the old Denman Street (London Bridge) Club – for which I had played – in the process. I was elected club captain, and Neale took me with him to our AGM which closed the 1946-1947 season.

Things had not gone smoothly. The War had swollen the Civil Service, and personnel changes were continual. Before the War, club Secretaries arranged fixtures among themselves on an ad-hoc basis, which had served well enough then. I was smarting from having recently played in three matches on three nights running, Neale pleading that these fixtures were the best arrangement he could make. Incautiously, I held forth at the meeting, pointing out shortcomings the past seven months had brought to light. With little ado, and to my consternation, the meeting voted me into the post of honorary secretary.

The name Berkeley Square recalls London's finest plane trees – 30 of them – which girdle a green lawn overlooked on three sides by dignified houses. Philistines had destroyed those of the fourth (east) side in 1937 to erect Berkeley Square House, an agglomeration of pretentious plate-glass showrooms for luxury motor cars topped by a block of offices served from an overlarge concourse by a battery of lifts. The Square had been laid out in 1689 and the trees planted 109 years later. Came 1940 when the Government requisitioned those new offices, in one of which seven years later your Executive Committee was meeting at 5.30 pm on most Friday evenings, that room was Chairman A. G. Pockett's office. The half-dozen of us were Harry G. Poor, R. C. S. Taylor (Assistant Paymaster General), Harry Hoskin (Admiralty), Fred M. Norman (Captain), Jesse H. Garner (Treasurer) and your secretary.

We agreed that my immediate task was to produce a fixture list for 1947-1948, despite objections from Pockett who saw no merit in a departure from pre-War practice – seemingly unaware that a comparatively small static Civil Service, in which all chess club officials were well known to each other, no longer existed. One could urge in his defence that although he was attached to the Ministry of Transport, his official function was to run a Civil Service benevolent institution. Thus he had been isolated from the rapid expansion and resulting turmoil we had experienced.

A single roneo'd sheet sufficed for dates, venues, and the telephone numbers of secretaries and captains. As I recall, we only had three divisions with eight boards for the senior teams. Match results were published in the Civil Service Sports Council's *Journal* (a penny monthly). The Council's live wire Secretary, J. H. Middleton, had already resuscitated 'representative' matches in cricket, rugby, and soccer against Army, Navy and Air Force teams, the Council paying its own teams' expenses. Fred Norman felt that Chess should be similarly recognised but such teams as the fighting services were likely to muster would be sitting ducks. Traditionally, Oxford and Cambridge held an annual London chess week on the Friday evening of which, the eve of their inter-varsity match, they combined to play a Civil Service team. They could provide two opponents, and we had not far to look for the third – London University. Middleton warmly supported us, and

Council agreed to pay rail and road expenses of our team of 25 for three matches each season. In common with other representative teams, a player participating in all three matches during a season was entitled to a CSSC blazer pocket badge (with CHESS added in gold wire). I recall only two members wearing that badge – P. B. (Pip) Sarson and P. R. Vivian. The rest of us had invested clothing coupons in sports jackets. Non-subscribers to CSSC and non-civil servants were not eligible for representative matches although Norman included some in other matches he organised. Middleton also lent us £300 to replace equipment we had lost during the Blitz.

To herald our 1948-1949 season, I published our first printed annual *Handbook*. Three of its modest 16 pages were allocated to Rules and six to fixtures. Our progress in a twelve-month period had been remarkably rapid: 23 Clubs were fielding 46 teams in five divisions with ten boards for teams in divisions 1 and 2.

The *Handbook*, I later learnt, made an unforeseen contribution to inter-departmental efficiency. A pre-War music hall joke was that if one wished to cut oneself off from the world one had only to enter a public telephone kiosk and try to make a call. Frequently during 1948-1949 a colleague must have remembered that old joke when an attempt to get in touch with an appropriate officer in another department could lead nowhere. It seemed that an inexperienced switchboard operator had put his caller through to the first number coming to mind whereupon at two or three minute intervals (they seemed longer) his call was returned to the switchboard and out to another extension to no purpose. He felt that he was in the reign of Chaos and old Night. But the resourceful officer approaches his chess club Secretary. 'I say, old chap, you were playing the Department of Duskiness 'tother evening. I want to get in touch with someone there who is responsible for such-and-such.'. 'Leave it with me' says our stalwart wood-shifter. He consults his copy of our *Handbook*, rings his opposite number in Duskiness and is soon furnished with the required name and number.

Our history as an organisation did not begin in 1922 under the aegis of the newly formed Civil Service Sports Council. Minerva may have sprung fully-armed from the brain of Jupiter but our departmental chess clubs were fully organised and competing with each other long before the Sports Council came to power. We are as old as the British Chess Federation formed in 1904. In that year we brought into operation the London Civil Service and Municipal Chess League. Derived from the London League (formed in 1887) in which one or two of our clubs probably participated from the outset. In those days, bank and insurance company employees together with civil servants had an advantage over other workers in London; they left their places of employment earlier. Naturally that led in a few years to the formation of the London Early League. Nor did one change suffice, hence the hiving off in 1904 of a league restricted to central and local Government employees. Seemingly we started with two divisions and included clubs from the London County Council and the Metropolitan Water Board.

Notwithstanding changes the Sports Council required of us, we made none to that league. Thus it continued – apart from two wartime hiatuses – to the present day. Long may it flourish! Our wisdom in 1922 has given us a good precedent for dealing with subsequent changes in the status of certain departments.

In 1904 the Admiralty fielded the strongest team and repeated its winning of the league's first division two years later. Other winners to 1926, less 1916-1920 when War halted our activities, are:

Patent Office	1907, 1911, 1926, 1928 (equal with Admiralty);
GPO	1908, 1910, 1912, 1915, 1920;
P.O. Savings Bank	1909;
Inland Revenue	1913, 1914, 1923;
Board of Education	1921
Ministry of Health	1922, 1924

I notice, from a souvenir booklet, that R. P. Michell (born 1873) of Admiralty, and E. G. Sergeant (born 1881) of Inland Revenue, were in a London team of six players in the first chess match between London and Chicago, using a trans-Atlantic cable in 1926, and that W. Gooding of P. O. Savings Bank had been short-listed.

Mr. J. Du Mont edited a selection of R. P. Michell's games which Pitman's published.

When he was well into his seventies E. G. Sergeant continued to participate in league matches for Inland Revenue's first team.

A hazard which once confronted our team captains all too frequently may have been forgotten by their successors; it was the invasion of London's highways and byways by fog. As recently as 1952, during the Smithfield Market's Live Cattle Show a fog suffocated many of those beasts together with four thousand Londoners. That disaster led to the Clean Air Act of 1956. After another six years London had no more noxious fogs. The hazard had lain not so much in pulmonary perils as in disruptions to commuter train services: 'Get home as soon as possible' was the order on a foggy evening. Thus upon the forecast of such weather the captain of an away team for that night's fixture would ring his opposite number in the morning to postpone the match.

At one of our Council's meetings in 1950 we had to consider a claim by the Ministry of Transport's captain that Air Ministry had defaulted and should forfeit match points. Both captains had conferred on the morning of the match but had emphatically disagreed on the likelihood of a fog that evening. Our problem was complicated by their continuance of that argument in Council, for the respective captains were P. B. (Pip) Sarson and A. G. Pockett. Pip was a Met. Office man (that Office then being under Air Ministry's aegis). Naturally we regarded Pip as an authority of weather forecasting, except for our chairman who maintained that he had read the weather reports on the morning in question from coastal ports that visibility was good with no signs of deterioration. True, fog had not appreciably materialised in London that evening. Admittedly, Met. Office forecasts were not unfailingly accurate but they were what we relied on.

We asked them to leave the meeting while we considered the claim. Clearly Pockett would not relish team captains ringing him when the Met. Office forecasted fog to check whether harbourmasters agreed. We called them back to tell them that the match would be played as an Air Ministry's home fixture, on a mutually agreed date. They accepted our ruling without cavil.

Despite evidence which should have led to the contrary, at the end of World War 2 a feeling of euphoria pervaded our country and amid promises of what we may call a Beveridge future some heads of departments began to encourage such amenities as Further Education and Leisure Activities for their staff. London Telecommunications Region was a case in point: there Jimmy Neale, Secretary of the GPO club, co-operated with classes on chess for women telegraphists. A good teacher, he soon had 30 or so of them at a weekly lecture in the Refreshment Club on GPO Headquarters Building fifth floor. Many of them joined the chess club. Jimmy was soon to be appointed Engineer-in-Chief GCHQ, but by the time he reached Cheltenham their number had declined although his popularity had not diminished.

A possible cause was an incident one evening when he had set up a position on his demonstration board and his students had reproduced that position on boards where they sat silently concentrating on determining white's next move. Suddenly the stillness was shattered by high-pitched squeals. They turned their heads to see two rats fighting in the aisle between the rows of dining tables. The ladies jumped on to their chair seats, skirts clutched tightly around their legs. One or two vented their alarm by screaming. The few male students present angrily dashed like terriers towards those rats which stayed not upon the order of their going.

It transpired that a colony of black rats had found lodgement at the top of that building. Food had been scrupulously locked away each afternoon; nonetheless sufficient crumbs had fallen from the tables. A rat catcher was under contract to destroy them but had for years prudently ensured a steady income by regularly culling them though not drastically enough to render them an endangered species. The urbane club manager retired soon after that incident and a resolute manageress took his place. She soon had those rats exterminated. She also refused to allow the chess club a tea urn and tin of biscuits on match nights. Rather than incur visiting teams' reproaches the club moved from that room, which it had regularly used from the building's opening in 1895, to a room in the basement where refreshments could be served and, incidentally, visitors would not have to climb five flights of stairs whenever the lift broke down (an uncommon occurrence but inevitably coincident with match nights).

GPO fielded a ladies team in our league (division 6) from 1951 for a few seasons during which time our Association ran a Ladies individual championship (won on each occasion by Jean Craker of Inland Revenue) until insufficient entries terminated that annual event.

In 1951 our total London membership was 790 and included 33 women, usually only one, treasured, club member apart from GPO's fourteen and Government Chemists' four. By 1962 that membership had levelled off at around 1050 but only 17 ladies were on that roll.

At our General meeting of the Association in 1946 A. G. Pockett had been elected chairman, Harry Hoskin (Admiralty) elected secretary although he was stationed at Bath, Jesse H. Garner was treasurer, Fred M. Norman was captain, and G. P. S. Coy was press correspondent. Harry had to stay in Bath longer than he had expected; I have forgotten what made our press correspondent ineffective but that job was tacked on to my secretarial work in 1947. Civil Service chess was most unlikely to provide stories for Fleet Street, and the *British Chess Magazine* could not always find space to record results of representative matches. I placed a few general articles in staff journals such as *Civil Service Opinion*. Nevertheless, it was no surprise to me when at our 1950 April AGM Council urged that we should run a news bulletin of our own. With few, if any, fully appreciating the amount of work involved, we were fortunate in finding a volunteer for that post in Harry Hoskin who had been brought back to London. He discussed what was involved at our next Committee meeting where the majority of us favoured giving him a free hand – mindful of the biblical injunction not to muzzle the ox that treads our corn. Harry quickly produced a two-page issue which included final league tables of five divisions for our 1949-1950 season. He also trod on our chairman's corns by complaining about the way he had conducted the AGM. A second General meeting of the Council was immediately necessary to arrange 1951-1952 match details: in the absence from London of our chairman that meeting was conducted by A. F. C. Taylor (Assistant Paymaster-General) and went very smoothly. Harry left the meeting very pleased because of the compliments paid him there on his maiden effort as *Bulletin* editor. His second issue contained names of 48 entrants to our individual summer competition and dates of a dozen matches which Fred Norman had already arranged for the coming season, including 50-board home and away with the Counties of Essex and Kent.

Next spring our chairman had yet to forget Harry's *lèse-majesté* and pushed a draft resolution for the AGM through Committee (he was a chairman who engaged each successive speaker in debate) that our *Bulletin* editor should restrict himself to news and eschew comment. Most of us had private reservations that Council would reject it. Those Committee meetings were on Friday nights (the five-day week had not yet arrived) and rarely did I catch a train earlier than 10.00pm.

Harry had the last word. A few days before the AGM he issued a *Bulletin* in which he drew attention to our chairman's resolution and said that should he be muzzled then the Association could look elsewhere for a *Bulletin* editor. The Council of course supported him. Harry retired from the Admiralty within a few years to South Devon, and Pip Sarson began a long reign in his stead as editor of our by then established *Bulletin*.

Our practice before World War 2 had been to hold a General meeting immediately after the close of each season, a practice we resumed as the 1946-1947 season ended. When it came to handing over trophies to their winners at that meeting we found we were in trouble. Several of those trophies were missing, including the Barstow cup – an impressively heavy silver cup – for the individual championship. In 1922 at the inception of our Association, Sir George Barstow of the Treasury who had taken a leading part in the creation of the Civil Service Sports Council, had then presented that cup coincidently with Prime Minister Bonar Law presenting a silver trophy for a team knockout competition. Silversmiths based its design on an ivory rook in an 18th Century Indian chess set in the Victoria and Albert Museum. Bonar Law was an enthusiastic chess player well known for lively, if not always sound, attacking play. Patent Office provided, in 1923, the first winning team and Ministry of Health supplanted them for the following two seasons.

One needs to examine the division 1 shield to determine by how many years it pre-dated trophies acquired on the formation of the Sports Council. The league certainly gave annual prizes to winning teams for I remember seeing a framed chessboard with a small silver plate on it dated 1910 for the winners of division 2.

Percy A. Cooke, pre-War Secretary and Captain of the Ministry of Health gave me invaluable help in my search for those missing trophies. He was able to state that the Barstow cup had been won by F. G. T. (Tims) Collins in 1938 and 1939 but, for some reason, not the individual gold medals which went with that award, for Percy had discovered them in a Ministry of Health safe.

Alas, Tims Collins had been shot down while on a night

bombing raid over Germany. Percy had the address of Tims's parents: I seem to remember it was in Eltham (an unknown suburb to me, but who is there familiar with all of London's suburbs?). With considerable reluctance I set out one evening to retrieve the Barstow cup, but I felt I had no choice in the matter. At an hour when the Collins family were likely to have finished their evening meal, I knocked diffidently on the door at which Tims's father identified himself and invited me in. I was glad I had those two gold medals with me when I explained why I had called. Mrs Collins had clearly supposed the cup to be Tims's personal property but her careful examination, probably for the first time, of its engraving clearly showed that it could not be won outright. I handed over the gold medals, making some excuse for their belated appearance. She said she would keep them for Tims's child, a fair-haired little girl of about six years, then playing quietly before the fireplace. My visit had, most regrettably, brought sorrow to the surface and she was in tears as she excused herself and left the room.

I apologised to Mr. Collins who fully appreciated my embarrassment. He talked about Tims who had played for Oxford University from where he went to the Board of Trade. He was commissioned in the RAF and at 22 had the prospect of a very short life before him. Mr. Collins spoke with approval of his son's whirlwind courtship and marriage which meant evading all those time-consuming formalities and ceremony so dear to the heart of a mother. He and I parted in a most friendly manner but that glimpse of a wartime tragedy had saddened me, though I knew that 50,000 of Tims's colleagues had perished with him on such missions. My report to our Executive Committee was brief.

I thought it would be well to have two General meetings each year: in addition to the traditional end of season meeting we could have an essentially social meeting just before the season began at which trophies could be formally presented. That suggestion was readily adopted.

The division 3 shield eluded us for yet another season: won by Inland Revenue II in 1936-1937 it still escaped discovery. I even went to Somerset House in office hours to stimulate a rigorous search which in the event proved successful: wrapped in brown paper, it was lying under a sloping drawing board.

The Post Annual cup was presented to us in 1926 by the Union of Postal Workers (recently renamed Communication workers I believe). For several years in the 1920s they had published a special magazine at Christmas time on the pattern of the popular *Strand and Pearson's* monthly magazine. Named the *Post Annual*, it comprised articles and illustrations on the manifold postal services of past and present. Profits from its sales were given to charities but in 1926 the UPW Executive Council decided to patronise sports and games. We put it up for competition among clubs with teams below the Bonar Law standard.

One of London's leading evening papers the *Star* (a penny a copy) put up a cup for a one-off competition among business and professional organisations in London. After winning it we decided in 1929 to make it a trophy for members not competing in the Barstow cup.

We had to buy additional shields later in the 1950's as we increased the number of league divisions. We also instituted trophies, with some help from the clubs immediately concerned, in memory of two well-known members: Jesse H. Garner, pre-War Secretary of the Central Telegraph Office Club and Association Treasurer from 1947 until his death seven years later (when R. D. Fleming took over), and J. (Jimmy) T. Curtis,

Secretary of Labour and National Service Club after World War 2, until his untimely death in 1960.

Jacob Bronowski put up a trophy for which we still compete with certain London business organisations. He became a television personality, and his series *The Ascent of Man* is unforgettable. What is not so well known is that he, a keen chess player, turned out in representative matches for us until 1950 when he was transferred from the Department of Works to the National Coal Board as Director of Research.

Were John H. Watson, M. D., late of the Army Medical Department, writing this narrative he would perhaps call it 'The Adventure of the Bleeding Chess Player'. My story begins on a Tuesday evening thirty-five winters ago. Big Ben had ponderously struck seven hours and the sound of his seventh stroke was still jangling in my ears as I came to the main entrance of the Ministry of Local Government and Planning on the west side of Whitehall after I walked from Trafalgar Square. I was leaving work late that night when I decided not to catch a train at Holborn but to go instead to Victoria for my train calling in to see GPO III en route. I had recently been elected club captain, and it seemed appropriate that I should make a token appearance at such an away match when an opportunity could be created.

Whitehall was deserted; pools of light at street lamps disclosed no pedestrian nor was a bus or private car in sight as I entered the building. The doorkeeper in his brightly lit little cubbyhole just inside the entrance knew about the match, apologised for there being no lifts working, and gave me detailed instructions on how to get to the scene of conflict. As I ascended the stairs, flights became narrower with each storey, and in my imagination risers became higher. Eventually I found myself in a room lined with bookshelves: in its central area were eight small tables bearing chess boards. There was plenty of space between the tables but nonetheless it seemed clear to me that I was in one of the corner turret rooms the cupolas of which I had often seen from the opposite side of Whitehall where I had an impression that they surmounted far less than that in which I then found myself. The sixteen contestants were so absorbed in their games that none noticed my arrival.

I stood near one board to watch a game between W. H. Goonatilleke, a newcomer to the GPO Club and a young lady whom I later understood to be a Miss Brown. Goonatilleke, a graceful slightly built Sinhalese, who rejoiced in the same surname as Ceylon's Chief Commissioner in London, had an opponent even smaller and more slightly built. Miss Brown was decorously dressed in a serge suit and white shirtwaist; her warm brown hair was neatly arranged, she wore no earrings and I judged her, despite her attractive appearance, to be shy and reserved. I could not but reflect how pleasant it was that her club could recruit such a member to participate in the king of games. As I stood there her attention did not for a moment waver from the board.

I moved silently around the room looking at each position in turn, nor during that time did any player look up from the board before him. Several minutes must have elapsed before I returned to see how Goonatilleke had fared. The strange sight which then confronted me gave me quite a shock. He lay supine behind his chair on the parquet flooring. I bent over him. His eyes were closed. And the lower part of his face was covered with blood. Wildly improbable thoughts flashed through my mind. Had he behaved in less than his usually impeccable manner? Had Miss Brown struck him? Manifestly she was not to be equated with a Russian lady discus thrower capable of administering a lethal clout to a far stouter man than

Goonatilleke. I looked at Miss Brown; she was imperturbably concentrating on the chessboard before her.

I bent closer over him. Blood was seeping from his nostrils. He opened his eyes, looked up at me and whispered 'A sudden attack of nose bleed. I lay down on the floor to stop it.'. 'That won't stop it. Get up and press a handkerchief hard against your nose.'. By this time one of the home players had come over and helped me to lift the bleeder to his feet and led him out to a lavatory to wash his face. In a very little time he returned, handkerchief pressed against his nose, and sat down at this table. ('Remarkable, Watson.'. 'Elementary my dear Holmes.'.)

Miss Brown, who had not spoken a word, gave him a fleeting smile, made her move and set his clock going. He had plenty of time on it. That would not always be so.

As a player, Goonatilleke could be classed among the smaller fry but in all our clubs each dependable member is equally valued, thus there is no call for me to apologise for relating another incident in which he figured – an international incident no less. One Sunday the GPO Club had been given use of a wireless telephone circuit to Brussels to play a team of 20 Belgian PTT players: terminals were in the PTT Headquarters in Brussels and the GPO Headquarters building in St. Martins le Grand. The Belgians were not at that time as strong, for instance, as the Netherlands PTT, so our strongest players were not participating. I recall that St. Paul's Cathedral bells, unheard on weekdays above the hum of the street traffic, became loud enough just before morning service to interfere with our transmitting moves so we had a few minutes break during which our Belgian colleagues listened to those bells and then allowed us to listen to those of St. Michael et Ste. Gudele which was near their building.

As the afternoon wore on, I noticed that Goonatilleke had

clocked far more time than anyone else. It is within a captain's province to draw a team member's attention to his clock. I did so. Twice. But he did not speed up, and a few minutes later I informed Brussels that his flag had fallen. Nor do I know of another instance where a player in a telegraphed or telephoned match has lost on time.

A chess book which in recent years has become a collector's item is *1. P-KB4* by R. E. Robinson. The only publishers' information on its title page is 'Printed by Daily Post Printers, Liverpool'. In fact it was published by its author, in 1950, in unusual circumstances. Additional to a discussion of Bird's Opening, it contains a collection of 201 games from 1831 to 1945, lightly annotated, plus five Swiss gambits (1. f4 f5, 2. e4 fxe4, 3. Nc3 Nf6, 4. g4), 31 From gambits, and ten games at odds of QKt. Robinson also included a brief biography of Henry Edward Bird (1830-1908).

Robinson (a Vice-President of the GPO Club) had collected over many years from far and wide a vast number of Bird's opening games. In his retirement he had selected and edited from that accumulation to produce an MS which, in 1948, he had submitted to B. H. Wood who agreed to publish it. Nor does your correspondent in any way suppose that Wood was deterred in reaching his decision when he found the scores of two of his own games among those by Masters from Alekhine to Zukertort.

But B. H. Wood was troubled with a serious problem concerning what is now generally referred to as 'cash flow'. Liverpool Post Printers had set up *1. P-KB4* in type in May 1949 and sent a bill of £175 to him. He found himself unable to pay it (in those years many had regarded B. H. Wood's attempt to make a living by chess as unduly optimistic: they were agreeably surprised when he eventually made a success of his venture).

Disappointed, Robinson determined to be his own publisher, paid the type setting bill, and plunged into a field quite new to him which included proof reading, designing a dust wrapper, and conducting a publicity campaign. In the latter he was helped by many of our members, including his brother-in-law W. S. Wallis (Inland Revenue). He had an edition of a thousand (including copies for review) to dispose of. Dr. J. M. Aitken (Cheltenham) who served on our adjudicators' panel for many years, was responsible for a review in *British Chess Magazine* (September 1950). R. J. Broadbent reviewed it in the *Western Morning News* (15th July): that particularly pleased Robinson for he had been born in Plymouth when his father was on the *WMN* staff during 1890-1895. Possibly as effective to Robinson's purpose as any was our Editor, Harry Hoskins' review in our *Bulletin*. During 1950, Robinson sold 430 copies and the following year 366, at which point he confessed to a gross profit of a few shillings less than £2. That he sold the remaining 194 copies at the published price of 12/6 each during the next few months did not make it a successful commercial venture, but his satisfaction with his first (and last) venture as a publisher was not to be assessed in terms of money.

Andrew Bonar Law (1868-1923) disdained the minor arts of popularity and therefore has faded from public memory, with what I think we may fairly call a notable exception. Throughout the 70 years since his death his name has frequently been on the lips of members of our Association for did he not present us with our most prestigious trophy? He was by birth a Canadian and became the first man from the Commonwealth to be elected Prime Minister of the United Kingdom. Throughout World War 1 – and during the earliest years of peace – his was the arduous task of dealing with the problems of our country's finances. The resultant strain had undermined his constitution to cause him on 23rd May 1923 after only 209 days as Prime Minister, to resign from that office completely shattered in health. Less than six months later he died.

The Liberal Party leader, Lloyd George, when he learnt that the Conservatives had chosen Bonar Law as their leader, tactfully observed 'The fools have stumbled on their best man by accident.'.

We can picture the situation in 1922 when the Civil Service Sports Council was formed and Ministers and senior Civil Servants were invited to present trophies to be competed for among the organisations coming under the aegis of the central Council. Bonar Law noticed the appeal, and remembering the recreation he had derived from playing chess, decided to present us with a trophy. He could have ordered one from the shelves of, say, Fattorini which would have made little inroad on his valuable time. He chose to consult the Victoria and Albert Museum which possessed historical sets of chessmen. He selected a rook from an 18th Century Indian set and had that ivory piece sent to Mappin and Webb whose silversmiths produced an enlarged exquisite copy. The beauty of that artefact is appreciated by all who have seen it outside its oak, glass-fronted container, topped with a small brass carrying handle.

On the opening page of our first printed yearbook in 1948 I reproduced a photograph of the trophy. It showed the rook with its square pediment, each of its four slightly tapering sides having a framed pointed-arch (blind) window; a cornice of dentils supported a roof with a very high dome of incurving foliage. The delicately chased silver piece surmounts a stepped ebony plinth with silver straps engraved with the names of winning clubs.

It is possible to infer from the foregoing that Bonar Law had a lively appreciation of art but the DNB records that 'literature, art, music, scenery had no interest to him'. An erstwhile colleague of his once told me that Bonar Law greatly enjoyed off-hand games of chess and favoured attacking play. If any score of a game of his was made it seems unlikely that it has survived. He was an outstanding, entirely unemotional, speaker. Kindly and considerate in his dealings, another quality of his should endear his memory to those of us with experience of officials who are intolerant of even the slightest criticism. He told a newspaper editor in 1922, 'My experience is that all Prime Ministers suffer from suppression. Their friends do not tell them the truth; they tell them what they want to hear... people are always apt to think that what has been will be. I am less inclined perhaps than most to that error... I was in the iron trade, a highly speculative business with frequent violent fluctuations in prices.'.

These few observations should have particular point with members who hitherto have taken trophies for granted. As for the clubs which won Bonar Law's trophy; first was Patent Office in 1923 followed by Ministry of Health in 1924 and 1925. The earliest details of team members which I have, is for the final played at the Patent Office in June 1926.

Patent Office		Somerset House
1. W O Woodfield	0-1	E G Sergeant
2. F W Dunn	½-½	D Miller
3. P Clarkson	0-1	M A Prentice
4. R F Whitehead	1-0	W H Taylor
5. E W Hilliar	0-1	W S Wallis
6. S F Chisholm	½-½	E W Harris
7. N A Burne	1-0	W W Brougham

8. W Langstaff	1-0	G E Master
9. E A Lynn	½-½	W S Jackson
10. G H Green	1-0	E Roberts
	5½-4½	

Boards 7 and 9 were adjudicated by E. Znosko-Borovsky, a professional player.

W O Woodfield was a vice-president from 1922 until his death in 1968.

When we elected Dr H R Calvert to our Executive Committee in 1951 our Association had rapidly grown to 40 clubs since its resuscitation in 1946. The majority of club officers were newcomers, hence our Committee found plenty of questions to answer at its monthly meetings which prevented the bad practice of introducing Rules to meet unusual situations. Our chairman thought we could continue in the free and easy manner of pre-War days when all club officials were well known to each other. His view found no favour. In such an atmosphere, H R (Doc) Calvert with his own quiet, good-humoured, practical suggestions, made a valuable contribution. His own club, UNATS, was made up of members from half a dozen ministries each hoping to gain enough members to hive off and form its own club. He was captain of UNATS first team which included P S Milner-Barry.

He became vice-chairman in 1959 and acted as chairman from mid-1962 when the holder of that office took up an overseas post, although our *Handbook* did not show him as chairman until its 1964 issue. He retired four years later to be forthwith elected a vice-president.

Throughout those years he had played regularly in our representative matches, and among the treasured memories of fellow team members are pleasant pre-match strolls with him in Oxbridge and relaxation, following home matches, at venues such as 'The Printer's Devil' in Fetter Lane (which did for the history of printing what 'The Yorker' in Piccadilly had done for cricket). There we chatted, not about games we had just played but of fringe scientific subjects when we were not prompting him to reminisce on his student days in Germany.

A number of our members used to play in the London Chess League, and others may still do so. Its Headquarters was St. Bride Institute, Bride Lane, Fleet Street. We call to mind Dr G A C Ashcroft (Patent Office), P A Cooke (Housing & Local Government) who had for years turned out for Battersea, and R J Broadbent (GPO) who played for Clapham Common. J H van Meurs (Baltic Exchange) was secretary of the league and of Clapham: he was usually at the Institute well before matches to check that boards and clocks were in order. So when your Correspondent found himself in Fleet Street soon after five o'clock one winter's evening in 1958, and with a Clapham Common match due to start at six o'clock, he turned into the Institute on the chance of having a chat with 'Van'. That Area had been heavily blitzed and was rebuilt and tidied up, but the St Bride building had escaped structural damage and now only too obviously needed renovation. Climbing to the first-floor landing (chess matches were on the top floor) he came upon a blackboard chalked 'World Draughts Championship'. Following an indicated direction he entered a smallish room with a dais under its cracked glass, cobwebby windows on which were seated on kitchen chairs with a small table between, the two contestants. Behind them were two officials, one operating a demonstration board and the other holding a large stopwatch in one hand. Your Correspondent sat himself in one of the thirty or so chairs arranged in rows before the dais.

No other chair was occupied. He was the audience. A solitary steward sat beside him and sotto voce put him in the picture. 'Thirty seconds to move' announced the man with the stopwatch. One contestant was faultlessly attired in a conventional business suit; the other wore a loose yellowed woollen jersey and baggy flannels.

Your Correspondent did not so much watch the play as think of what little he knew of draughts. The Clapham Club was originally the Clapham Common Open Air Chess and Draughts Club which suggested a more rural setting than now, and a better summer climate. The originator of the English detective stories, Edgar Allen Poe, had in his philosophic preamble to 'The Murders in the Rue Morgue' (1841) asserted that the higher powers of a reflective intellect are more decidedly tested by the unostentatious game of draughts than by all the more elaborate frivolity of chess. At this point it dawned upon me that the scruffily attired contestant was the English challenger. Unfortunately, 'the audience' had promised to participate in frivolity that night so he escaped to join the Clapham team.

He learnt later that Marion Tinsley, born in Kentucky in 1927, a Doctor in Mathematics, winning the World Draughts Championship in 1953, overwhelmed his challenger and in the event was never defeated, not even by a computer. Regrettably he fell a victim to cancer in 1995.

CLUB HISTORIES

INLAND REVENUE CHESS CLUB Short history of the Inland Revenue Chess Club by Roland Smith

LADY MEMBERS - Two made their mark in the club.

JEAN CRAKER - played during the 1950s and after she left to work for North Thames Gas the league rules were changed so that former members were still permitted to play. Jean was BCF under 18 Girls Champion in 1949 and 1950.

MARY INGLIS (nee HAY) - Mary played for the 2nd team and as 1st team reserve and she often shocked her male opponents with her strong attacking style of chess. She represented Scottish Ladies and was a fine postal chess player.

ECCENTRICS AND CLANGERS

Chess has had a fair share of eccentrics and our club was no exception. In the 1950s we hoped that a certain Middlesex county player did not pass too many pubs en route to the match as he liked his tipple! There was one classic night when he literally 'rolled into the room', played at lightning speed and won in a few minutes. In a match at Government Chemists we nearly got into serious trouble. Having passed through security I took several players the wrong way and as a member of staff came through a door I led the players into a corridor where there was no escape as we didn't know the pin code. Along the corridor were several warning notices, 'Danger- radioactive – keep out'. Eventually our shouts were heard and we were released by a very irate security guard.

WONDERFUL MATCHES

We had many tough matches against the GPO who had the former British Champion R J Broadbent on board 1 and in addition to county players they also had two or three former Civil Service champions. The most memorable for the strength of both teams was in April 1956 (see below) in which our board 10 was a Surrey county player. The most unexpected victory, despite defaulting board 10, was in November 1959. GPO had Broadbent who won as usual but on boards 2 to 4 their former Civil Service champions only scored ½ point – Percy Cook 1-0 C G Butcher; P Tillson ½-½ N A Perkins; Roland Smith 1-0 G P S Coy.

Inland Revenue **GPO**
(April 1956)

Board

1	E G Sergeant	0-1	R J Broadbent
2	D Miller	½-½	C G Butcher
3	P B Cook	½-½	N A Perkins
4	R Smith	1-0	E C Baker
5	P Tillson	½-½	A C Lynch
6	J Gilchrist	½-½	E A Taylor
7	W S Wallis	1-0	H L Mimardiere
8	E H Gordon	½-½	W H Leech
9	L Barford	½-½	N E A Moore
10	B Lyons	1-0	E H Bourne
		6-4	

HENRY GREATOREX TROPHY - this was presented by the Inland Revenue Sports Association in 1994/95 to the chess club for being the most successful club in that year for the performance of the team and individual achievements.

The successes were division 1 champions, Bonar Law trophy, Barford trophy (lightning chess) and British Postal Chess champions. The individuals who merit a mention were Nick Down (CS individual lightning chess champion), Nigel Fleming (Star trophy) and in postal chess Nick Down was selected for England in the European Championships and North Atlantic Treaty Tournament (NATT); Joe Watson (Scottish Champion and selected for Scotland in the NATT); Roland Smith scored 7/14 in a World Championship qualifier and played board 1 for the BPCF in friendly internationals.

POSTAL CHESS

In 1958 the Revenue succeeded in organising postal chess on a national basis and at one time had five teams competing in the British Correspondence Chess League (BCCL), but currently only have two teams. We first qualified for the British Championship in 1974, and won it in 1978, 1984, 1985 and 1995. We also won the Civil Service Postal chess championship but this competition was not popular and eventually abolished.

Many of our postal chess players participated in international matches or at county level and some won best game prizes. The following players deserve a mention:

Nick Down (Scottish Postal Chess champion 1993 but selected by England); David Edney (Scotland); Roy R Greenfield – best game prize; Alan Heaton (played for the Revenue team from 1970 to 1995 and only lost two games out of 50); Mary Inglis; Barry S Jefferies; A Phil Primett (board 1 Herts); Roland Smith (England, Kent board 1, and 6 best game prizes); Joe Watson (IM grade 2500). He represented Scotland, was twice Scottish champion and won the two other Scottish tournaments he entered and has a victory against a GM; A Howard Williams (Wales and best game prize). Last but by no means least Peter Coleman - Peter joined Revenue 1972 – 74 and the chess club from 1973 – 1980. He then gave up chess but in 1995 started postal chess and rapidly climbed the ranks and is now a GM with a grade of 2606 and currently one of the strongest postal / email chess players in the UK.

PERSONALITIES

The club has been fortunate that our membership has always included many strong players of county or British Championship standard and also a few who gained international honours either over-the-board or at postal chess. Inevitably the list which follows is restricted to those of exceptional chess ability or because their long association with the club as an officer or player deserves recognition.

W S Wallis - joined the club in 1912 and was chairman from 1953 to 1958. For 46 years he was a regular first team player and in his last 10 years he played 48 games for the club and only lost 4. What an amazing record. In 1958 he resigned because of his wife's ill health. He was a Middlesex county player for many years.

M G Walker – Martin was only in the Revenue for two years but since joining the chess club in 1998 he has continued to support us. He is a strong county player and currently represents Herts. In 2001 he played in the British Championship and scored 5/11 with wins against IM's Gary Lane and Colin Crouch and draws against grandmasters Chris Ward and Joseph Gallagher. He qualified to play in the British Championship in 2007. Martin has had many championship successes - Norfolk 1991, Herts. 2004 and 2005, CSSC 1998, 2000 and 2002 and several rapid-play tournament wins in 1995 Kings Lynn, 1999 Great Dunmore and Letchworth 2005.

J Watson – Joe joined the Revenue and the chess club in

1967 and has continued to play despite leaving the Revenue in 1972 - what loyalty especially as he had to travel from Marlow and now from Bath. He still plays on board 1 or 2. Postal chess is another of his strengths and he won all four Scottish postal tournaments he entered, two Candidates tourneys and twice became joint Scottish postal chess champion. Gained his IM grade 2500 and represented Scotland.

D Lees - David was only in London from 1967 to 1969 but had an excellent record on board 1 scoring 61% in 23 games including a draw against R J Broadbent. David was Civil Service champion in 1968.

OTHERS

There are other strong players or officials who made their contribution to the club who deserve a mention -

P Hare - Paul did well on board 1 and represented his county. He was a wizard at lightning chess and finished 5th in the British Lightning Chess Championship and in 1995 scored 10/10 on board 1 in the Barford trophy.

D Edney – David joined the club in 1993 became secretary in 1995 and also treasurer from 2005. David has represented Herts at postal chess scoring 3 wins and 2 draws and since 1993 he has played 24 games for the Revenue scoring 16 wins & 6 draws. In an international tournament he finished joint 1st. He became well known on TV as captain of the Revenue quiz team in the University Challenge 'The Professionals' where they were the first winners of this new competition.

R W G Fletcher - Ron first became an Essex county player at the tender age of 17 and also played for the Essex Boys v Brighton Schools. He twice played in the London Boys' chess championship and his best result was in 1950 when he won the Best Game Prize but was denied winning his section by another of our members Ian Hunter. Little did either realize that in 1954/5 they would both be playing for the Revenue 2nd team. He was 1st team captain from 1982/3 until 1985 but he played very few games after his move to the Guildford office. Ron also played postal chess for the Revenue.

D G Mackay - last played for us in 1953 but was the C S champion in 1952.

R Ryan - Bob only played for the club during his short spells in London 1960-62 and 1975- 78. But his services to postal chess both for the Revenue and nationally were considerable. He captained the Revenue postal chess 2nd team for 12 years and in addition was Controller for the British Correspondence Chess League Premier Division from 1991 - 2006 and Conductor of the BCC League from 2002 - 2006

D J Rawlings – Dave joined the club was 2nd team captain for more than 20 years to 2006. He also played many games as reserve for the 1st team and for the postal chess team.

INLAND REVENUE CHESS CLUB by Ron Fleming (written before the merger with HM Customs and Excise to form 'Revenue and Customs')

'Since the Revenue Chess Club drew its members from various individual offices it necessarily varied its players as members got posted into the provinces or got posted to London offices. It started life as the Somerset House Chess Club but then the Surtax Office was in Turnstile House, the A & CG in Bush House, and the EDO was in the West wing of Somerset House. The War meant that much of the Revenue went to Llandudno and, on its return, scattered around the countryside. Surtax went to Hinchley Wood, the A & CG went to Barrington Road, Worthing, and the EDO went first to Rayners Lane,

Harrow and then to Minford House in Shepherds Bush. Control was still exercised from the New Wing of Somerset House, and we played matches in the basement of the West Wing for a while players came too from the various Tax Offices. In the 1950's I took over as secretary and treasurer and, because of the problems over storing equipment and bringing it out for matches, I asked the club to move its HQ to Minford House and to play its home matches there. This meant that the CSCA Rules had to be varied to allow matches to be played (as I recall) within six miles of Central London, and this was agreed. When I gave up the Offices and other arrangements were made the club returned to Somerset House.'

'Being myself a player of only mediocre strength I was listed around 11/12 in the early nominations: Phil Primett was listed immediately above me so we filled the top boards of IR II at the beginning of the season. Quite often a division 2 team had one or two strong players and then tailed off on the lower boards. So we were regularly pitted against very good opposition and could only concentrate on 'going down with our flag flying'. I recall playing Admiralty whose top board was Surgeon Commander (now Surgeon Admiral) Holford who had at one time been the National Champion of South Africa. Whether he took me too easily or was having an off day I cannot say but I in fact won that game to my great surprise!'

'One last anecdote about the Revenue. Jean Craker was a regular player for the Revenue and 'quite good for a woman'. But then she gave up her appointment and joined the North Thames Gas Board, but we still wanted her services and continued to play her. Someone queried her eligibility to turn out for us since she was no longer a current revenue officer. So we had to redraft the eligibility clause of the CSCA Rules to provide that players shall be or have been a member of the department represented. This clause was very useful anyway because the Government of the day had a habit of amalgamating or hiving off various organisations with little regard to its consequence on Chess Teams! For instance, the Ministry of Aircraft Production was absorbed by the Air Ministry which gave that team three very strong players that they had not had before. The Ministry of Supply got players from the Ministry of Works. The CSCA turned a blind eye on any changes in current allegiances and allowed players to stay with a club even after they had moved to a different Ministry. However, those had all been internal moves within the Civil Service whereas Jean Craker had left the Civil Service to join a commercial concern.'

BTHQ CHESS CLUB By John McAllister

Details of the origins of the BTHQ Chess Club are lost in the mists of time. They certainly go back before the First World War, in fact an old letter heading states that the club was founded as far back as 1883. It was originally known as the GPO Chess Club, which became just the 'Post Office' in 1970. On its one hundredth anniversary, in 1983, after the separation of Post Office Telecommunications from The Royal Mail, it became BT&PO. In 1986 the name changed again, to its current BTHQ, removing the last trace of the Post Office from its modern identity (all but one of its members at that time was employed by BT).

Over the years a host of chess clubs playing in the London area have arisen from within the ranks of the Post Office and BT, all existed in parallel with GPO/PO/BT&PO/BTHQ, and most have long since gone. These include EC Test Section (GPO), GPO & Post Office Factory, PO Regional HQ, PO Savings, PO Supplies, PO North West Regional

HQ, Cable and Wireless (GPO), SWDO (GPO), POHS (Post Office Howland Street), NWPSC (North West Postal Sports Club), PO Contracts, Fortels, Western District PO, London Telecommunications Region (later BT Westminster), London Postal Region, Eastern Knights, BT (Stats), BT West End District and Centre Area (BT).

Not all of these clubs played in the Civil Service League, but of those that did only Eastern Knights and BTHQ have survived to this day - sadly however, even they no longer compete in the Civil Service. The only other club from this list that remains active today is BT West End District, and while members of that club have also been members of BTHQ in the CSCL, BT WED, as a club, has only ever played in the sister league to the CSCL, the London Commercial Chess League.

In past times, such activities as chess were taken very seriously indeed within the GPO and PO, and those representing the company in such activities bore a heavy load. On one occasion, after a particularly poor season (1970-71) in which the first team was relegated, the main culprits were brought before a senior manager and given a dressing down for letting the company down. And they were told in no uncertain terms, that they had better pull their socks up and get themselves promoted back to the first division or else. Or else 'what' was not explained, but you didn't argue with the pin-striped suited bosses in such organisations as the Post Office back then. That 'talking to' obviously had the desired effect as PO were promoted back to division one the following season.

Generally speaking, GPO did very well in the CSCL, winning division 1 eleven times between 1908 and 1949. It took BTHQ until 1988 to recapture the title, in the year in which they took the double, winning the Bonar Law trophy as well. Not bad considering that the season before they had only just recovered from their second spell in division 2 (this time lasting two years). The club also pulled off the double the following year, but this time it was their second team, who won division 5 and the Jesse Garner cup, doing so without losing a single match.

In BTHQ's double winning year of 1988, the struggle for the league title went down to the last match of the season against the Inland Revenue. Inland Revenue had to win that match to take the title, if BTHQ avoided defeat they would win the title on board points (helped it must be said, by two clubs defaulting their matches 10-0). It was a very tense evening at BTHQ's fortress Gresham Street, and although BTHQ were well outgunned on paper, they did extremely well to reach the end of the evening still in with a fighting chance, being just 5-4 down, with only the top board to finish. This was between Tim Kett of BTHQ and Welsh IM Howard Williams representing the Inland Revenue. Tim needed to win to draw the match and things did not look promising – he was the exchange for a pawn down with only queens and a few pawns left to complicate the issue. It was one of those occasions where everybody hung around, and the top board was literally surrounded by the other 18 players. Both Tim and Howard were very short of time, but Tim as usual was the coolest man in the room and laid a subtle trap, and with his flag hovering Howard stepped into it, lost a rook, and had to resign. It was one of those rare occasions in club chess when spontaneous applause broke out amongst the onlookers (BTHQ onlookers that is).

For the next ten years the club was very active, and at one point managed to field three teams in each of the Civil Service and London Commercial leagues. During that time the club was always a powerful contender in the leagues, and while it came second on a number of occasions, it never quite managed to take the top prize again.

Ten years further down the line and the club, along with so many others, was in decline as more and more of BT's central London buildings were closed and increasing numbers of staff were relocated or released. In 1990 BTHQ were relegated from division One, bounced straight back in 1991, but dropped back again in 1995, and stayed in division Two until their demise from the CSCL during the 2004-2005 season. The club still competed in the LCCL, but now had only one team of six boards, and even that number of boards was often difficult for the captain to fill.

HOME OFFICE CHESS CLUB By James Toon and Tony Ashby

League records show that the Home Office Chess Club was in existence as early as 1921, when the Home Office won the division 3 league title. However, the club must have ceased to exist some time after that. By the early 1980s, chess players in the Home Office – such as Tony Ashby and Graham Sandiford – were playing for UNATS, which had been formed in 1947 for those departments which did not have their own chess club.

In 1984, a small group of people in the Home Office Prison Department (as it then was) came together to play social chess during the lunch break. Two of them, Ron Matthews and Paul Haughton, advertised the group's existence in a Home Office newsletter and appealed for more players. This came to the attention of James Toon, who had joined the Home Office from university in late 1984 and had immediately started playing for UNATS. He contacted Ron Matthews and Paul Haughton, and the three of them agreed to form a new Home Office Chess Club drawing on the existing group of social players. The current Home Office Chess Club therefore dates from 1984.

It was natural that the members of the new club should want to play league chess for their own department. Discussions with Ian Pheby, the league's senior recorder, in 1985 resulted in a Home Office team entering division 4 of the league in the 1986/87 season. James Toon captained the team in its first season, leaving UNATS after only one year. He was followed by Tony Ashby and Graham Sandiford. The departure of three experienced players all at once was controversial – the UNATS captain, Renate Wilson, was very unhappy about it. However, under the league rules at the time, the Home Office three had no choice, since players whose own departments were represented in the League were not eligible to play for UNATS. (This restriction was removed a few years later so that players whose departments did have their own clubs could choose to play for UNATS instead.)

The Home Office team proved too strong for division 4 and indeed was soon promoted to division 1, where it has stayed ever since apart from a two-year break in division 2. Other experienced players emerged in the first few years to strengthen the team further: Richard Fries, Chris Carew, and Harry Carter. The nucleus of strong players ensured a steady stream of good results, although the club was not strong enough in the 1990s to challenge for honours in division 1 or the Bonar Law trophy. Club membership was settled at about 15 to 20 for a long period and this helped to create a strong sense of club identity and mutual commitment.

One incident stands out from the club's early years. In the early 1990s, the team was struggling in division 1 and was due to play an away match against a very strong Inland Revenue team featuring Craig Thomson and Howard Williams on the top boards. On arrival, the Home Office team found the Inland Revenue captain, Roland Smith, and his team-mates in an empty room with no chess equipment set out. Roland admitted that the Inland Revenue chess equipment was in a cupboard in a locked room and the room key had not been returned to the security desk by the previous user. The Home Office could have claimed the match on default, easing their relegation worries, but after a short discussion the team decided to re-arrange the match on a mutually-convenient future date. All of them would rather play chess than win in this manner. A few weeks later, they duly played and lost the postponed match. However, their actions earned the Home Office team a reputation for sportsmanship, and subsequent matches between the Home Office and Inland Revenue have all been played in a very good spirit.

The Home Office Chess Club has had its low points. A number of players have left over the years, weakening the league team. The saddest moment, however, was the premature death of Graham Sandiford in the mid-1990s from cancer. A special issue of the club's newsletter 'Across The Board' carried a chess obituary and some of Graham's finest games against other club members.

The club's membership gradually increased over the years and eventually it was decided to enter a 2nd team in the league. Peter Biggs, one of the most reliable and organized members of the club, agreed to captain this team. One of the club's founders, Paul Haughton, played for this team, but the other one did not. Ron Matthews had dropped out of chess by then. The team enjoyed moderate results over the years, once reaching the final of the Post Annual cup, but turning out a full team proved increasingly difficult and the 2nd team eventually withdrew from the league. It reappeared in 2005 following a membership drive, again under the captaincy of Peter Biggs.

As far as internal events were concerned, a club championship operated in the earlier years. This tended to be played over the summer as a series of rapid games in successive rounds. It seems to have been last contested in 1993, when Harry Carter and Richard Fries were the joint winners. The championship was revived in the summer of 2006 with an experimental scoring system that aggregated results and the number of games played. Tim Pelling was the clear winner.

Blitz chess has always been popular in the Home Office Chess Club. The AGM in April or May has for many years been followed by the annual blitz championship. Club members have also recently competed with success in league blitz events. The league's annual individual blitz tournament has been won by a Home Office player for the past four years: Chris Briscoe in 2003, Tony Ashby in 2004, James Toon in 2005 and Alistair Compton in 2006. James Toon also won the league Christmas blitz tournament in 2005. And a Home Office team consisting of Tony Ashby, Harry Carter, Alistair Compton and James Toon won the league annual team blitz tournament in 2006, finishing just ahead of a strong Metropolitan Police team.

The club's best season in the Civil Service League was in 2003/04, when the Home Office 1st team achieved the league and cup double. The team beat the Department of Environment in the cup final, and learned on the same night that a crucial adjudication had gone their way and they had won the league as well. The team was no stronger than in other years but for once the captain, James Toon, had been able to turn out his strongest team in almost all fixtures.

On the back of this success, the club obtained a grant from the Home Office Sports and Social Association to buy new wooden sets and boards and some digital clocks. The sets in particular are quite beautiful and for the Home Office Chess

Club they are a reminder that chess is, or should be, a beautiful game.

All club members have their biographies. James Toon is the only founding member of the Home Office Chess Club to be still active in the chess world. He taught himself to play at the age of 10 and started playing for Loughborough in the Leicestershire League when he was 13. Captaincy was thrust upon him at an early age and he took charge of the Loughborough 3rd team when he was 15. He made it to the Leicestershire 1st team, but was not one of the stars of Leicestershire junior chess: future GMs Mark Hebden and Glenn Flear were playing at a much higher level.

On arrival at Oxford in the early 1980s, James again found himself overshadowed by an exceptionally talented group of players including Peter Wells, Ken Regan, Will Watson, John Cox, John Hawkesworth, Jon Levitt and Colin McNab. But his organizational ability (or his willingness to volunteer for things) was soon recognized and he captained the University team to the Oxfordshire League title in 1983/84. He also played for Oxfordshire on a few occasions.

On joining the Home Office in 1984, James soon became involved in Civil Service League business. He was league grader for nine years, and a league adjudicator for a shorter period. He captained the Home Office 1st team in most seasons. He also turned out for the Home Office in the London Commercial League, for Hackney in the Middlesex League, for Streatham and then Athenaeum in the London League, and for Streatham and then for Ashtead in the Surrey League. He also played some matches for Surrey. All this can only be explained as an addiction to chess.

MET OFFICE CHESS CLUB Based on information provided

to ChessDevon website by Gareth Ward (later updated by him, and with further information from David Thomson, Steve Murray, Wilf Taylor)

Gareth Ward's original material is based on paper documents for 1946-94 rediscovered at Met Office HQ in 2008, engraved trophies, www.berkshirechess.org.uk and his recollections between 1993 and 2009.

The Meteorological ('Met') Office was formed by the Admiralty in 1854, as part of the Board of Trade, but it seems a chess club was not formed until 92 years later. (Admiralty did play in the league in the early years of course.) Pip Sarson founded a Met Office Chess Club in Harrow in 1946 as an offshoot of the Air Ministry Chess Club, with a plan to compete in the London Civil Service League. 22 players showed initial interest but attendance soon fell away. A club championship was run in 1947-48, won by Sarson (who also won in 1980), ahead of David Dicks, who won the club championship in 1996. He continued to play for the club until it moved to Devon in 2003! In 1950, the club was very active, playing matches against local clubs and simultaneous displays. Imre Konig beat them 16½-1½ on 6th July 1950, EJ Axton being the sole winner. Met Office moved to Dunstable shortly afterwards, but the club folded. In 1961, the Met Office moved to a brand-new building in Bracknell, where the club was re-formed, although it was not active for eight years in the next two decades. Pip Sarson continued to play and organize into the 1980s. Two founder members (Brian Edkins and David Macklin) continued to play until 2003, when the Met Office moved to Devon. In the late 70s, the club ran two or three teams in the Berkshire League. Wilf Taylor and Will Hand started playing then and continued to do so up to 2005. The strongest player then was Frank Woolford, who scored over 85 % in club events until well into his 60s. He was also Berkshire Champion in 1969 and 1970. The team oscillated between division 1 and 2 (which is now named after Frank Woolford), with the second team usually just missing promotion from division 3. Met Office won the Berkshire division 2 trophy in 1962, 1985, 1988, 1993 (shared) and 2003. The B team won division 3 in 1981 and 1987.

From 2000, the club started playing in the Border League (where Surrey, Hampshire and Berkshire meet). The move to Devon in 2003 resulted in only 5 players arriving in Devon, but more players joined, so in 2008 the club was able to run four teams, although was not very active by 2015. There was individual success for Andreas Keil, who won the CSSC national individual championship in 2008, having finished third for the preceding two years. He was the first qualifier from South-West to win the event. Other Met Office Chess Club qualifiers have been Adrian Pickersgill, Neville Lane and Ian Simpson. Wilf Taylor finished second in the national CS Postal tournament.

MINISTRY OF LABOUR CHESS CLUB (based on their Minutes Book)

An inaugural meeting was held on 22nd February 1926 starting at 5.15pm to consider the advisability of forming a chess club. F Davey chaired the meeting which was attended by 45 members. It appears that internal tournaments had been previously held. Although it seems a Ministry of Labour Chess Club existed with their Headquarters based at the Claims and Records Office, Kew, it was considered that there was room for a Club whose Headquarters would be based at Montague House, Richmond Terrace or Queen Anne's Chambers.

Mr A J Spencer, Secretary of the Civil Service Chess Association, addressed the meeting and gave details of the Objects of the Association. It was agreed that membership of the Club should be open to ladies(!) The first Annual General Meeting was held on 25th March 1926. The chairman stated it was intended to invite senior officers of the Ministry to become president and vice-presidents of the club.

A Committee meeting held on 16th July 1926 agreed that the league's secretary should be asked whether or not the Club's first team could be placed in division 1. A Half-Yearly General Meeting was held on 30th September 1926. The Chairman announced that Sir Horace Wilson had accepted the post of President. The club now had 66 members. It was announced that a 500-board match of Civil Service versus The Rest was to be held on 22nd October 1927 and that the club was seeking volunteers. It was said that the match would be the largest ever played.

At the Annual General Meeting held in September 1937, it was announced that the first team had finished third in division 3, and the second team had finished last in division 4. The Wilson trophy had again been won by the club. (This is not known as a CS chess trophy, but as Sir Horace Wilson was president, it may be that it was a Ministry of Labour Sports/Social Club trophy.) Mr Hodgson had finished runner-up in the CSCA individual championship.

At the Annual General Meeting of 2nd October 1946, it was announced that the Civil Service Chess Association had held meetings on 26th April 1946 and 6th September 1946.

Ministry of Labour changed its name to Department for Employment later.

BRITISH MUSEUM CHESS CLUB By Geoffrey S Barker

16th February 1951	Club inaugurated (Club nights Wednesday and Friday)
2nd November 1951	First match against East Sheen Chess Club
October 1952	Provisional club rules proposed
April 1954	Affiliated to CSCA and thereby access to LCS&M League
April 1956	Two teams in LCS&M League
	Purpose built equipment storage cupboard proposed
May 1957	10 wooden chess boards constructed by club member WS Deane
	WA Smith died
June 1957	Club committee post of Librarian started. Library created on book donations from RA Slade. Club nights restricted to Wednesday.
September 1957	Notice of retirement of founding member WS Deane
May 1958	Club Committee post of tournament controller considered
May 1959	Amalgamation with Natural History Museum Chess Club. Three teams in the LCS&M League.
June 1960	Club constitution adopted.
May 1962	Notice of retirement of founding member EL Sinclair.
May 1964	Club night changed to Monday. Two teams in LCS&M League.
	Notice of transfer of AW Newton to

	HM Customs and Excise.
April 1967	Untying of club from Natural History Museum. Amalgamation with Department of Education and Science rejected.
May 1969	Notice of retirements of founding members A Digby & AG Hudd.
May 1972	One team in LCS&M league.
May 1975	Club renamed British Museum/British Library Chess Club.
June 1977	Club library audit – 6 books missing compared to previous audit in 1971. Notice of retirement of RA Slade.
May 1978	Two teams in LCS&M League.
April 1979	Library audit – 8 books including one belonging to club secretary.
May 1985	Library audit – 9 books including one belonging to club secretary.
May 1989	CSCA disaffiliates from CSSC. One team in LCSPO&M League. Library audit - 9 books.
May 1990	CSCA funded by CSSC on an informal basis.
May 1991	Notice of retirement of SN Lal.
May 1995	Creation of new CSCA.
May 1996	Library audit – 10 books. Notice of resignation of TS Pattie.

DHSS CHESS CLUB By David Gilbert

We are technically the Health & Social Security Recreation Association (London) Chess Club. In 1972 when the two chess clubs merged, teams in the Civil Service League played under their departmental names so we naturally defaulted to DHSS. When the two departments split in 1988 HASSRA remained in place representing both departments. We chose to retain the DHSS name rather than take the HASSRA (London) Chess Club name.

(*DHSS Chess* published brief articles on the two bodies – ed.)

MINISTRY OF SOCIAL SECURITY CHESS By John James (First published in *DHSS Chess*, Volume 1, Issue 3, Christmas 1984)

Tired of raiding Russian chess magazines for material, the editors agreed that, as almost the last surviving member who can remember playing chess for the Ministry of Social Security prior to its merger with the Ministry of Health in 1968, I should write a short piece describing the chess club of those days. (Rather more survivors of the Ministry of Health club are still around and one, Raymond Gedling, is writing about them for the next issue.) The only other MoSS active survivor (I think) is Harry Cutler, retired now, but still on the pawn-pushing list.

MoSS chess was played in the recreation room under Ivybridge House. This meant we had to put away the table tennis table and often enough disentangle the boards and sets from odd items of the Carlton Players' props and dresses. Club home night was fixed – it had to be with so many other users.

The team, so far as I can recall, played in the fourth division in those days, except when it was playing in the Fifth. In other words, it was of a modest standard, though, as those were the days before a recognized grading system, I can't test my gut feeling that the league team was of a higher standard. There was no second team, and no exploitation of local office talent.

Top board was a Deputy Accountant General, a Mr Worrall (no relation of the cricketing gentleman). Board 2 was an elderly retired player. Harry was often to be found on about Board 3 or 4. Below him was Sir John Walley, a fearsome Deputy Secretary who strode like a mini-colossus over the little department, although he had to play to his strength in the chess team, since this game is nothing if not a great leveller. To prove the point, the next board was occupied by an elderly male shorthand-writer from the pool. If he was a day, he was 70, and if it was a choice between him or the blonde 18 year-old to take my dictation, you can imagine which choice I... but I digress. It left something of a hole in the team when he was dismissed for fighting the only other male typist. Dangerous days. Arthur Dinnis came next, a large untidy solicitor, who deserted us (the original cad!) when he joined the Department of Employment from where he is about to retire. The only other player I remember was Eddie Dare, who retired a year or so back, the only principal in the department, I should think, who was also a master-baker. He was remarkable for taking both the *Financial Times* and the *Morning Star*. And me? I played on the lower boards. The height of my ambition was to get the odd draw. I seem to remember one on a gloomy night in Rosebery Avenue against the Metropolitan Water Board.

I was away on a very long course when the departments merged and consequently I missed the funeral rites of the MoSS Chess Club. As you can see it has been almost totally interred in the new super-duper DHSS Club that was created.

One of the most awkward survivals was Sir John Walley who was elected president of the DHSS Club and re-elected in absentia every year. After we had heard not a peep from him for about six years, we finally plucked up courage to conclude that he wouldn't be too disappointed not to be re-elected for a further term!

CHESS IN THE MINISTRY OF HEALTH By Raymond Gedling (First published in *DHSS Chess*, Volume 1, Issue 4, Spring 1985)

The revival of the Ministry of Health Chess Club after the war was due in no small measure to the efforts of a small number of enthusiasts who had been playing for the club in 1939. Among them were men who had retired and made difficult journeys to help the club. The names of Pearman and Cordingley will mean nothing to present day players but they deserve honour for their part in keeping the game going. Both were of an old school, favouring King's Pawn openings and ever ready to try an Evans Gambit. The first post-war captain was P A Cooke, a great man for drawing a game. In a younger generation, McC Armstrong usually played top board. For the first year or two, I doubt whether we had more than 12 members for which to find 8 players for our first team. There was no woman member. Why were there so few then – and now?

There was a strong tradition in the club. It was demonstrated by the appearance of various trophies in a glass cabinet on the staircase of the Whitehall building. They included one which had been given before the war for competition between various branches, including Acton (the old Ministry had included what became the Ministry of Housing and all the insurance and pensions work except war pensions). Old hands made clear to us that we had inherited the mantle of Atkins, possibly the greatest of English amateur players and seven times English champion, who had played for the club. But was this a false tradition? When I checked up Atkins in the 'Encyclopaedia of Chess' recently, he was described as a school teacher. Can anyone tell me whether folk memory or the encyclopaedia should prevail?

The club started its post-war career in the first division of the Civil Service League. I can recall only two divisions and no second teams. For a number of seasons we finished about the middle of the league. The departments in the league were fewer than now but the larger offices were included and, to justify the 'Municipal' in the league's title, we had not only the London County Council but the Metropolitan Water Board which meant an occasional safari to Rosebery Avenue. The outstanding club of those years was the Post Office. I can recall them turning out against us (on eight boards) seven county champions. One of them, Broadbent, had been English champion. Post Office names of repute included Wernick (Surrey), Butcher (Midlands), Neale, Boxall and Perkins. The latter may still be active – he was present when I last played against the Post Office. Other strong sides were the Patent Office and the Board of Trade. It was a year or two before the Inland Revenue – dispersed during the war – came together to form a strong team.

These were the days before grading, which incidentally, owed a great deal in this country to a civil servant, the late Otto (Sir Richard) Clarke who had a prominent hand in creating the first grading list. Grading has contributed immensely to the improvement (and professionalism, in both good and bad senses) of English chess, but some of us think that it has killed a lot of the fun. Before grading, we did not argue much over about probably drawn positions if the team result was not in doubt. It was chess for fun, not chess for blood.

For the enthusiast there were a few Civil Service representative games to be had for the asking. Occasionally, they produced odd opponents. One of mine walked out and was not seen again in the match because I swapped off queens at move 6. Another took out his teeth and placed them where they faced me throughout the game. They positively grinned when I made a dubious move.

There were few opportunities for any of us to get any chess apart from our team games. We started a club championship but I doubt whether we ever had more than eight entries. There was no club night. Having started my chess in a club into which one could drop, at random, on two nights each week and always find an opponent, I noticed this. I noticed also the absence of any handicap tournament to encourage new players. Games at odds seem to have vanished from the chess scene, probably because standards have improved too much to make this practicable.

And there were very few books except the chess classics by Nimzowitsch and world champions like Alekhine and Lasker. I treasure my fourth edition of Modern Chess Openings but cannot recall any book of those days on a specific opening.

Open tournaments were few, not the weekly round that goes on all over the country these days. Hastings was the only place to go. One of our members retired and became, I think, treasurer of the Hastings club. One year, feeling unwell, he entered a very lowly section. He found all his opponents were from a local school. They played all games to a finish regardless of whether they were a queen down. He played into the night. He had no rest period.

And of course, we did not even think of the chess computer.

GOVERNMENT CHEMISTS CHESS CLUB By Edward

W Godly & Kevin J Thurlow

A Government Laboratory team played in the first season of the Civil Service League, although it is not clear if this were a Customs or Inland Revenue Laboratory. It had ceased to appear in the league by the time the First World War started. The Laboratory of the Government Chemist (LGC) was a separate body from 1911, although a lot of its work was done for Customs. In 1950 a chess club was formed, and the legendary JC Thompson was a founder member. There was nobody left from the old club, so they thought it was a completely new club. JC Thompson was Head of Calibrations section at LGC for 30 years and an ever-present in the first team. During WWI, he had flown in the Royal Flying Corps, only to be shot down and taken prisoner. He discovered in captivity that socks rotted quickly, so he got out of the habit of wearing them, and continued to be sockless for the rest of his life. On rainy days, he would happily walk through deep puddles, not fearing soggy socks for the rest of the day. 'Tommy' used to visit local shops in luncheon-breaks in a quest for old books and prints. The Hippopotamus came about as he was unhappy that so many opponents relied on opening theory and did not really think for themselves. Many of the games ended completely blocked and time-limits in league chess meant there were frequent draws. But there were violent tactical battles. He published (at his own expense) a booklet on the opening in June 1957, priced 6d, which included 18 games, including a win against Tartakower. Boris Spassky played a Hippo-type system against Petrosian in the World Championship and the editor of *Chess* said it was a pity JC Thompson had not lived to see this happen. As he was not only alive, but playing rather successfully, the match captain wrote to *Chess*, whose editor was happy to retract his comment!

The team started in division 5 (the lowest) in 1951-52, but won all 8 matches so convincingly, that the club was promoted straight to division 3, where it stayed for several years. The club's first team languished in division 4 for a while, but gained promotion in 1962-63, and again in 1963-64. In 1965, LGC became part of the Ministry of Technology, which did not have a club, so several good HQ players joined Government Chemists. After strong performances in division 2, the club gained promotion to division 1 for one year in 1966/67. Meanwhile, the second team was promoted in four successive seasons. It was the tradition that the Government Chemist was president of the club, and the Deputy Government Chemist a vice-president. When a Mr Longwell became DGC in 1966, he was invited to be VP, and to play chess for the club. He accepted the post of VP, but said, 'One sure way to lose all your matches would be to have me play in them. If it were snakes and ladders perhaps I might help.' Government Chemists did attract members from other bodies in due course, partly as LGC kept changing Government departments, and 'Government Scientists' might have been a better club name. National Physical Laboratory (NPL) had formerly played in the CS League, but when their CS League team folded, some of their members joined Government Chemists, including the NPL Director, Paul Dean. NPL still played in the Thames Valley League, and there was an annual start of season Chemists vs Physicists friendly match. Propellants, Explosives and Rocket Motor Establishment (PERME) also supplied players and by the 1970s, Government Chemists were starting to make their presence felt. After one victory, the opposition complained about the eligibility of some of the members of the team, but the CSCA immediately threw out the complaint. In 1972/73 promotion was gained to division 1 again, and by now the club was running four teams. The internal club championship attracted over 60 entries from a total of about 450 staff. Government Chemists managed to win the league in 1974-75, when leading clubs were fielding players graded over 170 on board 10. The second team came second in division 3, and the third team was second in Division 6. Within two years, we were running four teams, in division 1, 3, 5 and 7 (by then the lowest). This was to be the zenith as the policy of dispersal took effect and two years later, we were down to two teams. LGC was threatened with expulsion to Cumbria, and some staff members wisely got jobs in the London area. The early 1980s saw victory in the Bonar Law trophy, when several players produced stunning individual results to despatch the mighty Revenue in the Final. But by the mid-1980s, it was a struggle to field two teams and only a dozen players contested the internal events. An approach was made to Patent Office to merge, but this was declined. The Cumbria move was shelved when it became clear to everyone it made no sense. The club folded when LGC left Waterloo in 1988/89 and moved to Teddington, to share a site with NPL. An attempt was made to run an internal event, but there was only a handful of entries and very few games played. Those interested played for NPL or UNATS, but they were a minority. Over the years, many individuals from the club took on senior posts in the CSCA and the London CS League, including successive Chairmen, EW Godly and IM Pheby.

GREATER LONDON CHESS CLUB by Tim Pelling

The origins and early activities of what is now the Greater London Chess Club have, alas, been lost in the mists of time. Its earliest incarnation was formed in 1887 – of this at least we can be fairly certain – as part of the social life of the Metropolitan Board of Works. The self-appointed MBW came into existence in 1856 to deal with the day-to-day running of London's affairs. Starting with the best of intentions (the great Victorian, Joseph Bazalgette, did much valuable work for them), the body became prone to corruption which, in its last months, reached alarming proportions. The MBW was abolished in 1889, and the newly elected London County Council took over; and the chess club acquired a new name.

It is our club's strong belief that the LCC chess club was a founder member of the Civil Service Chess League. But it must be admitted that diligent research by the editor has failed to unearth any hard evidence to substantiate this. However, the inclusion of the word 'Municipal' in the full title of the league is a boost to our claim. It should be remembered that the LCC was a Local Government organization – not, strictly speaking, part of the Civil Service – and therefore the league needed to expand its remit so we could play in it.

The Civil Service League was formed in 1904, but there is no specific mention of an LCC team until 1907. A 'Local Government' team appeared earlier, but there is no proof that it was us although the writer thinks it very likely was.

Our real history begins in 1922 when the LCC moved into the new grand County Hall beside Westminster Bridge, and the chess club found its spiritual home. About this time too emerges the first name we can quote with confidence: the formidable John Foley. In his prime Foley was a strong player and he was a major force in Civil Service chess for many years. Probably he competed in the British Championship. With advancing years his playing strength decreased, but not his competitive spirit. He continued to represent LCC (and the later GLC) until 1974, at the grand age of 92. His last win in the club championship was in the 1961-2 season in his 80th year. This larger-than-life character was President of the club for many decades and always insisted on chairing all meetings. He brooked no opposition and it was amazing how his hearing aid malfunctioned when someone had the temerity to voice a different view! It took a long time that actually the elected Chairman (at the time, Bill Bush) should chair the meetings.

Some twenty years younger was the equally strong A Bernfield. Even now we don't know for certain what his first name was. He told the writer it was Abraham, but other evidence suggests it was Aaron. No matter – he was always known as Bernie. Bernie was an entirely different character from Foley. A tiger at the board certainly, but self-effacing away from it; and a true gentleman. He would always buy the first round at the post-match drink-up and, if you didn't tie him to his chair, the second and third as well. He was a regular competitor in the British Championship (a tradition in the club), by the way, continued to this day by James McDonnell), but ill-health sapped his energy and playing strength in later years. Nevertheless he and Foley dominated LCC chess for many years. Both names are justly commemorated by the premier competitions within the club.

In 1965 the London County Council was superseded by the Greater London Council. This had little effect on the chess club other than a change of name. It was another ten years though to the best period of the (now) GLC chess club. The new President was Geoff Ashelford. And by this time the mantle of the club's top rated player had been taken over by Tim Pelling. But there was strength in depth too. The GLC became the dominant force in Civil Service chess, and remained so from about 1975 to 1985. During this period too the GLC and the chess club hosted two major international tournaments in harness with the Lambeth Arts and Recreation Association (LARA). In 1980 and 1982 the public was able to come to County Hall and witness some of the world's top players in action, in events sponsored by Phillips and Drew. But all things come to an end; LARA disappeared, the tournaments – despite being both popular and successful – ceased; and the GLC chess club was about to suffer a double blow.

In 1986 the Greater London Council was abolished - a political decision without any obvious benefits to Londoners. The GLC's sister organization – the Inner London Education Authority (ILEA) – was allowed to survive for a while. So, under their aegis, the chess club continued at County Hall. Then, in 1990, ILEA was abolished too. This time there was no clear successor body. The new Greater London Authority was far too small to take over the roles of either GLC or ILEA (nor was it intended to) and there was certainly no room for a chess club.

It was just as well that the club was financially well-off for it suddenly had to pay large rents for a room at the Civil Service Recreation Centre – first at Monck Street then (when that was closed) at Chadwick Street. The club changed its name to the somewhat grandiose Greater London Chess Club (GLCC) and staggered on. The arrangement with the CSRC was initially uneasy and gradually became untenable: after all we weren't really a Civil Service club to begin with, and saying we were founder members of the CS Chess League cut little ice.

The years from 1990 to 2006 were a twilight period. We seemed unable to decide what sort of club we wanted to be. Indeed, many members expected it to fold within a few years when the money ran out.

In 2006 several members attempted to move the club out

of Chadwick Street and start anew as an independent club. A new member, Nigel Blades, who has probably done more than anyone to get the club looking forwards rather than backwards, was able to find a likely venue at St George's Church, Bloomsbury. Despite considerable (and in the circumstances, surprising) opposition, the move was completed later that year. We may consider this time as being the start of the modern era of the GLCC.

We finally began to come to grips with looking to the future, beyond the confines of the CS League. Additionally, we were thrown a lifeline by the league itself. The CS League, under its Chairman Ian Pheby, were sympathetic to the GLCC's problems and relaxed the conditions for playing in it. So we have been able to maintain all our links with the CS League while expanding our horizons.

We have been extraordinarily lucky as a club in having so many members willing to devote their time to it. But the brunt of the work falls typically to the team captains, treasurers, and particularly the secretaries. In the past 50 years tremendous secretarial stints have been worked by John Gorton, Geoff Ashelford, Gordon Broadbent and Paul Efstathiou. Derek Hadley has done so much for so long (whether as tournament director, general dogsbody, and briefly chairman) that he must be mentioned. So must our current treasurer, Phil Zammit, many times team-captain. Other long-time captains are Gerry Shapson (sadly no longer with us), Ken Huddart and Tom Fleming. Jim Robinson has been the club's 'meeter and greeter' for years and has worked strenuously to boost our recruitment drive. Several of the club's internal competitions have gone open, and other open blitz tournaments (some for the CS League) have joined the list; these are professionally run by Nigel Blades. Traditionally the chairman has had little to do beyond chairing meetings, but the present incumbent Tony Packham – another long-standing member – is well on the way to being the most active chairman in our history.

Were I to list everyone who has contributed, the roll-call would last for pages. But the club is grateful to all whether mentioned or not.

Correspondence Chess

(Based largely on information received from Ray Pomeroy)
Individual departments had played correspondence chess for some time, notably Inland Revenue, who continue to play to this day. Ministry of Social Security, Ministry of Health, Ministry of Aviation were active in the 50s and 60s, and Prebond played in the British Correspondence Chess League (BCCL). It was not until 1969 that Civil Service Chess Association played a friendly postal match against RAF and won by the narrowest possible margin, 15½-14½. Peter Bond (Secretary of CSCA) then organised the first CS Correspondence team tournament the following year, featuring Credex, Customs & Excise A and B, Health (London), Inland Revenue, Norcross DHSS A & B, Prebond A & B, Post Office (London), Rosyth CS and Rutherglen DHSS. Health won. CSCA beat RAF again, by the same score. In 1971, there were ten entries in the team event, Environment (Marsham Street) winning. In 1972, Ray Pomeroy took over the running of the event and was rewarded with 20 entries, the holders just losing to Inland Revenue. CSCA then affiliated to the British Postal Chess Federation, and in 1973 entered the BCCL, finishing second in division 2. The team was R Myers, R Williams, D Townley, CH Veale, R Pomeroy, T Edwards, F Ellison and K James. The 1974 CSCA Team event attracted 46 entries and National Giro won the top division. 'Only' 28 teams entered the following year and this time UNATS won. At this point, Prebond stopped playing in BCCL, and their players joined the CSCA team, leading to third place in the Premier Division, the B team was

5th in division 1, C team 7th in division 2 and the D team 8th in division 2. Players like Len Gibbins, Gordon Hickford and John Weir played for the next 30 years. In 1976, CSCA entered seven teams and the D Team (N Kent, D Moore, W Williams, R Bauld, K Lovel, S Smith, N Phillips and A Smith) won division 1. JT Pascoe won the BCCA Best Game Prize. CSCA beat the British Correspondence Chess Association (BCCA) 31½-26½. Ian Pheby started playing that year.

UNATS won the CSCA Team event in 1977, the first team to win it twice. Eight CS teams played in the BCCL, and Bob Ryan started playing, and he continues to do so. BCCA gained their revenge in the annual friendly match, winning 38½-29½. Peter Morton took over the CSCA Team event in 1978 and Inland Revenue won. Eleven CS teams played in the BCCL. The A Team (F Cartmel, R Borland, D Banks, J Calleja, D Willmets, K James, D Moore and M Firth) were third in the championship, thus qualifying for the British Postal Chess Team Championship (BPCTC), the top national competition. BCCA won the friendly by 52½-21½. 1979 saw the CSCA's debut in the BPCTC and in a fantastic performance were joint first with Sutton Coldfield and Streatham and Brixton. Sutton Coldfield won on Board Count and CSCA had to settle for second, still the highest placing CSCA has achieved. The very strong CSCA team was T Thomas, D Vaughan, G Mitchell, D Lees, JT Pascoe, DV Mardle, J Sargent, G Young and R Pomeroy. Trevor Thomas was good enough to beat the mighty Jonathan Penrose in CC five years later. Despite the fact that this team was entered, we managed to put 12 teams in the BCCL, the best CSCA ever managed. The friendly against BCCA grew again, but CSCA lost 38-40, also losing to British Correspondence Chess Society (BCCS) 15-37.

In 1980, Inland Revenue became the first team to win

the CSCA championship three times. CSCA were 5th in the BPCTC, and had three teams in BCCL's top division, the Championship (the Premier Division is below the Championship). The B team (F Cartmel, R Borland, D Banks, R Price, I Pheby, K Thurlow, S Smith, R Bauld) came second and the A team (M Prizant, D Lynch, S Gillam, B McCague, J Sargent, M Wiggett, D Townley, R Pomeroy) was third. The C team finished 7th. Kevin Thurlow and Dave Scuffam started their unbroken runs of playing for CSCA. CSCA beat BCCA 60-32 and Open University 18-6. The CS Team event did not take place in 1981. CSCA A were 4th in BPCTC and the B team were 9th. CSCA C team (S Gillam, D Willmets, P Curbishley, R Ryan, Dr A Islam, R Hulme, M Wiggett, D Moore) won the BCCL, (CSCA's first victory), ahead of the A team who were 5th and the B team who were 7th! CSCA A (S Gillam, F Cartmel, J Sargent, P Curbishley, D Cooper, R Ryan, M Corrigan, R Pomeroy, S Smith, D Moore) were equal first with the mighty Mushrooms in the Postal Chess League (PCL). CSCA lost 43-47 to BCCA and 16-20 to Sussex. CSCA had three teams in BPCTC in 1982, but the best position was 5th. Inland Revenue won the BCCL, with CSCA C again being the top CSCA team, but only finishing 7th. There were only nine CSCA teams in BCCL this season. John Sargent took over running the CSCA team event, and DHSS were first out of 14 teams. Inland Revenue won the BPCTC in 1983, just ahead of Sutton Coldfield and CSCA. Inland Revenue also won BCCL, just ahead of CSCA A. There was more of the same in 1984, IR winning the BPCTC, with CSCA A 3rd equal and CSCA B 8th. CSCA A were second in BCCL, but more importantly, we entered eleven teams in BCCL, and five in the PCL, CSCA D (M Burn, F Wilding, R Jones N Talbot, K Middleditch, E Lyon, F Deeks, I Howard, J Weir, J Moran) winning division 4.

1985 saw the disappearance of the CSCA team event again, but CSCA A were 3rd in BPCTC. CSCA A (M Prizant, B McCague, D Banks, M Burn, J Sargent, D Smith, R Bauld, R Pomeroy) won the BCCL at last. The D team (F Wilding, R Gedling, C Veale, G Tinnams, D Williams, M Duck, G Coy, R Mears) won the Premier Division. The final CSCA team event took place in 1986. Only ten teams participated. DHSS had their third win, making them the second most successful club after Inland Revenue, who had five wins. Bob Ryan, Ken Medcalf and Ray Pomeroy all took on Controller duties in various BCCL divisions. At this stage, Ray Pomeroy decided the team names were a bit confusing (and maybe boring) so new names were introduced, viz. Administrators, Bureaucrats, Civilians, Diplomats, Enthusiasts, Friends, Gentlemen, Hansards, Jugglers, Knights. There was no team beginning with 'I' as it looks like a '1'.

The 1987 BCCL was shared by Inland Revenue and the Bureaucrats (R Bauld, C Moore, J MacKness, M Firth, K Thurlow, R Hulme, M Duck, G Coy), the Administrators (M Prizant, I Pheby, D Banks, M Burn, D Pearce, J Sargent, D Moore, R Pomeroy) coming 3rd. The Diplomats (P Barrow, H Duff, S Halliday, N Twitchell, C Veale, F Wilding, R Gedling, G Tinnams) won the Premier Division again, but with different players. The following year the Administrators (M Prizant, M Burn, I Pheby, D Pearce, D Moore, J Sargent, T Packham, R Pomeroy) lost to Mensa A on board count in BCCL. In 1989, the BPCF started the British Postal Chess Federation Club Championship, (not to be confused with the BPCTC) which PCL won with 13½, ahead of BCCA 12½ and CSCA (D Vaughan, M Burn, I Pheby, K Thurlow, D Pearce, D Moore, J Sargent, G Pugh, R Bauld, R Pomeroy) on 12. The BPCFCC allowed organisations to participate as well as clubs.

In 1990, the Administrators (I Pheby, C Moore, T Packham, D Pearce, G Pugh, J Sargent, M Firth, R Pomeroy) won the BCCL. In 1991, Kevin Thurlow organised the inaugural CS individual CC championship, which was won by Ian Pheby. Harrow Land Registry wanted to play in the defunct CSCA team event, so entered the BCCL as CS Land Registrars. Alwyn O'Hare, Tony Rixon and Mike Bland still play for CSCA. Ian Pheby took over as controller of PCL. CSCA finished 4th in the BPCFCC but an unpleasant dispute soured the atmosphere. CSCA hoped it was an isolated problem, and continued to play, but again there were problems and so we withdrew. CSCA and Inland Revenue accepted a challenge from an European Commission team, which CSCA won 20-12. Chess and Bridge suddenly ended their support for PCL in 1992, and Fred Fenner took over running the much reduced competition. 1993 saw the third CS individual championship, won by Chris O'Bee and Kevin Thurlow on 5½/8. The Administrators (P Trussler, M Burn, C Moore, K Hyde, J Sargent, I Pheby, D Vaughan, R Pomeroy) again won the BCCL, and the Diplomats (M Duck, A Yavash, F Clarke, R Stephenson, E Lyon, P Pickering, M Corrigan, D Scuffam) won the Premier Division, but were not allowed to be promoted as CSCA already had three teams in the top division! Ray reorganized the teams so that the players were promoted, even if the team were not. 1994 saw Ian Pheby win the fourth and final CS individual championship. This season also marked the last friendly match played by CSCA, a close 15½-14½ win against BCCA. The following season, CSCA ran only seven teams in BCCL, but in the BPCFC, we finished 2nd, the best ever performance, with a team comprising K Hyde, M Burn, J Sargent, I Pheby, P Trussler, D Pearce, R Bauld, C O'Bee, G Pugh, R Pomeroy. In 1996, there were further problems with BPCFCC, so CSCA decided not to enter again. The event no longer exists, having merged with BPCTC in 2004. For the next few years, success was elusive, although some CS teams finished in the top three of their respective competitions. The number of teams fell gradually over the years. The Civilians (R Mitchell, G Bicknell, A O'Hare, D Scuffam, J Williams, R Mirams, R Gedling, V Hubbuck) won BCCL division 1. Individual success came for Ian Pheby who became a CC international master in 2002, and then a senior international master in January 2003. He then represented England in the 15th Olympiad. Bob Ryan became Chief Controller of BCCL.

The merger of the BPCTC and BPCFC (but still called the BPCTC) in 2004 allowed the organisations to dominate and the clubs fell away. The PCL disappeared at the same time, so our two teams transferred to the BCCL. As there was some overlap, we ended up fielding seven teams. In 2005 the Diplomats (C Duddy, I Calvert, D Scuffam, A Smith, R Bauld, P Barrow, V Hubbuck, P Pickering) won the Premier Division. The Scottish Correspondence Chess League (SCCL) took non-Scottish teams, so we entered two teams in their division 2, the B team (K Hyde, D Scuffam, G Bicknell, A O'Hare, V Hubbuck) winning, and the A team (D Laing, R Ryan, P Barrow, C Duddy, R Bauld) finishing 2nd. The 2006/7 season brought spectacular success. The Administrators (K Thurlow, J Sargent, C Walton, A Ashby, I Calvert, J Cooper, D Vaughan, G Coy) finished 2nd in the BCCL Championship, but Civilians (C Portman, N Lane, P Solomons, N Twitchell, G Pugh, K Hyde, D Scuffam, R Price) won the Premier Division, whilst the Diplomats (R Bauld, R Saunders, P Deeks, M Duck, P Coast, P Pickering, R Mirams, R Pomeroy) were 2nd. Friends (R Ryan, L Gibbins, R Johnson, R Haggett, S Brown, G Bicknell, V Hubbuck, R White) won division 2, with Gentlemen (R Lovelock, J Woodruff, A O'Hare, A Rixon, M Bland, G

Mill-Wilson, I Goodhand, R Pomeroy) just behind. Teams continued to perform well, without actually winning anything, the best performance coming from the Administrators (I Pheby, C Walton, K Thurlow, A Ashby, J Cooper, J Sargent, C Duddy, G Coy, K Norman) coming 3rd in the BPCTC in 2008.

The following year the SCCL set up a 'web server' league in addition to their postal league. The BPCTC and BCCL have now followed suit, and most players now say they will only play on web servers. Despite the increasing influence of computers, CC is still quite popular. There have been other changes to CC, but there has been a decline in the number of players and teams. Some quite successful leagues no longer exist. Web servers are reversing the decline to some extent. There have always been problems with genuine and claimed postal delays and disappearances, now you can make a move on a board in South East England and you know your opponent in Tahiti has received it in a matter of seconds.

Biographies

Over the years the *Bulletin* and the *Information Sheets* have published a number of obituaries of well-known members of the Civil Service Chess Association and the London Civil Service, Post Office and Municipal Chess League. These are given below, generally as published, but with the occasional explanatory note, e.g. giving the identity of an official merely denoted by title. Obituaries for the majority of past members were never published. Their absence is in no way poor reflection on those members. Biographies of well-known members have been added to the list.

JAMES MACRAE AITKEN (27/10/1908 – 3/12/1983)

He was 10 times Scottish Champion and represented Scotland many times in Olympiads. He retired from the Foreign Office about 10 years ago and moved to Cheltenham where he continued to play with enthusiasm. At Guernsey in late 1983 he scored 4/7 gaining a share of the 'Veterans' prize. He was his usual friendly self and still a good player. He defeated the author in an opposite-coloured bishop ending in the lightning tournament. When the author mildly suggested that he had been hoping to draw the ending, his distinguished opponent chuckled and said, 'Were you now!'

Kevin Thurlow, Bulletin Editor, February 1984

CONEL HUGH O'DONEL ALEXANDER CMG CBE (19/4/1909 – 15/2/1974)

By now many will have been saddened to learn of the

death, at the age of 64, of Mr. Alexander, but the loss of such a distinguished vice-president of the CSCA must be reported in our own news *Bulletin*. He was perhaps the most competent British chess player in recent years having defeated two World Champions and twice, in 1938 and 1956, taken the British Championship. More recently he was chess correspondent to the *Sunday Times* and became one of our leading chess authors. He served in the Government Communications HQ of the Foreign Office and had a distinguished war record in British Intelligence.

Tom West, July 1974

CHO'D Alexander was born in Cork, and studied mathematics at Cambridge University and taught at Winchester College. According to *Chess*, (January 1938), he 'still preserves a trace of Irish brogue and Celtic excitability – his hair sometimes begins to resemble a wild garden shrub at tense periods of the game and he constantly jerks intermittent remarks at his opponent.' If the last part of the comment is true, it is surprising nobody complained.

Mikhail Botwinnik wrote, '...with his urge for overcoming and taming opposition, with his enthusiasm for uncompromising struggle, Alexander pioneered the way for British players to modern, complicated and daring chess; chess players will never forget him.'

Alexander won Hastings in 1946 and finished equal first in 1953 and defeated such players as Botwinnik, Euwe and Bronstein during his career, a measure of his ability. The war and his work (which prevented him visiting Moscow for the 1956 Olympiad, or indeed playing anywhere behind the iron curtain ever) meant he never realized his full potential. Milner-Barry commented on the fact that Alexander had only won the British Championship twice, which he felt was a sign that

Alexander needed a challenge, and that playing Botwinnik and Bronstein was much more interesting than playing in British events. Certainly his results back up this theory.

JOHN MAURICE ALLAIN QPM (? – 2008)

John Allain achieved the unusual dual feat of being both a very high-ranking police officer and a very prominent chess player.

On the police side he joined the Metropolitan Police in the 1950's after National Service. He rose to the rank of Commander which was one of the top 30 positions in the Metropolitan Police. He was Commander on the old Q district which covered Brent. He retired in the early 1990's. Before he retired he was awarded the highly prestigious Queens Police Medal which is only awarded in the Queen's birthday and New Year's Honours list.

On the chess side he was a member of the Metropolitan Police chess club for many years. He was in the first team in the 1970's and 1980's and during that period regularly had a grade in the 160/170 area. He held several positions in the club and was chairman for a number of years. He finished playing in the early 1990's when he retired from the police. However after this he was chairman of the London Commercial League for many years and only stood down in 2005. He was also involved in junior chess at one or two schools in the London area. He also played a major role in correspondence chess and was until recently President of the British Correspondence Chess Association.

John had suffered from major health problems in recent years and had undergone quadruple heart bypass surgery. Nevertheless he remained one of the most approachable men you could hope to meet, and had time for everyone.

Adrian Barron, Metropolitan Police Chess Club Captain, January 2008

Awarded Queen's Police Medal 1987 when he was Commander in Metropolitan Police.

JEFFREY ANSELL

He was active in the resusciation of our Association in 1946-1947 after seven years of inactivity. He then started a chess club in the Ministry of Supply which had been created during the War. He could always be counted on if extra help were needed in the CSCA. He was also an adjudicator from 1956/57 to 1984/85.

E C Baker, CSCA Vice-President, November 1985

ANTHONY ASHBY (1947-)

Tony Ashby joined the Home Office in 1965 and played for UNATS until the Home Office started its own club in 1986. He played many times for the Civil Service on top board in representative matches against Oxbridge Colleges and in the Bronowski trophy. He was 1st team captain for the Home Office for a number of years. When the Home Office club had to disband, because of increased security measures at their venue, the members started the Pimlico Chess Club and introduced a new league, called the Central London League. Tony was elected chairman of Pimlico Chess Club and continued in office for eight years.

He won the national Civil Service championship four times, as well as the league blitz and lightning championships a number of times. He was for many years an adjudicator for the league.

A Surrey county player, in 2007 he was awarded the Frank Parr Memorial Prize for the best game played in the Surrey

League that season. A long-time member of Battersea Chess Club he won their 5-minute championship 8 years in succession, a record that has not yet been equalled.

When he retired from the Home Office the league created the 'Tony Ashby Shield', awarded annually to the player who had most improved their grade during the year.

Internationally, he competed in the 18th World Senior Chess Championship in 2008 in Bad Zwischenahn, Germany, scoring a creditable 7/11, coming 54th out of over 200 competitors. The following year (2009) he won the British Senior Championship at Torquay jointly with David Anderton and has since played for the England Senior Teams in World and European Senior Team championships. He was awarded the FIDE Candidate Master title for three international tournament performances over 2200, his highest rating being 2265.

GEOFF ASHELFORD (30/9/1929 – 2/11/2011)

Geoff was born in Jersey, adopted at a young age, and endured the German occupation in WWII. When his adoptive parents died, he was adopted again and moved to the mainland after the war. He joined the army and saw service in Korea. In 1960, he joined London County Council, which he said was rather like the army with its various ranks and disciplines. He became captain and secretary and was elected president in 1976. He was controversial at times. In addition to his official duties, he did much voluntary work for the RASC (Royal Army Service Corps) and the British Legion. He also helped staff who were at odds with the management.

Based on tributes by John Gorton and Phil Zammit.

EDWARD CECIL BAKER MBE (11/7/1902 - May 1997)

Distinguished and hard-working CSCA official. Secretary

(1948-1951), additional committee member (1951-1956), vice-chairman (1956-1958), and chairman (1958-1965), vice-president 1968. He played for the Post Office and was one of the leaders who resurrected the league after WWII. He also masterminded the *Handbook*, which appeared then. His articles for the *Bulletin* which appear elsewhere in this volume give a flavour of his splendid work for CS chess.

From personal correspondence between EC Baker and the author,

'During the course of the war and for several years after I was one of Churchill's historians and from thence went on to documentation (European P & T), archive, and special library work before getting a university appointment in America.

Chess has been a relatively minor interest in my life, but I've done far more than the measured mile for CS Chess.' (Considerably more than that – KJT)

SIR LEONARD BARFORD (died 3/4/1992, aged 83)
   Deputy Chief Inspector of Taxes, Inland Revenue 1960 - 64
   Chief Inspector 1964 – 73
   Commissioner, Inland Revenue 1970 – 73
   Deputy chairman, Horse Totaliser Board 1974 – 77
   President CSCA 1964-1992
   Knighted 1967

I first met Leonard Barford when I was transferred to London in February 1953 and joined Revenue Chess Club where Leonard was already an established first team player. Although I played a few games for the Revenue first team, it was not until September 1953 when I took over the captaincy that I really began to appreciate his many virtues.

To put my following comments in perspective one must

understand that Leonard Barford (at that time a young Grade 5) was already destined for greatness. Everyone spoke of him as the heir apparent for the ultimate job as Chief Inspector of Taxes, a mere three further promotions! He shortly assumed the onerous task of President of the Association of Tax Inspectors (now merged with the First Division Association) and took responsibility for negotiating the terms and conditions for Inspector of Taxes, and at the same time holding an official post. A man of great mental energy and ability.

Leonard not only fulfilled all the forecasts of his career by becoming Chief Inspector of Taxes, but was soon Knighted (1967) and then became the first Chief Inspector to be appointed a Commissioner of Inland Revenue.

It was very encouraging for me as a young captain to discover that all the trappings of high Revenue office were completely forgotten when Leonard sat behind the chessboard. He was then just one of the loyal members of a team, and he did his best by battling with lost positions until his gritty perseverance often carried him either to victory or a draw. He do not mind cramped positions and liked nothing better than swapping pieces and reaching an endgame. It did not matter to him whether he had an inferior position because he understood endgames and usually won. Although he played for the team before 1953, I only have records from 1953 to 1961: played 83, won 33, drew 32, lost 16. Indeed a hard man to beat.

Even after ceasing playing for the Revenue, he did not sever his interest in the game. In 1962 he became our President and then in 1964, President of the CSCA, both offices being held until he died at the age of 83. Despite the heavy calls on his time his interests extended beyond chess and he was also a fine bridge player.

Perhaps my most abiding impression of him was his kind

words of encouragement to me as a young captain: 'Make your own decisions about the positions for adjudication as I will never complain if you agree to a loss on my board'.

He joined the club in 1951 and played for the first team until 1960. His elevation to the most senior posts including Chief Inspector and on the Board of Inland Revenue brought his playing days to an end. He continued his interest in chess becoming President of the club and in 1964 President of the Civil Service Chess Association and this continued until his death. In 1968 he presented the Barford trophy for competition by teams of four at lightning chess. Sir Leonard was an authority on the Old Testament and a leading figure in the Sussex Masonic lodges.

Roland Smith, April 1992

SIR RICHARD BARNETT (6/12/1863 – 17/10/1930)

Barnett won the Ulster Championship aged only 12, and was Irish rifle champion three years later. He went on to be President of the Oxford University Chess Club and Irish Chess Champion. He finished 4th in the 'Men's Free Rifle at 1000 Yards' in the 1908 Olympics, only one point behind the silver medallist. He was President of the House of Commons Chess Club and it was reckoned that Bonar Law was the only stronger player in the House.

SIR GEORGE BARSTOW KCB (20/5/1874 – 29/1/1966)

Barstow was born in York on 20th May 1874 and was educated at Clifton College and Emmanuel College, Cambridge. He then entered the Civil Service. He worked for Local Government Board in 1896, but joined Treasury in 1898. In 1909 he was appointed a principal clerk in HM Treasury and shortly afterwards became an assistant secretary.

He was appointed Companion of the Order of the Bath (CB) in 1914 and in 1919 he was appointed controller of supply services at the Treasury, serving in the post until 1927. He received the KCB in 1920. In 1927 he became government director of the Anglo-Persian Oil Company (later the Anglo-Iranian Oil Company), holding the post until 1946. He also joined the board of the Prudential Assurance Company, and was chairman 1941-1953.

His name lives on in the form of the Barstow cup, which was presented to the CS individual champion. Strangely, he was not elected vice-president.

JY BELL CB (1877 – 14/12/1966)

Vice-president of CSCA, Surrey CCA and Guildford CC. Principal assistant secretary GPO. Spent the last 30 years of his life in Guildford, even winning the club championship in his 70s.

ABRAM BERNFIELD (1910 - 1982)

I am sure all who knew Abram Bernfield (retired 1976) will be saddened as were members of GLC Chess Club to learn of his death, at the age of 72, in the Bethnal Green Hospital on 27th December 1982. He was buried in the Jewish Community Cemetery at Bushey Green on 3rd January 1983. Regrettably, I learned of this only after several telephone calls to try to establish why 'Bernie' had not attended a chess club committee meeting on 11th January 1983. He had always been punctilious in presenting his apologies in advance if unable to attend a meeting or club event.

Bernie was one of the real characters in our club, someone I came to know, respect and warmly regard over the past twenty years. He was an inveterate chain smoker, a strict vegetarian and an avid chess player all of which, to a greater or lesser degree, doubtless accounted for his slightly emaciated appearance. He invariably carried a large, heavy briefcase which contained, among other things, packets of cigarettes, chess books and a small chess set. I marvelled that he could go around thus laden when he weighed only some seven stones. He was generous to a fault. An endearing habit he had in the pub was meticulously to write down a drinks order in Pitman's shorthand on an old envelope or odd scrap of paper. He was of the generation that had had to learn shorthand and typing within two years of entering the old general grade in order to remain in the Service!

In his time Bernie played against some of the great British chess masters such as CHO'D Alexander, Sir PS Milner-Barry and Sir George Thomas, and had some of his games published. He participated in chess congresses up and down the country over many years and had intended to play in the Lambeth congress organised by the club in February. He always acquitted himself well in these events but failed to win a major prize. However, he fared better in the club and won the championship seven times. I have not been able to establish the exact date on which he joined the club, but assume it was before the 1939-1945 War. He was appointed to the Committee in 1947 and was elected a vice-president at the 1972 AGM to mark his 25 years' committee service.

Bernie's close relatives predeceased him and he died a bachelor. Typically, he has bequeathed £100 and his not inconsiderable library of books on chess to the club. He will be greatly missed by all who knew him.

G P Ashelford, November 1983

I was sorry to learn of the demise of A Bernfield. He joined the LCC at the time of our Association's resurrection after the 1939-1945 War. He always played readily and cheerily on board 2 although he was a stronger player than John Foley who as doyen of the club and pioneer of social welfare in LCC regarded Board 1 as his prescriptive right. We remember Bernfield as unobtrusively courteous and friendly, a gentleman it was always a pleasure to meet.

E C Baker, CSCA Vice-President, November 1983

A further measure of Mr Bernfield's courtesy was when he played Anne Sunnucks in a representative match. She played a move which appeared to lose a piece, so he sportingly suggested she take the move back as it spoiled the game. She politely declined as she had already played the move, so the game continued, and Bernie soon realized that he was in trouble. Unbeknownst to him, it was the latest Soviet theory. (This incident pre-dated 'Women's Lib' by many years, so was genuine courtesy, not a grave insult.)

K J Thurlow 2011

PETER A BOND (21/6/1941-2003)

Peter was one of life's characters and a person with a heart of gold. He had a great love for his dogs, the Church and chess. He lived in New Southgate and was a tower of strength at the local Church Trinity at Bowes Methodist Church. Not only did he make the refreshments for Church meetings but washed up afterwards. One of his guiding principles was to help others less well off than himself and he often repaired electrical appliances or broken tools for the elderly parishioners or for those who had fallen on hard times. But despite all these good works not all the congregation appreciated Peter taking his dogs into the Church for Sunday morning service!! Peter also found time to bombard the local MP with letters if local matters needed attention and had been neglected.

Peter was a member of both Southgate and Inland Revenue

chess clubs. He did a lot of good work in both clubs and also helped the Braille chess club by putting games on tape for the blind chess players. I first met Peter when he joined the Inland Revenue club in 1965 and was elected 4th team captain. He then held a series of offices until 1979 including tournament controller, postal chess captain, 2nd and 3rd team captain. He won the club's minor championship in 1972/3 but his greatest victory was winning the 'Star Chess Galactic Championship' competition in 1979 – a national tournament for a three-dimensional space age game based upon chess. His prizes included a computer and printer, a holiday for three in the Isle of Wight but he declined a free trip to USA on Concorde. The photographs of Peter being awarded his prizes showed him surrounded by two very attractive Star Wars dolly birds and the robot dog K9. When I asked Peter what he thought of the Star War maidens he replied that he had only noticed the dog! His victory received wide press coverage in which Peter mentioned that he had held 44 offices in various chess clubs over the years. Peter continued to support the club as organiser of the lightning tournament which was held each year following the Annual General Meeting. He was elected a Vice-President of the club in 2000 in recognition of his long and valuable services to the club.

Peter's services to Civil Service chess were not confined to the Revenue club. He also gave outstanding service to the Civil Service Chess Association. In the period 1966-1976 he was divisional recorder (1966-1967), secretary (1968-1972), *Bulletin* editor (1968-1969), postal chess controller (1970 and 1971), lightning tournament controller (1974 and 1975), representative to the Civil Service Sports Council (1971, 1875 and 1976) and officer without portfolio (1985-1990). In all 22 years' service to add to what he did for the Revenue and other chess clubs. In 1991 he was made a vice-president of the Civil Service Chess Association and became vice-president of the London Civil Service Chess League in 1994 when the CSCA and the league split into separate bodies. What an amazing record of service to help others enjoy their chess!

Peter was a member of other chess clubs - Southgate, Nomads and Morley College. He had a heart of gold and for many years helped the Braille chess club and his local church where he was always mending electrical appliances for the needy members of the parish. But not all appreciated his eccentricity when he took his two dogs to church every Sunday morning especially when the big one caused havoc during an anthem by the choir.

But my abiding memory of Peter was at his funeral which was attended by a 92 year old friend in a wheelchair paying his own personal tribute to Peter who went to play with him most weeks. That is the stature of Peter who dedicated himself to help others.

Thank you Peter for all your good works.

Roland Smith (Secretary of CSCA and the London Civil Service League, and captain of Inland Revenue Chess Club), August 2003

Note – Peter was elected vice-president of Beckton Rooks Chess Club to his delight – 'I have always wanted to be president of vice!' (Kjt)

Ron Fleming (IR) commented, 'I will give you my recollections on Peter Bond. He and I moved in different circles in the Estate Duty (now Capital Taxes) Office, and I have little knowledge of his official activities. I recall him as an eccentric and not one with whom I was in tune. So let it rest.'

EC Baker said, (personal correspondence) 'Bond, on the contrary, is a lively character - mad as a hatter.'

RJ BROADBENT (3/8/1906 – 29/10/1988)

RJ Broadbent, one of our vice-presidents, died at the end

of October 1988 aged 82. He had been Northern Counties Champion for several years when, in 1946, he was transferred from Manchester to London. He made many contributions to Civil Service chess thereafter until pressure of official work on his promotion to assistant secretary forced him to give up chess except for an unobtrusive Saturday column in the *Western Morning News* which he had started to contribute in 1948 when he first won the British Championship.

He served on our adjudicators' panel for a number of years and in that capacity for Oxford and Cambridge University matches. His ability to assess positions was exceptional in that he viewed positions in his own games equally dispassionately. He found little time to play in tournaments but did accept an invitation to the London Congress in 1946 and the Staunton Centenary Congress in 1957. On neither occasion had he managed to make much preparation. His most remarkable international performance was in the Britain v Holland ten- a-side double round, annual matches. By 1947 after four such matches the Dutch led with two wins and a draw, but Broadbent had won seven games and had drawn the eighth. The BCM Editor, J H du Mont who had earlier described him as the English Capablanca in reporting on the match wrote '... it must be a matter of great astonishment to the Dutch that we do not play Broadbent No. 1.'.

Only occasionally did he play for the Civil Service in Saturday matches as when he successfully led a 50 board team against Essex in 1947. More importantly, since our Association exists primarily to serve its constituent clubs, he rarely, if ever, missed a club match, though he often arrived at an away venue within a few minutes of the allowable half hour on the clock. Nor would he demur from conceding a draw to his opponent in an unfinished game if GPO had already won the match for he was never interested in grading figures. He did draw the line at one match where John Foley (LCC) claimed a draw having managed to retain an equal force during 36 moves at the cost of a position which made Dr Thompson's 'hippopotamus' defence look like an open game. Broadbent then demonstrated a forced mate in eight moves.

E C Baker, March 1989

JACOB BRONOWSKI (18/1/1908 – 22/8/1974)

He was born in Poland and read Mathematics at Cambridge. Became Scientific Deputy to the British Chief of Staff Mission to Japan, and wrote the classical report on the effects of the atomic bomb attacks in Hiroshima and Nagasaki. It is reported he visited Hiroshima as part of this work, and possibly Nagasaki as well. He joined the National Coal Board in 1950. In 1973, he presented the classic BBC Television series, The Ascent of Man, which many people regard as the best TV programmes ever made. He was interviewed for a role in Intelligence in the early part of World War II, but was not accepted, for unknown reasons. He is perhaps best known in CS chess circles as the presenter of the Bronowski cup (in 1964).

KJ Thurlow 2012

DAVID BURFORD

Members will be saddened to learn of the death of David Burford who had represented Treasury Chess Club for over 25 years. As well as being a regular member of the Second Team David made a significant contribution to the well-being of the club, most notably by looking after its finances for a number of seasons, assisting in the purchase of the club's current sets and donating the Summer cup.

Ian M Pheby, March 2008

WILLIAM L BUSH

Bill Bush joined the then London County Council Chess Club in 1955. He served as an administrative officer in the Treasurer's department of the LCC and subsequently the GLC from 1941 to 1983 when he opted for early retirement. Since joining the chess club he became successively 1st team captain, 2nd team captain, vice-chairman, chairman and vice-president. He was also chairman and treasurer of the club's sub-committee responsible for organising the LARA Chess Congresses from 1978 to 1985. Additionally, he was a past member of the CSCA Executive Committee. Bill was a quietly spoken person, but when occasion demanded, could be vigorous in pursuit of an argument if convinced of the justice of the cause. He was a well-respected member and staunch supporter of his club, and he will be missed.

Geoff Ashelford, May 1994

Rt. Hon. SIR ALEXANDER CADOGAN, PC OM GCMG KCB (25/11/1884 – 9/7/1968)

Vice-president of CSCA

Cadogan had been a career diplomat. He was a director of the Suez Canal company and a friend of the Prime Minister Anthony Eden. He did not hold public office after retiring in 1957. He was the first former civil servant to be chairman of BBC when appointed in 1952 aged 67. At that stage he had never watched a BBC programme. He asked Churchill what to do, and received the reply, 'Just be fair.' Cadogan, who had joined the Diplomatic Service in 1908, had spent all but two of the following years in the Foreign Office. Between 1934 and 1936 he was first minister and then ambassador to China, and since October 1936 assistant under-secretary in London. In the 1930s, he rejected suggestions that Hitler should be shot with high-powered rifles from the British Embassy in Berlin. Cadogan also presided over an Office facing fundamental administrative change. In conversation with Cadogan in the late autumn of 1940, Ernest Bevin, the new minister of Labour, urged on him the need for the Foreign Office to take a greater interest in industrial and labour matters. Bevin soon recognised Cadogan as an adviser of exceptional value.

DR HENRY REGINALD CALVERT (25/1/1904 – 15/8/1992)

I am very sorry to report the death of Henry Calvert. *The Times* carried an appreciation on 29th August which reported a varied scientific education at St. John's College, Oxford, University of Göttingen and London University. After a spell with industry, he entered the Science Museum in 1934. During the War he joined Ministry of Supply to do research into ballistics, returning to the Science Museum in 1946 to be a Deputy Keeper. In 1949 he became a Keeper in the department of Astronomy and Geophysics, and retired (gradually) by 1969. He was also treasurer of British Society for the History of Science from 1952 to 1963.

He played chess for Department of Education and its predecessors for many years and became chairman and vice-president of CSCA. He joined Redhill Chess Club in 1946 and finally left in 1981 when he found his enjoyment hampered by losing to inferior opposition due to tiredness at the end of a long evening. He was still a force to be reckoned with in the 1970s. He retained an interest both in the CSCA and Redhill Chess Club thereafter. I shall remember him for his kind good humour and his complete absence of 'side'. He was always very encouraging and supportive and he will be greatly missed.

Kevin J Thurlow, Bulletin, September 1992

He played for some years with UNATS and then became a

founder of the Ministry of Education/DES Chess Club, as well as its first chairman. He will be remembered as a good club player, though never of the highest rank, a man whose quiet humour never allowed him to take the game, or himself, too seriously. During the quiet of the match we would hear his heavy sigh and his stage-whisper 'Chess is a silly game!' when both his colleagues and his opponent would know he was laying some deep-laid trap. I expect that when he approached the pearly gates he gave a similar groan with the comment 'Mine has been a silly life!', but St. Peter was not deceived either. He let him in at once.

Eric Croker, September 1992

When we elected Dr H R Calvert to our Executive Committee in 1951 our Association had rapidly grown to 40 clubs since its resuscitation in 1946. The majority of club officers were newcomers, hence our Committee found plenty of questions to answer at its monthly meetings which prevented the bad practice of introducing rules to meet unusual situations. Our Chairman (AG Pockett) thought we could continue in the free and easy manner of pre-War days when all club officials were well known to each other. His view found no favour. In such an atmosphere H R (Doc) Calvert, with his quiet, good-humoured, practical suggestions, made a valuable contribution. His own club (UNATS) was made up of members from half a dozen Ministries each hoping to gain enough members to hive off and form its own club. He was captain of UNATS first team which included P S Milner-Barry.

He became vice-chairman in 1959 and acted as chairman from mid-1962 when the holder of that office (AG Pockett) took up an overseas post, although our *Handbook* did not show him as chairman until its 1964 issue. He retired four years later to be forthwith elected a vice-president. Throughout those years he had played regularly in our representative matches, and among the treasured memories of fellow team members are pleasant pre-match strolls with him in Oxbridge and relaxation, following home matches, at venues such as 'The Printer's Devil' in Fetter Lane (which did for the history of printing what 'The Yorker' in Piccadilly had done for cricket). There we chatted, not about games we had just played but of fringe scientific subjects when we were not prompting him to reminisce on his student days in Germany.

E C Baker, November 1992

FREDERICK CAMM (ca 1887 – 9/7/1966)

Frederick Jackson Camm (Ministry of Labour) was a barrister and member of the Inns of Court and was awarded the Military Cross during service with the Essex Regiment in World War I. He was a member of West London CC, had won their championship many times and had occupied all the leading committee posts at one time or another.

SIR ARCHIBALD CARTER (1887-????)

Vice-president of CSCA

Sir Richard Henry Archibald Carter, KCB, KCIE, Permanent Under Secretary of State for India [*from 1947*] and Joint Permanent Under Secretary of State for Commonwealth Relations [*from 1948*].

SIR RICHARD WILLIAM BARNES CLARKE, KCB, OBE (usually known as Otto Clarke) (13/8/ 1910 – 21/6/1975).

He was a Cambridge graduate and sat the examinations of the Royal Statistical Society in 1932, being awarded the Frances Wood prize. He later worked for the *Financial News*, which was taken over by the *Financial Times*, and he devised the Ordinary Share Index, now known as the Financial Times Ordinary Share Index. He was in the Ministries of Information, Economic Warfare, and Supply and Production, during World War II, with a spell in the Combined Production and Resources Board in Washington DC. He was awarded the OBE in 1944 and joined the Treasury in 1945. He ended his career as permanent secretary in the Ministry of Technology, retiring in 1971. He was a fine player – Cambridge University's team in 1930 – 32 started CHO'D Alexander, RWB Clarke, J Bronowski. Clarke gave up playing chess when he left Cambridge. He is best known as the originator and mainstay of the British grading system. He was well aware that it was only a measure of performance and warned against using it as an absolute judge of players' ability. The background mathematical work he carried out was most impressive.

KJ Thurlow 2012

HAROLD GODFREY COLE (1879 - 27/1/1922)

He had played for England and was a noted player, finishing 2nd in the 1912 British Championship. He played above EG Sergeant in the Somerset House team in 1912. Ill-health reduced his activity later.

F G TIMS COLLINS (3/6/1915 – 27/11/1943)

His father was George Collins and his mother Beatrice Collins (nee Tims), who married in 1913, so his name was an amalgam of the two surnames, although the Tims was used as a forename. He died in a Mark III Lancaster bomber (DV289), which was shot down over Heuchelheim, en route to Berlin. Two of the eight crew survived. Collins was a member of 101 Squadron, based at Ludford Magna, Lincolnshire, with the fitting motto 'Mens agitat molem' (mind over matter). This squadron bombed Peenemunde (home of the V1s) the month before his death. His epitaph reads, 'With the wings of a bird and the heart of a man he compass'd his flight.' (from 'The New Icarus' by Ernest Rhys.)

He was London Boys Champion in 1933, and joint first in the 1933 British Boys championship, with 2½/3, but lost the play-off. He went on to become Civil Service Champion, winning the Barstow cup on both the occasions he played in it, in 1938 and 1939. He also played top board for the CS.

EUGENE ERNEST COLMAN (11/10/1878 – 20/7/1964)

Played top board for Cambridge U vs Oxford U in 1901, and later received acclaim from Pillsbury for his game in a match against leading American Universities. He joined the Indian Civil Service, and headed for Singapore, becoming in due course, a magistrate, a barrister and 'Currency Commissioner', whose signature adorned the currency. During World War II, Japan overran Singapore and he was sent to the notorious Changi prison. Here, he worked out the Colman variation of the Two Knights Defence, which he used to great effect in the London League, when he had recovered sufficiently from his war time ordeal. When Changi was liberated, the Japanese Commander committed hari-kiri and left a note saying, 'I lose at chess. No flowers bloom in the garden.'

DEIDRE COLMER (1912 – 26/8/1968)

Members may have heard the sad news of the death recently of Deidre Colmer who, as her many friends and acquaintances in Civil Service chess circles will know, bore a serious illness bravely and cheerfully for many years. Deidre had a distinguished record as a player, having been, on one occasion (1950), third in the British Ladies championship. She was also the first Civil Service Ladies champion and, on a number of occasions, played for the Civil Service representative team. In the Ministry of Power Chess Club she will be remembered as a leading player who gave generous encouragement and advice to younger players. Her memory will be kept alive by 'The Colmer Cup', a trophy she presented to the club and is awarded annually to the winner of the handicap championship.

PA Bond, Bulletin, December 1968

Note – Eileen Tranmer reported visiting her in hospital a few weeks before her death and found her, 'entertaining three guests and also playing a game on her pocket board with a medical student.'

PERCY B COOK (ca.1920 – 1985)

It was with great sadness that we heard that Percy Cook had at last succumbed to the illness that had afflicted him since he retired. Percy had spent his life playing chess, over 30 years with the Inland Revenue, for Civil Service, Ilford and Kent. He played at the BCF and Hastings congresses most years and still found time to play at many others. The effort that Percy put into making the Inland Revenue Club a successful and happy one will always be remembered. Quite apart from being ever present in the first team, he gave a considerable amount of his time helping weaker players and assisting the match captains of the lower teams. His results in the club championship were astounding with an incredible 16 victories. When Percy was at the height of his powers in the 1950s and the 1960s he competed in the British Championship on more than one occasion, as well as playing in some of the very strong tournaments at Hastings and elsewhere. He has left behind a meticulous record of over 3000 match games and one is immediately struck by the strength of his play with the white pieces where he always commenced with Pawn to King four. The record of his best games where he either won or drew includes such opponents as J Penrose, CHO'D Alexander, I Konig, N Littlewood, AY Green, A Phillips, PS Milner-Barry and many others who have graced the top echelons of British chess. Percy was one of those players who became a legend in his lifetime and he will forever remain a legend in the annals of the Inland Revenue Chess Club.

Percy joined the club in 1947 and held various offices, including first team captain (1959 and 1966 – 1982). He first won the club championship in 1948 and added a further 13 victories. Although Percy liked country walks he devoted his life to chess playing also for Ilford and represented Kent and the Civil Service. He played regularly in tournaments and several times qualified for the British Championship where he played with distinction against many of the finest players in the UK.

Percy was undoubtedly a loveable eccentric but one with a heart of gold. He will long be remembered for the help and guidance he gave to other players by attending second and third team matches, giving lectures and so on. His ill health in 1982 shortly before he was due to retire sadly brought an end to his competitive chess and he spent his final years at the Star and Garter Home at Richmond where he encouraged many of the disabled residents to play chess.

Roland Smith, August 1985

He passed me one afternoon in Kew Gardens, carrying a string bag bulging with assorted groceries. He was quite oblivious of the flowers and trees and of passers-by, day dreaming I supposed of some chess position. I turned and stopped him and he blinked amiably at me as if I were some friendly visitor from Mars.

E C Baker, November 1985

Ian Pheby recalls playing Percy on Board 5 in a Government Chemists vs Inland Revenue match in 1979. The latter were leading 5-0, when Ian offered a draw. Percy was most perturbed, and said, 'You know if I accept the offer of a draw, your team will lose the match.' Ian responded that he was well aware of this, but he was struck by Percy's sportsmanship. IR won 8½-1½.

PERCY A COOKE

Housing and Local Government. Did a great deal for CSCA before WWII. Died of heart failure on the train home after a London League match.

SIR JOHN WARCUP CORNFORTH (7/9/1917- 8/12/2013)

Cornforth joined National Institute of Medical Research (NIMR) at Hampstead and then at its Mill Hill Research Laboratories in London, where he remained until 1962. He subsequently won the Nobel Prize for Chemistry in 1975. He was a similar chess strength to Aitken and Mardle.

GEORGE PHILIP STANLEY COY (28/5/1917 – 12/8/2019)

Philip Coy played in the Civil Service championship (Barstow cup) in 1935 not expecting to get far. He met the experienced veteran BHN Stronach in the semi-final and played for five hours and 85 moves in a single session after work. He won the final as well and retained his title the following year, and won the Kent championship in 1939 but the start of World War II prevented the South of England tournament scheduled for November 1939. He moved to Sussex in 1979 and played on Board 2 for Hastings below Stuart Conquest. He gave up over the board chess in 1980, but continued playing correspondence chess until he reached his 100th birthday. He was an adjudicator for the league until quite recently before that. He passed away a father, grandfather, great-grandfather and great-great-grandfather.

SIR ERIC CRANKSHAW KCMG MBE (1885-????)
Vice-president of CSCA

Appears to have been responsible for the Government Hospitality Fund during WW2.

ERIC CROKER (3/11/1923 – 18/12/2014)

BCF Senior Arbiter and President of Middlesex CCA. Long and distinguished career in chess, played for Department for Education and Science, and was member of CSCA Committee. After he was arbiter at the European Deaf championship, Eric commented, 'This is the noisiest event I have ever been in charge of.' He was arbiter at Guernsey Festival for many years and his calm demeanour and helpful attitude endeared him to all. Received BCF President's Award for Services to Chess in 1991.

JAMES T CURTIS (1897 – 26/10/61)

Many of our members knew JT Curtis, Ministry of Labour & National Service, and they will be sorry to learn that he died on 26th October 1961. He had been ill for some time but had returned home from hospital a week or two earlier.

We remember with gratitude Jim's assistance when our Association was reformed after the War. Without it we could not have restarted our representative matches. It was thanks to him that we were given the use of attractive premises in St. James' Square on Saturday afternoons. Refreshments for our visitors were a problem and Jim used to spend the whole of Saturday morning preparing these himself. Alas, no more shall we hear 'Would anyone like another cup of tea or another sandwich?' in his quiet friendly tones.

He shared the Association auditing task with FJ Dadd for many years. At our annual meeting in May 1960 we elected him vice-president with, I remember, some acclaim. Undoubtedly he was pleased by our tribute but his simple self-effacing acknowledgement was characteristic. He has given us many happy hours and will remain in our affections.

That no flowers should be sent to his funeral was a long-spoken wish. Your Committee agreed to send a contribution to the Cancer Research Fund instead. He was commemorated with one of the individual trophies.

E C Baker, November 1961

FREDERICK JAMES DADD MVO (3/3/1894 - 1977)

Secretary of UNATS when it was founded, but most impressively Auditor of CSCA accounts for more than 50 years.

ARTHUR STOKES DAMERELL (1877 – 1952)

Born in Bodmin, Cornwall. Joined the Excise branch of Inland Revenue and learned chess in Carlisle, then later became Senior Chief Clerk of Customs and Excise, Bristol. He joined Bath Chess Club and spent his final years in Bath.

Bath Chronicle & Weekly Gazette (20th August 1938) and KJ Thurlow

SIR WILLIAM SCOTT DOUGLAS, GCB, KBE (20/8/1890 – 17/2/1953)

We regret to announce the death, at the age of 62, of our late President, Sir William Scott-Douglas, GCB, KBE, only two years after his retirement.

P B Sarson, Bulletin, 1953

He was permanent secretary of Ministry of Supply during the

war and then in Ministry of Health from 1945 – 1950, being very much involved in the implementation of the National Health Service, working closely with Aneurin Bevan. Bevan specifically mentioned Douglas in his tenth anniversary of the NHS speech to the House of Commons. (KJT)

SIR HAROLD EMMERSON GCB, KCVO (7/4/1896 – 2/8/1984)

Vice-president of CSCA

Harold Emmerson joined the Civil Service as a junior clerk as he felt that his family's financial circumstances prevented acceptance of a university scholarship. This proved no barrier to a very successful career. After service in the First World War, he joined Ministry of Labour. By 1926, after the General Strike, he was secretary of a Government Mission sent to USA and Canada to study industrial relations. He continued to progress, being Principal Officer Civil Defence for Northern Region, at the start of the Second World War, but returned to London in 1940 as Chief Industrial Commissioner under Ernest Bevin (then Ministry of Labour), and dealt with conflicting needs for manpower from the armed services. He became permanent secretary at Ministry of Works from 1946 – 1956, when he intended to retire, but was persuaded to continue as permanent secretary of Ministry of Labour (when Iain MacLeod was Minister) from 1956 – 1959. He was awarded the GCB as soon as he accepted the post and retired when his Minister moved to other work. Sir Harold was vice-president of the CSCA from 1949 and startled the organisation by attempting to resign this 'post' in 1969.

(Sources for the above include the *Times*)

SIR ALFRED FAULKNER, CB, CBE (3/7/1882 – 15/7/1963)

He left King's College, London and joined the Admiralty in 1901 in a low clerical grade, but became Director of Sea Transport in 1920. He left this post in 1927 to become permanent under-secretary for Mines in 1927. He was a practical man and solved problems sometimes with methods, 'a bit arbitrary by some Civil Service notions', but they worked. Although he did become a Knight Bachelor, he was never a 'Knight of the Order of the Bath, or even of the British Empire, and he felt these discriminations acutely.' The *Times* Correspondent suggested that Faulkner suffered from not being an Oxbridge or Public School type, which held him back. He retired in 1942. He became a vice-president of CSCA in 1949.

(Sources include the *Times*)

SIR WARREN FISHER (22/9/1879 – 25/9/1948)

Head of the Home Civil Service 1919 - 1939. He was a prime mover in the start of the Civil Service Sports Association (later Council). His approach to his political masters was unusual. When a man called Bullock was disciplined on an ethical matter, Fisher wrote to his Minister (Neville Chamberlain),

'Neville Dear – I did enjoy getting a little note from you – it gives such a cosy feeling. Bless you.

That's a truly delightful paper about Bullock isn't it? But there's no escape from the consequences.

With fond love, Warren'

Not quite the 'I remain, sir, your obedient servant' style that one associates more with the era.

NIGEL FLEMING

Joined Inland Revenue (which became HMRC) in 1982, left in 1985 for private sector and moved in 1996 to work in USA.

The chess scene was much different there as team chess was not real aimed at non-grandmasters. He joined the legendary Marshall Chess Club in New York, as well as playing in the 'World Open' in Philadelphia, where even the Under 2000 section had a first prize of $20000, and playing chess in the parks. Returned to UK about ten years later, where he became treasurer of the league.

R D FLEMING (1919 – 1/1/2006)

Ron was brought up in a chess environment as his father was a keen chess player and secretary of the Southern Counties Chess Association. In 1932 his father arranged for the annual British Chess Congress to be held at Ronald's school and the celebrated Sultan Khan won the tournament. To commemorate the congress the BCF awarded a medal to the school for a chess competition which Ron won three times. Ron's father played for East Kent and Ron would go to watch, but on one occasion Ron played to avoid the team losing a game by default. Although a Bishop and Knight down he played on and checkmated his opponent! Ron won a boys tournament at Margate and often played at Hastings and one year he represented the SCCU in the British Boy's championship. Until 1938 when he left home to work in London Ron played correspondence chess for Bucks/Northants and thereafter played in matches for Kent.

In 1938 Ron started work in the Revenue at the Estate Duty Office (EDO) and this entailed studying while working and attending law lectures at King's College where he gained a LLB (Hons). The proximity to Somerset House led him to join the Inland Revenue Chess Club based next door at Somerset House. When war came, the EDO moved to Llandudno but soon Ron was called up and joined RAOC. In 1946 he was given an early release to do 'work of national importance' – the need of the EDO was greater!! Ron returned to Llandudno but in 1947 EDO returned to London where Ron stayed until his retirement in 1980. On retiring, Barbara and Ron bought a bungalow in Ferring but Ron then got a job at the Stamp Duty Office in Worthing until November 1981 when he finally retired !!

Ron played chess for the Revenue, Kent and Civil Service, and until recently he also played postal chess for Kent. In the Revenue's golden period in the 1950's and 60's Ron played for both the 1st and 2nd teams. I well remember his marvellous results during my captaincy in the years 1953/4 to 1957/8 when he scored 21 wins in 24 matches. He played even more games in the period 1958/9 – 1969/70 scoring 61½ from 96. An amazing record for someone who professed that he couldn't take chess seriously and was more interested in his family life !!

Ron's contribution to chess administration has been enormous as secretary (1950–1956) and treasurer (1950–1953) of the Revenue Club. For the CSCA he was treasurer from 1951 to 1984, controller of the ladies championship until it ceased in the 1970's and vice-chairman 1980-1983. In recognition of his services he was made a vice-president in 1984 and in 1995 became president of both the CSCA and the London Civil Service, Post Office and Municipal Chess League. He was the first untitled holder of the office of president but no one was more deserving of this honour.

Personal condolences have been sent by me and our Chairman Ian Pheby to his widow Barbara and the family, and also on behalf of the CSCA, the London CS Chess League and the Revenue Chess Club.

Roland Smith, January 2006

JOHN FOLEY (ca 1889? -1/2/1976)

When we reorganised in 1947 after the War John was a member of the London County Council Club which, with a roll of fifty members, was our largest club. The LCC in 1951 elected John as its President and in 1957 he was elected to our Executive Council, a position he held until 1969 by which time, handicapped as he was with increasing deafness, he was finding travel between his home in West Dulwich and London something of a trial, and his name was added to our roll of vice-presidents.

As a chess player he was noted for his tenacious play – his forebears were from Yorkshire – and for years the LCC to his satisfaction played him on its top board. John missed no opportunity to further chess in LCC and missed no meeting of our Council. Only when he gave me a MS of his on *Welfare Work in London* to submit to a publisher did I learn that he was London's original professional welfare officer being appointed in 1900. Thus he must have been not that far short of qualifying for a telegram from the Queen when he died. A little below medium height, slightly built, white haired but with a fresh complexion, he looked younger than his years, a thought that occurred to me when he was playing off-hand charity games one afternoon at a Dulwich charity fete. He invited challengers at a shilling a game and offered a travelling set as a prize. At the end of the day he still had the set and the charity an extra two or three pounds.

As a Council member he looked forward each year to accompanying our team to Cambridge where he made the point of calling on EM Forster, the GOM of English letters, at his rooms in King's College. They had been colleagues years before at the Working Men's College, Mornington Crescent. Forster had taught English and John had given introductory lessons on the same subject. The tutors at that College did their work for no pay whatsoever. John gave me a conducted tour one evening in the mid-fifties; the enthusiasm of Forster's day had long since disappeared, but clearly the College was still serving a useful social purpose. John was always punctilious in providing an obituary sketch for its magazine on anyone, of the many he had known, who had at some time served the College. It seems only just, therefore, that we should attempt such a tribute to a good-hearted man, who for all his stubborn hang-on-at-all-costs chess play was self-forgetful in his interest in the welfare of his fellows.

E C Baker, CSCA Vice-President, May 1976

John Foley, President of the GLC Staff Chess Club and a vice-president of the Civil Service Chess Association died after a short illness in King's College Hospital on 1st February 1976 at the ripe old age of 87. His passing marks the end of an era; many Civil Service players who have been participating in the Association's activities for some time will recall the familiar white haired and black jacketed figure whose 'whispers' reverberated around the playing area.

He has been a force in the chess world for many years past, his activities extending far beyond the confines of the LCC/GLC and the CSCA. Although his powers inevitably declined somewhat in the latter years, he was at one time a very fine player and the regular top board for our club. How many of us would like to think that we could achieve on our eighties the standard he still maintained to the end? As he often said himself, he still 'knew the moves'.

It was not only John's prowess as a player that earned our respect and admiration; his loyalty to our club imposed on him the duty of appearing for nearly every club activity to lend his moral support even if not actually playing. It was perhaps not generally known that this was at the cost of much suffering from rheumatic pain. We at the GLC Club are now very glad we were able last year to commemorate his 25th year as our President with a suitably engraved memento – he was obviously much moved by this ceremony and we like to think he may have died a little more content in knowing the high esteem in which he was held. If there is a Valhalla for chess players we are sure he will be there, perhaps perpetrating one of his famous 'swindles'.

John Foley was laid to rest on 12th February at Streatham Park Cemetery. The GLC Club and the Working Men's College with which he was also associated were very well represented.

W L Bush, GLC Staff Chess Club Chairman, May 1976

RICHARD FRIES

Richard Fries joined the Home Office straight from university in 1965. He worked in most parts of the Home Office (extending much wider than the Home Office now), including policing, criminal justice and immigration, as well as race relations, charity and the voluntary sector, and even horse racing!

In 1992 he became Chief Charity Commissioner, as the head of the Commission was called until it was reformed in 2005. He retired from that post in 1999, though he continued to be active in charity matters, including being a visiting fellow in the Centre for Civil Society at the London School of Economics until 2006.

Chess playing in the civil service came late in his career, though he learnt chess at the age of 4 and was an enthusiastic player at school (Kingston Grammar School, one of the leading London chess schools when he was a pupil there). After university he gave up active chess playing until his children took it up at school themselves. Accompanying them to tournaments brought him back to the board and, encountering a Home

Office colleague over the board at an Evening Standard weekend tournament he was drawn into the Home Office team, then starting up the Civil Service League divisions. Since then he has been actively involved in CS chess both as a player and administrator. (RF)

SIR THOMAS GARDINER Vice-president of CSCA

Director General of the Post Office 1936-1945. The Munich crisis of 1938 provided an agonising trial run for much of the national war planning, and a new urgency and new machinery were called forth. Sir J. Anderson (after governing Bengal), returned to enter the Government as Lord Privy Seal, with headquarters in the Home Office to develop the war planning. Sir T. Gardiner from the G.P.O. was appointed his chief of staff and designated permanent secretary of the new Ministry of Home Security, whose necessity in war was now recognised.

JESSE H GARNER (?? – 16/8/54)

Vice-president of CSCA

The CSCA has suffered a very great loss in the death of Mr. J H Garner, one of our vice-presidents, on 16th August 1954.

Mr. Garner had been a stalwart in Civil Service chess for longer than most of us can remember. For many years before the War he was secretary and match captain of the Centels club, one of the oldest clubs in the league. Soon after the Association was started up again after the War in September 1946, Mr. Garner became our treasurer. This was a difficult period of reconstruction; and the courteous, efficient and business-like way in which he carried out the duties of his office contributed greatly to the restoration of the affairs of the Association. We were all conscious of a great loss when his failing health made it necessary for him to relinquish the post of treasurer last year.

Garner was a fine chap to know – a man of great character and integrity. His passing is a loss not only to Civil Service chess but to all those who had the pleasure of knowing him personally.

A trophy was presented in his name.

A G Pockett, September 1954

JAMES GILCHRIST (5/5/1894 – 4/10/1963)

James Gilchrist worked for Inland Revenue in Scotland, Ireland and London, and played in some very strong events. He was a close friend of William Winter. Gilchrist finished 7th = in the Scottish Championship on 2½/9, remarkably 2½ points behind the players immediately ahead of him.

BERNARD E GLAZE (1915? - 2006)

Bernard died in August aged 90, and he spent his working life at the Estate Duty Office, later the Capital Taxes Office where he became a Chief Examiner. Although he gave up competitive chess for the Inland Revenue and Metropolitan some years ago he was the oldest member of the Revenue club. Bernard joined in 1940 while the department was in Llandudno of which he became secretary in 1946. When the department returned to London in 1947 Bernard was the driving force in restarting the club at the inaugural meeting held at Somerset House on 25 July 1947 when he was appointed secretary and treasurer. The membership was only 9 and the team had to play in division 2. They won immediate promotion to division 1 and in 1948/49 won the Bonar Law trophy. Under his leadership the membership increased rapidly and soon the club had five teams.

For many years Bernard represented Middlesex and the Civil Service and played in many Bonar Law finals for the Revenue. But for me his unique claim to fame was his win in the final of the Bonar Law in 1956/57 which enabled the Revenue to achieve the league and cup double for the first time. 36 years later two strong Revenue players withdrew on the morning of the Bonar Law final and Bernard agreed to play. He again won which enabled us to do the league and cup double. This victory was quite a surprise as the Revenue team was weakened by the absence of 3 of their top 5 players and we had previously lost 3 finals to Eastern Knights.

In his later years Bernard played for the Revenue 2nd team but often as first team reserve. Despite his age he was a marvellous team player and made light of travelling from Princes Risborough to London. In 1998 in recognition of more than 50 years Civil Service chess he was appointed a vice-president of the Civil Service Chess Association and of the London Civil Service, Post Office and Municipal Chess League. What a wonderful record.

Roland Smith, September 2006

LAJ GLYDE (1906-1983)

Laurie Glyde was associated with the Hastings and Ilford congresses for many years. His career was in the Ministry of Housing and he then retired to his native Hastings. Joe Soesan summed it all up, 'Laurie Glyde was a tireless worker for chess and he will be sadly missed by all who worked with him and played under his captaincy.'

The author was playing the last game at the Hastings congress in the early 80s, trying to win an ending with rook and six pawns each and was rather startled to be approached by Mr Glyde with a suggestion that the game should be agreed a draw as everyone wanted to go home. It became clear he was deadly serious, but the game continued and victory was achieved.

EDWARD W GODLY (?/11/1929 - ?/12/2020)

Distinguished career at Laboratory of the Government Chemist, represented UK at European and World Customs meetings, also was heavily involved in chemical nomenclature at international level. He was involved in the early days of the reformed Government Chemists CC, held several committee positions and became chairman of CSCA. He qualified several times for the finals of the *Times* crossword competition. Despite taking early retirement in the late 80s through ill-health, he was still playing a quarter of a century later.

IJ GOOD (9/12/1916 – 5/4/2009)

A mathematical genius from childhood, he became Cambridgeshire champion in 1939. He was at Bletchley Park with Turing etc from 1941, and worked on programmable computers and Bayesian statistics. Later he worked at GCHQ and the Admiralty Research Laboratory, before going to Oxford University and then taking a chair at Virginia Polytechnic Institute and State University (Virginia Tech). His 1964 paper on intelligent machines was quoted by Arthur C Clarke in *2001: A Space Odyssey* to explain the activities of HAL, and Good advised Kubrick during the making of the film. Good played in the Varsity matches of 1939 and 1940, and later for Cheltenham and Civil Service.

(from *Daily Telegraph* obituary)

HERBERT GOSLING (1887?- ?/2/1968)

Died aged 81. He won two championship medals in Home Office Chess Club during World War I. He played for a number of clubs and Essex and regularly attended congresses. He was very popular, and courteous in victory and defeat. One player said, 'I could never imagine chess without him.'

A YORWARTH GREEN (1904? - ?/11/1963)

AY Green was a chartered accountant and entered the Ministry of Supply during World War II, later he moved to the Board of Trade and at his death he was in Ministry of Aviation. He was champion of Yorkshire, Middlesex and Civil Service. He never reached the prize list in the British Championship, mainly due to inconsistency, as he was a danger to all his opponents.

ROY R GREENFIELD (1921 – 2009)

Roy, who died in September aged 88, played chess at Somerset House and Llandudno during the years 1939 -1941 and again in 1946/7 after service in the RAF. He rejoined the Inland Revenue chess club in 1953 when I was 1st team captain. He was so keen that he played for our 1st, 2nd, 3rd and 4th teams. The Rules were then changed and this limited his 1st team appearances. Until 1998 Roy played for the 2nd team and as reserve for the 1st team. He also played for a few seasons in the Hammersmith League in a Revenue team based at the Estate Duty Office in Shepherds Bush.

Roy was 2nd team captain 1956 – 1960 and then secretary for 6 years. Between 1957 and 1981 he played many times in the Revenue and Civil Service tournaments winning the Star trophy in 1957 and 1960 and represented the Civil Service in the Bronowski matches. Very few knew that he learnt Russian so that he could read Russian chess books which were not translated into English. He was deservedly elected a vice-president in 1993.

He had a wonderful record for the Revenue teams competing in the British Correspondence Chess League and in the British Postal Chess Championship in which he won a Best Game Prize. What a record – played 50 games from 1977/8 to 2008/9 and only lost 3 scoring more than 70% and did not lose a game after 1991/2. In the period 1992/3 to 1996/7 he scored 7.5/10 and then had a break. On returning to the team in 2003/4 – 2008/9 he scored 11/14. Roy was a member of the Revenue teams which won the British Postal Chess Championship in 1978, 1984, 1985 and 1995.

Roy had an exceptional career in the Revenue in which he was Deputy Controller of the Capital Taxes Office. He was editor and co-editor of Dymond's Death Duties (renamed Capital Taxes) from 1963 – 2003 and from 1986 – 2000 Roy was editor of the monthly Capital tax Planning. He acted as consultant editor or as a regular contributor to these publications until well into his 80's.

What can one say about Roy who succeeded in everything he undertook – the person I knew for 57 years was the gentle kindly giant. Thanks for all you have done for the club.

Roland Smith, Revenue & Customs, November 2009

ERIC W HAMMOND (???? – 1996)

It is with regret that I must inform you that Eric Hammond, a founder member of Government Chemists Chess Club, died recently. He served his club as secretary and match captain for a number of years. He retired from active chess when his club folded in 1988.

Ian M Pheby, December 1996

Note – Government Chemists Chess Club started in 1950, but it was discovered later that there had been an earlier club.

PETER W HEMPSON (18/2/1936 -)

He won the IR championship once with 100 % score. He also won county championships of Cumberland and Westmorland in 1957 and Yorkshire in 2000, and played in the British Championships many times.

JOHN MORLEY HOLFORD (10/1/1909 – 4/11/1997)
CB(1965) OBE(1954) BA Cantab(1930) MRCS LRCP(1933) MB BCh(1939) MRCP(1939) FRCP(1954)

Qualified as Doctor in 1933, and joined the Royal Navy in 1935. After distinguished war service, he worked ashore, including RNH Simonstown, Cape of Good Hope from 1944-1946, becoming joint South African chess champion in 1946, having earlier earned a half blue at Cambridge. (Half blue is the maximum you can achieve for chess.) In August 1947 he was awarded the King Haakon VII liberty medal bestowed by the King of Norway for services rendered during the war. He transferred to Admiralty in 1949 until 1957, before returning to naval work as a principal medical officer at a submarine base. Considered to be 'the best brain in the Royal Naval Medical Service', he was appointed a consultant in medicine, promoted to the rank of Surgeon Rear-Admiral in April 1963 and in the same month was appointed an honorary physician to Her Majesty the Queen. He retired in 1966, but went on to be Senior Principal Medical Officer, Department of Health and Social Security 1973-1974. Played chess for Admiralty.

GEORGE ARCHER HOOKE (28/2/1857 – 4/12/1934)

George Archer Hooke was born in Chelsea, and died in Barnes. Hooke was the Assistant Registrar General of Shipping and Seamen, part of the Board of Trade. He worked earlier for the Board of Trade as a Staff Clerk, and was then based in Streatham. He married Ellen Farmer in 1889, and they had five children between 1891 and 1896. He played for England in a cable match against USA in 1903.

IAN HUNTER (?? – 2004)

Ian who died in November aged 71 first became a serious chess player while at school and became the first captain of the London University College chess team. After receiving his degree in English, he entered the Inland Revenue in 1953. Ian joined the chess club in October 1954 and played for the 2nd team and also as a successful 1st team reserve for 50 years. He became chairman in 1981 and in recent years also treasurer until he relinquished these posts when his health deteriorated in 2004. Ian was a wise and very efficient chairman. He enjoyed nothing more than the crazy lightning chess tournament which followed the AGM when it was customary to have a glass of wine while playing each round!!

Ian was the youngest Inspector of Taxes to be promoted to principal inspector (assistant secretary grade) and after a further promotion he became Head of the International Division of the Inland Revenue. This involved the most complex legislation and many trips abroad to negotiate double taxation agreements. After his retirement in 1993 he worked as a consultant for both OECD and Price Waterhouse and then finally as Clerk to the Commissioners. His brilliant mind and encyclopaedic knowledge extended to his work and outside interests such as literature where he could quote from Shakespeare to meet any situation.

Ian's friends were well aware of his love of red wine, whisky and good food, and there are many happy memories of visits to *El Vinos* and the *Gay Hussar*. One aspect of Ian which came as a surprise was his culinary skills creating delicious sauces for his guests. His son paid a moving tribute at the funeral and hoped that St Peter had got in a decent supply of good claret for when Dad arrived.

Roland Smith, President, Inland Revenue Chess Club, January

2005

PHIL JEFFRIES 1953-2008

Both myself and Phil joined the then GLC. Chess Club within a few months of each other in the mid-1980s when the club was based at County Hall and in those days had over 100 members and ran as many as seven teams in the Civil Service League. Being of similar standard we found ourselves getting regular games for both the 5th & 6th teams and usually sat next to each other on consecutive boards whenever we both played. This, amazingly, continued for most of the next 20+ years as our grades rose and fell almost in unison throughout that period.

I well remember the first game I played against Phil, we had both finished our league games quickly and to kill an hour we played a friendly, as black I played a Queen's Gambit accepted which led to a tremendously open and knife-edged game, the type you rarely played in league games but wish you had the nerve to. It was the first of many enjoyable clashes we had over the years in internal club tournaments with honours fairly even over that period. We both had a preference for d4 openings and must have exhausted every Queen's pawn opening in the book and probably several besides. Phil was a far better player than his grade would suggest and he was capable of quite deep analysis of complex positions. He was such a quick player I'm sure if he'd really put his mind to it he could have been an exceptionally good player, often he'd be listening to something on his earphones and even reading a newspaper as well whilst playing, disconcerting indeed for his opponent, but that was Phil, always busy in some way.

He always struck me as someone who got a grasp of things so quickly and so well that it was almost effortless. As a fellow trade unionist we often chatted about various things he was involved with, in particular his efforts with the proposed redevelopment of the King's Cross area for the Channel Tunnel rail link and subsequent plans in which he put his exceptional skills in preparing appeals and other legal work over more than a decade to such effective use. His neighbours owe so much to his selfless efforts over this period and it is likely that things in that area would have been very different without his input.

A quiet, gentle and very knowledgeable man, Phil would always chat easily to opponents, new members or whoever was about and his helpful nature was clear to all who met him. Our team has missed him greatly this season, not just in results but a true absence.

We extend our deepest sympathies to Diana Shelley, his partner of 32 years, and the rest of his family.

Paul Efstathiou, GLCC, January 2009

ET JESTY MBE (1885 – 7/1959)

He won the Civil Service championship in 1923, 1925 and 1927 and played for Ministry of Education. Tribute was paid to him thus, 'His kindness and modesty made him extremely popular and he will be missed by many.'

D LE B JONES CB (18/11/1923 -)

A strong chess player, who worked in Ministry of Power, (which became Ministry of Technology, which became Department of Trade and Industry, which became Department of Industry), rising to a very senior level. He then joined the Cabinet Office and the Department of Energy, before becoming Director, Long Term Office, of the International Energy Agency from 1982 – 1988.

(Based on notes from John Saunders)

WILFRED HM KIRK (1877?-1946)

He was born in Devon, spent some time in America, then returned and joined the Civil Service as a 'Temporary Boy Copyist' in 1892, and became a 'Second Division Clerk' in the Local Government Board in September 1894 after an Open Competition. Later he worked for Ministry of Health from 1918 - 1938. In October 1927, he organized the massive match of more than 1000 players in Ministry of Health's building in Whitehall. He was one of the 12 players in the 1929 British Championship, finishing 11th. He retired from work and CS chess in 1938, travelling round Europe for a year, and then moved to Hastings, where he had Civil Defence duties during the war. He was secretary of the Civil Service League (from 1906 - 1938), a very strong player, and carried on organizational work after he retired, including the first Hastings Congress after the war.

(David Gilbert and KJT)

A H LAMERTON (?? – 12/10/54)

We regret to have to report the sudden death of Mr. A H Lamerton, Treasurer of GPO Chess Club, on 12th October 1954. A comparatively young man who had done a great deal towards the organisation of the GPO Chess Club, he will be missed by his club and all who have met him in league matches. He was very pleasant to know.

P B Sarson, Bulletin, October 1954

ANDREW BONAR LAW (16/9/1858 – 30/10/1923)

Andrew Bonar Law was born in Canada. Andrew and Bonar are both forenames and the latter is pronounced to rhyme with 'honour'. He was generally known as 'Bonar' to his friends. He worked in Glasgow in his early career and regularly had lunch at Lang's Coffee House nearby, and sometimes had a game of chess there before afternoon work. Although he played golf and tennis, he was devoted to indoor games like chess, bridge, billiards and whist. When travelling on trains, he solved chess problems if there were nobody to play. He was a Conservative MP from 1900 – 1923 and was the Leader of the Party from 1911 – 1923. He was trailing in the leadership battle between Walter Long and Austen Chamberlain (half-brother of Neville), but the latter two both withdrew as they feared their neck and neck battle would split the party. In 1911, he was staying at Windsor Castle and played chess against Sir Walter Parratt (ex-Organist at Windsor Chapel), who won. At dinner, the king (George V) said, 'I hear old Parratt beat your head off.' This may seem uncharitable, but the king did not like BL, as the latter had already more or less told the king what action he should take over a political problem. Law took no prisoners in Parliament. Asquith's Government and Ministers were accused of insider dealing in shares. Lloyd George and Sir Rufus Isaacs were prominent in this. Four months after the furore, Isaacs was appointed Lord Chief Justice! There were other accusations against Government ministers, and Law attacked them in a speech in Belfast. Back in Parliament, *Hansard* reported:

'The Prime Minister: Let us see exactly what it is. It is that I and my colleagues are selling our convictions.

Mr Bonar Law: You haven't got any.'

When the Government appeared to be about to order British troops to attack Ireland, which became known as the 'Curragh Incident', there was some outrage, several officers threatened to resign, and this exchange followed as the Government backtracked.

'Mr Winston Churchill: It is admitted that a misunderstanding on this point arose.

Mr Bonar Law: Rubbish.

Mr Winston Churchill: Do I understand the Rt. Hon. Gentleman to say, 'Rubbish'?

Mr Bonar Law: Yes.'

Law was appointed colonial secretary in 1915 as part of Asquith's Coalition Government, but became chancellor of the exchequer from 1916 – 1919, when Lloyd George was prime minister. Apparently Asquith was also a keen player. At the end of the war Law gave up the exchequer for the less demanding office of lord privy seal 1919 – 1921, and resigned the leadership through ill health in 1921. During a trip to Paris to recuperate, he played chess at the fames Café de la Regence, and apparently, he played with

'Great recklessness, flashes of brilliance, but in a manner dangerously unsound by ordinary standards.'

Bonar Law became prime minister on 23 October 1922. A General Election resulted in victory, but Bonar Law was diagnosed with throat cancer and resigned on 22 May 1923. He remained the 20th century prime minister who served for the shortest time, and also the only prime minister to be born outside the British Isles (New Brunswick, Canada).

He was renowned for his integrity (although there were claims that Max Aitken, later Lord Beaverbrook, 'ran' him) and powerful speeches, but of course for CS chess players, he is remembered best for the trophy that bears his name.

W H LAW (????-16/1/1953)

We regret to announce the death of Mr. W H Law (HM Stationery Office) on 16th January 1953. Mr. Law played in a match against GPO II on Thursday evening and collapsed on his way home; he was taken to hospital and died early the following morning. Mr. Law was a keen chess player and has been a stalwart member of the Stationery Office Club since it was reformed in 1945. A Lewisham player, he played regularly for the Civil Service and Kent County Association. He will be missed by his many friends in both Associations.

P B Sarson, Bulletin, 1953

IHOR LEWYK

The CSSC disbanded the chess committee and advertised for a national organiser instead. Ihor was encouraged to volunteer for the role and took up the position around 2009. The budget was slashed for events but he continued the CSSC individual championship at Edinburgh Chess Club. The qualifiers were not given full funding as in the past and this saw a steady slump in entries so that by 2015 there were only four entries. He decided to resign the role that season.

From 2011 to 2015 he ran chess at the CSSC games. The first one was a well-attended team event for four players and there were eight teams. Again the lack of participants led to this being dropped from the games.

Ihor was President of the Yorkshire Chess Association from 2000 to 2015 and received the ECF President award for services to chess in 2012, and a CSSC Volunteer of the Year nomination.

NORMAN ALASDAIR MACLEOD (6/12/1927 – 2/10/1991)

GM of chess composition (awarded posthumously) and International Judge of chess composition. He was a strong player, finishing 2nd in the Scottish Championship three times in the 1950s behind Aitken each time. Worked for the Foreign

Office at GCHQ and also in Washington DC. He became Maryland champion during his stint in USA. He played for Scotland in the 1958 Olympiad and bravely essayed the King's Gambit twice.

JAMES MAHOOD CBE, ISO (8/9/1876 – 14/3/1950)

Although the death of Mr J Mahood was included in the Executive Committee's Report, the Chairman (AG Pockett) in his wisdom did not see fit to mention the matter. In addition to his brilliancy in his official capacity as Assistant Paymaster General, 'Jimmy' Mahood – as he was known to his friends – was also brilliant at chess, winning the Civil Service chess championship for 3 years in succession in 1928, 1929 and 1930.

Usually one minute's silence is asked for. You won't forget next time, will you? Thank you.

H Hoskin, Bulletin, 1950

Note – It is clear from this (and other comments) that Hoskin and Pockett were not friends. In fact, one gets the impression that Pockett was generally disliked by other members of the Executive Committee. He was accused of not moving with the times, in particular opposing the publication of a *Handbook*, which many thought essential for a rapidly expanding CSCA after World War II.

James Mahood had played a high board for Civil Service as well as being a prominent member of Hampstead. He even finished second in the 1913 British Championship. BCM reported that, 'He was an excellent shot at rifle and was several times in the King's Hundred at Bisley.' The King's Hundred started as the 'Queen's Prize' in 1860, and is regarded as the most coveted prize in the shooting world. Queen Victoria gave a prize of £250 for the winner, and this amount has not changed to this day. The winner is allowed to quote the letters 'GM' (for Gold Medal, not grandmaster...) after his name. The winner is chaired off by other competitors to 'See the Conquering Hero Comes', following a military band and the range officials, which must be a splendid sight. Usually, over a thousand people enter, the top three hundred qualifying for the second round, and then the top hundred (hence the title) shoot in the final round at 900 and 1000 yards. Unfortunately, the National Rifle Association has no record of James Mahood competing in this event, which left something of a mystery, which was solved by John Saunders. Mahood reached the last 300 in 1906, but did not qualify for the final 100. According to *The Times* of Thursday 19th July 1906, page 11, Lance-Corporal J Mahood (12th Middlesex) scored 96/100 in the first round of the competition. Mahood was a vice-president of CSCA.

DENIS VICTOR MARDLE, CBE (9/8/1929 – 31/7/2000)

It is with much sadness and regret that I must inform our members of the death of one of our vice-presidents, Denis V Mardle CBE., on 31 July 2000. He was 70.

Denis was a cryptanalyst at GCHQ in Cheltenham, and was appointed Head of the cryptanalysis division in 1982. He was a strong player whose grade reached 2b in 1959 (equivalent to BCF 217-224). He was known to many of our members as one of the panel of adjudicators. He became an adjudicator in 1957 and thus gave the league and the Civil Service Chess Association 43 years' service. A remarkable achievement! His evaluation of a position was always accompanied by a couple of pages of detailed analysis in support of his decision. Though I never met him, I had many conversations with him over the past eighteen years. I always found him to be a friendly person who was prepared to help our league and association in any way he could.

Ian M Pheby, October 2000

BCM mentioned that he contracted polio aged 15 and was badly disabled for the rest of his life. He played for England in the late 50s and early 60s and won the Stevenson Memorial in 1964, with 9½/11, 1½ clear of a strong field. Possibly as a result of this he was invited to play in the next Hastings Premier, where he struggled, and then gave up major chess activity the following year. He said, when appointed a vice-president, 'I have played very little over the board for the last 25 years, due mainly to a need to concentrate on my work, retiring in 1989 from the same post filled before his retirement by CHO'D Alexander. I remember playing him (I lost) on board 1 for Cambridge University against the Civil Service in 1950 or 1951 in a 50 a side match.' It is possibly at that match that Alexander spotted him as a potential recruit for GCHQ.

SIR ALEXANDER MAXWELL (1880 - 1963) Vice-president CSCA He was permanent under-secretary to the Home Office 1938-1948 and former tobacco adviser to the Board of Trade.
He was involved in the drafting of the Criminal Justice Bill in 1947. The plan was to introduce the bill without a clause abolishing capital punishment. Then, the suggestion would be made that, since the question aroused differences of opinion transcending party lines, the government would leave the matter to a free vote of the entire House. Maxwell thought this was wrong. 'To leave the matter to a free vote of the House,' he argued, 'would be an indication that the Government had not made up its mind on the question.' If an abolitionist clause were introduced on a free vote, this would only inspire the House of Lords to delete the clause from the bill and defend their action on the ground that the government had given no

clear lead to Parliament.

KENNETH CHARLES MESSERE (16/4/1928 – 31/3/2005)

He played for Customs. In 1964, he went to work for the Organization for Economic Cooperation and Development and was head of fiscal affairs from 1971 – 1991. In 1954 he began playing postal chess and became a leading player. He won a semi-final of the 5th World Correspondence Championship (1961-64) and became the first English player to compete in a World Championship Final.

REGINALD PRYCE MICHELL (9/4/1873 – 19/5/1938)

He was born in Penzance and was taught to play chess by his aunt, and before he left for London aged 17 to study for the Civil Service, he had made his name as an expert chess player. He won the Metropolitan championship seven years later, and two years later won the City of London club championship, having finished second for the previous six years! In 1902 he won the British Amateur Championship. Michell played for Middlesex, Surrey, Admiralty and also represented England eight times. He played for England in 1937 Olympiad, won City of London, Middlesex and Surrey championships, and twice finished second in the British Championships. He was President of Kingston Chess Club and their champion for many years. Michell retired from the Admiralty in 1933 with the rank of superintendent clerk. According to *Chess*, 'his serious devotion to his duties as a civil servant effectively prevented his penetrating beyond the fringe of masterdom.' He took up croquet on retirement. He died five years later after a short illness and is buried in Kingston upon Thames, along with his wife, Edith (nee Tapsell, 1872?-1951), also a strong player. J du Mont subsequently published a book entitled, 'RP Michell, a Master of British Chess' in 1947, which *Chess* scathingly reviewed, 'Britain is far from the top of the chess tree and there must be a hundred British players with better justification for the publication of a book of their games than Michell. Mr du Mont's graceful pen has made the most of his subject. The price of the book (10/6 for 108pp, 36 games) is so extraordinarily high that one feels some appeal is being made to sentiment.'

KJ Thurlow, Western Morning News, Chess, Surrey Comet.

DAVID MILLER (4/11/1881 – 31/1/1972)

Mr David Miller, who died in January 1972, so long outlived most of his contemporaries in Civil Service chess that the majority of readers may not have known of him. Nevertheless, he was, when in his prime, one of the leading players of the country having participated in a number of British Championships in the days when this was the prerogative of a select few, and also in the strong International tournament held at Hastings in 1919 to celebrate the victory in the 1914-1918 War.

The late Mr WS Wallis told me that David Miller joined the Somerset House (now Inland Revenue) Club in 1901 and he continued active membership until 1960. At this stage he retired from Civil Service chess but continued to play for the Hampstead Club, near his home. However, he remained a vice-president of the Revenue Club until his death, so the connection with the club lasted more than 70 years!

Mr Miller was known as a charming and courteous opponent, but he was also a stern and tenacious one. A recent issue of the *British Chess Magazine* refers to a game of his in the 1913 British Championship which went to 168 moves! Like others among the best players of his generation he did not seek superiority through a vast knowledge of a plethora of opening variations but relied on a few sound openings and his considerable skill in combinative middle games. So successful was he that he remained among the leading players in the London area for more than fifty years.

Those of us that can remember our first tentative steps in competitive chess at the time of the flight of the Revenue Headquarters Offices to Llandudno during the 1939-1945 War recall with gratitude the privilege of meeting Mr Miller over the board and the benefit we derived from his kindly advice and sterling example.

A P Primett, November 1972

Thanks to 'Britbase', which informs us that David Miller was born in Russia, (to Russian parents, Samuel and Freda) arrived in UK by 1891 and naturalized British in 1899.

Kjt

Miller played Board 2 (or 1) for Revenue for 37 years. He represented Middlesex and also played Board 2 for Metropolitan. He had the distinction of holding the record for the longest game ever played in the British Championship! When I became captain of the Revenue first team in April 1953 Miller made it clear that if I ever demoted him from board 2 he would leave the club, but perhaps one can forgive someone who has been the unchallenged board 2 since at least 1923!

Roland Smith

DAVID G MILLS

A noted chess enthusiast from Yorkshire. He joined the Civil Service in 1973 and worked for DHSS/DWP. He captained the CS team for 11 years and his magazine 'Time Trouble' started in 1982. He also campaigned very hard for a national individual championship and ran it for the first three years. David is a dedicated organiser, who puts a few backs up along the way, but nobody doubts his passion. He has also done a lot of work for chess in Hull over the years and assisted at the European Chess Championship for Visually Impaired Players at Durham in 2007. He is an Associate Member of the Braille Chess Association. He retired from work in 2013, but continues to be active in chess, captaining two Hull and District teams in the Yorkshire League, and the Under-120 and Under-140 Yorkshire teams in the counties championship. He also runs the HASSRA national individual tournament as well as the Yorkshire and Humberside regional championship.

SIR P S MILNER-BARRY, KCVO, CB, OBE (20/9/1906 – 25/3/1995)

Members will have read in the National press of our President's death at 88 years. When his friend and fellow vice-president (as he then was), Hugh Alexander, died 21 years ago at the age of 65 after two years struggle against disease, Milner-Barry wrote of Hugh's astonishment at the sympathy and devotion of his friends during his illness 'for he had little idea of the affection and admiration which he inspired'.

The modest and kindly Milner-Barry, who often played in our representative matches against Oxford and Cambridge Universities, inspired comparable feelings, though during his many years of retirement from the Civil Service must have become aware of the fact. His name can be heard among echoes of names of contributors to opening theory e.g. the Milner-Barry variation to the Nimzo-Indian Defence which he introduced at Hastings in 1928-29. Many of his games have been recorded in *British Chess Magazine*, but we may well stay a moment to look at one he played on 4-5 October 1947 when the Australian High Commissioner courteously made Australia House available to a Great Britain team from which to play a radio match against an Australian team in

Melbourne and Sydney. The *British Chess Magazine* Games Editor rated Milner-Barry's game against F C Crowl as 'the most brilliant and satisfying game of the match'. The venue for the match could scarcely be bettered; never was such comfort afforded players, officials and onlookers. Your correspondent was Milner-Barry's by proxy. In the earlier hours of the match fortified with sandwiches and coffee he made each of Crowl's moves with confidence but as the hours crept on he, not being a nightjar, began to regard the surrounding comfort as a threat. Never before or since has he drunk in the course of a single night so many cups of black coffee. At five o'clock in the morning he checked each incoming move several times before transmitting that move and operating M-B's clock as that prince amongst chess players silently and absorbedly brooded over his position. They also serve who only stand and keep awake. During a long and very active life, Milner-Barry has somehow found time to promote chess in our country. We are all grateful to him.

E C Baker, April 1995

Milner-Barry learned chess at the age of eight, but did not play seriously for some years. He was *Times* chess columnist in 1937 and became OBE in January 1946, for his work at Bletchley Park. After the war he went to Treasury, becoming assistant secretary within two years. At Sir Stuart's memorial service, someone who had worked for Milner-Barry related that he had a stress-related illness, and asked for time off to recover. Sir Stuart immediately agreed, 'Take as much time off as you need'. When a refreshed staff member resumed work, he discovered a message saying that he had been docked annual leave for his time away from the office! He played in a Lloyds Bank Masters late in his life, when the fire-alarm went off. The lone arbiter (his colleagues had all left the room at the same time unfortunately) instructed everyone to get out, and then realized Sir Stuart was still thinking about his move, probably not having heard the alarm. He approached and tried to attract the player's attention, only to be waved away as the great man was concentrating.

JI MINCHIN (? – 1902)

Civil servant in India who was a prime mover in the 1883 London Chess Congress.

GRAHAM RUSSELL MITCHELL CB, OBE (4/11/1905 – 19/11/1984)

Mitchell was a contemporary of several leading English players at Oxford, and took up postal play during the war, shortly after joining the Security Service. He rose to be Deputy Director of MI5, but retired early. He was accused of being a Soviet agent, but no compelling evidence for that has ever been forthcoming. He became the first British player to become an IM at postal chess (in 1953) and took the game up again when he retired. There was some excitement in 2009 when a number of postcards belonging to Mitchell were sold at auction. One of these (against a Dr Edmund Adam of Frankfurt), commented that he was likely to lose to Collins and politely enquired how Adam was faring. Then it said '9....5435 10.1432 12-16/6 16/6'. Postal players will recognise that as saying 9....Nc5, 10.B(or Q)c2. The other numbers are received and sent dates. Postcards were commonly used for playing postal chess, and were preferred by serious players as they provided proof of moves and dates, unlike the 'shuttling score-sheet'. Someone said that the Russians favoured chess as a means of communication, and there was a section on it in the KGB Handbook. 'The chances are that these were instructions or intelligence to a Soviet agent or an informer.' The writer did concede they might just be chess moves! Mitchell was a good enough player to win a game against Purdy.

SIR DAVID MONTEATH, KCB, KCSI, KCMG, CVO, OBE. (7/4/1887 – 27/9/1961)

After education at Oxford University, he entered the Admiralty in 1910, before transferring to the India Office in 1911. He returned to Admiralty in 1915 and two years later became Deputy Director of Naval Sea Transport, before spending two years in the RNVR, seeing active service in the Baltic. In 1919, he returned to the India Office, rising to high office. In 1941, he was under-secretary of state for both India and Burma. He was a key figure in partition of the sub-continent in 1947, and continued as under-secretary of state for Burma until its independence in 1948. He became vice-president of CSCA in 1949.

(Based on information in the Times)

FREDDIE NORMAN

Played for Admiralty Chess Club and was a prime mover in resurrection of the league after WWII. Became match captain for CSCA.

PAT O'SHEA

Pat played for UNATS for some thirty years and sadly died on Easter Sunday. He had been ill but seemed to be over the worst of it. Unfortunately, it struck back earlier this year. His team mates and all who knew him are saddened by this loss.

Kevin J Thurlow, Bulletin, April 1995

E H OSBORNE

With regret we have to announce the death of the President of ECGD Chess Club, Mr. EH Osborne, ISO. A Founder Member, he died suddenly in December 1964 after a short illness. Before he joined ECGD in 1953, he had been a member of the board of Trade Chess Club for many years. Although he had retired from the Service in 1962, he continued playing regularly for ECGD until he was taken ill. He will be sadly missed.

J Loften, Bulletin, March 1965

GEORGE PAGE (27/20/1890 – 26/6/1953)

Played for Edinburgh CS from 1912 and won the Scottish Championship in Edinburgh in 1925. Also played for Edinburgh and won their championship nine times in succession. He was also a renowned problemist, composing over 250 problems and winning prizes on a number of occasions. Wrote a chess column for the *Scotsman* from 1920 – 1939.

(BCM)

N ANTHONY PERKINS (7/12/1912 – 29/4/1991)

With great regret we record the death on 29th April 1991 of Tony Perkins who for many years served on our panel of adjudicators and played for us in representative matches. He played on third board for Oxford against Cambridge during 1931-34 when at St. John's College, winning three of his four games. With a residential qualification he played several times in the Scottish Championship and was in Scotland's team at the 13th Olympiad in Munich. He played for Middlesex and was organiser of their team tournaments. For a number of years he was chairman of our GPO Club. Most recently he was President of British Telecom HQ.

Early in 1940 CHO'D Alexander had recruited him

among other young mathematicians and chess players to the cipher-breaking group at GCHQ which had such astonishing successes against the German cipher machine *Enigma*.

He continued to play in Congresses from time to time and was on the Baltic Cruise event during April in the course of which he was a welcomed visitor at the Leningrad Club. He died suddenly two days after returning home.

Tony delighted in combinations and to him the board was a source of aesthetic pleasure rather than a battlefield; that pleasure he shared unobtrusively with many of us.

E C Baker, August 1991

IAN M PHEBY (20/04/1951 -)

He was shown how to play chess at the age of 6 but never really took chess seriously until he joined Government Chemists Chess Club in 1969. He was soon playing at county standard. In 1970 he showed an interest in chess administration and became 2nd team captain for his club. He started on the Executive Committee as individual tournaments controller in the 1973-1974 season and later progressed to divisional recorder, senior recorder (in the 1982-1983 season), vice-chairman and then chairman (in the 1989-1990 season). He was made a vice-president in the 2001-2002 season. He retired from league administration at the 2012 Annual General Meeting where he was presented with a variety of gifts in appreciation of his service over so many years. In fact at the end of the 2011-2012 season Ian had completed some 128 man-years of service in Civil Service chess which is a record which may stand for a very long time. In addition to his administration for this league he played a prominent role in Grays Chess Club and Essex chess for nearly twenty years.

Ian has been and remains a very strong correspondence

chess player. He is a Senior International Master with the International Correspondence Chess Federation (ICCF) and he also holds one Grandmaster norm. His highest rating of 2621 some years ago meant he was the highest rated player in England and 48th in the world at that time. He has been a Commissioner of the ICCF, and he is the President of the English Federation for Correspondence Chess (EFCC). He won the 2011-2012, 2013-2014 and 2014-2015 British Veterans' Championships. He regularly represents England and has captained his country which he regards as a great honour.

In 2009 Ian was recognised by the English Chess Federation when he received the President's Award that year for his services to chess.

ARTHUR GERALD POCKETT OBE (1903 – 2004)

'Temporary Boy Clerk', June 1919. Chairman of the league for 12 years. Vice-president of CSCA from 1959, when retired as chairman. OBE (New Year 1947) for work as secretary, Civil Service War Distress Fund.

RAY POMEROY (1944 -)

Vice president of CSCA and the league. Correspondence chess match captain of the CSCA, knock-out tournament controller of the Social Correspondence Chess Association, controller of division 2 of the British Correspondence Chess League, and member of the Macclesfield Chess Club, the National Correspondence Chess Club and the Social Correspondence Chess Association.

Played water polo and cricket, played and refereed rugby, also interested in bird-watching. Started organizing chess in 1961 at school and has continued ever since. He joined Export Guarantee Credit Department (ECGD) in 1963 and played for

Credex. As a representative of the London Hostels Association Sports & Social Committee he was on the committee that founded the Monck Street Civil Service Sports & Social Club in the late sixties. He ran the CS Correspondence Chess League from 1973 - 1978 and in his second year the number of teams playing had gone from 12 to 47. Ray organised the CS teams in the British Correspondence Chess League in 1974/5 and continues to this day! He was also the CS match captain in OTB matches from 1973/4 – 1976/7. He also took on work for various postal chess organisations.

CARL S PORTMAN (08/02/1964 -)Born in Birmingham on a freezing February in 1964 Carl was brought up on a diet of jam sandwiches and Aston Villa - his beloved football team. He moved to Shropshire in the hot summer of 1976 where he learned chess at Charlton School thanks to one John Lenton. He is proud to look back on his chess career (he still plays) and think that he has been school, club and county (Shropshire) champion. He has also represented the UK chess team at the NATO Chess Championships in France, Hungary and the USA - being captain at the last two events. He is a well-known organiser, securing the likes of Polugayevsky, Nunn, King. Sadler, Sachdev and Short for simuls. Carl worked in the Ministry of Defence in the UK and Germany for 30 years but now lectures on natural history and rainforests (he has written two books about travels in Ecuador and Australia), coaches chess in schools and manages chess in prisons for the English Chess Federation. He is the author of the book *Chess Behind Bars* and is a columnist for *Chess* as well as being the editor of the UK Armed Forces Chess Magazine *OPEN FILE*, (for MOD as well as Army, Navy and RAF). He received the ECF President's award for his services to chess in

2015. Carl retains a keen Brummie humour and his motto is 'Don't complain about the dark, light a few candles'.

ERNEST J PRICE (1880? – 16/3/1958)

He was formerly Board 1 for Ministry of Health and had won the Essex championship in 1924 and 1928. He died aged 78.

A PHILIP PRIMETT (18/06/1915 - ?/8/2002)

It is my sad duty to announce that A.P. 'Phil' Primett died in August, aged 87. Phil had represented Inland Revenue Chess Club for nearly sixty years and was still playing regularly in division 1 of the league with considerable success. He had also previously been an adjudicator giving many years of excellent service. He was made a vice-president of the league and the CSCA in 1998 in recognition of his services.

Ian M Pheby, October 2002

Phil was the perfect kindly gentleman, and it was my pleasure to have known him since February 1953. In all that time I have never known him get annoyed with his opponents nor speak unkindly of anyone. His service to Civil Service chess and particularly the Inland Revenue has been outstanding. Phil has played for the Inland Revenue for 59 years and most of that time in the first team. On numerous occasions the result of a match depended upon Phil winning and he did! A legend in his lifetime and a record that will never be surpassed. Even this past season at the ripe age of 87, he commanded a first team place with good results and finished the season with a BCF grade of 143. In 1993 a report for the Inland Revenue Sports Association described Phil as 'having the gift of eternal youth' but little did we realize that he would be playing as well 10 years later.

Phil first joined the Inland Revenue during the War when the Inland Revenue was moved to Llandudno. When the department returned to London after the War, Phil became match captain until 1953 and he took on the captaincy for another six years in the 1960's. His second spell as captain was the golden era for the Inland Revenue who won the division 1 championship and the Bonar Law trophy in four consecutive years. He represented Hertfordshire and the Civil Service for most of his playing career. He also excelled at postal chess and for many years was board 1 for Hertfordshire, and for more than 25 years he has been a member of the Inland Revenue postal chess team who were British champions four times.

Phil loved playing in chess tournaments and in addition to being a former Inland Revenue champion he often spent many weeks each year playing in chess congresses all over the UK. We often joked with Phil about what pills he was taking such was his enthusiasm and zest for the game. As match captain I often marvelled how he had the energy to travel from Haywards Heath in the midst of winter to play in London knowing that he would not get home until midnight.

'Thanks' seems a small word Phil for all you have done for Civil Service chess and the Inland Revenue chess club.

You will never be forgotten.

Roland Smith, Inland Revenue Chess Club, October 2002

Phil was commemorated with a trophy that was awarded for the centenary weekend congress.

ERIC AUGUSTUS COAD PRYOR (or COAD-PRYOR) (1890 – 1958)

He was a former Kent champion and was an expert on glass at NPL, publishing several papers on the subject and being granted a number of patents, where he signed his name as EAC

Pryor. He married the daughter of the Director of NPL, Sir Richard Glazebrook in 1919.

SIR GORDON RADLEY KCB, CBE (1898-1970)

He joined the General Post Office as a Junior Research Engineer and rose to Director-General. He was an outstanding engineer, and did pioneering work in telecommunications relating to warfare. He became President of the Institute of Electrical Engineers. The only criticism that was voiced was that he was ahead of his time in making decisions and failed to reckon on the inertia of organizations and slowness of introduction of new technology. He was president of CSCA for eight years.

WILLIAM EDWARD COLE RICHARDS (12/10/1907? – 14/4/1989)

When our editor reported that W E C Richards, vice-president and for many years a member of our adjudicators' panel had died on 14th April 1989, he confessed to knowing little about him and asked that someone better placed contribute an obituary.

W E C Richards served Patent Office and CSCA well for more than forty years and deserves a place in our memories. During that time he did not miss a representative match nor the return 'mirror' matches we played against the three universities. Other members of the teams in those years will recall him as tall, slim and good humoured. Invariably at those Saturday matches he wore grey flannels and an olive green blazer with a Hertford College shield on its breast pocket. I have not established that he played for Oxford in the Oxford v Cambridge matches when he was a student.

We valued the impression we left with our opponents even

above match results and therefore greatly appreciated his unfailing good manners over the board. In the team he played from board 4 to board 9 depending of course on who else had turned out. He reached our individual championship final in 1947, losing to CG Butcher who had been Midlands champion. For a number of years he was captain of the Patent Office Club and its president in his retirement years.

Surrey County also had his name on its adjudicators' panel. He certainly took an active part in inter-county matches and took a high board in Surrey's Correspondence team. I have no record of him in Surrey club competitions, unlike his office colleague GAC Ashcroft who was an influential member of the famous Battersea Club.

E C Baker, December 1990

WEC Richards lived in Stanmore, Middlesex and was an active member of the Harrow Chess Club for many years during which he played over 800 competitive games for them. Even in later years the then white haired figure was often seen jogging (even in the coldest winters) around his home district, something he had kept up since his youth when he could do a respectable sub 5 minute mile. He had an active mind and at matches was able to recall personal experience of meeting the 'old masters' and 'how it was' in pre-War years.

David Groffman, December 1990

WEC Richards was an adjudicator from 1951/52 (or earlier) to 1983/84.

CHARLES A ROEDER (1922 -   )

Vice-president of CSCA

Foreign Office 1939 – 1942. Served in the RAF 1942 – 1946, then rejoined the Foreign Office, but was transferred to the Ministry of Transport in 1950, when the FO staff were told they could be transferred anywhere in the world! He was senior recorder from 1964 for many years. Remarkably, he won his club's half-hour tournament at the age of 82!

SIR ARTHUR RUCKER, KCMG, CB, CBE (1895-????)
Vice-president of CSCA

1945 - Deputy secretary at the Ministry of Health. Chamberlain's principal private secretary, both at Health and when Chamberlain was prime minister.

CHARLES ARTHUR RUSSELL, BARON RUSSELL OF KILLOWEN (10/11/1832 – 10/8/1900)

Irish Statesman, and later Lord Chief Justice, was 'interested in chess'.

From *The Standard*

GRAHAM SANDIFORD

The Home Office Chess Club lost one of its most active and committed members when Graham Sandiford died at the start of the year. Graham had been ill for a long time, but bore it manfully and continued to play in and for the club right up to the end.

Graham joined the club shortly after its formation in 1984. At the time he was playing in the Civil Service League for UNATS but he switched allegiance when we entered our first team in division 4 of the league in 1986. He turned out regularly from then on, and his presence was significant in the team's rapid rise to reach division 1 in 1990.

Inside the club, Graham competed enthusiastically in our internal competitions. He stalked his opponents relentlessly and always tried to play all his games. He won the championship three years running from 1988 to 1990, finishing runner-up in 1987 and 1991. In 1989 he won the summer Blitz tournament as well, finishing runner-up in 1990.

Although he enjoyed tactical play in knockout games, Graham really stood out as a strong positional player. His games were simple, logical and clear, and the best were marked with profound manoeuvring in the style of Steinitz. He won so many games as white with 1.c4 through the accumulation of small positional advantages. As black he played the Nimzo-Indian, or systems with ...d5 against 1.d4. Against 1.e4 he played the Caro-Kann for a long time. This resulted in too many draws, however, and for a short while he tried the Scheveningen variation of the Sicilian Defence. In the last two years he turned to the French Defence and, as was his way, immersed himself in black's strategy. The idea of positional pressure against white's weakened pawn structure appealed to him. He was also attracted to the tactical possibilities available against a white player with an over-extended centre. His last games were exciting tactical victories in which he used his better development to launch sacrificial attacks against the white King.

Graham was also very keen on analysing adjourned positions. He spent many hours going through his middle games and end games striving to find the best continuation. In this as in other things, Graham's commitment and enthusiasm were an inspiration. We shall all miss him very much.

James Toon, March 1992

JOHN M SARGENT (9/12/1945 -)

Vice-president of the league. Long time and enthusiastic match captain (1978 – 2000) and organiser of tournaments, especially unusual ones, like the 'all-play-all simultaneous', selected openings, selected endings, and superstars – comprising chess, draughts, darts, pool, backgammon, table tennis etc. He organized the first Civil Service weekend tournament at Monck Street, which attracted over well over 100 players, and was opened by Sir Stuart Milner-Barry. He continued to organize many such tournaments. He is also a strong correspondence chess player.

PB 'Pip' SARSON (died 1984)

AP Primett wrote, 'In the late 1940s and early 1950s he and PM Shaw were the joint mainstays of the old Air Ministry team which functioned in Kingsway before that office became merged in the Ministry of Defence. Later he was transferred to Bracknell and, as far as I know, played only infrequently in matches and congresses thereafter. 'Pip' was not one of the strongest CS players but was well capable of refuting unsound opening play. He was a likeable man and courteous opponent and I have pleasant memories of some congresses at Hastings spent in his company in the old days.'

He won the Meteorological Office club championship in 1980! The Met Office was at one stage part of the Air Ministry.

JOHN SAUNDERS (1954 -)

He worked for Treasury before leaving to be a Chess journalist, and subsequently editor of BCM and then Chess. He has always been an entertaining and talented writer. His 'Britbase' database of games is an essential tool for serious chess players. When Michael Heseltine appeared on BBC's 'Question Time' to call the Soviets a 'cold, calculating, chess-playing people', John was sufficiently irritated by the pejorative metaphor that he wrote to the *Guardian* asking if the Conservative Government were thinking of banning chess, just as Iran had. Unfortunately, his CS management spotted the letter and told him 'in an oblique, informal and Sir Humphreyish way' that it was not a great idea for civil servants to publicly castigate Ministers.

N BALIOL SCOTT (?/?/? -19/9/1956)

We regret to announce the death of the President of the Ministry of Supply Chess Club, Mr. N Baliol Scott, as a result of a traffic accident. The club will experience the sad loss of a fine player and sterling club member.

A H Rawlings, October 1956

He was an under-secretary at the Ministry of Supply, and president of the Supply Chess Club.

EMIL SEMM-SKRZYPECKI (31/10/1918 – 17/9/2005)

Emil joined Redhill and GLCC chess clubs in about 1970 and made an immediate impact. Chess players are supposed to be dull, cautious individuals. A lot of them conform to this stereotype and play well-documented systems without taking risks. They treat higher–rated players with respect and lose gracefully. It soon became apparent that Emil didn't subscribe to any of these theories. He played aggressively in every game, only aiming for a draw if it were quite impossible to try for a win. He didn't bother with theoretical lines, just playing what he wanted, and he had the admirable attitude that you take turns to move and why shouldn't the opponent make a mistake before he did? He just loved the game, and that was much more important than the result. This is not to say he was a weak player.

He was always eager to pass on his enthusiasm to others. In the last couple of years, he was coaching children at an infant school. When some of them moved on to the next school, they were sorry that Emil would no longer be teaching them chess. He helped others as well and was keen to explain to people that it was important that they enjoy the game.

He and I played in a tournament in his native Poland. He was the oldest player in the tournament by some distance, but the legendary Victor Korchnoi was also there, one of the best players ever, and still an amazingly good player in his 70s. Many chess players think it's wrong to talk to stronger players, but Emil walked up to Korchnoi at lunch and said, 'I can't understand why you're a better player than me, I was playing before you were born.' Victor laughed.

Every time Emil finished a game, whatever the result, he wanted to set the pieces up and play again.

Kevin Thurlow, October 2005

EDWARD GUTHLAC SERGEANT OBE (3/12/1881 – 16/11/1961)

Three anecdotes from Ron Fleming:-

1. On one occasion when Revenue I was playing LCC Sergeant was set to play John Foley. Foley, all cheerful, said 'I see we are to meet again, Mr Sergeant.' EGS in his quiet and unassuming way countered 'Oh, have we played each other before? Did you beat me?'.

(Mr Sergeant was not in the habit of losing in the CS League – KJT)

2. Revenue was matched to play Woolwich Arsenal away. I explained to Sergeant that the Arsenal was just across the square from the railway station and quite easy of access. When we met there for the match I said to him concernedly, 'Did you have any difficulty in finding your way here, Mr Sergeant?' to which he replied 'No – I took a cab.'.

3. One season when Percy Cook was match captain I was concerned that he had not collected the tea money for the home games at Somerset House, being too occupied with his own game. He had, I knew, paid the refreshments bill himself

so I wrote around to all the first team members telling them of my concern and suggesting that if for some reason they had omitted to pay their dues they might like to send me the missing sum (and I gave a maximum sum based on that player's appearances at home games times the evening charge which was something like 1/6d [7½p]) so that I could pass it on to Percy. Sergeant sent me a cheque for £1 – far more than he could have owed – but forgot to sign it!

Roland Smith reported –

He may well have been a founder member of the club formed at Somerset House in 1911. I first met Sergeant when I became captain in 1953. He was an unassuming elderly gentleman who at no time mentioned that he had competed against many of the world's finest players. I did not become aware of his exceptional prowess until 2007 when researching this article. From 1921, such was his standing in British chess that he was often invited to play in the international tournaments at Hastings and Margate and these tournaments attracted many of the world's leading players. Before the war he had wins against Tartakower, RP Michell, Menchik, Colle and Sir George Thomas, but perhaps his best win was at Margate in 1935 against Mieses. He drew with even more illustrious players, including world champions. His great games include draws against Euwe, Spielmann, Golombek, Capablanca, Mieses, Reti, Koltanowski, Winter and Gruenfeld. The chess stage he performed on included a who's who of chess, and although he lost, his opponents included such immortals as Janowski, Alekhine, Maroczy, Rubenstein, Reshesvsky, Szabo, Pirc, Keres, Flohr, Najdorf and Prins. Sergeant won on Board 2 for Middlesex on 12/12/1925 against CR Gurnhill when Middlesex beat Yorkshire in the counties championship final. Sergeant also won the Middlesex championship in 1947 (aged 66!), and won the London championship in 1951. He represented England, Middlesex and Civil Service as well as competing several times in the British Championship. Sergeant was Inland Revenue's Board 1 for more than 37 years (possibly nearer 50.) During the last 10 years, he lost only three games playing for Revenue, and these were to RJ Broadbent (Post Office) – an England international and former British Champion. His final fling was in the 1959 British Championship at the age of 78, where he made the excellent score of 6½/11 against strong opposition, including a draw against Alexander. In October 1960, ill health ended his incredible chess career.

Sergeant was a very famous member of the Board of Inland Revenue Solicitors' Office and whose published work, 'Sergeant on Stamp Duty' is still a leading reference work.

BCM gave further information. He died three months after he finally retired from work for the Revenue! Sergeant drew in a simultaneous display against Blackburne in 1898. In the British Championship of 1907, played at Crystal Palace, Atkins won with 7½/11, second were the legendary Blackburne equal with three CS players, Sergeant (joined Revenue 1910), Michell and Wainwright on 6½. In 1938, he was just half a point behind the winner (Alexander). He continued to play with great distinction for the rest of his life, but he treated chess as a hobby, always analysing with opponents irrespective of the result. Gerald Abrahams said, 'Incapable of gloating and grumbling, he loved the game so much that the result was relatively unimportant to him.'

SIR JOHN SIMON (1873 – 1954)

He was attorney-general, home secretary, foreign secretary, chancellor of the exchequer and lord chancellor, but never prime minister. He was very keen on chess and was frequently called on to open chess events, where he made a number of well-received speeches. Having recently returned from a political conference, he commented that a chess congress had the advantage that it would be conducted in silence and would achieve a definite result.

BRIAN H SMITH (died 1995)

It is my sad duty to inform you that Brian Smith of Trade Chess Club died in early October. I have sent a letter of condolence to his widow on behalf of the London Civil Service, Post Office and Municipal Chess League and the Civil Service Chess Association. Brian had held several posts within his club and had been treasurer of the Civil Service Chess Association. More recently, he was auditor of both the league and the association.

Ian M Pheby, October 1995

DAVID SMITH (died 2004)

When I received the news of Dave's tragic death I had just returned to work after a two week break. I began the day in what has become common practice these days – wading through a pile of emails, beginning at the earliest. It was about the tenth in the pile, from BTHQ's chairman, and I could not quite take it in. Only a couple of lines, but I had to read it a dozen times.

I had known Dave for nearly twenty years, and come to know him as a genuinely decent guy. I passed on the sad news to those not on the chairman's distribution list and received a number of comments from others in BTHQ who are as saddened as I am by his death and some of those comments have been woven in the following paragraphs.

One of my earliest memories of Dave was at the 1986 BT chess club AGM when Dave was secretary and I had yet to take on my first role with the club. It was held in a central London pub, where about a dozen of us had taken over a sizeable corner. We were voting in a club constitution to satisfy the BT Recreation Association and changing out name from BT&PO to BTHQ, but even then I got the impression that Dave could not take this too seriously, and was as much interested in enjoying the company and exchanging amusing anecdotes.

Dave was a modest player who tended to understate his abilities, but there is no doubt that he was a strong player. While his grade was always around 180, he once said that if he wanted to, he could get it above 200 by carefully selecting his opposition and 'duffing up all the 150s and 160s'. But that was not his style and as one of BTHQ's top boards he was always happy to take on any opposition. His style was very dynamic, but also accurate and precise, and while he obviously lost games, I cannot remember him ever blundering.

During his time with BTHQ we had some of our best years. A top three boards of Tim Kett, Dave Smith and Roger Stockwell was a match for any team, and when supported by an assortment of erstwhile 'duffing' material, we had several league and cup victories (including a Civil Service double), and finished in the top three of one or other of our leagues for the best part of a decade.

It was a rare occasion indeed that Dave missed a match, and he was the kind of person you were always glad to see in your team - not just because he was a good player but for the energy and enthusiasm he brought with him. There are those that turn up for matches and disappear afterwards, but Dave was always keen to discuss the other games, the merits of various opening lines and swap and absorb new ideas, not to mention a variety of other subjects away from the chessboard.

Post-match analysis down the pub was always the high spot

of every match evening, and in an era when the post-match pub session was starting to decline he was the most determined to keep it going. We had many happy sessions reviewing our games over a pint (or two) on his little pocket set with the flat pieces that he seemed to carry with him everywhere.

As well as post-match analysis, Dave was also very willing and generous with his time in helping others in the team come to decisions about adjourned and adjudicated games. He was happy to go over any analysis and was always gentle in pointing out the flaws we had missed - even the obvious ones.

By the mid-nineties when chess was in general decline, particularly in London as many companies were relocating out of London, Dave was always there – playing his last game for me on 11th May earlier this year, beating N Holroyd of Railways in the LCCL Champions v The Best of the Rest.

Dave was also a Mushrooms player, in fact he revitalised Mushrooms 2 – a great achievement considering the club has no base. One or two BTHQ players who wanted some London League experience also played for him there as well.

Dave's interests were not limited to chess. On one occasion he took up Go, and was an enthusiastic advocate of the game, and how it could be compared in complexity to the great game itself. He would gladly explain the rules and strategy with the same enthusiasm he had for chess.

Whatever downsides he had in his life, chess gave him much pleasure and he transmitted that to others. I am immensely saddened by Dave's death, but I know I am not alone. Like everyone else who knew him well, Dave will be sadly missed and never forgotten.

John McAllister, October 2004

ROLAND SMITH (1931 -)

He joined Inland Revenue CC in 1953 (becoming first team captain in April 1953), and had many years' service as captain, secretary, correspondence chess organizer and IR National team championships organizer. The Inland Revenue Sports Association gave him a Merit Award in 1991. In addition, he spent 20 years as secretary, treasurer and president of London CS League and CSCA. He received a BCF President's Award in 2003. He had the rare distinction of receiving a CSSC Merit Award in 2007, after 53 years' service to CS chess, and he did not stop there... He undertook the major task of rewriting the rules when the CSCA split into the league and a separate CSCA. He has also played postal chess to a high level.

He has played for Northumberland, Surrey, Kent and Civil Service, and was joint winner of the Barstow cup in 1971. Subsequently, he concentrated on correspondence chess, where he has won three Counties and other best game prizes. He played top board for Kent for more than ten years, and has represented England in the North Atlantic Treaty Tournament and in the European Team Preliminaries. In 2004, he played Board 6 in the European Team Finals, and scored 6½/12 for 4th place and his first International Master norm, drawing with all three grandmasters.

BERNARD HENRY NEWMAN STRONACH (ca 1880 – 21/7/1962)

Readers will be sorry to learn of the death on 21st July 1962 of Bernard Henry Newman Stronach at the age of 82. Through his chess activities in the Civil Service he became known to a wide circle of friends as a sound player, very hard to beat, especially in his heyday in the twenties and thirties. He was an outstanding exponent of the simultaneous display and of blindfold chess.

He began his Civil Service career in the War Office in 1895, moving four years later to the Board (later Ministry) of Education where he stayed for over forty years. When the Board's chess club was first formed in 1908 he was elected captain and was club champion in 1925 and 1928. Stronach was champion of the whole Civil Service in 1926, 1931, 1933 and 1934 and was runner-up in 1938 and 1939. He was a vice-president of the CSCA from 1949 until his death.

After the break for the Second World War when he served for a time in the office of the War Damage Commission, he played top board for UNATS and he went several seasons without losing a game for them.

No report would be complete without a reference to his power of analysis and skill in adjudication. He is said never to have been defeated in correspondence chess although he played some fifty games. He was an adjudicator for the Surrey and Civil Service leagues, and there were seldom successful appeals from his decisions.

The chess world is much the poorer for his going.
HR Calvert /T J Soutar, September 1962

COLIN BERNARD STRONACH (02/04/1921 - ????)
Son of BHN Stronach. Chairman of the league.

HERBERT HENRY STRUTT (1907? – 1939)

Mr Herbert Henry Strutt, of 4, London Road, Hailsham. died on Sunday in the Princess Alice Hospital. Eastbourne. The eldest son of the late Mr. and Mrs. H H. Strutt, he was 32 years of age, and bachelor, and was clerk at the Hailsham Employment Exchange He was an accomplished chess player, and was captain of the Hailsham Chess Club. He had played for Sussex in matches against Kent, Surrey, Middlesex, Essex and Herts. Last year, he reached the semi-final of the Sussex championship, and he also played correspondence chess for Great Britain.

Sussex Agricultural Express 17 February 1939

CREASSEY EDWARD CECIL TATTERSALL (ca 1877 – 26/10/1957)

We regret to announce the death on 26th October 1957 at the age of 80 of Mr. CEC Tattersall, an old Civil Service player. He was runner-up to ET Jesty in the first Civil Service individual championship in 1923.

Mr. Tattersall was a successful player of the Cambridge University Chess Club winning all four possible times against Oxford, and an enthusiastic president of that club nearly 60 years ago. He worked in the Victoria and Albert Museum specialising in carpets; he eventually became Keeper of the Department of Textiles.

He played for the Board of Education Chess Club, a club which only this year has revived under its new title of the Ministry of Education Chess Club. Mr. Tattersall will best be remembered in chess circles for his well-known *'A Thousand End-Games'* which was published in 1910-1911, and is still one of the most important works in English.

P B Sarson, Bulletin, December 1957

The *Times* obituary commented, 'His *Notes on Carpet-Weaving and Knotting*, written for the Victoria and Albert Museum, has proved a very popular little book. Tattersall also wrote on chess.'

R C S TAYLOR, CBE (16/7/1886 – 2/2/1953)

We regret to announce the death on 2nd February 1953 of Mr. R C S Taylor, CBE, a vice-president of the Association, who had been a well-known figure in Civil Service chess circles and in representative matches for over 30 years.

Mr. Taylor started his chess career with Hampstead Chess Club where he acquired a brilliant, dashing style of play which he never abandoned. When the Paymaster-General's Office Chess Club was founded around 1920, he became its first match captain, and he played for the club without a break right up to 1953. With Mr. James Mahood, CBE, another brilliant player, who died in 1950, also a member, this small office club achieved a considerable degree of success against the clubs of far larger departments, and won the championship of the second division on several occasions.

Mr Taylor retired from the post of Assistant Paymaster-General, at the age of 66, on 30th September 1952, and his death so soon after retirement will be greatly deplored by his many friends in the chess world. The loss of his services will be keenly felt by his own club for whom he continued to play after his retirement.

P B Sarson, Bulletin, 1953

The *Times* added that, 'His relations with his staff were rendered cordial by his unfailing kindness, courtesy and consideration, and his keen sense of duty and responsibility impelled him to do all in his power to promote their welfare. He had an exceptional mathematical brain and was a brilliant chess player.'

Paymaster-General's Office had a team before World War 1, but the league did not start again until 1919-1920, so people may have forgotten its previous existence. (KJ Thurlow)

JOHN CRITTENDEN THOMPSON (24/1/1889 – 22/7/1971)

Known usually as Tommy, he is best known for his espousal of the 'Hippopotamus' system, whereby he would put most of the pawns on the third rank, develop his pieces behind them, then try to break out. He published a booklet on the system in 1956. He was a bit of a character, and tended to wear a three-piece suit, the waistcoat fully-buttoned, and boots with no socks. This was a relic of the First World War, where he was a Prisoner of War, and where socks quickly rotted in the appalling conditions, and he never got back in the habit of wearing them. He had served in the Royal Flying Corps as Navigator, Bomb-Aimer and Rear Gunner in two-seater bombers, and he could land the aircraft in an emergency. He regarded the pilot as a mere chauffeur. He had a very large beard so nobody knew if he wore a collar and tie. He smoked an enormous pipe, so opponents had to cope with a cloud of smoke and a capacious beard if they wished to view his pieces. He joined Laboratory of the Government Chemist and spent most of his career in the Calibrations Division.

STEPHEN F THORPE-TRACEY (27/12/1929 -)

Career in Army then DHSS, reaching rank of controller of Newcastle Central Office. Much voluntary work also. Secretary CSCA 1974 – 1977, chairman of Tiverton Chess Club 1994 onwards, President of Devon County Chess Association. A keen and regular player in his mid-80s.

KEVIN J THURLOW (1/61953 -)

Joined Laboratory of the Government Chemist in 1975, and made debut for the club two days later. A long career at LGC followed in foods, Customs, calibrations (same role as JC Thompson), chemical nomenclature, reference materials, chemical safety and technical author. There were many years of organizational work for Government Chemists CC, and CS League and CSCA, as well as elsewhere. *Bulletin* editor 1981-1995, continued as committee member until 2011, vice president of league and CSCA, national championship organizer for many years, national postal championship organizer. Won CS championships at lightning, blitz, rapid play, (including selected openings and selected endings), standard chess and postal. Received ECF President's Award in 2011. Represented England in European Team Seniors Championship. Won Surrey Correspondence Chess championship, and represented Civil Service, Surrey, England and Europe at Correspondence Chess.

JAMES MG TOON (1962? -)

James Toon was one of the founding members of the new incarnation of Home Office Chess Club. He taught himself to play at the age of 10 and started playing for Loughborough in the Leicestershire League when he was 13. Captaincy was thrust upon him at an early age and he took charge of the Loughborough 3rd team when he was 15. He made it to the Leicestershire 1st team, but was not one of the stars of Leicestershire junior chess: future GMs Mark Hebden and Glenn Flear were playing at a much higher level.

On arrival at Oxford University in the early 1980s, James again found himself overshadowed by an exceptionally talented group of players including Peter Wells, Ken Regan, Will Watson, John Cox, John Hawkesworth, Jon Levitt and Colin McNab. But his organizational ability (or his willingness to volunteer for things) was soon recognized and he captained the University team to the Oxfordshire League title in 1983/84. He also played for Oxfordshire on a few occasions.

On joining the Home Office in 1984, James Toon soon became involved in Civil Service League business. He was league grader for nine years, and a league adjudicator for a shorter period. He captained the Home Office 1st team in many seasons. He also turned out for the Home Office in the London Commercial League, for Hackney in the Middlesex League, for Streatham and then Athenaeum in the London League, and for Streatham and then for Ashtead in the Surrey League.

When the Home Office club lost its venue, due to increased security issues, James was the principal driving force in the formation of Pimlico Chess Club, open to all, and the introduction of the Central London Chess League. He also made a significant contribution to the work involved in transforming the Civil Service League to the Public Service League, ensuring enough clubs could be involved and adapting the rules of governance for the new league.

JOHN TOOTHILL (9/5/1938 – 22/11/2017)

He secured a scholarship for his place at the University of Oxford, originally intending to study French. However, with National Service still in effect, Mr Toothill joined the Joint Services' School for Linguists in order to learn Russian in just two months. In 1958 he was posted to Gatow Airfield in Berlin, where he worked with the RAF to spy on Russian aircraft traffic for two years. Upon returning from Berlin, he took up his place at Oxford, choosing to study Russian as well as French and graduating with a 2:1.

After a spell in industry, he then moved to Kendal, working for Westmorland County Council as an administrative assistant in 1970.

In 1985, aged 46, he reached the top of his career ladder and took up the dream role of National Park Officer for the Lake District. Mr Toothill's work was far reaching, including time spent examining the country's National Parks for an influential government report. An OBE came in 1995 for his services to the environment and he took his retirement in 1998, aged 60. Mr Toothill was also a bridge player, passionate about cricket, enthusiastic about architecture and he continued to walk into his retirement.

Since his school days, Mr Toothill had been a keen chess player and he continued to play throughout his retirement. A strong correspondence player, Mr Toothill was part of the gold winning Great Britain team at the 1982 Correspondence Chess Olympiad. In over the board chess, he became a British master in 1980, played Board 1 for Cumbria as match captain and captain of the county's Chess Association, was captain and chairman of Windermere Chess Club and became British Senior Champion in 2000.

In fact, Mr Toothill was playing chess right up until the end of his life. He was taken ill on November 21, while in the middle of a game at the Windermere club.

'The guy (David Phillips) he was playing chess with offered him a draw in the ambulance,' Dr Jane Toothill said. 'But he was doing well and he said no.'

(*Westmorland Gazette*)

GEORGE EDWARD WAINWRIGHT (2/11/1861 - 31/8/1933)

He was secretary of Oxford University Chess Club in 1881, and President in 1882. He was a strong player, and played a high board in the very strong Admiralty team and had a best of 2nd place in the British Championship as well as being part of the England team. Wainwright played fairly quickly, but he did once take 45 minutes over a single move. BCM reported, 'His attacks, even when unsound, were very difficult to meet, inspired as they were by a strong personality, very rapid sight of the board and a healthy confidence.'

SIR JOHN WALLEY (3/4/1906 – 1/11/2002)

Played chess for DHSS (and its predecessors). He joined the Ministry of Labour as assistant principal in 1929; promoted under-secretary, to take charge of legalization and other preparations for the Beveridge National Insurance Scheme, in the new Ministry of National Insurance, 1945; deputy secretary, Ministry of Social Security, 1966; retired. He wrote a book in 1972 with the eye-catching title, *Social Security: Another British Failure?*, which was regarded as a very fine history of Social Security in the UK.

GEORGE WERNICK (31/12/1875 – 16/2/1958)

George William John Wernick, known in the chess world as George Wernick, died on 16th February 1958. A vice-president of GPO, he was in the team at the inception in 1904 of the London Civil Service and Municipal League. He won the Civil Service championship in the second season of our Association (1923-1924). He appeared again in the final ten years later. A record of which he was immensely proud was that of his five personal games with EG Sergeant, Inland Revenue, three wins and two draws. He was playing for GPO regularly as late as two seasons ago, and he celebrated his 82nd birthday on the last day of 1957.

All of our readers who have played him will agree with Mr. WH Watt's opinion recorded in *'Fifty Years of Chess at Battersea'* (1935): 'Never have I encountered a more sporting or more pleasant opponent.'.

Some will remember his mate in eight moves with black against a Customs opponent in a division 1 match in 1950. A trophy has been named after him for one of the Surrey individual competitions in recognition of his services to chess in that County.

EC Baker, March 1958

He played for GPO from 1900 to 1956. His playing style was described as 'fishing in troubled waters', as he preferred tactical positions. (KJT)

TOM WEST (1900? – 1978)

All members will be saddened to learn that our former Chairman Tom West collapsed over the chess board in a match for Surbiton Chess Club and died soon afterwards. Tom gave up the chairmanship of CSCA in 1976 and was elected a vice-president. He was chairman of DHSS Chess Club for many years and only resigned a few months ago. He was a dedicated chess player and intended to continue this season playing for DHSS and CSCA. All who played with Tom liked and respected him and we shall feel his loss deeply. Those of us who had the privilege of working closely with Tom when he was chairman will always remember his unfailing good humour and the firmness with which he kept us to the point. He was a wise leader, full of common sense and always ready to encourage others. When we met him last at the Autumn Meeting, we could not have foreseen that this was to be his last appearance at a CSCA function. He will be sadly missed both by his club and by CSCA.

S F Thorpe Tracey, Bulletin, November 1978

May I add a few words to your tribute to Tom West. He learnt to play chess in 1935, soon after joining the General Register Office, and was a great asset to the Ministry of Health Chess Club. He became chairman in 1970 and vice-president last year when he retired from the Civil Service.

Tom won the Star trophy in 1967 and the DHSS championship in 1971. He was always a tower of strength and we were hoping that he would continue to play and enjoy his other hobbies of watching cricket and repairing clocks for many years to come. He is greatly missed and our sympathy goes to his wife and family.

K W Lovell, DHSS Chess Club, April 1979

GEOFF WHITE (1926? – 19/6/2012)

Vice-president of the league from 2008-2012. He gave many years' service to UNATS chess club, being on the committee with a variety of posts, including chairman, vice-chairman, secretary and match captain, from 1966 – 2012, and his enthusiasm was matched by his good nature and courteous manner. He probably kept the club going when times were difficult. He rarely played in later years but he continued to work hard for the club.

Players from outside UNATS will recall the magnificent refreshments he provided when UNATS hosted the cup finals for some 15 years. He produced a wide variety of sandwiches, and cakes, and kept the tea and coffee coming. Not many people would give up their evening just to feed chess players.

KJ Thurlow 2012

SIR HAROLD HERBERT WILES KBE, CB (1893 – 1965)

Obtained a First-Class Honours Degree in Classics at Christ's College in 1914, then served as a captain in The Wiltshire Regiment in the First World War, where he was gassed, causing life-long health problems. He joined the Ministry of Labour as assistant principal in 1920, and achieved the rank of deputy secretary in 1946, and held that post until he retired in 1955. He was renowned for his common-sense approach and courteous manner. He went about his work quietly and unobtrusively, an approach which clearly worked in those days. He was vice-president of CSCA from 1956.

'Times' 1965 and KJ Thurlow 2011

A HOWARD WILLIAMS (1950 -)

Started playing chess at the age of 13, and won the Welsh Championship 17 times between 1968 and 1994, did not play again until 2005, and then not until 2011, when he won again! He represented Wales at Olympiads in 1972 – 1986 inclusive on Boards 1 and 2, with an overall plus score, even achieving a draw with Polugaevsky. He played seven times in the British Championship, never scoring less than 6.5/11, and finishing in the prize list four times, including one joint first, but unfortunately did not fare well in the play-off. He achieved victories over Raymond Keene and Jonathan Penrose. Wrote a much-respected book on the Alekhine Defence with Richard Eales in 1972. He represented Wales in the 1972 FIDE Zonal tournament finishing 4th equal (10/17) ahead of the other home country representatives Ray Keene and Craig Pritchett.

He joined Inland Revenue in 1982, when he was already recognised as a very strong player, and between then and 1993, he played 106 games, with only six losses. He had a similar record until he left London in 2001. He represented Wales at correspondence chess and was top board for Inland Revenue when it was 4 times British Champions.

WP WILLIS (1885-1970)

It is with regret that I write requesting an amendment to this club's entry in the CSCA *Handbook* in connection with the entry for vice-presidents where it is necessary to delete the name of WP Willis. WP Willis, Senior Vice-President of GLC Chess Club, died at the age of 85 on 3rd November 1970. He was secretary of the club as long ago as 1912 and played for the first team for many years. He was elected vice-president of the club at the Annual General Meeting on 5th October 1937. Although he retired from the former London County Council's Education Department on 28th May 1950, he retained an interest in the club's affairs, though this was restricted for the last two years of his life due to the loss of his eye sight.

G P Ashelford, GLC Chess Club, May 1971

SIR HORACE WILSON (23/8/1882- 19/5/1972)

Vice-president of CSCA

Joined the Civil Service in 1900 and had an impressive career. He was permanent secretary in Ministry of Labour (1921-30), being awarded a knighthood in 1924, chief industrial adviser to the Government (1930-1939), seconded for special service with Stanley Baldwin (1935-1937) and Neville Chamberlain (1937-40) (even having a room in 10 Downing Street), and finally permanent secretary of the Treasury, head of the Civil Service (1939-1942).

Chamberlain seemed to regard Wilson as more important than members of the Cabinet. Wilson warned Chamberlain of the danger of Mrs Simpson and feared she was a Nazi sympathiser. He accompanied Chamberlain to the 1938 Munich Conference with Hitler, Mussolini and Daladier (French Prime Minister). Chamberlain's policy of appeasement is and was widely regarded as a sign of weakness, even treason. That a British government was prepared to conspire with Nazi Germany to instruct the Czech government to surrender land to Germany was disgraceful. But appeasement did buy time so Britain could manufacture weapons. There was no doubt how a senior MP in 1939 felt. As Wilson walked past, the MP said loudly, 'There goes the man who has betrayed his country.'

WILLIAM WOODFIELD (28/4/1885 – 5/1/1968)

Essex Champion 1923, 1933, 1934.

His granddaughter reported that he had left a book on bridge inscribed, 'This book and a radio set were presented by members of the Patent Office Chess Club as a token of esteem and good wishes on the occasion of his retirement in April 1950 to William Oliver Woodfield, Hon Sec of the club 1919-1939 and ten-times winner of the Office chess championship. Autographed by fellow members of the Patent Office team winning the Bonar Law trophy in 1950. (Signed W Lamplast, GAC Ashcroft, FT Kemsly, Rowbotham, H Harding, W Richards, SD Sillies and two indecipherable names)' Vice-president CSCA 1948-68.

C WOOLLAM (ca 1950 – 10th February 2006)

It is with sadness that I report that Chris Woollam died on 10th February, aged 56. Chris, a member of the no longer active Government Chemists chess club, was a divisional recorder from 1974 to 1978, and he also served on the EC as an additional committee member from 1976 to 1979.

Ian M Pheby, February 2006

J XUEREB (???? – 2010)

It is with sadness that I report that Joe Xuereb has died. Joe was a member of Cable & Wireless which had success in league and cup competitions from the mid-1950s to the early 1980s. He served the league as secretary from 1966 to 1968 and as an additional committee member from 1968 to 1969.

Joe represented Malta in the 1992 (Manila) Olympiad and the 1994 (Moscow) Olympiad where he scored a total of +6 =2 -4.

Ian M Pheby, January 2010

Note - Joe got an automatic 2200 FIDE rating (much higher

than his BCF equivalent) from these events for scoring over 50 %. Many players would have protected the rating, by not playing, but not Joe – he regularly played strong events like the Hastings Challengers because he wanted to play chess.

Kevin Thurlow 2010

Trophy Winners & Officials

YEAR	DIVISION 1	DIVISION 2	DIVISION 3	DIVISION 4	DIVISION 5
1905	ADMIRALTY	-	-	-	-
1906	ADMIRALTY	-	-	-	-
1907	PATENT OFFICE	-	-	-	-
1908	GPO NORTH	-	-	-	-
1909	PO SAVINGS BANK	-	-	-	-
1910	GPO	PATENT OFFICE	-	-	-
1911	PATENT OFFICE	PAYMASTER GENERALS OFFICE	-	-	-
1912	GPO	GPO NORTH	-	-	-
1913	INLAND REVENUE	PATENT OFFICE	-	-	-
1914	INLAND REVENUE	CUSTOMS	CUSTOMS	-	-
1915	GPO	BOARD OF AGRICULTURE & FISHERIES	SOMERSET HOUSE	-	-
1916-19	-	-	-	-	-
1920	GPO	POST OFFICE STORES	-	-	-
1921	BOARD OF EDUCATION	POST OFFICE ENGINEERING	HOME OFFICE	-	-
1922	MINISTRY OF HEALTH	PATENT OFFICE	TRADE	-	-
1923	INLAND REVENUE	GPO NORTH	MINES DEPARTMENT	CROWN AGENTS FOR COLONIES	-
1924	MINISTRY OF HEALTH	HEALTH	HIGH COMMISIONER FOR INDIA	TRADE	-
1925	}ADMIRALTY }PATENT OFFICE	HIGH COMMISSIONER FOR INDIA	PO SAVINGS BANK II	-	-
1926	PATENT OFFICE	PENSIONS	CAFCO	CENTELS	PENSIONS (WESTMINSTER)
1927	GPO	PAYMASTER GENERALS OFFICE	PO ENGINEERING (DENHAM)	SOMERSET HOUSE	TRADE III
1928	PATENT OFFICE	GPO NORTH	WAR OFFICE	AIR MINISTRY	WORKS II

					PO LONDON ENGINEERING DISTRICT II (DENMAN)
1929	GPO	ROYAL ARSENAL	HEALTH	CUSTOMS & EXCISE	
1930	PATENT OFFICE	METROPOLITAN WATER BOARD	ADMIRALTY	POST OFFICE SAVINGS BANK III	STATIONERY OFFICE II
1931	ADMIRALTY	WAR OFFICE	AIR MINISTRY	}LONDON COUNTY COUNCIL	AIR MINISTRY II
				}MINISTRY OF PENSIONS	
1932	GPO	ADMIRALTY II	CENTELS	SOMERSET HOUSE II	HEALTH IV
1933	INLAND REVENUE	AIR MINISTRY	PO SAVINGS BANK	ROYAL ARSENAL II	TRANSPORT
1934	ADMIRALTY	WAR OFFICE	INLAND REVENUE II	TRANSPORT	CUSTOMS III
1935	ADMIRALTY	ADMIRALTY II	CUSTOMS II	CUSTOMS III	LCC V
1936	HEALTH	CUSTOMS II	TRANSPORT	TRADE II	UNEMPLOYMENT ASSISTANCE BOARD
1937	PATENT OFFICE	}ADMIRALTY II	INLAND REVENUE II	TRADE II	LCC V
		}CUSTOMS II			
		}LCC II			
1938	GPO	CUSTOMS & EXCISE II	LABOUR (KEW)	TRADE III	STATIONERY OFFICE
1939	PATENT OFFICE	PAYMASTER GENERALS OFFICE	NALGO	MINISTRY OF LABOUR(HQ) II	TRADE III
1940-46	-	-	-	-	-
1947	GPO	H M STATIONERY OFFICE	TRANSPORT	-	-
1948	SUPPLY	INLAND REVENUE	FUEL & POWER	}MINISTRY OF LABOUR & NS	-
				}MINISTRY OF FUEL AND POWER	
1949	GPO	UNATS	P O SAVINGS DEPARTMENT	LCC IV	UNATS II
1950	SUPPLY	METROPOLITAN WATER BOARD	GPO II	GPO III	UNATS III

1951	INLAND REVENUE	LABOUR & NATIONAL SERVICE	TRADE	PO SUPPLIES	GOVERNMENT CHEMISTS
1952	PATENT OFFICE	CUSTOMS	WORKS	INLAND REVENUE II	NATIONAL INSURANCE
1953	INLAND REVENUE	HLG	INLAND REVENUE II	PENSIONS & NATIONAL INSURANCE	CUSTOMS III
1954	INLAND REVENUE	INLAND REVENUE II	AIR MINISTRY	NEW SCOTLAND YARD	INLAND REVENUE III
1955	INLAND REVENUE	TRADE	CAFCO	INLAND REVENUE III	LCC III
1956	CUSTOMS	CAFCO	LCC II	PATENT OFFICE II	HOUSING AND LOCAL GOVERNMENT II
1957	INLAND REVENUE	INLAND REVENUE II	PENSIONS & NATIONAL INSURANCE	SUPPLY II	EXCHEQUER AND AUDIT
1958	CUSTOMS	INLAND REVENUE II	CUSTOMS II	HEALTH	SAVINGS BANK III
1959	INLAND REVENUE	SUPPLY	CABLE AND WIRELESS	SBD II	BRITISH MUSEUM
1960	LCC	AIR MINISTRY	HOUSING AND LOCAL GOVERNMENT	BRITISH MUSEUM	CADESSA
1961	INLAND REVENUE	CABLE AND WIRELESS	NSY	POWER	FORTELS
1962	INLAND REVENUE	INLAND REVENUE II	BRITISH MUSEUM	FORTELS	EDUCATION
1963	INLAND REVENUE	METROPOLITAN POLICE	TRADE	HEALTH	ECGD
1964	INLAND REVENUE	SBD	SBD II	}CUSTOMS II	FORTELS II
				}EXCHEQUER & AUDIT	
				}TRANSPORT	
1965	HLG	CAFCO	TRANSPORT	EXCHEQUER & AUDIT	FORTELS III
1966	INLAND REVENUE	CABLE AND WIRELESS	HEALTH	DEFENCE	CUSTOMS III
1967	INLAND REVENUE	INLAND REVENUE II	UNATS II	BRITISH MUSEUM	FORTELS III
1968	INLAND REVENUE	}INLAND REVENUE II	GLC II	CUSTOMS II	}INLAND REVENUE III
		}EDUCATION			}TRADE II
					}WORKS II

Year	Col1	Col2	Col3	Col4	Col5
1969	INLAND REVENUE	TRADE	EMPLOYMENT & PRODUCTIVITY	GPO II	METROPOLITAN POLICE II
1970	INLAND REVENUE	HLG	INLAND REVENUE II	}METROPOLITAN POLICE II	NSY
				}PATENT OFFICE II	
1971	INLAND REVENUE	HEALTH	PATENT OFFICE II	}NEW SCOTLAND YARD	PATENT OFFICE III
				}TRADE II	
1972	DOE MARSHAM	PATENT OFFICE	EDUCATION	NORDIS	GOVERNMENT CHEMISTS II
1973	}GLC	DHSS	EMPLOYMENT	DHSS II	CAFCO
	}INLAND REVENUE				
1974	INLAND REVENUE	METROPOLITAN POLICE	BRITISH MUSEUM	CAFCO	CSD
1975	GOVERNMENT CHEMISTS	DHSS	CABLE AND WIRELESS	UNATS III	CAFCO II
1976	UNATS	UNATS II	GLC III	EDUCATION	CUSTOMS II
1977	UNATS	CABLE AND WIRELESS	EMPLOYMENT	PATENT OFFICE II	NALGO
1978	GLC	}PATENT OFFICE	DHSS II	CSD TREASURY	EASTERN KNIGHTS
		}UNATS II			
1979	INLAND REVENUE	GLC II	CSD TREASURY	EASTERN KNIGHTS	GOVERNMENT CHEMISTS II
1980	INLAND REVENUE	CUSTOMS	EASTERN KNIGHTS	EDUCATION	CABLE AND WIRELESS II
1981	GLC	CABLE AND WIRELESS	BML	CABLE AND WIRELESS II	METROPOLITAN POLICE III
1982	GLC	TRADE	INLAND REVENUE III	METROPOLITAN POLICE III	PONWD
1983	GLC	EASTERN KNIGHTS	PATENT OFFICE	LTR II	UNATS IV
1984	GLC	EMPLOYMENT	BML	WDO	GLC V
1985	INLAND REVENUE	ENVIRONMENT	GLC II	GLC V	ENERGY I
1986	GLC	BTPO	GLC III	TREASURY II	DHSS IV
1987	GLC	METROPOLITAN POLICE	EDUCATION	HOME OFFICE	DHSS V
1988	BTPO	UNATS	HOME OFFICE	DHSS V	DHSS VI
1989	EASTERN KNIGHTS	HOME OFFICE	CUSTOMS	EMPLOYMENT II	BT & PO II

Year					
1990	EASTERN KNIGHTS	HOME OFFICE	CUSTOMS	EDUCATION	BT & PO II
1991	GLCC	BTHQ	TREASURY	BTHQ II	ENVIRONMENT II
1992	INLAND REVENUE	METROPOLITAN POLICE	INLAND REVENUE II	UNATS II	DHSS V
1993	INLAND REVENUE	GLCC II	DHSS II	EMPLOYMENT	METROPOLITAN POLICE II
1994	INLAND REVENUE	UNATS	ENVIRONMENT	GLCC III	TREASURY II
1995	INLAND REVENUE	TREASURY	TRADE	BTHQ II	HOME OFFICE II
1996	}EASTERN KNIGHTS	METROPOLITAN POLICE	UNATS II	HOME OFFICE II	DHSS IV
	}HOME OFFICE				
1997	EASTERN KNIGHTS	DHSS	INLAND REVENUE II	TREASURY II	BML
1998	UNATS	INLAND REVENUE I	ENVIRONMENT	CUSTOMS	METROPOLITAN POLICE II
1999	UNATS	DETR	TRADE	DHSS III	-
2000	UNATS	GLCC	UNATS II	UNATS III	-
2001	INLAND REVENUE	DHSS	TREASURY I	GLCC II	-
2002	EASTERN KNIGHTS	METROPOLITAN POLICE	DHSS II	GLCC III	-
2003	INLAND REVENUE	HOME OFFICE	INLAND REVENUE II	-	-
2004	HOME OFFICE	SPARTA	DHSS II	-	-
2005	UNATS	GLCC	DFEE	HOME OFFICE II	-
2006	UNATS	TRADE	TREASURY II	-	-
2007	UNATS	METROPOLITAN POLICE	SPARTA	-	-
2008	REVENUE & CUSTOMS	GLCC	GLCC II	-	-
2009	REVENUE & CUSTOMS	TREASURY	TREASURY II	-	-
2010	UNATS	DHSS I	HOME OFFICE & JUSTICE II	-	-
2011	HOME OFFICE & JUSTICE	GLCC	REVENUE & CUSTOMS II	REVENUE & CUSTOMS III	-
2012	PIMLICO	BUSINESS & INNOVATION	DHSS II	GLCC III	-
2013	PIMLICO	TREASURY	REVENUE & CUSTOMS II	-	-
2014	GLCC	DHSS II	PIMLICO II	-	-

YEAR	DIVISION 6	DIVISION 7	DIVISION 8	DIVISION 9
1905-50	NO CONTEST	-	-	-
1951	TRADE III	-	-	-
1952	P O SAVINGS III	-	-	-
1953	INLAND REVENUE IV	-	-	-
1954	INLAND REVENUE (WESTMINSTER)	-	-	-
1955	SAVINGS CERTIFICATES DIVISION	EXCHEQUER & AUDIT	-	-
1956	EXCHEQUER AND AUDIT	POST OFFICE SUPPLIES II	EXCHEQUER AND AUDIT II	-
1957	UNATS II	EXCHEQUER & AUDIT II	CADESSA II	-
1958	}BRITISH MUSEUM }CADESSA	CADESSA II	FORTELS	-
1959	ECGD	FORTELS	EDUCATION	INLAND REVENUE V
1960	SAVINGS BANK DIVISION IV	EDUCATION	INLAND REVENUE V	CUSTOMS V
1961	SAVINGS BANK DIVISION IV	CUSTOMS IV	HOUSING & LOCAL GOVERNMENT II	GPO IV
1962	}CABLE AND WIRELESS II }CUSTOMS IV	HOUSING & LOCAL GOVERNMENT II	NEW SCOTLAND YARD	FORTELS IV
1963	TRADE II	FORTELS III	CABLE AND WIRELESS III	NORDIS
1964	SAVINGS CERTIFICATES DIVISION	NEW SCOTLAND YARD	TRADE III	TRADE IV
1965	CUSTOMS III	INLAND REVENUE III	CACO IV	WTA
1966	BRITISH MUSEUM II	METROPOLITAN POLICE II	PATENT OFFICE III	PATENT OFFICE IV
1967	WEST TELEPHONE AREA	NEW SCOTLAND YARD		-
1968	NEW SCOTLAND YARD	POCOMPS	NATURAL HISTORY MUSEUM II	-
1969	SAVINGS BANK DIVISION III	NATURAL HISTORY MUSEUM II	-	-
1970	GLC IV	BRITISH MUSEUM II	-	-
1971	}BRITISH MUSEUM II	-	-	-

	}GOVERNMENT CHEMISTS II			
1972	CAFCO	-	-	-
1973	}CAFCO II	-	-	-
	}POST OFFICE II			
	}PONWD			
1974	DHSS III	}CHARLES HOUSE	-	-
		}EMPLOYMENT II		
		}GOVERNMENT CHEMISTS III		
1975	EASTERN KNIGHTS	WESTERN DISTRICT OFFICE	-	-
1976	LTR	}NATURAL HISTORY MUSEUM II	-	-
		}UNATS IV		
1977	WESTERN DISTRICT OFFICE	CABLE AND WIRELESS III	-	-
1978	METROPOLITAN POLICE III	POST OFFICE MOUNT PLEASANT	-	-
1979	EDUCATION & SCIENCE	CSD/TREASURY II	-	-
1980	LONDON TELECOMMUNICATIONS REGION II	-	-	-
1981	PONWD	-	-	-
1982	GLC VI	-	-	-
1983	INLAND REVENUE IV	-	-	-
1984	EMPLOYMENT II	-	-	-
1985	BT & PO III	-	-	-
1986	TRADE III	-	-	-
1987	DHSS VI	-	-	-
1988	-	-	-	-
1989	-	-	-	-
1990	DHSS VI	-	-	-
1991	METROPOLITAN POLICE II	-	-	-
1992	GLCC V	-	-	-
1993	BTHQ III	-	-	-
1994	TRADE II	-	-	-

1995	UNATS III	-	-	-
1996	TRADE II	-	-	-
1997	TREASURY III	-	-	-
1998 - 2014	NO CONTEST	-	-	-

YEAR	BONAR LAW TROPHY	POST ANNUAL CUP	JESSE GARNER TROPHY	TEAM LIGHTNING/ BLITZ (BARFORD TROPHY)
1905-22	NO CONTEST	-	-	-
1923	PATENT OFFICE	-	-	-
1924	MINISTRY OF HEALTH	PATENT OFFICE II	-	-
1925	MINISTRY OF HEALTH	GPO NORTH II	-	-
1926	PATENT OFFICE	PATENT OFFICE II	-	-
1927	INLAND REVENUE	GPO NORTH II	-	-
1928	PATENT OFFICE	PO STORES	-	-
1929	PATENT OFFICE	PO STORES	-	-
1930	PATENT OFFICE	GPO NORTH II	-	-
1931	BOARD OF EDUCATION	PATENT OFFICE II	-	-
1932	ADMIRALTY	LABOUR (KEW)	-	-
1933	G.P.O.	AIR MINISTRY	-	-
1934	ADMIRALTY	CUSTOMS II	-	-
1935	MINISTRY OF HEALTH	NPL	-	-
1936	PATENT OFFICE	CUSTOMS II	-	-
1937	}PATENT OFFICE }G.P.O.	PATENT OFFICE II	-	-
1938	PATENT OFFICE	ADMIRALTY II	-	-
1939	PATENT OFFICE	PATENT OFFICE II	-	-
1940-46	-	-	-	-
1947	G.P.O.	NPL	-	-
1948	G.P.O.	LABOUR AND NATIONAL SERVICE	-	-
1949	INLAND REVENUE	PO SAVINGS DEPARTMENT	-	-
1950	PATENT OFFICE	CROWN AGENTS	-	-
1951	PATENT OFFICE	TRADE	-	-
1952	PATENT OFFICE	TRADE	-	-
1953	GPO	INLAND REVENUE II	-	-
1954	GPO	UNATS	-	-

Year				
1955	SUPPLY	CABLE AND WIRELESS	-	-
1956	INLAND REVENUE	CABLE AND WIRELESS	-	-
1957	INLAND REVENUE	UNATS	EXCHEQUER & AUDIT	-
1958	PATENT OFFICE	INLAND REVENUE II	BRITISH MUSEUM	-
1959	GPO	TRADE	BRITISH MUSEUM	-
1960	SUPPLY	CABLE AND WIRELESS	CADESSA	-
1961	INLAND REVENUE	HOUSING & LOCAL GOVERNMENT	EXCHEQUER & AUDIT II	-
1962	INLAND REVENUE	INLAND REVENUE II	GENERAL POST OFFICE III	-
1963	INLAND REVENUE	}TRADE }WORKS	TRANSPORT	-
1964	INLAND REVENUE	TRANSPORT	MINISTRY OF WORKS II	-
1965	AVIATION	TRANSPORT	PATENT OFFICE II	-
1966	INLAND REVENUE	CUSTOMS	GENERAL POST OFFICE III	-
1967	INLAND REVENUE	FORTELS	HLG II	TRANSPORT
1968	INLAND REVENUE	INLAND REVENUE II	NEW SCOTLAND YARD	EDUCATION & SCIENCE
1969	UNATS	GOVERNMENT CHEMISTS	NORDIS	INLAND REVENUE
1970	INLAND REVENUE	PATENT OFFICE	SBD	UNATS
1971	INLAND REVENUE	GOVERNMENT CHEMISTS	PATENT OFFICE III	INLAND REVENUE
1972	TRADE	GOVERNMENT CHEMISTS	DOE (MARSHAM STREET) III	INLAND REVENUE A
1973	POST OFFICE	EMPLOYMENT	CREDEX	INLAND REVENUE
1974	INLAND REVENUE/ POST OFFICE	GOVERNMENT CHEMISTS II	DOE (CROYDON)	UNATS
1975	UNATS	}GOVERNMENT CHEMISTS II }INLAND REVENUE II	GLC V	UNATS A
1976	UNATS	INLAND REVENUE II	ENVIRONMENT (MARSHAM STREET)	INLAND REVENUE
1977	POST OFFICE	EMPLOYMENT	}WESTERN DISTRICT OFFICE }TRADE II	NACS
1978	UNATS	ENVIRONMENT	CREDEX	INLAND REVENUE
1979	INLAND REVENUE	CUSTOMS	UNATS IV	NACS

1980	HEALTH AND SOCIAL SECURITY	CUSTOMS	INLAND REVENUE III	NACS
1981	INLAND REVENUE	CABLE AND WIRELESS	CSD/TREASURY II	GLC
1982	UNATS	TRADE	EDUCATION & SCIENCE II	CABLE AND WIRELESS
1983	GOVERNMENT CHEMISTS	POST OFFICE II	INLAND REVENUE IV	-
1984	INLAND REVENUE I	DHSS III	EMPLOYMENT II	GLC
1985	EASTERN KNIGHTS	EDUCATION I	ENERGY I	GLC
1986	DHSS I	TRADE	UNATS IV	GLC
1987	EASTERN KNIGHTS	GOVERNMENT CHEMISTS II	DHSS V	GLCC
1988	BT & POST OFFICE	DHSS V	DHSS VI	GLCC
1989	EMPLOYMENT	CUSTOMS I	B T & POST OFFICE II	GLCC
1990	INLAND REVENUE I	BT & POST OFFICE II	-	-
1991	EASTERN KNIGHTS	DHSS IV	-	-
1992	EASTERN KNIGHTS	BML	-	HOME OFFICE
1993	INLAND REVENUE	METROPOLITAN POLICE III	-	-
1994	EASTERN KNIGHTS	ENVIRONMENT II	-	GLCC
1995	INLAND REVENUE	EDUCATION	-	INLAND REVENUE
1996	EASTERN KNIGHTS	BTHQ II	BML	GLCC
1997	EASTERN KNIGHTS	ENVIRONMENT	TREASURY III	GLCC
1998	UNATS	CUSTOMS	METROPOLITAN POLICE II	INLAND REVENUE
1999	INLAND REVENUE	TRADE	-	UNATS
2000	EASTERN KNIGHTS	UNATS II	UNATS III	-
2001	UNATS	TREASURY I	DHSS III	-
2002	UNATS	UNATS II	DHSS IV	UNATS
2003	DTLR	DFEE	-	UNATS
2004	HOME OFFICE	DFEE	-	UNATS
2005	INLAND REVENUE	DFEE	-	UNATS
2006	REVENUE & CUSTOMS	UNATS II	-	HOME OFFICE
2007	UNATS	REVENUE & CUSTOMS II	-	REVENUE & CUSTOMS
2008	HOME OFFICE & JUSTICE	HOME OFFICE & JUSTICE II	-	METROPOLITAN POLICE
2009	REVENUE & CUSTOMS	TREASURY II	-	HOME OFFICE & JUSTICE
2010	HOME OFFICE & JUSTICE	UNATS II	-	HOME OFFICE & JUSTICE

2011	HOME OFFICE & JUSTICE	UNATS II	-	HOME OFFICE & JUSTICE
2012	HOME OFFICE & JUSTICE	UNATS II	-	METROPOLITAN POLICE
2013	DHSS	REVENUE & CUSTOMS II	-	METROPOLITAN POLICE
2014	PIMLICO	PIMLICO II	-	DHSS

Other Events

YEAR	INDIVIDUAL LIGHTNING/ BLITZ (BOND TROPHY)	INDIVIDUAL LIGHTNING/ BLITZ UNDER 150 (BOND TROPHY)	BARSTOW CUP	STAR TROPHY (PREVIOUSLY JUNIOR CHAMPIONSHIP OR GROUP II)	JAMES CURTIS TROPHY (PREVIOUSLY GROUP III)
1905-22	NO CONTEST	-	-	-	-
1923	-	-	E T JESTY	-	-
1924	-	-	G WERNICK	-	-
1925	-	-	E T JESTY	-	-
1926	-	-	B H N STRONACH	-	-
1927	-	-	E T JESTY	-	-
1928	-	-	J MAHOOD	-	-
1929	-	-	J MAHOOD	J WEBB	-
1930	-	-	J MAHOOD	H P JAMES	-
1931	-	-	B H N STRONACH	W T E TAYLOR	-
1932	-	-	W G CROCKETT	P A COOKE	-
1933	-	-	B H N STRONACH	G W HENLEN	-
1934	-	-	B H N STRONACH	C W ROBERTS	-
1935	-	-	J C THOMPSON	W H BAILEY	-
1936	-	-	G P S COY	E G FENELON	-
1937	-	-	G P S COY	H HOSKIN	-
1938	-	-	F G T COLLINS	W J GILLIES	-
1939	-	-	F G T COLLINS	T E DENBEIGH	-
1940-46	-	-	-	-	-
1947	-	-	C G BUTCHER	W H LAW	-
1948	-	-	C G BUTCHER	B DENNIS	-
1949	-	-	C G BUTCHER	E L LEESE	-
1950	-	-	N A PERKINS	E A TAYLOR	-

Year					
1951	-	-	A Y GREEN	W T E TAYLOR	P HENLEY
1952	-	-	D G MACKAY	J R GREENING	E W GODLY
1953	-	-	A H CHALLIS	}H J PHILLIPS	C J LAW
	-	-		}P G MARK	
1954	-	-	A Y GREEN	J EYRE	I J BENSON
1955	-	-	E C HUGHES	L GODZIKOWSKI	T H MALLETT
1956	I P RUSSELL	-	G B LEWIS	D H REED	J A FRESHWATER
1957	-	-	G P S COY	R R GREENFIELD	W A HOBBS
1958	I P RUSSELL	-	W E C RICHARDS	K A R DRANE	S MARKHAM
1959	-	-	R A SLADE	J GILL	G ASHBY
1960	J EYRE	-	K C MESSERE	R R GREENFIELD	P HANDSAKER
1961	W E C RICHARDS	-	R A SLADE	G ASHBY	W A WALSH
1962	W E C RICHARDS	-	P R VIVIAN	R C PENTECOST	C J TISDELL
1963	-	-	R J STOCKWELL	A F STIMSON	E D BERRY
1964	-	-	R J STOCKWELL	R C WILSON	I W V J HURRY
1965	-	-	G B LEWIS	P ST. QUINTON	J M XUEREB
1966	-	-	R E SPURGEON	H F FISHER	-
1967	-	-	}R E SPURGEON	S C DOWNTON	C B ROBSON
1968	-	-	D LEES	T B WEST	R HULME
1969	R J STOCKWELL	-	R STOCKWELL	}R HULME	}J ANWAR
				}A KNAGGS	}J YEO
1970	R J MYERS	-	G P S COY	R C O'NEALE	P A BOND
1971	R J STOCKWELL	-	}E W AYLING	}P S MORTON	J MCKENZIE
			}R LOWEN	}D J TOWERS	
			}R SMITH		
1972	R J MYERS	-	E W J AYLING	G HICKFORD	C WOOLLAM
1973	R J MYERS	-	E W J AYLING	}K E CREER	B CHAMBERLAIN
				}C WOLFE	
1974	}P B COOK	-	G LEE	}J H JAMES	D GRIFFIN
	}A F STIMSON			}B STUART	
1975	}P B COOK	-	-	T B PACKHAM	R BOWMAN
	}A F STIMSON				
1976	}J T PASCOE	-	-	IAN M PHEBY	K TUCK
	}K J THURLOW				
1977	}D BANKS	-	R SEFTON	J H JAMES	R BELLETTY
	} D L BARASI				
	}K J THURLOW				

Year					
1978	R REDDIN	-	A F STIMSON	M J COWLEY	A R CHAPMAN
1979	G HAYES	-	T B PACKHAM	J XUEREB	R L D SKRINE
1980	K J THURLOW	-	S GILLAM	M J O'NEILL	D GILBERT
1981	S GILLAM	-	A C ASHBY	-	D SCUFFAM
1982	O S PHILLIPS	-	T B PACKHAM	-	S PRESTON
1983	J GIBB	-	A C ASHBY	K POGSON	M MOISSINAC
1984	S CROWDY	-	J MCDONNELL	E YOUNG	J JORDAN
1985	S CROWDY	-	A C ASHBY	M LUNN	E HAZELL
1986	G BOLT	-	-	-	-
1987	-	-	-	-	-
1988	A C ASHBY	-	-	-	-
1989	-	-	-	-	-
1990	A C ASHBY	-	-	-	-
1991	-	-	-	-	-
1992	K J THURLOW	-	-	-	-
1993	-	-	K J THURLOW	D T JOHNSON	E BOSSLEY
1994	-	-	K J THURLOW	J J MCDONNELL	I ALLGOOD
1995	N DOWN	-	-	N D FLEMING	B SKINNER
1996	T PHILLIPS	-	-	-	-
1997	A C ASHBY	-	-	-	-
1998	-	-	-	C DUDDY	-
1999	M SHEPHARD	-	-	-	-
2000	} A C ASHBY	-	-	-	-
	} M WALKER	-			
2001	-	-	-	-	-
2002	K J THURLOW	-	-	-	-
2003	A LEDGER	-	-	-	-
2004	C BRISCOE	-	-	-	-
2005	A C ASHBY	-	-	-	-
2006	J M G TOON	-	-	-	-
2007	A COMPTON	-	-	-	-
2008	A C ASHBY	-	-	-	-
2009	A EILERS	-	-	-	-
2010	A EILERS	-	-	-	-
2011	J ROBINSON	P BIGGS	-	-	-
2012	J ROBINSON	R JOHNSON	-	-	-
2013	R HALDANE	P MORTON	R HALDANE	E ORSAGOVA	K HENDRIKSE
2014			J MCDONNELL	A FRASER	B GITTENS

YEAR	GROUP IV	GROUP V	TONY ASHBY SHIELD	TEAM CORRESPONDENCE TOURNAMENT DIVISION 1	TEAM CORRESPONDENCE TOURNAMENT DIVISION 2	TEAM CORRESPONDENCE TOURNAMENT DIVISION 3
1905-51	-	-	NO AWARD	-	-	-
1952	F OPPENHEIMER	-	-	-	-	-
1953	W PETHYBRIDGE	J H WALLACE	-	-	-	-
1954	-	-	-	-	-	-
1955	T J SOUTAR	-	-	-	-	-
1956	-	-	-	-	-	-
1957	A ROBERTSON	-	-	-	-	-
1958	-	-	-	-	-	-
1959	M J BRESLIN	-	-	-	-	-
1960	A G B BAKER	-	-	-	-	-
1961	D J HOWARD	-	-	-	-	-
1962-70	-	-	-	-	-	-
1971	-	-	-	HEALTH (LONDON)	-	-
1972	-	-	-	ENVIRONMENT (MARSHAM STREET)	-	-
1973	-	-	-	INLAND REVENUE	-	-
1974	-	-	-	POST OFFICE A	CUSTOMS (SOUTHEND)	TRANSPORT AND ROAD RESEARCH LABORATORY (CROWTHORNE) A
1975	-	-	-	NATIONAL GIRO A	TRANSPORT AND ROAD RESEARCH LABORATORY (CROWTHORNE) A	CREDEX B
1976	-	-	-	UNATS A	ENVIRONMENT (SWANSEA)	LTR (SOUTH CENTRAL)
1977	-	-	-	DHSS	DHSS (LONDON) B	LTR (CENTRE & WEST)
1978	-	-	-	UNATS A	CUSTOMS (NORTHAMPTON)	WESTERN DISTRICT OFFICE
1979	-	-	-	INLAND REVENUE A	DHSS (BRISTOL) A	INLAND REVENUE C
1980	-	-	-	INLAND REVENUE A	GOVERNMENT CHEMISTS	GOVERNMENT CHEMISTS B
1981	-	-	-	INLAND REVENUE A	INLAND REVENUE B	UNATS B
1982	-	-	-	-	-	-
1983	-	-	-	-	-	-
1984	-	-	-	DHSS I	TRADE	INLAND REVENUE II
1985	-	-	-	INLAND REVENUE	GOVERNMENT CHEMISTS	GOVERNMENT CHEMISTS II

1986	-	-	-	DHSS 1	UNATS II	TRADE
1997-2008	-	-	-	-	-	-
2009	-	-	D GLEAVE	-	-	-
2010	-	-	M J COWLEY	-	-	-
2011	-	-	A MANUCHERI	-	-	-
2012	-	-	J SLATTERY	-	-	-
2013	-	-	D BYRNE	-	-	-
2014	-	-	S HUMPHREYS	-	-	-

YEAR	LADIES CHAMPION	LONDON LADIES CHAMPION	SELECTED OPENINGS TOURNAMENT
1905-49	-	-	-
1950	MISS J CRAKER		-
1951	MISS J CRAKER		-
1952	-		-
1953	-		-
1954	-		-
1955	MISS J CRAKER		-
1956-69			-
1970	} MISS JOAN BURRELL } MISS SHARON WALLS	MISS JOAN BURRELL	-
1971	-	MISS JOAN BURRELL	-
1972	-	} MISS JOAN BURRELL } MISS BETTY GARDNER	-
1973	MISS JOAN BURRELL		-
1974	-		-
1975	-		-
1976	MRS SHARON A FURLONG	MRS MARGARET PHEBY	-
1977	MISS B J GARDNER	MISS B J GARDNER	-
1978	-	-	-
1979	-	-	A F STIMSON
1980	-	-	} G HAYES
			} S GILLAM
1981	-	-	K J THURLOW
1982	-	-	S GILLAM

Year			
1983	-	-	J GIBB
1984	-	-	-
1985	-	-	B SMITH
1986-2014	-	-	-

YEAR	DIVISION 1 BEST PERFORMANCE AWARD	DIVISION 2 BEST PERFORMANCE AWARD	DIVISION 3 BEST PERFORMANCE AWARD	DIVISION 4 BEST PERFORMANCE AWARD
1905-98	NO AWARD	NO AWARD	NO AWARD	NO AWARD
1999	A P PRIMETT	A LEDGER	M BAKER	}G ANDREWS
				}M FULLEYLOVE
				}K REEVE
2000	N BLADES	J J MCDONNELL	P JASZKIEWSKI	K REEVE
2001	A H WILLIAMS	N BLAKE & D M GROFFMAN	C O'CONNOR	}G M BROADBENT
				} K SEAR
2002	A LEDGER	J M G TOON	}MARTIN BAKER	P EFSTATHIOU
			}T PIKE	
2003	J WATSON	D W HADLEY	P JASZKIEWSKI	NO AWARD
2004	M KEANE	K NORMAN	P JASZKIEWSKI	NO AWARD
2005	A EILERS	N MCMURDO	R HULL	P JASZKIEWSKI
2006	T W PELLING	W K OSBORNE	K NEVOLS	NO AWARD
2007	N TWITCHELL	M BENJAMIN	M CARSON	NO AWARD
2008	M WALKER	T W PELLING	K HUDDART	NO AWARD
2009	A C ASHBY	MISS S TIDMAN	L FARRINGTON	NO AWARD
2010	MATTHEW BAKER	G COOK	D STAPLES	NO AWARD
2011-14	NO AWARD	NO AWARD	NO AWARD	NO AWARD

YEAR	SELECTED ENDINGS TOURNAMENT	ONE DAY RAPIDPLAY TOURNAMENT	CSSC NATIONAL CHAMPIONSHIP	NATIONAL INDIVIDUAL CORRESPONDENCE CHAMPIONSHIP
1905-80	-	-	-	-
1981	-	K J THURLOW	-	-
1982	-	-	-	-
1983	-	}J GIBB	-	-
		}A GALLAGHER		
1984	-	K J THURLOW	-	-
1985	}J HELPS	G MOORE	-	-

	}M J ROSE			
1986	-	E GERBER	-	-
1987-1990	-	-	-	-
1991	-	-	C STOREY	-
1992	-	-	A DUNN	-
1993	-	-	A C ASHBY	-
1994	-	-	J TOLAN	IAN M PHEBY
1995	-	-	A C ASHBY	C O'BEE
1996	-	-	D WOLSTENCROFT	}C O'BEE
				} K J THURLOW
1997	-	-	A LEDGER	IAN M PHEBY
1998	-	-	M WALKER	-
1999	-	-	K J THURLOW	-
2000	-	-	M WALKER	-
2001	-	-	A LEDGER	-
2002	-	-	M WALKER	-
2003	-	-	J WAGER	-
2004	-	-	P JOWETT	-
2005	-	-	K NORMAN	-
2006	-	-	D WOLSTENCROFT	-
2007	-	-	A C ASHBY	-
2008	-	-	A KEIL	IAN M PHEBY
2009	-	-	K J THURLOW	-
2010	-	-	J WAGER	-
2011	-	-	R ARCHER	-
2012	-	-	?	-
2013	-	-	?	-
2014	-	-	J WAGER	-

League Officers

YEAR	PRESIDENT	CHAIRMAN	VICE-CHAIRMAN	SECRETARY
1905-38	NOT KNOWN	NOT KNOWN	NO POST	W H KIRK
1939	-	-	-	PERCY A COOKE
1940-46	-	-	-	NOT KNOWN
1947	-	A G POCKETT, OBE	-	H HOSKIN

Year				
1948	-	A G POCKETT, OBE	-	H HOSKIN
1949	SIR WILLIAM SCOTT DOUGLAS, KCB, KBE	A G POCKETT, OBE	-	E C BAKER
1950	SIR WILLIAM SCOTT DOUGLAS, KCB, KBE	A G POCKETT, OBE	-	E C BAKER
1951	SIR WILLIAM SCOTT DOUGLAS, KCB, KBE	A G POCKETT, OBE	-	E C BAKER
1952	SIR HAROLD WILES, KBE, CB	A G POCKETT, OBE	-	D H LAW
1953	SIR HAROLD WILES, KBE, CB	A G POCKETT, OBE	-	D H LAW
1954	SIR HAROLD WILES, KBE, CB	A G POCKETT, OBE	-	D H LAW
1955	SIR HAROLD WILES, KBE, CB	A G POCKETT, OBE	-	D H LAW
1956	VACANT	A G POCKETT, OBE	-	H S HOLMES
1957	SIR GORDON RADLEY, KCB, CBE, PhD	A G POCKETT, OBE	E C BAKER, MBE	H S HOLMES
1958	SIR GORDON RADLEY, KCB, CBE, PhD	A G POCKETT, OBE	E C BAKER, MBE	F E LEREW
1959	SIR GORDON RADLEY, KCB, CBE, PhD	E C BAKER, MBE	G BRIDDON	F E LEREW
1960	SIR GORDON RADLEY, KCB, CBE, PhD	E C BAKER, MBE	DR H R CALVERT, MA	F E LEREW
1961	SIR GORDON RADLEY, KCB, CBE, PhD	E C BAKER, MBE	DR H R CALVERT, MA	A SPENCER TONKS
1962	SIR GORDON RADLEY, KCB, CBE, PhD	E C BAKER, MBE	DR H R CALVERT, MA	A SPENCER TONKS
1963	SIR GORDON RADLEY, KCB, CBE, PhD	E C BAKER, MBE	DR H R CALVERT, MA	A SPENCER TONKS

1964	SIR GORDON RADLEY, KCB, CBE, PhD	E C BAKER, MBE	DR H R CALVERT, MA	G JESSUP
1965	LEONARD BARFORD	E C BAKER, MBE	DR H R CALVERT, MA	T MCDADE
1966	LEONARD BARFORD	DR H R CALVERT, MA	A SPENCER TONKS	T MCDADE
1967	LEONARD BARFORD	DR H R CALVERT, MA	A SPENCER TONKS	J M XUEREB
1968	SIR LEONARD BARFORD	DR H R CALVERT, MA	F C BLACKMAN	J M XUEREB
1969	SIR LEONARD BARFORD	C B STRONACH	F C BLACKMAN	P A BOND
1970	SIR LEONARD BARFORD	C B STRONACH	F C BLACKMAN	P A BOND
1971	SIR LEONARD BARFORD	C B STRONACH	F C BLACKMAN	P A BOND
1972	SIR LEONARD BARFORD	C B STRONACH	F C BLACKMAN	P A BOND
1973	SIR LEONARD BARFORD	T B WEST	VACANT	P A BOND
1974	SIR LEONARD BARFORD	T B WEST	-	K E CREER
1975	SIR LEONARD BARFORD	T B WEST	-	K E CREER
1976	SIR LEONARD BARFORD	T B WEST	-	S F THORPE-TRACEY
1977	SIR LEONARD BARFORD	E W GODLY	-	S F THORPE-TRACEY
1978	SIR LEONARD BARFORD	E W GODLY	-	S F THORPE-TRACEY
1979	SIR LEONARD BARFORD	E W GODLY	-	S F THORPE-TRACEY
1980	SIR LEONARD BARFORD	E W GODLY	ROGER SEFTON	S F THORPE-TRACEY
1981	SIR LEONARD BARFORD	E W GODLY	RONALD D FLEMING	D SCUFFAM
1982	SIR LEONARD BARFORD	E W GODLY	RONALD D FLEMING	D SCUFFAM
1983	SIR LEONARD BARFORD	E W GODLY	RONALD D FLEMING	D SCUFFAM

Year				
1984	SIR LEONARD BARFORD	E W GODLY	RONALD D FLEMING	D SCUFFAM
1985	SIR LEONARD BARFORD	E W GODLY	IAN M PHEBY	D SCUFFAM
1986	SIR LEONARD BARFORD	E W GODLY	IAN M PHEBY	D SCUFFAM
1987	SIR LEONARD BARFORD	E W GODLY	IAN M PHEBY	D SCUFFAM
1988	SIR LEONARD BARFORD	E W GODLY	IAN M PHEBY	R L TURNHAM
1989	SIR LEONARD BARFORD	E W GODLY	IAN M PHEBY	R L TURNHAM
1990	SIR LEONARD BARFORD	IAN M PHEBY	JAMES M G TOON	R L TURNHAM
1991	SIR LEONARD BARFORD	IAN M PHEBY	JAMES M G TOON	R L TURNHAM
1992	SIR LEONARD BARFORD	IAN M PHEBY	JAMES M G TOON	R L TURNHAM
1993	SIR P S MILNER-BARRY, KCVO, CB, OBE	IAN M PHEBY	JAMES M G TOON	R L TURNHAM
1994	SIR P S MILNER-BARRY, KCVO, CB, OBE	IAN M PHEBY	JAMES M G TOON	ROLAND SMITH
1995	SIR P S MILNER-BARRY, KCVO, CB, OBE	IAN M PHEBY	JAMES M G TOON	ROLAND SMITH
1996	RONALD D FLEMING	IAN M PHEBY	JAMES M G TOON	ROLAND SMITH
1997	RONALD D FLEMING	IAN M PHEBY	RICHARD J FRIES	ROLAND SMITH
1998	RONALD D FLEMING	IAN M PHEBY	RICHARD J FRIES	ROLAND SMITH
1999	RONALD D FLEMING	IAN M PHEBY	RICHARD J FRIES	ROLAND SMITH
2000	RONALD D FLEMING	IAN M PHEBY	RICHARD J FRIES	ROLAND SMITH
2001	RONALD D FLEMING	IAN M PHEBY	RICHARD J FRIES	ROLAND SMITH
2002	RONALD D FLEMING	IAN M PHEBY	RICHARD J FRIES	ROLAND SMITH

2003	RONALD D FLEMING	IAN M PHEBY	RICHARD J FRIES	ROLAND SMITH
2004	RONALD D FLEMING	IAN M PHEBY	RICHARD J FRIES	ROLAND SMITH
2005	RONALD D FLEMING	IAN M PHEBY	RICHARD J FRIES	ROLAND SMITH
2006	RONALD D FLEMING	IAN M PHEBY	RICHARD J FRIES	ROLAND SMITH
2007	ROLAND SMITH	IAN M PHEBY	RICHARD J FRIES	ROLAND SMITH
2008	ROLAND SMITH	IAN M PHEBY	RICHARD J FRIES	ROLAND SMITH
2009	ROLAND SMITH	IAN M PHEBY	RICHARD J FRIES	ROLAND SMITH
2010	ROLAND SMITH	IAN M PHEBY	RICHARD J FRIES	ROLAND SMITH
2011	ROLAND SMITH	IAN M PHEBY	RICHARD J FRIES	ROLAND SMITH
2012	ROLAND SMITH	IAN M PHEBY	J ROBINSON	NIGEL BLADES
2013	ROLAND SMITH	RICHARD J FRIES	J ROBINSON	NIGEL BLADES
2014	ROLAND SMITH	RICHARD J FRIES	J ROBINSON	MARIA SANT

YEAR	TREASURER	SENIOR RECORDER	GRADER	MATCH CAPTAIN
1905-46	NOT KNOWN	NOT KNOWN	NO POST	NOT KNOWN
1947	J H GARNER	NOT KNOWN	-	F M NORMAN
1948	J H GARNER	F M NORMAN	-	F M NORMAN
1949	J H GARNER	F M NORMAN	-	F M NORMAN
1950	J H GARNER	F M NORMAN	-	F M NORMAN
1951	J H GARNER	F M NORMAN	-	F M NORMAN
1952	J H GARNER	F M NORMAN	-	F M NORMAN
1953	J H GARNER	F M NORMAN	-	F M NORMAN
1954	RONALD D FLEMING	P M SHAW	-	F M NORMAN
1955	RONALD D FLEMING	G BRIDDON	-	F M NORMAN
1956	RONALD D FLEMING	G BRIDDON	-	F M NORMAN
1957	RONALD D FLEMING	G BRIDDON	-	F M NORMAN
1958	RONALD D FLEMING	A L SYMES	-	F M NORMAN
1959	RONALD D FLEMING	G W EAST	-	F M NORMAN
1960	RONALD D FLEMING	G W EAST	-	F M NORMAN

Year				
1961	RONALD D FLEMING	G W EAST	-	F M NORMAN
1962	RONALD D FLEMING	G W EAST, OBE	-	F M NORMAN
1963	RONALD D FLEMING	S N OWEN	-	F M NORMAN
1964	RONALD D FLEMING	S N OWEN	-	F M NORMAN
1965	RONALD D FLEMING	CHARLES A ROEDER	-	J W SCANLAN
1966	RONALD D FLEMING	CHARLES A ROEDER	-	J W SCANLAN
1967	RONALD D FLEMING	CHARLES A ROEDER	R CREAMER	J W SCANLAN
1968	RONALD D FLEMING	CHARLES A ROEDER	R CREAMER	J W SCANLAN
1969	RONALD D FLEMING	CHARLES A ROEDER	R HULME	DR R H S PHILLIPS
1970	RONALD D FLEMING	CHARLES A ROEDER	R HULME	DR R H S PHILLIPS
1971	RONALD D FLEMING	CHARLES A ROEDER	R HULME	DR R H S PHILLIPS
1972	RONALD D FLEMING	CHARLES A ROEDER	R HULME	DR R H S PHILLIPS
1973	RONALD D FLEMING	CHARLES A ROEDER	R HULME	DR R H S PHILLIPS
1974	RONALD D FLEMING	CHARLES A ROEDER	R HULME	RAYMOND POMEROY
1975	RONALD D FLEMING	CHARLES A ROEDER	R HULME	RAYMOND POMEROY
1976	RONALD D FLEMING	CHARLES A ROEDER	R HULME	RAYMOND POMEROY
1977	RONALD D FLEMING	CHARLES A ROEDER	R SEFTON	R SEFTON
1978	RONALD D FLEMING	CHARLES A ROEDER	R SEFTON	J M SARGENT
1979	RONALD D FLEMING	CHARLES A ROEDER	R SEFTON	J M SARGENT
1980	RONALD D FLEMING	CHARLES A ROEDER	R SEFTON	J M SARGENT
1981	RONALD D FLEMING	CHARLES A ROEDER	R SEFTON	J M SARGENT

1982	RONALD D FLEMING	CHARLES A ROEDER	R SEFTON	J M SARGENT
1983	RONALD D FLEMING	IAN M PHEBY	R SEFTON	J M SARGENT
1984	RONALD D FLEMING	IAN M PHEBY	R SEFTON	J M SARGENT
1985	A Z BEECH	IAN M PHEBY	R SEFTON	J M SARGENT
1986	A Z BEECH	IAN M PHEBY	R SEFTON	J M SARGENT
1987	B H SMITH	IAN M PHEBY	IAN M PHEBY	J M SARGENT
1988	B H SMITH	IAN M PHEBY	JAMES M G TOON	J M SARGENT
1989	M W WILES	IAN M PHEBY	JAMES M G TOON	J M SARGENT
1990	A HAINES	IAN M PHEBY	JAMES M G TOON	J M SARGENT
1991	A HAINES	IAN M PHEBY	JAMES M G TOON	J M SARGENT
1992	A HAINES	IAN M PHEBY	JAMES M G TOON	J M SARGENT
1993	A HAINES	IAN M PHEBY	JAMES M G TOON	J M SARGENT
1994	A HAINES	IAN M PHEBY	JAMES M G TOON	J M SARGENT
1995	A HAINES	IAN M PHEBY	JAMES M G TOON	J M SARGENT
1996	J BURROWS	IAN M PHEBY	JAMES M G TOON	J M SARGENT
1997	NIGEL D FLEMING	IAN M PHEBY	C GOULDEN	J M SARGENT
1998	M J KEOHANE	IAN M PHEBY	C GOULDEN	J M SARGENT
1999	M J KEOHANE	IAN M PHEBY	C GOULDEN	J M SARGENT
2000	M J KEOHANE	IAN M PHEBY	IAN M PHEBY	J M SARGENT
2001	CHRIS J REEVE	IAN M PHEBY	IAN M PHEBY	VACANT
2002	CHRIS J REEVE	IAN M PHEBY	IAN M PHEBY	-
2003	CHRIS J REEVE	IAN M PHEBY	NIGEL BLADES	-
2004	CHRIS J REEVE	IAN M PHEBY	DAVID T JOHNSON	-
2005	CHRIS J REEVE	IAN M PHEBY	DAVID T JOHNSON	-
2006	CHRIS J REEVE	IAN M PHEBY	DAVID T JOHNSON	-
2007	CHRIS J REEVE	IAN M PHEBY	DAVID T JOHNSON	-
2008	CHRIS J REEVE	IAN M PHEBY	DAVID T JOHNSON	-
2009	CHRIS J REEVE	IAN M PHEBY	DAVID T JOHNSON	-
2010	CHRIS J REEVE	IAN M PHEBY	DAVID T JOHNSON	-
2011	CHRIS J REEVE	IAN M PHEBY	DAVID T JOHNSON	NO POST
2012	NIGEL D FLEMING	IAN M PHEBY	DAVID T JOHNSON	-
2013	NIGEL D FLEMING	JAMES TOON	DAVID T JOHNSON	-
2014	NIGEL D FLEMING	JAMES TOON	JAMES TOON	-

YEAR	CORRESPONDENCE CAPTAIN	DIVISIONAL RECORDERS	INDIVIDUAL TOURNAMENT CONTROLLER	LIGHTNING/ BLITZ TOURNAMENT CONTROLLER
1905-51	NOT KNOWN	NOT KNOWN	-	-
1952	-	S MILLER, F M NORMAN, G E RUGLESS, P M SHAW, L STEPHENS	-	-
1953	-	MISS J CRESSWELL, F M NORMAN, H F J PRIBYL, P M SHAW, A L SYMES	-	-
1954	-	MRS J GODLY, P M SHAW, A L SYMES	-	-
1955	-	G BRIDDON, MRS J GODLY, A L SYMES	A H LORMAN	-
1956		G BRIDDON, G S HUMPHRY, A L SYMES	D H REED	A L L WINTERS
1957	-	R E ASHBOURNE, G BRIDDON, A L SYMES	D H REED	-
1958	-	R E ASHBOURNE, K G FRY, A L SYMES	D H REED	-
1959	-	R E ASHBOURNE, G W EAST, K G FRY, G SHAW	D H REED	-
1960	-	R E ASHBOURNE, J S CATTERALL, G W EAST, G SHAW	T L HERDMAN	-
1961	-	J S CATTERALL, G W EAST, S N OWEN, A L POLLARD	T L HERDMAN	-
1962	-	J S CATTERALL, G W EAST, OBE, S N OWEN, A L POLLARD	T L HERDMAN	-
1963	-	J S CATTERALL, V L HOLT, S N OWEN, A L POLLARD	T L HERDMAN	-
1964	-	E W HAMMOND, V L HOLT, P R VIVIAN	G MASKELL	-
1965	-	E W HAMMOND, V L HOLT, P R VIVIAN	G MASKELL	-
1966	-	E W HAMMOND, R A W MARSHALL, P R VIVIAN	G MASKELL	-
1967	-	P A BOND, I W V J HURRY, MISS Y D GUTHRIE	R E SPURGEON	R CREAMER, E CROKER

Year				
1968	-	P A BOND, I W V J HURRY, MISS Y D GUTHRIE	R E SPURGEON	R CREAMER, E CROKER
1969	-	I W V J HURRY, MRS Y D LITTLE, J WATSON	R E SPURGEON	R CREAMER
1970	-	A D BURGESS, I W V J HURRY, A I WAREING	R HULME	P A BOND
1971	P A BOND	F C BECKER, A D BURGESS, A I WAREING	R HULME	F C BECKER
1972	P A BOND	F C BECKER, K E CREER, A I WAREING	K E CREER	F C BECKER
1973	RAYMOND J POMEROY	F C BECKER, K E CREER, A I WAREING	K E CREER	C SERVANTE
1974	RAYMOND J POMEROY	F C BECKER, K E CREER, A I WAREING	IAN M PHEBY	P A BOND
1975	RAYMOND J POMEROY	B CHAMBERLAIN, A I WAREING, C WOOLLAM	IAN M PHEBY	P A BOND
1976	RAYMOND J POMEROY	K E CREER, A I WAREING, C WOOLLAM	IAN M PHEBY	P A BOND
1977	RAYMOND J POMEROY	I M PHEBY, A I WAREING, C WOOLLAM	IAN M PHEBY	P A BOND
1978	RAYMOND J POMEROY	I M PHEBY, A I WAREING, C WOOLLAM	IAN M PHEBY	J M SARGENT
1979	RAYMOND J POMEROY	I M PHEBY, A I WAREING, C WOOLLAM	A F STIMSON	J M SARGENT
1980	RAYMOND J POMEROY	I M PHEBY, R J POMEROY, A I WAREING	A F STIMSON	J M SARGENT
1981	RAYMOND J POMEROY	I M PHEBY, R J POMEROY, A I WAREING	A F STIMSON	J M SARGENT
1982	RAYMOND J POMEROY	I M PHEBY, R J POMEROY, A I WAREING	A F STIMSON	J M SARGENT
1983	RAYMOND J POMEROY	R J POMEROY, K J THURLOW	A F STIMSON	J M SARGENT
1984	RAYMOND J POMEROY	R J POMEROY, K J THURLOW	O S PHILLIPS	J M SARGENT
1985	RAYMOND J POMEROY	R J POMEROY, K J THURLOW	O S PHILLIPS	J M SARGENT
1986	RAYMOND J POMEROY	R J POMEROY, K J THURLOW	O S PHILLIPS	J M SARGENT
1987	RAYMOND J POMEROY	R J POMEROY, K J THURLOW	O S PHILLIPS	J M SARGENT
1988	RAYMOND J POMEROY	R J POMEROY, K J THURLOW	VACANT	J M SARGENT
1989	RAYMOND J POMEROY	K J THURLOW, P ZAMMIT	A C ASHBY	J M SARGENT

1990	RAYMOND J POMEROY	K J THURLOW, P ZAMMIT	VACANT	J M SARGENT
1991	RAYMOND J POMEROY	K J THURLOW, P ZAMMIT	VACANT	J M SARGENT
1992	RAYMOND J POMEROY	K J THURLOW, P ZAMMIT	VACANT	J M SARGENT
1993	RAYMOND J POMEROY	K J THURLOW, P ZAMMIT	DAVID T JOHNSON	J M SARGENT
1994	RAYMOND J POMEROY	DAVID T JOHNSON, K J THURLOW	DAVID T JOHNSON	J M SARGENT
1995	RAYMOND J POMEROY	DAVID T JOHNSON, C MORGAN	DAVID T JOHNSON	J M SARGENT
1996	RAYMOND J POMEROY	NONE	DAVID T JOHNSON	J M SARGENT
1997	RAYMOND J POMEROY	-	VACANT	J M SARGENT
1998	RAYMOND J POMEROY	-	B SKINNER	J M SARGENT
1999	RAYMOND J POMEROY	-	-	J M SARGENT
2000	RAYMOND J POMEROY	-	-	J M SARGENT
2001	RAYMOND J POMEROY	-	-	J M SARGENT
2002	RAYMOND J POMEROY	-	-	CHRIS J REEVE
2003	RAYMOND J POMEROY	-	-	CHRIS J REEVE
2004	RAYMOND J POMEROY	-	-	CHRIS J REEVE
2005	RAYMOND J POMEROY	-	-	CHRIS J REEVE
2006	RAYMOND J POMEROY	-	-	CHRIS J REEVE
2007	RAYMOND J POMEROY	-	-	CHRIS J REEVE
2008	RAYMOND J POMEROY	-	D GILBERT	N BLADES
2009	RAYMOND J POMEROY	-	D GILBERT	N BLADES
2010	RAYMOND J POMEROY	-	D GILBERT	N BLADES
2011	RAYMOND J POMEROY	-	D GILBERT	N BLADES, J M G TOON
2012	RAYMOND J POMEROY	-	D GILBERT	N BLADES
2013	RAYMOND J POMEROY	-	D GILBERT	N BLADES
2014	RAYMOND J POMEROY	-	D GILBERT	N BLADES

YEAR	CORRESPONDENCE TOURNAMENT CONTROLLER	ADDITIONAL COMMITTEE MEMBERS	BULLETIN EDITOR
1905-48	NOT KNOWN	NOT KNOWN	NO POST
1949	-	H HOSKIN, H G POOR, R C S TAYLOR, C.B.E.	NO POST
1950	-	MISS D COLMER, H HOSKIN, J ROWBOTHAM, L STEPHENS, R C S TAYLOR, C.B.E.	H HOSKIN
1951	-	MISS D COLMER, H HOSKIN, J ROWBOTHAM, L STEPHENS, R C S TAYLOR, C.B.E.	H HOSKIN
1952	-	E C BAKER, DR H R CALVERT, J NEALE, P B SARSON, P M SHAW, L STEPHENS	P B SARSON
1953	-	E C BAKER, DR H R CALVERT, J NEALE, P B SARSON, P M SHAW, L STEPHENS	P B SARSON
1954	-	E C BAKER, DR H R CALVERT, P B SARSON, P M SHAW, W A WALSH, A L L WINTERS	P B SARSON, W A WALSH
1955	-	E C BAKER, DR H R CALVERT, P M SHAW, A L L WINTERS	P B SARSON
1956	-	E C BAKER, DR H R CALVERT, MISS D COLMER, D LAW, A L L WINTERS	P B SARSON
1957	-	DR H R CALVERT, MISS D COLMER, D LAW, A L L WINTERS	P B SARSON
1958	-	F C BLACKMAN, G BRIDDON, DR H R CALVERT, J FOLEY	P B SARSON
1959	-	F C BLACKMAN, DR H R CALVERT, J FOLEY, A W NEWTON	T L HERDMAN
1960	-	F C BLACKMAN, J FOLEY, A W NEWTON, P B SARSON	T J SOUTAR
1961	-	F C BLACKMAN, J FOLEY, A W NEWTON, P B SARSON	T J SOUTAR
1962	-	F C BLACKMAN, J FOLEY, G MASKELL, P B SARSON	T J SOUTAR
1963	-	F C BLACKMAN, J FOLEY, G MASKELL, J W SCANLAN	T J SOUTAR
1964	-	F C BLACKMAN, J FOLEY, J W SCANLAN, A SPENCER TONKS	T J SOUTAR
1965	-	F C BLACKMAN, E CROKER, J FOLEY, A SPENCER TONKS	

1966	-	F C BLACKMAN, E CROKER, J FOLEY, G MASKELL	J LOFTEN
1967	-	F C BLACKMAN, R CREAMER, E CROKER, J FOLEY, R E SPURGEON	J LOFTEN
1968	-	P A BOND, A J BROOKS, E CROKER, J FOLEY, B C GOULD	J LOFTEN, P A BOND
1969	-	E CROKER, J FOLEY, J M XUEREB	P A BOND
1970	-	A D BURGESS, W L BUSH, E CROKER, F G DOYLE, I F RAMSEY	P A BOND
1971	P A BOND	A D BURGESS, W L BUSH, F G DOYLE, I F RAMSEY	G K SANDIFORD
1972	P A BOND	W L BUSH, F G DOYLE, R J MYERS, D POWER, I F RAMSEY	M R DAY
1973	RAYMOND J POMEROY	\	M R DAY
1974	RAYMOND J POMEROY	F C BECKER, W L BUSH, B CHAMBERLAIN, F S ROBINSON, A I WAREING	M R DAY
1975	RAYMOND J POMEROY	F C BECKER, W L BUSH, B CHAMBERLAIN, F S ROBINSON, A I WAREING	S F THORPE-TRACEY
1976	RAYMOND J POMEROY	F C BECKER, W L BUSH, K E CREER, R SEFTON, A I WAREING	S F THORPE-TRACEY
1977	RAYMOND J POMEROY	F C BECKER, W L BUSH, R HULME, A I WAREING, C WOOLLAM	S F THORPE-TRACEY
1978	RAYMOND J POMEROY	F C BECKER, W L BUSH, R HULME, A I WAREING, C WOOLLAM	S F THORPE-TRACEY
1979	RAYMOND J POMEROY	F C BECKER, W L BUSH, R HULME, R J POMEROY, C WOOLLAM	S F THORPE-TRACEY
1980	RAYMOND J POMEROY	F C BECKER, W L BUSH, R HULME, R J POMEROY, G A STEPHENSON, C WOOLLAM	S F THORPE-TRACEY
1981	P S MORTON	F C BECKER, A BEECH, W L BUSH, R HULME, J PAGE, G A STEPHENSON	G BULL
1982	P S MORTON	F C BECKER, A BEECH, W L BUSH, R HULME, J PAGE	G BULL
1983	VACANT	A BEECH, W L BUSH, R HULME, P JOLLY, J PAGE	KEVIN J THURLOW
1984	J M SARGENT	A BEECH, G BOLT, J JORDAN, J PAGE, A F STIMSON	KEVIN J THURLOW
1985	J M SARGENT	G P ASHELFORD, G BOLT, J JORDAN, J PAGE, A F STIMSON	KEVIN J THURLOW

Year			
1986	J M SARGENT	G P ASHELFORD, P BOND, M COLES, J JORDAN, A F STIMSON	KEVIN J THURLOW
1987	J M SARGENT	P BOND, J JORDAN, T B PACKHAM, A F STIMSON, P ZAMMIT	KEVIN J THURLOW
1988	VACANT	P BOND, J JORDAN, T B PACKHAM, A F STIMSON, P ZAMMIT	KEVIN J THURLOW
1989	VACANT	P BOND, T B PACKHAM, P ZAMMIT	KEVIN J THURLOW
1990	VACANT	P BOND, T B PACKHAM, P ZAMMIT	KEVIN J THURLOW
1991	VACANT	P BOND, P ZAMMIT	KEVIN J THURLOW
1992	KEVIN J THURLOW	G P ASHELFORD, P ZAMMIT	KEVIN J THURLOW
1993	KEVIN J THURLOW	G P ASHELFORD, MISS D WELLS, P ZAMMIT	KEVIN J THURLOW
1994	KEVIN J THURLOW, C J O'BEE	D J DUNFORD, R J FRIES, T W PELLING	KEVIN J THURLOW
1995	VACANT	D J DUNFORD, R J FRIES, T W PELLING	KEVIN J THURLOW
1996	-	R J FRIES, J McALLISTER, T W PELLING	IAN M PHEBY
1997	-	I ALLGOOD, C CHEEK, R A CLEAVE, J McALLISTER, T W PELLING	IAN M PHEBY
1998	-	I ALLGOOD, R A CLEAVE, J McALLISTER, T W PELLING, K J THURLOW	IAN M PHEBY
1999	-	R A CLEAVE, J McALLISTER, T W PELLING, K J THURLOW, P ZAMMIT	IAN M PHEBY
2000	-	R A CLEAVE, J McALLISTER, T W PELLING, K J THURLOW, P ZAMMIT	IAN M PHEBY
2001	-	N BLADES, J McALLISTER, T W PELLING, K J THURLOW, P ZAMMIT	IAN M PHEBY
2002	-	N BLADES, J McALLISTER, T W PELLING, K J THURLOW, P ZAMMIT	IAN M PHEBY
2003	-	T W PELLING, K J THURLOW, P ZAMMIT	IAN M PHEBY
2004	-	N BLADES, T W PELLING, K J THURLOW, P ZAMMIT	IAN M PHEBY
2005	-	N BLADES, T W PELLING, K J THURLOW, P ZAMMIT	IAN M PHEBY
2006	-	N BLADES, T W PELLING, K J THURLOW, P ZAMMIT	IAN M PHEBY

Year			
2007	-	N BLADES, T W PELLING, K J THURLOW, P ZAMMIT	IAN M PHEBY
2008	-	P EFSTATHIOU, N D FLEMING, T W PELLING, K J THURLOW, P ZAMMIT	IAN M PHEBY
2009	-	P EFSTATHIOU, N D FLEMING, T W PELLING, K J THURLOW, P ZAMMIT	IAN M PHEBY
2010	-	P EFSTATHIOU, N D FLEMING, T W PELLING, K J THURLOW, P ZAMMIT	IAN M PHEBY
2011	-	P EFSTATHIOU, N D FLEMING, T W PELLING, K J THURLOW, P ZAMMIT	IAN M PHEBY
2012	-	P BIGGS, P EFSTATHIOU, T W PELLING, K J THURLOW, P ZAMMIT	IAN M PHEBY
2013	-	P BIGGS, P EFSTATHIOU, T W PELLING, K J THURLOW, P ZAMMIT	VACANT
2014	-	P BIGGS, T W PELLING	VACANT

YEAR	AUDITOR	WEBMASTER	NATIONAL CHAMPIONSHIPS ORGANISER (CSSC POST)
1905-27	NOT KNOWN	NO POST	NO POST
1928	F J DADD	-	-
1929	F J DADD and W H HIPKISS		
1930 - 1956	F J DADD		
1957	J T CURTIS, F J DADD M.V.O.	-	-
1958	J T CURTIS, F J DADD M.V.O.	-	-
1959	J T CURTIS, F J DADD M.V.O.	-	-
1960	J T CURTIS, F J DADD M.V.O.	-	-
1961	F PURDY, F J DADD, M.V.O.	-	-
1962	F PURDY, F J DADD, M.V.O.	-	-
1963	F PURDY, F J DADD, M.V.O.	-	-
1964	F PURDY, F J DADD, M.V.O.	-	-
1965	F PURDY, F J DADD, M.V.O.	-	-
1966	F PURDY, F J DADD, M.V.O.	-	-
1967	F PURDY, F J DADD, M.V.O.	-	-
1968	F PURDY, F J DADD, M.V.O.	-	-

Year			
1969	F PURDY, F J DADD, M.V.O., J WATSON	-	-
1970	F PURDY, F J DADD, M.V.O.	-	-
1971	F PURDY, F J DADD, M.V.O.	-	-
1972	F PURDY, F J DADD, M.V.O.	-	-
1973	F PURDY, F J DADD, M.V.O.	-	-
1974	F J DADD, M.V.O., R C A PENTECOST	-	-
1975	F J DADD, M.V.O., R C A PENTECOST	-	-
1976	F J DADD, M.V.O., G W MASKELL, R C A PENTECOST	-	-
1977	F J DADD, M.V.O., G W MASKELL, R C A PENTECOST	-	-
1978	G W MASKELL, R C A PENTECOST	-	-
1979	G W MASKELL, R C A PENTECOST	-	-
1980	G W MASKELL, R C A PENTECOST	-	-
1981	G W MASKELL, R C A PENTECOST	-	-
1982	R C A LEE-PENTECOST, G W MASKELL	-	-
1983	R C A LEE-PENTECOST, G W MASKELL	-	-
1984	R C A LEE-PENTECOST, G W MASKELL	-	-
1985	R C A LEE-PENTECOST, G W MASKELL	-	-
1986	R C A LEE-PENTECOST, G W MASKELL	-	-
1987	R C A LEE-PENTECOST, G W MASKELL	-	-
1988	R C A LEE-PENTECOST, G W MASKELL	-	-
1989	R C A LEE-ANDERSON, G W MASKELL	-	-
1990	P M SHAW, B H SMITH	-	-
1991	P M SHAW, B H SMITH	-	DAVID G MILLS
1992	P M SHAW, B H SMITH	-	DAVID G MILLS
1993	P M SHAW, B H SMITH	-	DAVID G MILLS
1994	B H SMITH, R L TURNHAM	-	KEVIN J THURLOW
1995	B H SMITH, R L TURNHAM	-	KEVIN J THURLOW
1996	B H SMITH, R L TURNHAM	-	KEVIN J THURLOW
1997	G P ASHELFORD, R L TURNHAM	-	KEVIN J THURLOW
1998	G P ASHELFORD, R L TURNHAM	-	KEVIN J THURLOW
1999	G P ASHELFORD	-	KEVIN J THURLOW
2000	G P ASHELFORD	-	KEVIN J THURLOW
2001	G P ASHELFORD	-	KEVIN J THURLOW
2002	G P ASHELFORD	J MCALLISTER	KEVIN J THURLOW
2003	G P ASHELFORD	J MCALLISTER	KEVIN J THURLOW
2004	G P ASHELFORD	J MCALLISTER	ROBERT DENNINGTON

Year			
2005	G P ASHELFORD	J MCALLISTER	ROBERT DENNINGTON
2006	G P ASHELFORD	J MCALLISTER	ROBERT DENNINGTON
2007	LEWIS EDWARDS-WINSER	JAMES M G TOON	KEVIN J THURLOW
2008	LEWIS EDWARDS-WINSER	JAMES M G TOON	KEVIN J THURLOW
2009	LEWIS EDWARDS-WINSER	JAMES M G TOON	KEVIN J THURLOW
2010	LEWIS EDWARDS-WINSER	JAMES M G TOON	KEVIN J THURLOW
2011	LEWIS EDWARDS-WINSER	JAMES M G TOON	KEVIN J THURLOW
2012	T WOODS	JAMES M G TOON	KEVIN J THURLOW
2013	T WOODS	JAMES M G TOON	KEVIN J THURLOW
2014	T WOODS	JAMES M G TOON	IHOR LEWYK

LEAGUE VICE-PRESIDENTS	DATES
C H O'D ALEXANDER, CBE	1968 - 1974
E C BAKER, MBE	1968 - 1998
N BLADES	2009 - 2011
P A BOND	1992 - 2003
J Y BELL, CB	1949 - 1967
R BRAIN	1970 - 1989
R J BROADBENT	1970 - 1989
THE HON. SIR ALEXANDER CADOGAN, GCMG, KCB	1949
DR H R CALVERT, MA	1969 - 1992
SIR ARCHIBALD CARTER, GCMG, KCB, KCIE	1949 - 1968
COLONEL SIR ERIC CRANKSHAW, KCMG, MBE	1949 - 1950
J T CURTIS	1961 - 1962
F J DADD, MVO	1977
SIR WILLIAM SCOTT DOUGLAS, GCB, KBE	1952 - 1953
SIR HAROLD C EMMERSON, CB, KCB, KCVO	1949 - 1969
SIR ALFRED FAULKNER, CB, CBE	1949
R D FLEMING	1985 - 1995
J FOLEY	1970 - 1976
SIR THOMAS GARDINER, GBE, KCB	1949

J H GARNER	1955
B E GLAZE	1999 - 2005
E W GODLY	1990 - 2011
J MAHOOD CBE, ISO	1949
D V MARDLE, CBE	1993 - 2001
SIR ALEXANDER MAXWELL, GCB, KBE	1949
SIR P S MILNER-BARRY, KCVO, CB, OBE	1970 -1992
SIR DAVID T MONTEATH, KCB, KCMG, CVO, OBE	1949
F M NORMAN	1965 - 1967
I M PHEBY	2002 - 2011
A G POCKETT, OBE	1959 - 1993
R J POMEROY	1993 - 2011
H G POOR	1949 - 1963
A P PRIMETT	1999 - 2003
W E C RICHARDS	1987 - 1989
C A ROEDER	1987 - 2011
SIR ARTHUR N RUCKER KCMG, CB, CBE	1949
J M SARGENT	2003 - 2011
R SMITH	1992 - 2006
B H N STRONACH	1950 - 1962
C B STRONACH	1973 - 1997
R C S TAYLOR, CBE	1953
K J THURLOW	1995 - 2011
J M G TOON	2009 - 2011
T B WEST	1977 - 1979
G WHITE	2009 - 2011
SIR HAROLD WILES, KBE, CB	1956 - 1968
W O WOODFIELD	1922 - 1968
P ZAMMIT	2009 - 2011

YEAR	NUMBER OF CLUBS	NUMBER OF TEAMS	PLAYERS	DEFAULTS	DEFAULTS %	ADJUDICATIONS
1905	9					
1906	7					
1907	10					
1908	12	17				
1909	16	20				

1910		23				
1911		23				
1912		25				
1913-15						
1916		None				
1917		None				
1918		None				
1919		None				
1920	15	19				
1921		29				
1922	23	38				
1923-24						
1925	21	60	640			
1926		65				
1927	27	64				
1928	27	61				
1929	28	64				
1930						
1931		57				
1932	27	57				
1933	29	59				
1934	28	58				
1935	27	59				
1936-37						
1938	28	53				
1939		None				
1940		None				
1941		None				
1942		None				
1943		None				
1944		None				
1945		None				
1946		None				
1947	24					
1948						
1949	23	48				
1950	25	50				
1951	29	62	790			

1952	30	65				
1953	29	68				
1954	30	67				
1955	34	72	732			
1956	32	78	800			
1957	33	80				
1958	35	80				
1959	35	86				
1960	35	88				
1961	36	90				
1962	36	85	1050			
1963	36	90				
1964	31	86				
1965	34	84				
1966	34	85				
1967	34	80				
1968	34	77				
1969	33	69	830			54
1970	29	63	806			
1971	26	60	766			
1972	27	60	768			
1973	29	60				
1974	30	67				
1975	27	68	842			
1976	29	70	871			
1977	30	70	848			119
1978	29	68	820			94
1979	27	63	833			107
1980	26	62	730			81
1981	26	57	722			96
1982	22	55	679			81
1983	21	55	613	224	5.6	82
1984	20	58	610	344	8.2	95
1985	20	58	608	355	8.6	69
1986	20	55	575	423	10.1	71
1987	20	54	556	390	9.3	74
1988	18	46	532	419	11.1	81
1989	15	42	427	245	8.9	60

1990	15	39	408	280	9.7	79
1991	15	37	404	217	7.4	53
1992	15	37	392	213	7.5	76
1993	15	39	384	216	7.2	48
1994	15	38	394	201	7.0	55
1995	15	36	367	195	6.8	54
1996	15	38	360	287	9.9	78
1997	14	35	324	253	10.5	62
1998	13	30	290	291	11.7	28
1999	13	28	253	225	10.6	33
2000	14	25	251	209	10.1	32
2001	14	24	228	212	11.1	26
2002	14	23	223	193	10.7	25
2003	13	22	207	99	6.1	24
2004	12	22	202	144	9.1	33
2005	12	22	207	148	9.8	17
2006	11	21	202	72	4.8	29
2007	11	21	202	106	7.0	11
2008	11	20	196	64	4.6	17
2009	11	20	196	106	7.6	14
2010	10	21	200	83	5.8	28
2011	10	22	187	81	5.5	6
2012	9	22	176	89	6.2	6
2013	9	19	170	48	3.4	8
2014	9	20	176	50	4.1	0

NEW CSCA

YEAR	PRESIDENT	VICE-PRESIDENTS	CHAIRMAN	VICE-CHAIRMAN
1995	SIR P S MILNER-BARRY, KCVO, CB, OBE	E C BAKER, MBE; P A BOND; R D FLEMING; E W GODLY; D V MARDLE, CBE; R J POMEROY; C A ROEDER, R SMITH; C B STRONACH; K J THURLOW	IAN M PHEBY	-
1996	RONALD D FLEMING	E C BAKER, MBE; P A BOND; E W GODLY; D V MARDLE, CBE; R J POMEROY; C A ROEDER, R SMITH; C B STRONACH; K J THURLOW	IAN M PHEBY	-

Year				
1997	RONALD D FLEMING	E C BAKER, MBE; P A BOND; E W GODLY; D V MARDLE, CBE; R J POMEROY; C A ROEDER, R SMITH; C B STRONACH; K J THURLOW	IAN M PHEBY	-
1998	RONALD D FLEMING	E C BAKER, MBE; P A BOND; E W GODLY; D V MARDLE, CBE; R J POMEROY; C A ROEDER, R SMITH; K J THURLOW	IAN M PHEBY	-
1999	RONALD D FLEMING	P A BOND; B E GLAZE; E W GODLY; D V MARDLE, CBE; R J POMEROY; A P PRIMETT; C A ROEDER, R SMITH; K J THURLOW	IAN M PHEBY	-
2000	RONALD D FLEMING	P A BOND; B E GLAZE; E W GODLY; D V MARDLE, CBE; R J POMEROY; A P PRIMETT; C A ROEDER, R SMITH; K J THURLOW	IAN M PHEBY	-
2001	RONALD D FLEMING	P A BOND; B E GLAZE; E W GODLY; D V MARDLE, CBE; R J POMEROY; A P PRIMETT; C A ROEDER, R SMITH; K J THURLOW	IAN M PHEBY	-
2002	RONALD D FLEMING	P A BOND; B E GLAZE; E W GODLY; I M PHEBY; R J POMEROY; A P PRIMETT; C A ROEDER, R SMITH; K J THURLOW	IAN M PHEBY	RICHARD J FRIES
2003	RONALD D FLEMING	P A BOND; B E GLAZE; E W GODLY; D G MILLS; I M PHEBY; R J POMEROY; A P PRIMETT; C A ROEDER, J M SARGENT; R SMITH; K J THURLOW	IAN M PHEBY	RICHARD J FRIES
2004	RONALD D FLEMING	B E GLAZE; E W GODLY; D G MILLS; I M PHEBY; R J POMEROY; C A ROEDER, J M SARGENT; R SMITH; K J THURLOW	IAN M PHEBY	RICHARD J FRIES

Year				
2005	RONALD D FLEMING	B E GLAZE; E W GODLY; D G MILLS; I M PHEBY; R J POMEROY; C A ROEDER, J M SARGENT; R SMITH; K J THURLOW	IAN M PHEBY	RICHARD J FRIES
2006	RONALD D FLEMING	E W GODLY; D G MILLS; I M PHEBY; R J POMEROY; C A ROEDER, J M SARGENT; R SMITH; K J THURLOW	IAN M PHEBY	RICHARD J FRIES
2007	ROLAND SMITH	E W GODLY; D G MILLS; I M PHEBY; R J POMEROY; C A ROEDER, J M SARGENT; K J THURLOW	IAN M PHEBY	RICHARD J FRIES
2008	ROLAND SMITH	E W GODLY; D G MILLS; I M PHEBY; R J POMEROY; C A ROEDER, J M SARGENT; K J THURLOW	IAN M PHEBY	RICHARD J FRIES
2009	ROLAND SMITH	E W GODLY; D G MILLS; I M PHEBY; R J POMEROY; C A ROEDER, J M SARGENT; K J THURLOW	IAN M PHEBY	RICHARD J FRIES

YEAR	SECRETARY	TREASURER	GRADER
1995	ROLAND SMITH	JEREMY BURROWS	JAMES M G TOON
1996	ROLAND SMITH	JEREMY BURROWS	JAMES M G TOON
1997	ROLAND SMITH	JEREMY BURROWS	C GOULDEN
1998	ROLAND SMITH	JEREMY BURROWS	C GOULDEN
1999	ROLAND SMITH	ROLAND SMITH	C GOULDEN
2000	ROLAND SMITH	HEDLEY FEATHERSTONE (CSSC)	IAN M PHEBY
2001	ROLAND SMITH	HEDLEY FEATHERSTONE	IAN M PHEBY
2002	ROLAND SMITH	HEDLEY FEATHERSTONE	IAN M PHEBY
2003	ROLAND SMITH	HEDLEY FEATHERSTONE	NIGEL BLADES
2004	ROLAND SMITH	HEDLEY FEATHERSTONE	DAVID T JOHNSON
2005	ROLAND SMITH	HEDLEY FEATHERSTONE	DAVID T JOHNSON
2006	ROLAND SMITH	HEDLEY FEATHERSTONE	DAVID T JOHNSON
2007	ROLAND SMITH	HEDLEY FEATHERSTONE	DAVID T JOHNSON
2008	ROLAND SMITH	HEDLEY FEATHERSTONE	DAVID T JOHNSON
2009	ROLAND SMITH	HEDLEY FEATHERSTONE	DAVID T JOHNSON

YEAR	MATCH CAPTAIN	CORRESPONDENCE CAPTAIN	CORRESPONDENCE CHAMPIONSHIP CONTROLLER
1995	JOHN M SARGENT	RAYMOND J POMEROY	KEVIN J THURLOW AND C J O'BEE
1996	JOHN M SARGENT	RAYMOND J POMEROY	KEVIN J THURLOW AND C J O'BEE
1997	DAVID G MILLS	RAYMOND J POMEROY	C J O'BEE
1998	DAVID G MILLS	RAYMOND J POMEROY	NO TOURNAMENT
1999	DAVID G MILLS	RAYMOND J POMEROY	-
2000	DAVID G MILLS	RAYMOND J POMEROY	-
2001	DAVID G MILLS	RAYMOND J POMEROY	-
2002	DAVID G MILLS	RAYMOND J POMEROY	-
2003	DAVID G MILLS	RAYMOND J POMEROY	-
2004	DAVID G MILLS	RAYMOND J POMEROY	-
2005	DAVID G MILLS	RAYMOND J POMEROY	-
2006	DAVID G MILLS	RAYMOND J POMEROY	-
2007	DAVID G MILLS	RAYMOND J POMEROY	-
2008	VACANT	RAYMOND J POMEROY	IAN M PHEBY
2009	VACANT	RAYMOND J POMEROY	NO TOURNAMENT

YEAR	BULLETIN EDITOR	WEBMASTER	MEMBER WITHOUT PORTFOLIO	AUDITOR
1995	KEVIN J THURLOW	NO POST	DAVID G MILLS	B H SMITH AND R L TURNHAM
1996	COLIN CHEEK	-	VACANT	B H SMITH AND R L TURNHAM
1997	COLIN CHEEK	-	-	R L TURNHAM AND J WILLIAMS
1998	VACANT	-	-	R L TURNHAM AND J WILLIAMS
1999	-	-	-	DAVID J EDNEY
2000	-	-	-	CSSC
2001	-	-	ROBERT DENNINGTON	CSSC
2002	-	J MCALLISTER	ROBERT DENNINGTON	CSSC

2003	-	J MCALLISTER	ROBERT DENNINGTON	CSSC
2004	-	J MCALLISTER	-	CSSC
2005	-	J MCALLISTER	-	CSSC
2006	-	J MCALLISTER	-	CSSC
2007	-	JAMES M G TOON	-	CSSC
2008	-	JAMES M G TOON	-	CSSC
2009	-	JAMES M G TOON	DAVID G MILLS AND IHOR LEWYK	CSSC

Length of Service of Committee Members - All Posts until 2011 (Top Ten)

IAN M PHEBY	125
RAYMOND J POMEROY	110
KEVIN J THURLOW	89
RONALD D FLEMING	75
J M SARGENT	69
ROLAND SMITH	69
CHARLES A ROEDER	58
E C BAKER, MBE	52
F J DADD, MVO	51
EDWARD W GODLY	50

Literature Sources etc.

Alan Turing: The Enigma by Andrew Hodges, Vintage Books 1983, revised 1992.

Correspondence Chess Reminiscence No 7, by Eric Ruch

http://www.edochess.ca

The Emperor's Codes by Michael Smith, Bantam, 2000

Enigma – The Battle for the Code by Hugh Sebag-Montefiore, Weidenfeld and Nicholson 2000

Fifty Years of Chess at Battersea by LC Birch 1935

Head of the Civil Service – (A Study of Sir Warren Fisher) by Eunan O'Halpin (Routledge) 1989

King, Queen and Knight, by Norman Knight & Will Guy, Batsford 1975

The Secret Life of Bletchley Park by Sinclair McKay, Aurum 2010

The Spycatcher's Encyclopedia of Espionage, Peter Wright, Heinemann Australia, 1991.

Station X by Michael Smith, Channel 4 Books, 1998

The Unknown Prime Minister by Robert Blake, Eyre and Spottiswoode, 1955

A Web of Deception – The Spycatcher Affair by Chapman Pincher, Sidgwick and Jackson 1987

Weighed in the Balance, by PW Hammond and H Egan, HMSO, 1992